PAGE LAYOUT

PAGE LAYOUT

INSPIRATION • INNOVATION • INFORMATION

GENERAL EDITOR: ROGER WALTON

PAGE LAYOUT

First paperback edition published in 2002 by:
HBI, an imprint of HarperCollins Publishers
10 East 53rd Street
New York, NY 10022-5299
United States of America

Distributed in the United States
and Canada by:
North Light Books,
an imprint of F & W Publications, Inc.
4700 East Galbraith Road
Cincinnati, Ohio 45236
1-800-289-0963

Distributed throughout the rest
of the world by:
HarperCollins International
10 East 53rd Street
New York, NY 10022-5299
Fax: (212) 207-7654

ISBN 0-06-050609-1

Conceived, created, and designed by:
Duncan Baird Publishers
6th Floor, Castle House
75–76 Wells Street, London W1P 3RE

Designer: Sonya Merali
Editor: Simon Ryder
Project Co-ordinator: Tara Solesbury

10 9 8 7 6 5 4 3 2 1

Typeset in MetaPlus
Color reproduction by Scanhouse, Malaysia
Manufactured in China

NOTE
All measurements listed in this book
are for width followed by height.

CONTENTS

SECTION ONE 8
DESIGN FOR DESIGN

SECTION TWO 56
DESIGN FOR BUSINESS

SECTION THREE 74
DESIGN FOR EDUCATION AND THE ARTS

GLOSSARY OF USEFUL TERMS 140

INDEX 142

FOREWORD

The job of the graphic designer is to communicate; after that there probably aren't any hard-and-fast rules. You can refine this a little by asking what it is that needs to be communicated and to whom but essentially the remit of the designer in the pursuit of effective communication is as wide and deep as the designer's imagination and that of the client.

The foundation of any design job includes the brief (information, materials, and thoughts provided by the client), the schedule (how much time you have overall and how much of your client's time within that), and the budget. These are the parameters and ingredients within and upon which you must bring your imagination to bear. As the work shown in this book demonstrates again and again, of these three elements what ultimately makes a design successful is the designer's imagination—not the source material, the amount of money available, or the production process. Be it an item of stationery, a website, or a calendar to promote manufacturers of machinery used in the production of paperboard, what gives the designs in this book their edge is the way in which individual designers have analyzed the requirements and constraints of the job and responded with exceptional imagination and flair.

The title *Page Layout* has been interpreted in the widest sense possible. It is intended to be an expression more of the design process than of the format in which the final design is realized. Increasingly, among the questions under consideration by the designer is what form the communication should take—a book, leaflet, brochure, press announcement, website, series of billboard posters, television advertisement—or a sidewalk performance? I would say there are circumstances in which each of the above might be appropriate, along with many other possibilities.

Page Layout comprises a wide range of designs drawn from all over the world that show imagination working at the highest level. This work can be seen as a stepping-off point from which your imagination can roam freely and creatively—an inspiration for future designs.

RW

DESIGN FOR DESIGN

This opening section shows designers promoting themselves, the company they work for, or another company within the design sphere. The work ranges from the intensely personal—a book exploring the impact of new media on graphic design, for example—to more obviously commercial projects, such as posters to advertise typefaces, sets of stationery, and furniture-design brochures.

SECTION ONE

The different color of the cover close to the spine, combined with the red line of the elastic band, is reminiscent of traditional leather binding techniques. This suggests a link between the values involved in the making of handmade items and the company's own philosophy.

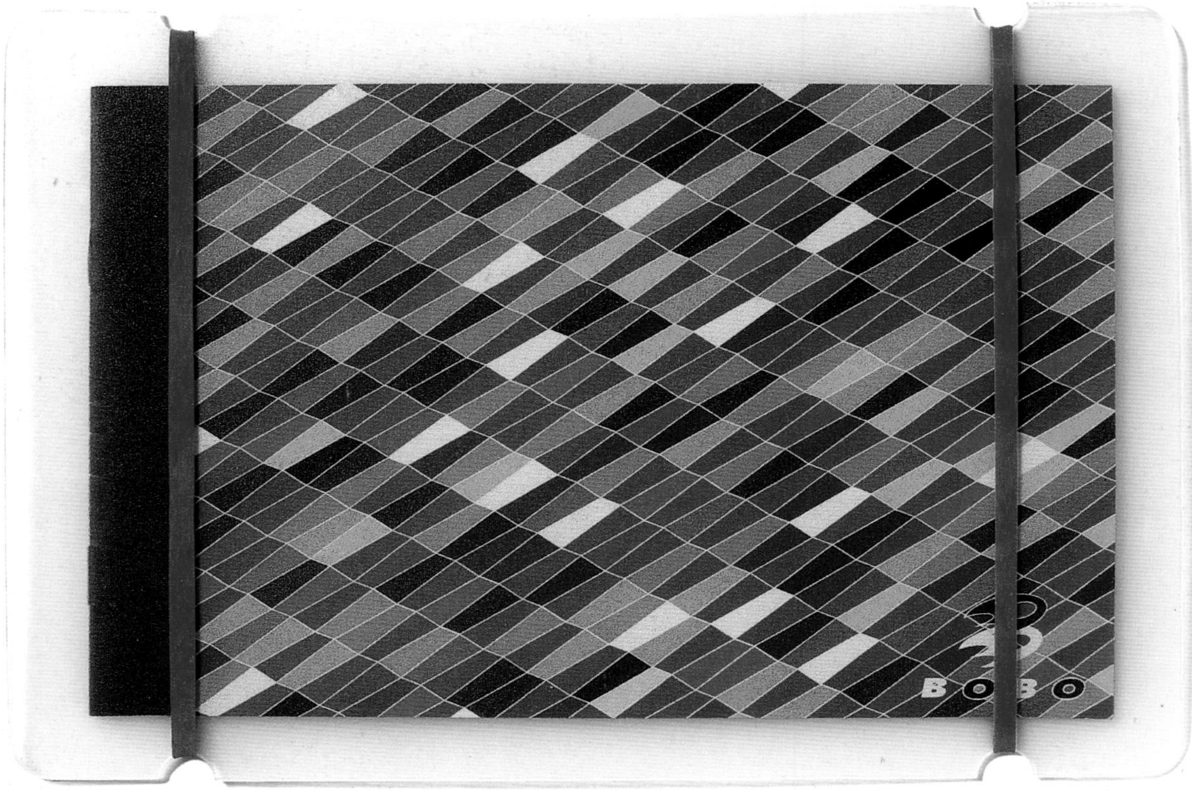

Designers
Red Design

Design Company
Red Design

Country of Origin
UK

Description of Artwork
8-page promotional brochure for the product design company Bo Bo.

Page Dimensions
210 x 135 mm
$8^1/_4$ x $5^1/_4$ in

Format
Brochure

Bo Bo Brochure

This stylish publication for a furniture design company comes attached to a piece of translucent polyurethane, a reference to the types of material used in the company's products. Inside, strong colors are used to set off the muted, almost monochrome, tones of the photographs, while on some lefthand pages a prismatic abstract background is suggestive of the way light passes through a translucent material. Shots of personnel, conceptual drawings, and images of furniture under construction are brought together under different headings to give a very full picture of the company philosophy and practice.

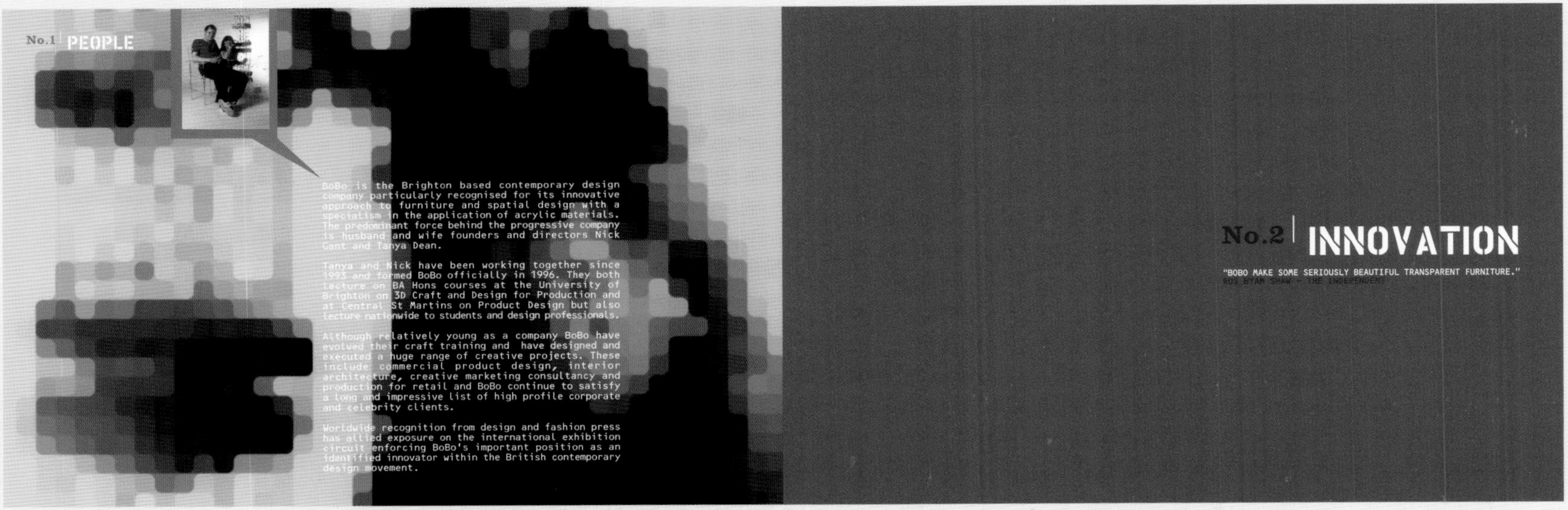

No.1 | PEOPLE

BoBo is the Brighton based contemporary design company particularly recognised for its innovative approach to furniture and spatial design with a specialism in the application of acrylic materials. The predominant force behind the progressive company is husband and wife founders and directors Nick Gant and Tanya Dean.

Tanya and Nick have been working together since 1993 and formed BoBo officially in 1996. They both lecture on BA Hons courses at the University of Brighton on 3D Craft and Design for Production and at Central St Martins on Product Design but also lecture nationwide to students and design professionals.

Although relatively young as a company BoBo have evolved their craft training and have designed and executed a huge range of creative projects. These include: commercial product design, interior architecture, creative marketing consultancy and production for retail and BoBo continue to satisfy a long and impressive list of high profile corporate and celebrity clients.

Worldwide recognition from design and fashion press has allied exposure on the international exhibition circuit enforcing BoBo's important position as an identified innovator within the British contemporary design movement.

No.2 | INNOVATION

"BOBO MAKE SOME SERIOUSLY BEAUTIFUL TRANSPARENT FURNITURE."
ROS BYAM SHAW - THE INDEPENDENT

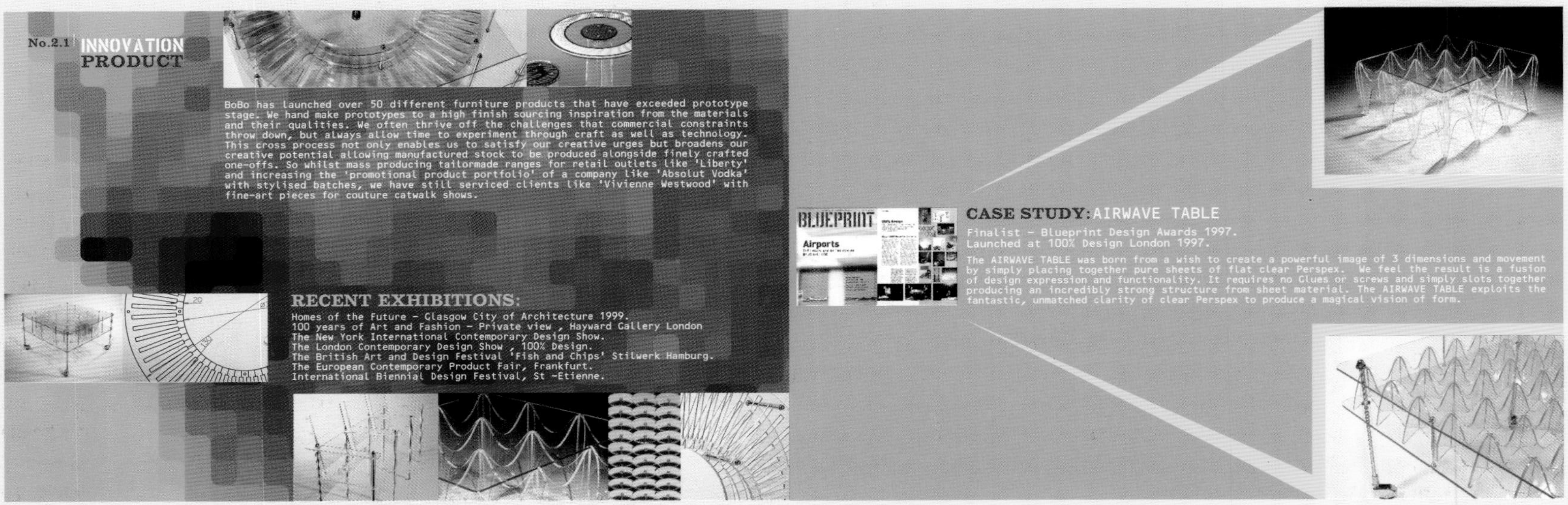

No.2.1 | INNOVATION PRODUCT

BoBo has launched over 50 different furniture products that have exceeded prototype stage. We hand make prototypes to a high finish sourcing inspiration from the materials and their qualities. We often thrive off the challenges that commercial constraints throw down, but always allow time to experiment through craft as well as technology. This cross process not only enables us to satisfy our creative urges but broadens our creative potential allowing manufactured stock to be produced alongside finely crafted one-offs. So whilst mass producing tailormade ranges for retail outlets like 'Liberty' and increasing the 'promotional product portfolio' of a company like 'Absolut Vodka' with stylised batches, we have still serviced clients like 'Vivienne Westwood' with fine-art pieces for couture catwalk shows.

RECENT EXHIBITIONS:

Homes of the Future - Glasgow City of Architecture 1999.
100 years of Art and Fashion - Private view , Hayward Gallery London
The New York International Contemporary Design Show.
The London Contemporary Design Show , 100% Design.
The British Art and Design Festival 'Fish and Chips' Stilwerk Hamburg.
The European Contemporary Product Fair, Frankfurt.
International Biennial Design Festival, St -Etienne.

CASE STUDY: AIRWAVE TABLE

Finalist - Blueprint Design Awards 1997.
Launched at 100% Design London 1997.

The AIRWAVE TABLE was born from a wish to create a powerful image of 3 dimensions and movement by simply placing together pure sheets of flat clear Perspex. We feel the result is a fusion of design expression and functionality. It requires no Glues or screws and simply slots together producing an incredibly strong structure from sheet material. The AIRWAVE TABLE exploits the fantastic, unmatched clarity of clear Perspex to produce a magical vision of form.

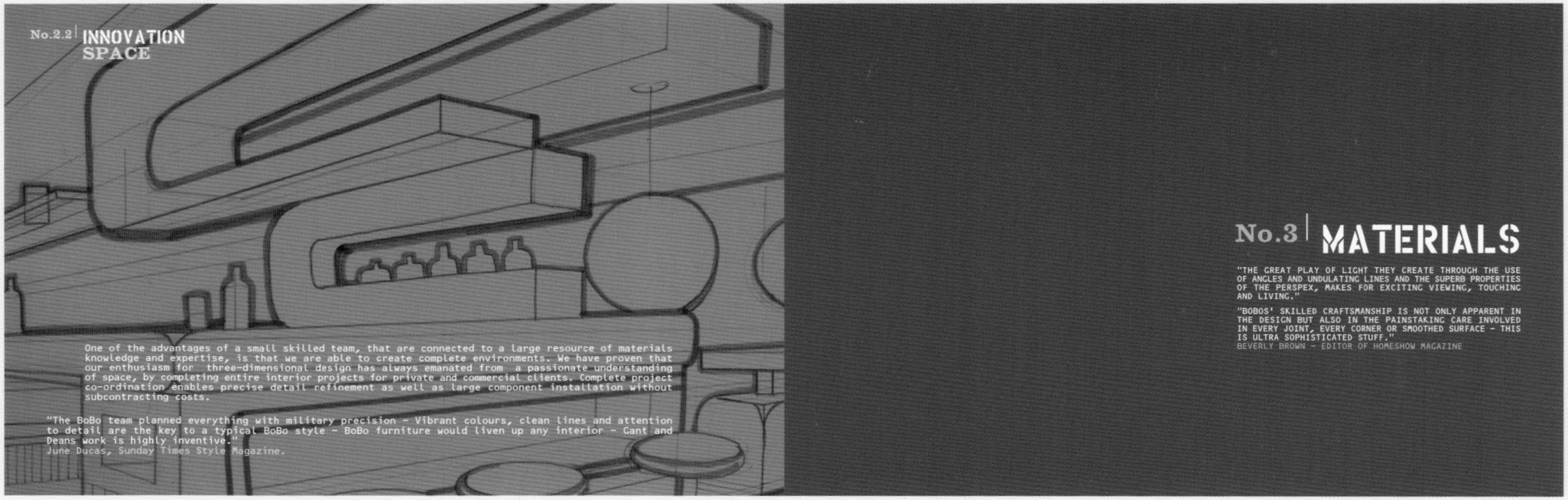

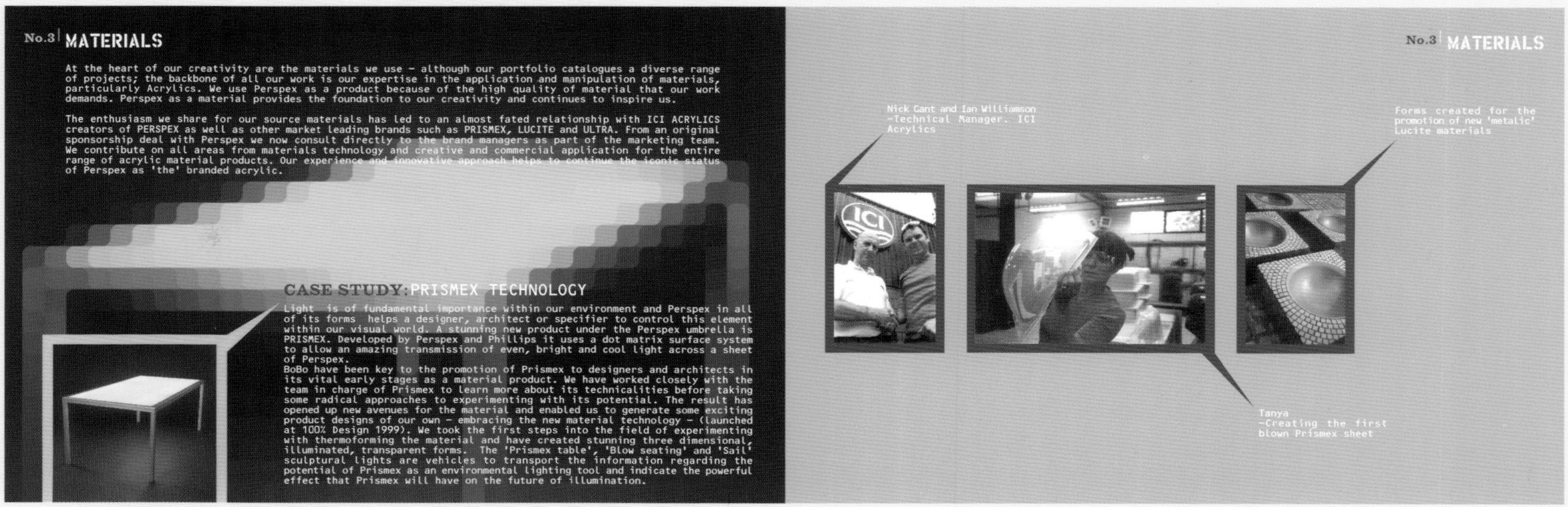

In a nice reversal of the way text bubbles are used in cartoon strips, here the images (photographs) are surrounded by a border and connected to the text with a tapering leader line.

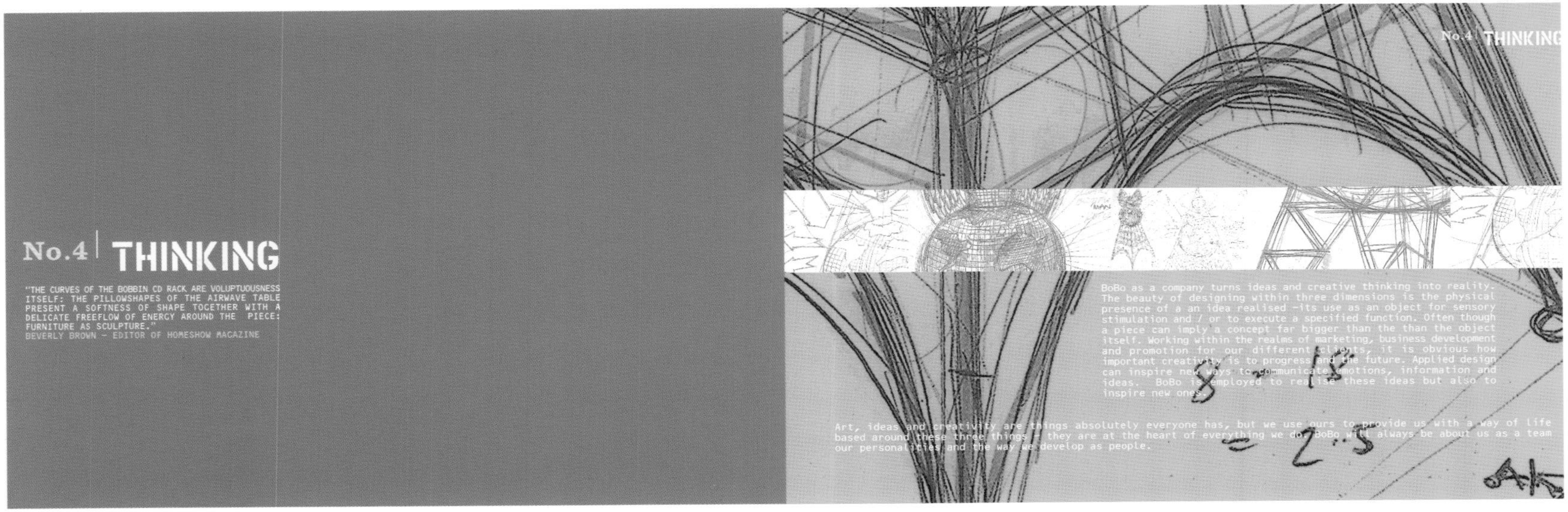

No.4 | THINKING

"THE CURVES OF THE BOBBIN CD RACK ARE VOLUPTUOUSNESS ITSELF: THE PILLOWSHAPES OF THE AIRWAVE TABLE PRESENT A SOFTNESS OF SHAPE TOGETHER WITH A DELICATE FREEFLOW OF ENERGY AROUND THE PIECE: FURNITURE AS SCULPTURE."
BEVERLY BROWN – EDITOR OF HOMESHOW MAGAZINE

No.4 | THINKING

BoBo as a company turns ideas and creative thinking into reality. The beauty of designing within three dimensions is the physical presence of a an idea realised –its use as an object for sensory stimulation and / or to execute a specified function. Often though a piece can imply a concept far bigger than the than the object itself. Working within the realms of marketing, business development and promotion for our different clients, it is obvious how important creativity is to progress and the future. Applied design can inspire new ways to communicate emotions, information and ideas. BoBo is employed to realise these ideas but also to inspire new ones.

Art, ideas and creativity are things absolutely everyone has, but we use ours to provide us with a way of life based around these three things – they are at the heart of everything we do. BoBo will always be about us as a team our personalities and the way we develop as people.

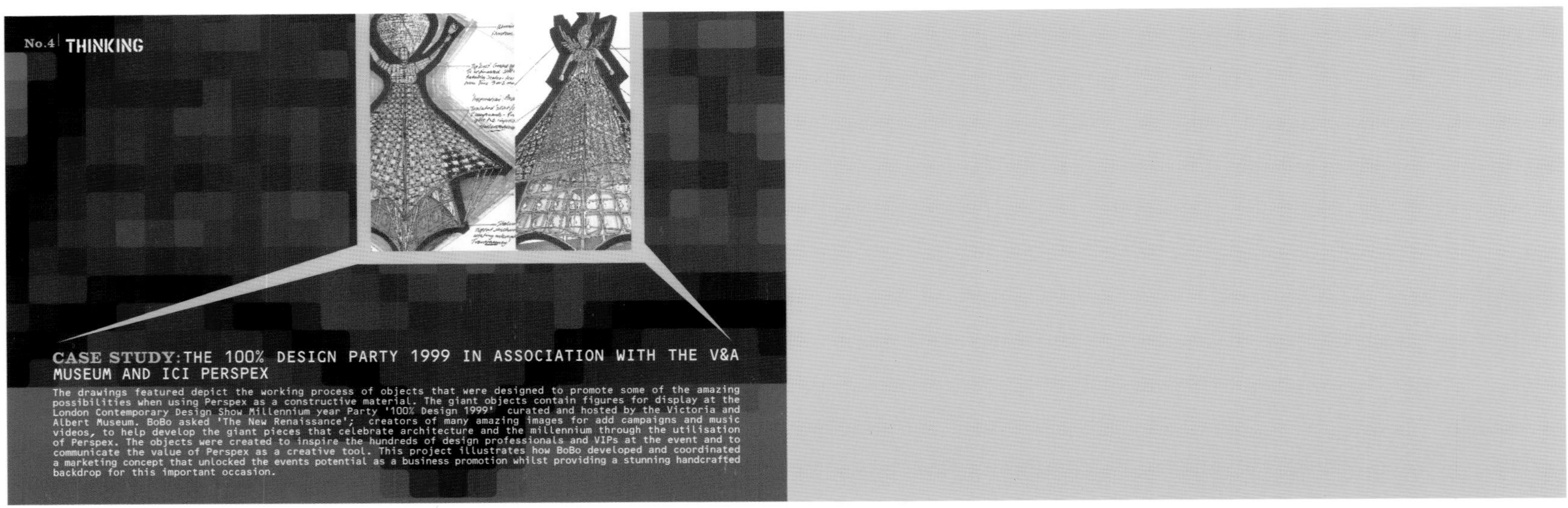

No.4 | THINKING

CASE STUDY: THE 100% DESIGN PARTY 1999 IN ASSOCIATION WITH THE V&A MUSEUM AND ICI PERSPEX

The drawings featured depict the working process of objects that were designed to promote some of the amazing possibilities when using Perspex as a constructive material. The giant objects contain figures for display at the London Contemporary Design Show Millennium year Party '100% Design 1999' curated and hosted by the Victoria and Albert Museum. BoBo asked 'The New Renaissance'; creators of many amazing images for add campaigns and music videos, to help develop the giant pieces that celebrate architecture and the millennium through the utilisation of Perspex. The objects were created to inspire the hundreds of design professionals and VIPs at the event and to communicate the value of Perspex as a creative tool. This project illustrates how BoBo developed and coordinated a marketing concept that unlocked the events potential as a business promotion whilst providing a stunning handcrafted backdrop for this important occasion.

Designers
Mark Allen, Dave Bravenec, Adrianne De Loia, Armando Llenado, Chris Martinez

Art Director
Dave Bravenec

Illustrators
Dave Bravenec, Adrianne De Loia, Alejandra Jarabo

Photographer
Dave Bravenec

Design Company
Kick Media

Country of Origin
USA

Description of Artwork
Stationery for C14 Design, the creative laboratory of Kick Media.

Dimensions
Sticker (*below left*), Business card (*below right, top & bottom*):
115 x 51 mm, 4 1/2 x 2 in
Postcards (*opposite*):
153 x 102 mm, 6 x 4 in

Format
Corporate identity

C14 Design

The strong graphic identity of this design group has two simple elements: a black C14 logo-type and the second-color hippopotamus. Two-color printing is used to maximum effect (*below*), with the second color appearing in three different percentage tints, and text reversed white-out-of-green in contrast to the black text used elsewhere. The postcards (*opposite*) immediately identify the company through its name and the hippopotamus, showing that consistent use of a word or symbol can identify, even when their connection to the activity of a company is not immediately obvious.

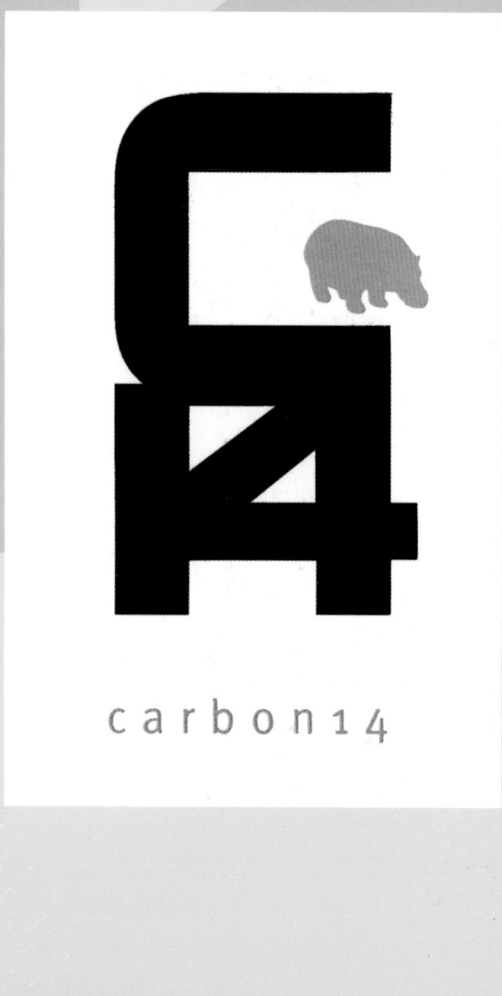

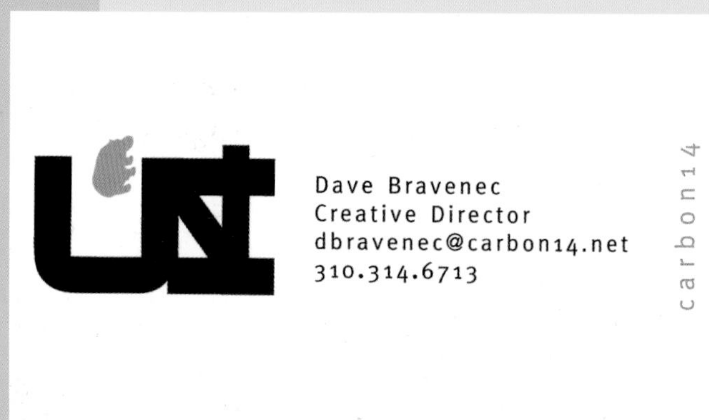

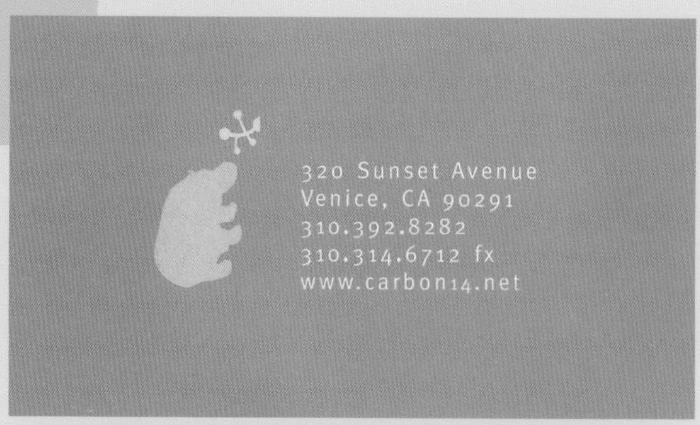

This side of the business card reveals how the varied use of the second color can produce a degree of subtlety within a bold design.

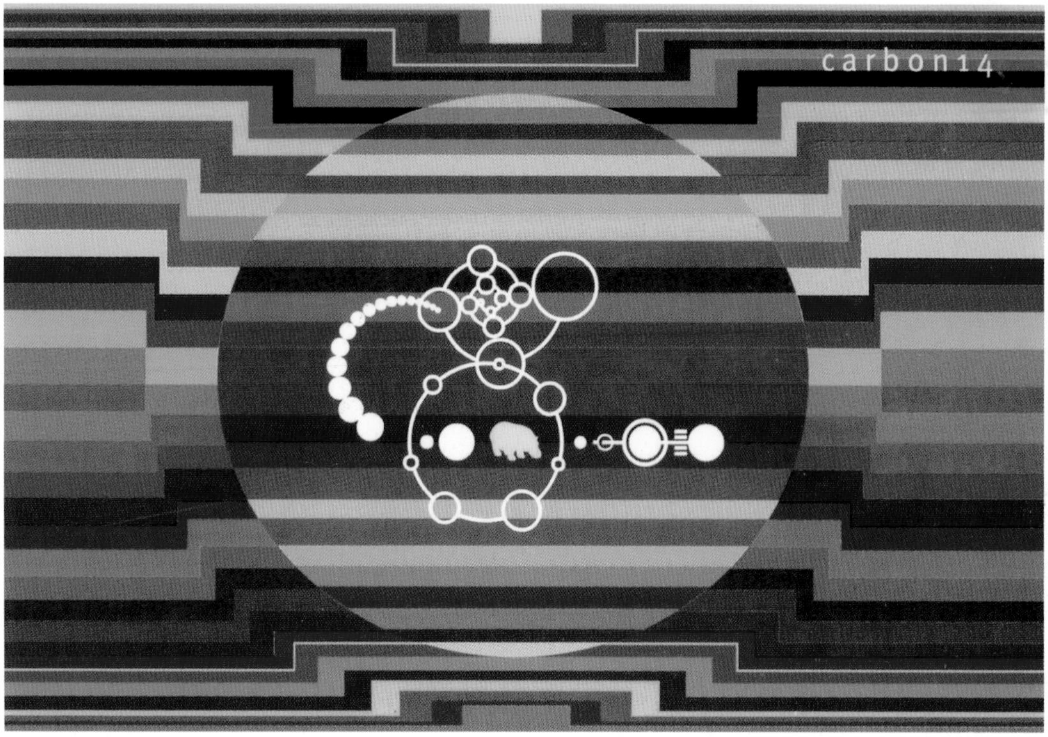

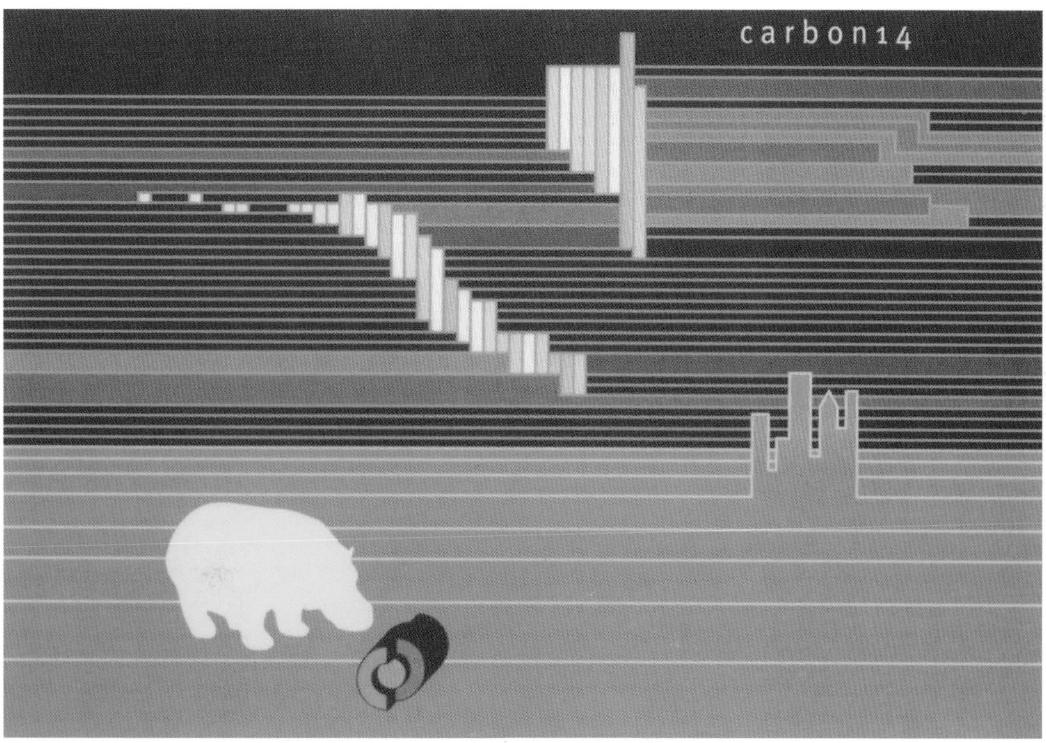

C14 mostly use the hippo symbol in a purely abstract way. However, on this postcard, its use is more directly linked to the design: it seems to be looking at the cylindrical object—which increases its flexibility and adds a touch of humor.

Thomas & Bohannon Stationery

Everything about this range of stationery has been inspired by tools of the printing trade—a simple idea, nicely executed. The centerpiece of the design is an industrial-catalog-style line drawing of a printing press which acts as the company logo. In addition, a number of graphic devices, all part of the printer's lexicon—crop marks, registration marks, density panels, and guide rules—work to produce a distinctive and extensive stationery range. The resulting design communicates a sense of specialist expertise and attention to detail that is a very good promotion of the company to potential clients.

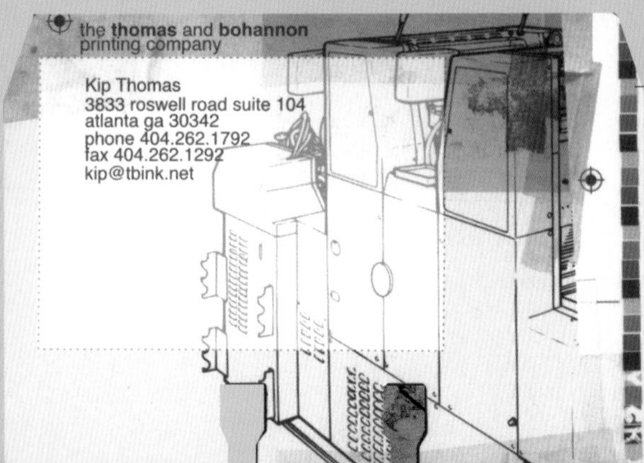

This color strip is derived from the color ink density panels used by printers to check color balance before starting a print run.

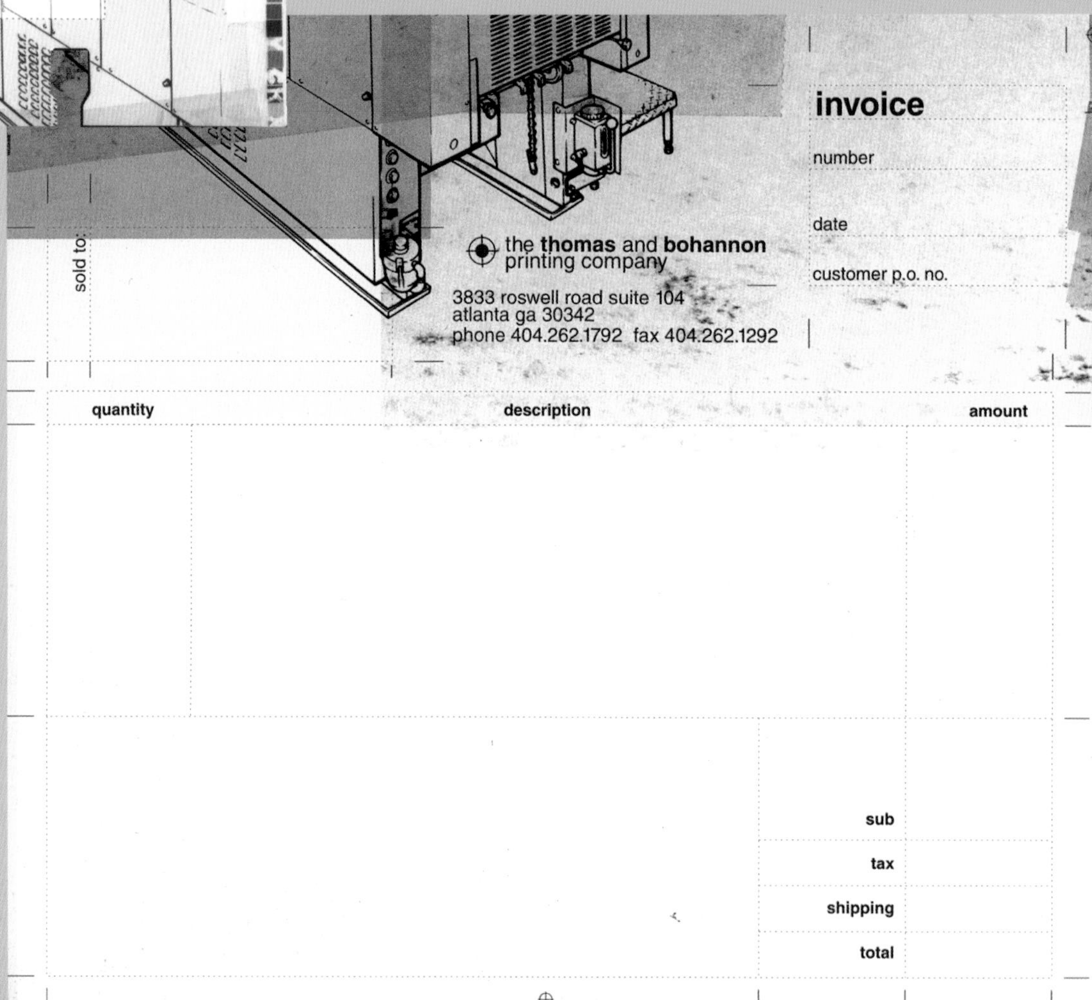

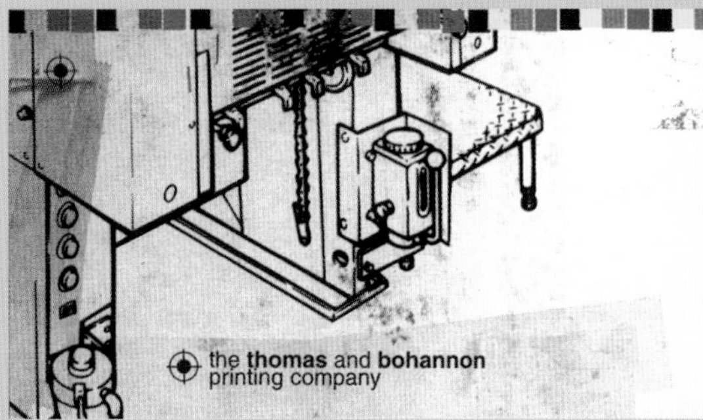

Crop marks, normally used to show where to trim the printed sheet, are used here to play with the space on the page by demarcating the area in which to type or write.

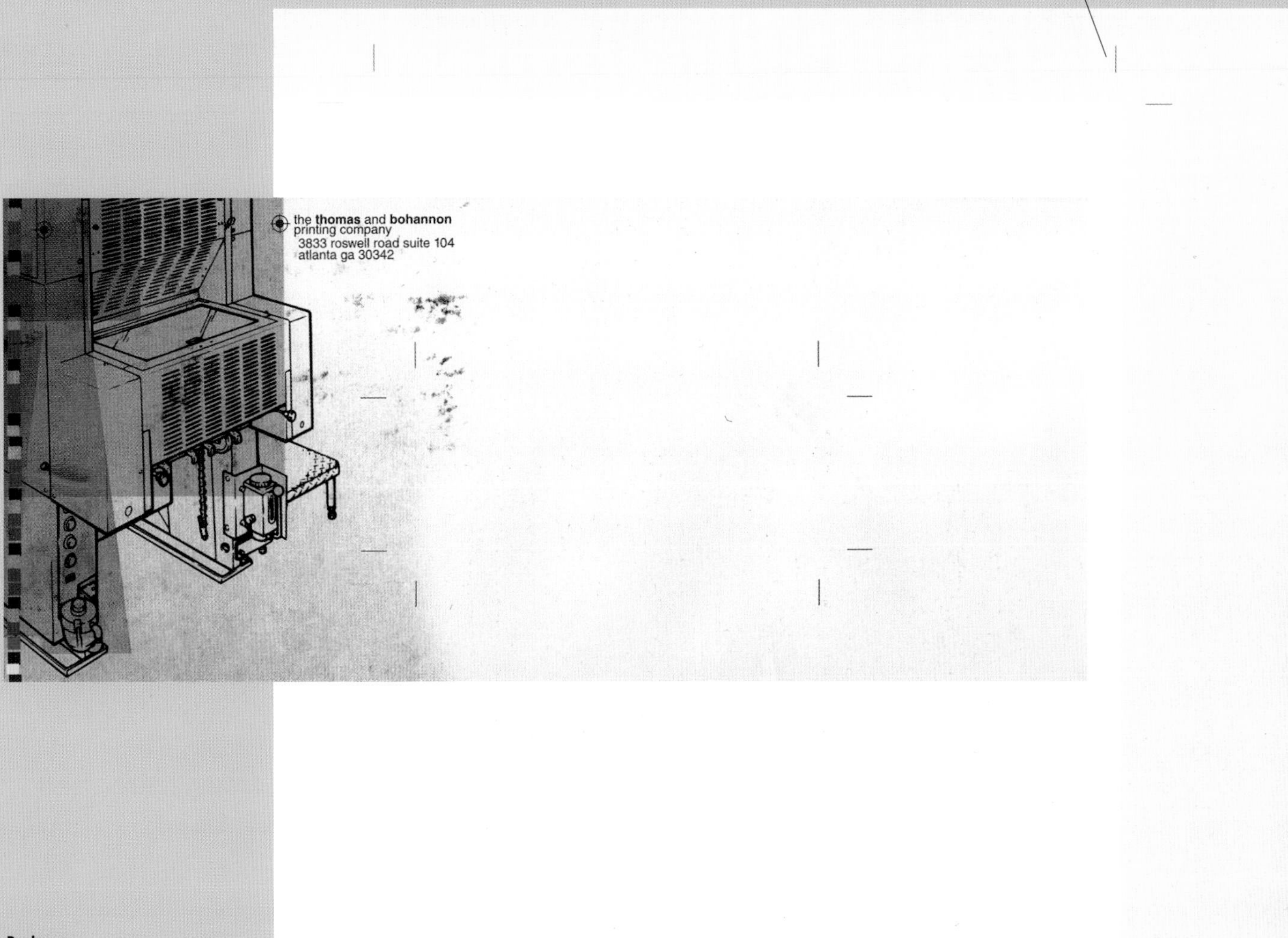

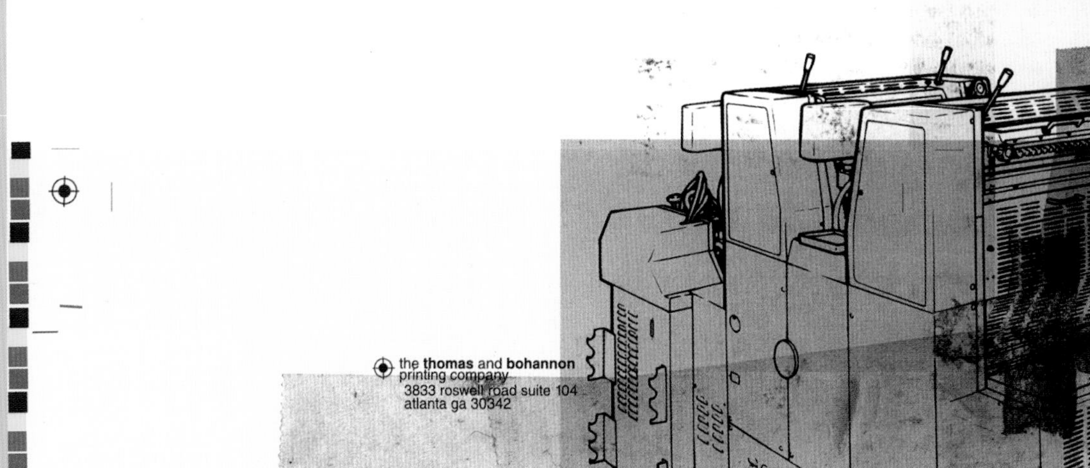

Designers
Graphic Havoc avisualagency

Illustrators
Graphic Havoc avisualagency

Design Company
Graphic Havoc avisualagency

Country of Origin
USA

Description of Artwork
Corporate identity package, including 'logo,' stationery, and website, for an offset lithography printing company.

Dimensions
Various

Format
Corporate identity

Designers
David Hand (*below, left*)
Seel Garside (*below, center*)
Hitch (*below, right*)
Ian Mitchell (*opposite*)

Design Company
Beaufonts

Country of Origin
UK

Description of Artwork
A set of posters featuring fonts created by Beaufonts.

Dimensions
297 x 420 mm
$11^{3}/_{4}$ x $16^{1}/_{2}$ in

Format
Poster

Don't Panic—This is Beaufonts

Advertising typefaces is not easy, as they are often required to be the unobtrusive building blocks of design. Here, Beaufonts' simple but witty posters serve their purpose very well, not only to promote their type library but also the company and its website. They succeed in promoting very different font styles by using disparate but always intriguing images together with recurring areas of flat color that give visual cohesion to the promotion.

Special Production Techniques

Designed specifically to be downloaded from their website, these posters have never been traditionally printed.

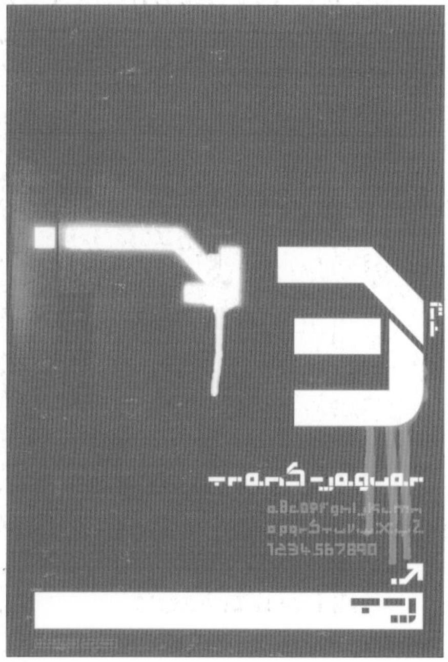

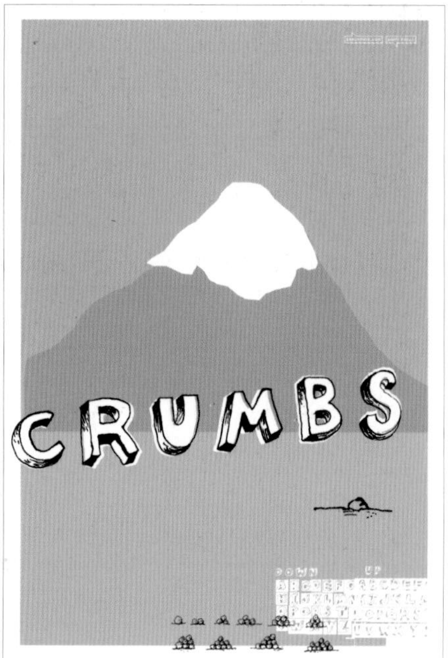

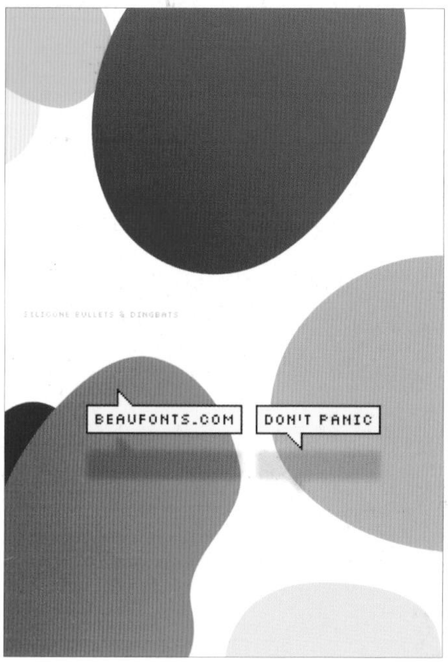

www.
beaufonts
.com

[letterforms,
symbols,
ideas and
interaction]

DON'T PANIC

BEAUFONTS.COM

Chercher/Trouver (Looking For/Finding)

Interesting self-promotion is achieved here without showing any of the designer's work. Instead, the activities of the group are presented conceptually. This book has been created alongside their website and therefore has been strongly influenced by it. The use of geometric line imagery creates a background texture upon which the text is overlaid. The central information bar acts as a stable backbone against which the other elements are varied and contrasted.

Opposite, center: the fluid background design successfully evokes movement, which is a key element of the accompanying interactive website.

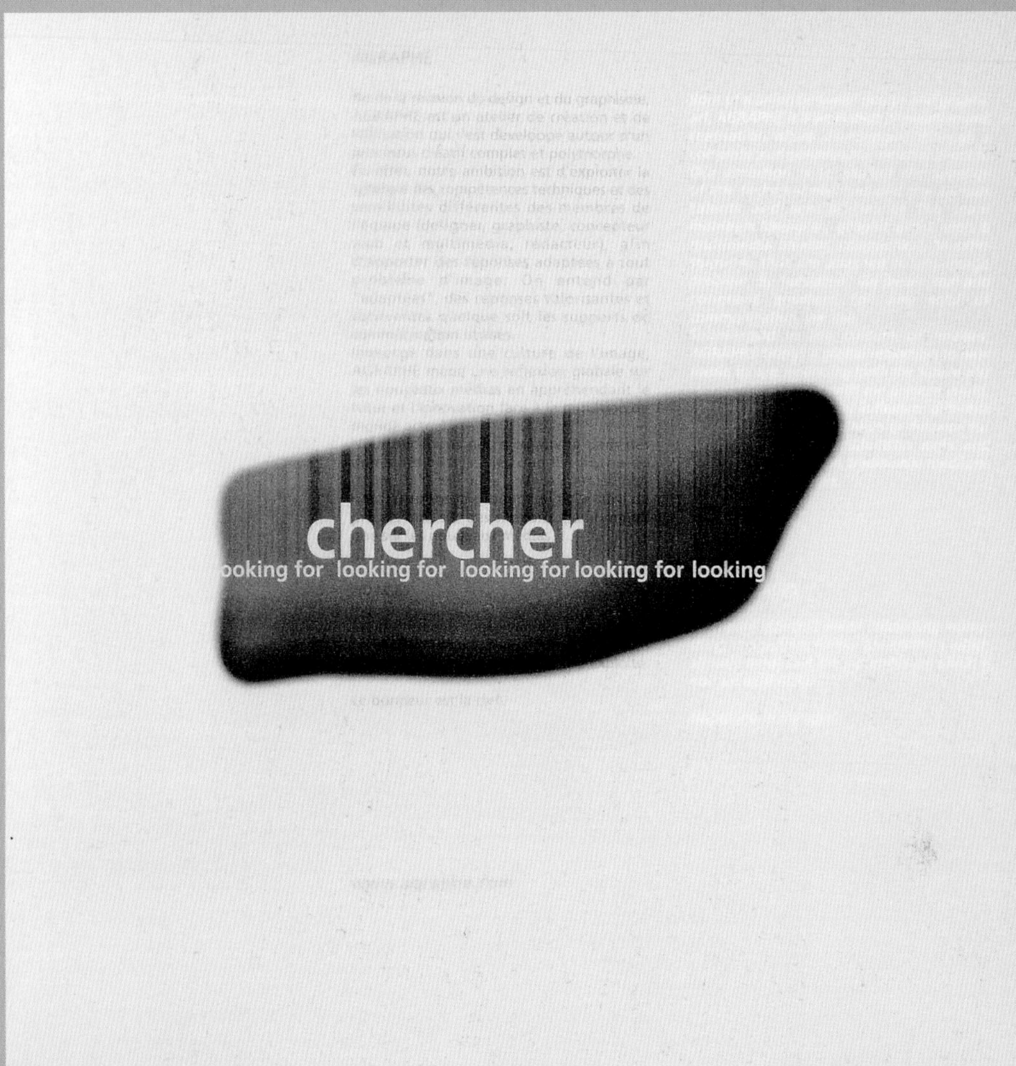

Designer
Agraphe

Art Director
Thomas Erhel

Copywriters
Laetitia Campana, Thomas Erhel, Luis Mizon

Illustrator
Ludovic Erhel

Photographer
Computer images and photographs by Agraphe

Design Company
Agraphe

Country of Origin
France

Description of Artwork
28-page self-promotional book

Page Dimensions
210 x 210 mm
$8^1/_4$ x $8^1/_4$ in

Format
Book

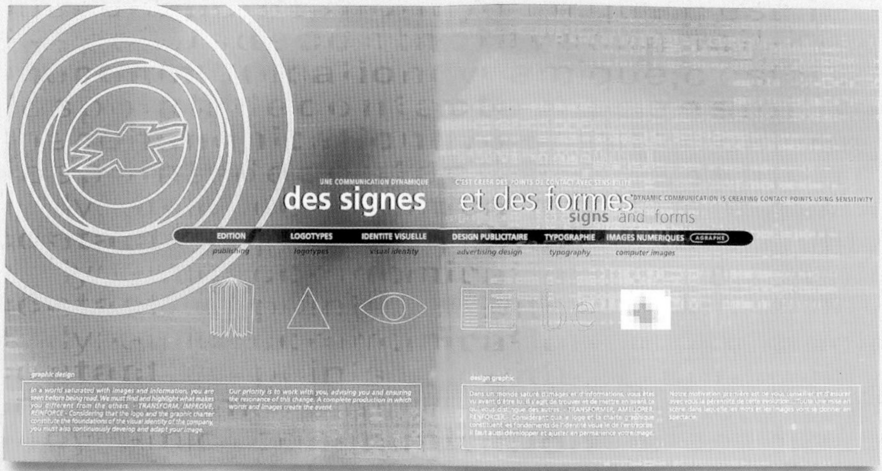

UNE COMMUNICATION DYNAMIQUE
des signes
et des formes
signs and forms
EDITION
LOGOTYPES
IDENTITE VISUELLE
DESIGN PUBLICITAIRE
TYPOGRAPHIE
IMAGES NUMERIQUES
AGRAPHE
publishing
logotypes
visual identity
advertising design
typography
computer images
graphic design
design graphic

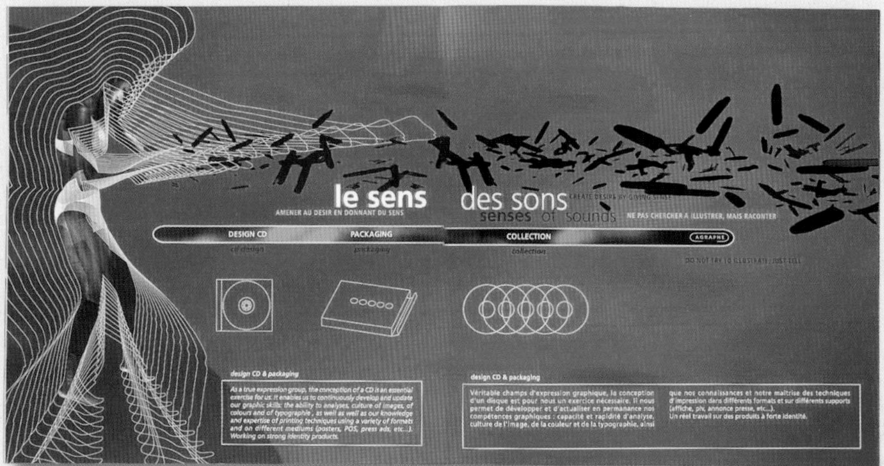

le sens
des sons
senses of sounds
AMENER AU DESIR EN DONNANT DU SENS
NE PAS CHERCHER A ILLUSTRER, MAIS RACONTER
DESIGN CD
PACKAGING
COLLECTION
AGRAPHE
design CD & packaging

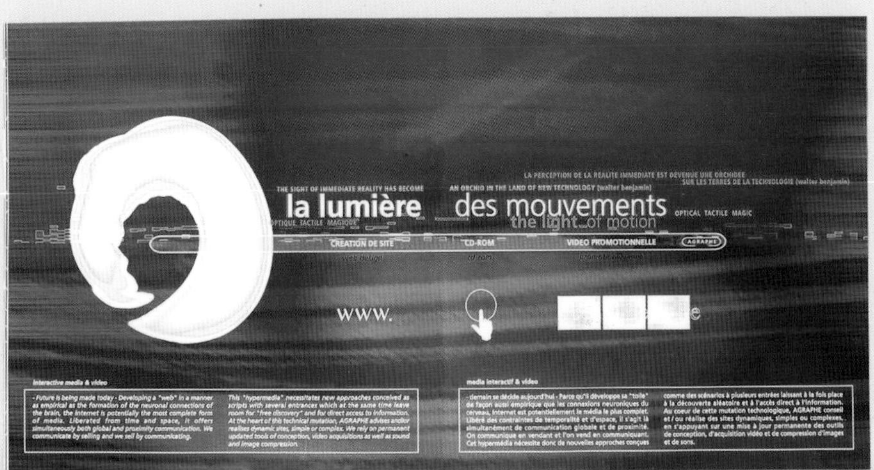

la lumière
des mouvements
the light of motion
OPTICAL TACTILE MAGIC
CREATION DE SITE
CD-ROM
VIDEO PROMOTIONNELLE
AGRAPHE
www.
interactive media & video
media interactif & video

Fuel Printed Matter

(See following spread for description)

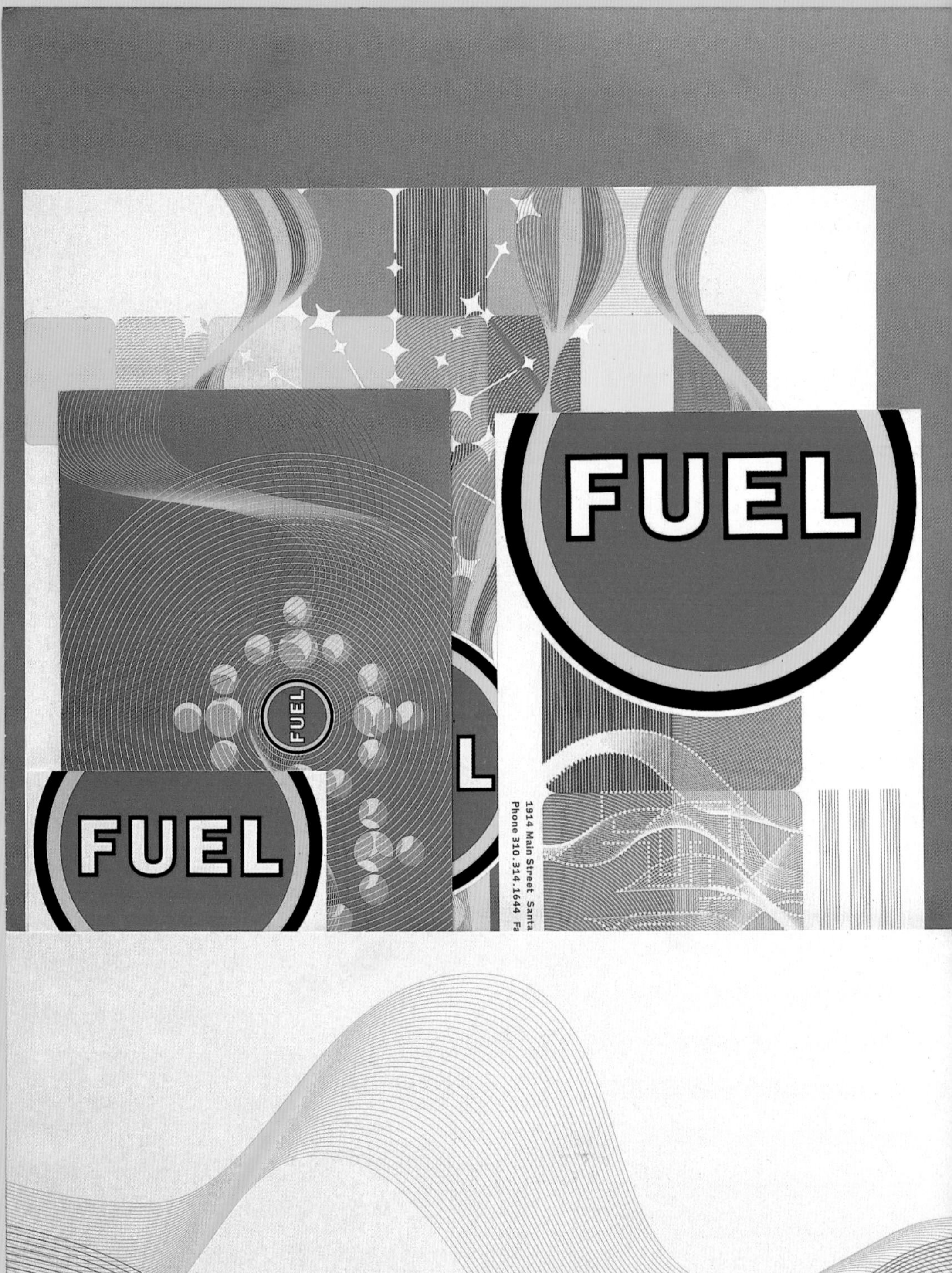

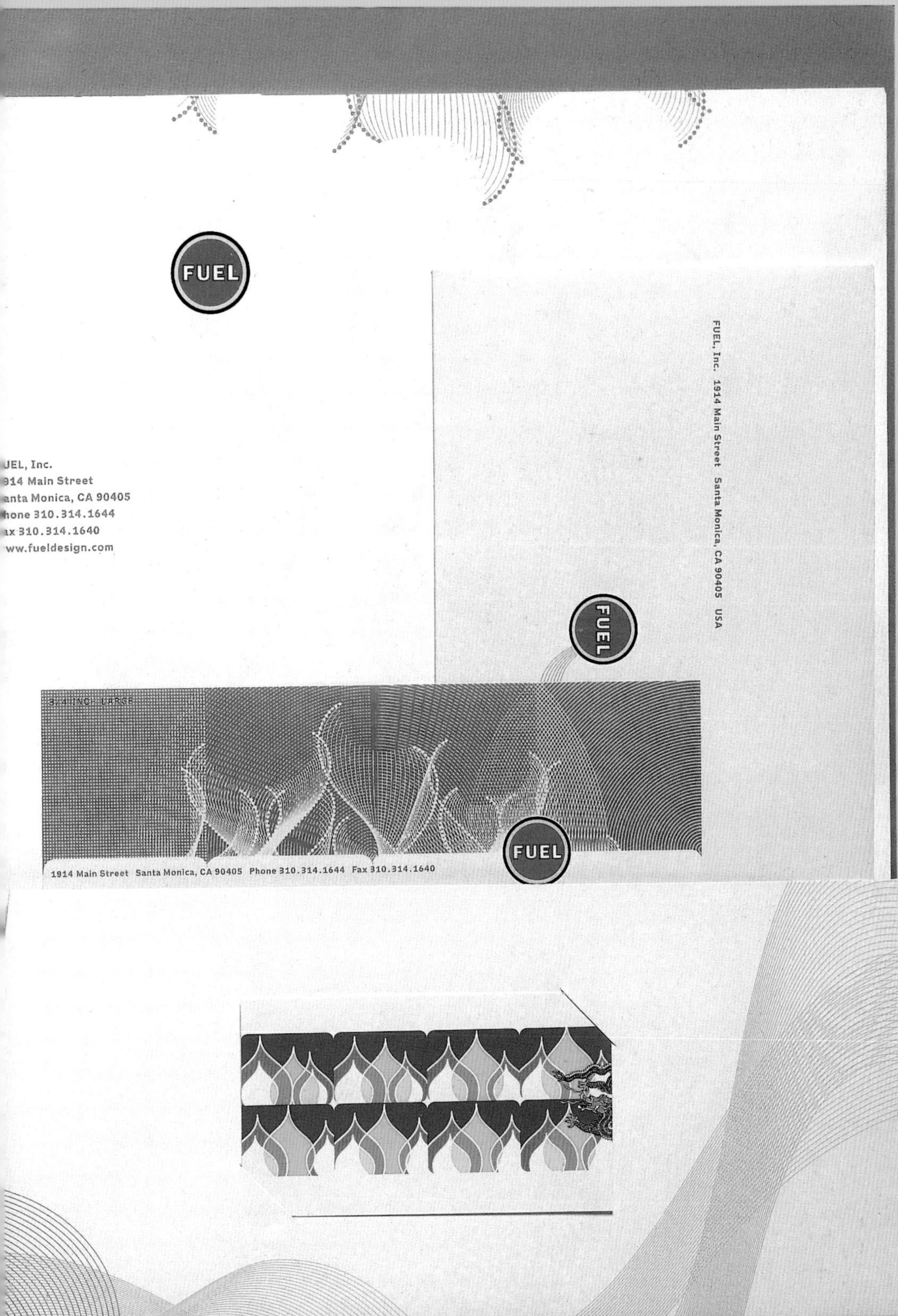

Designer
Jens Gehlhaar

Creative Director
Seth Epstein

Illustrator
Jens Gehlhaar

Design Company
Fuel

Country of Origin
USA

Description of Artwork
A range of stationery and packaging, including video labels and inserts, for the Santa Monica based motion graphics studio Fuel.

Dimensions
Various

Formats
Stationery, packaging

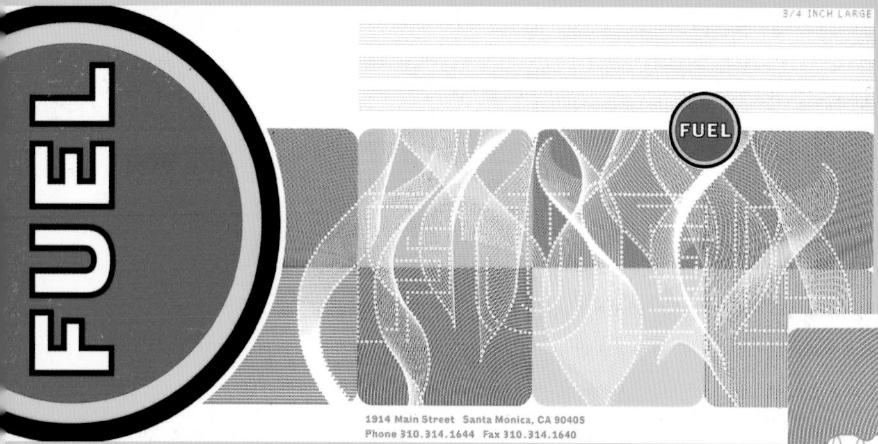

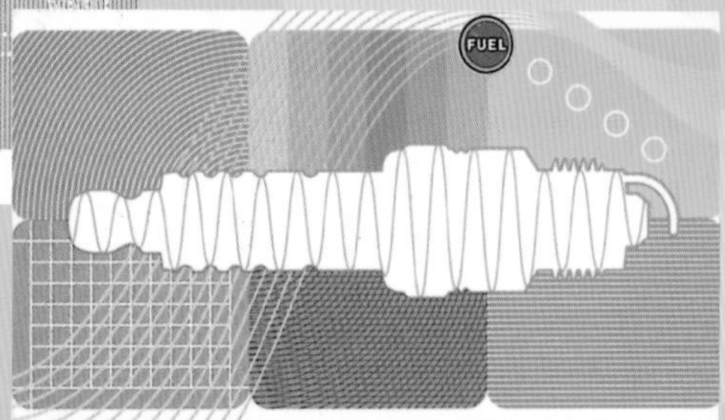

Flowing curves keep the whole design in motion and reinforce the dynamic nature of the company's output.

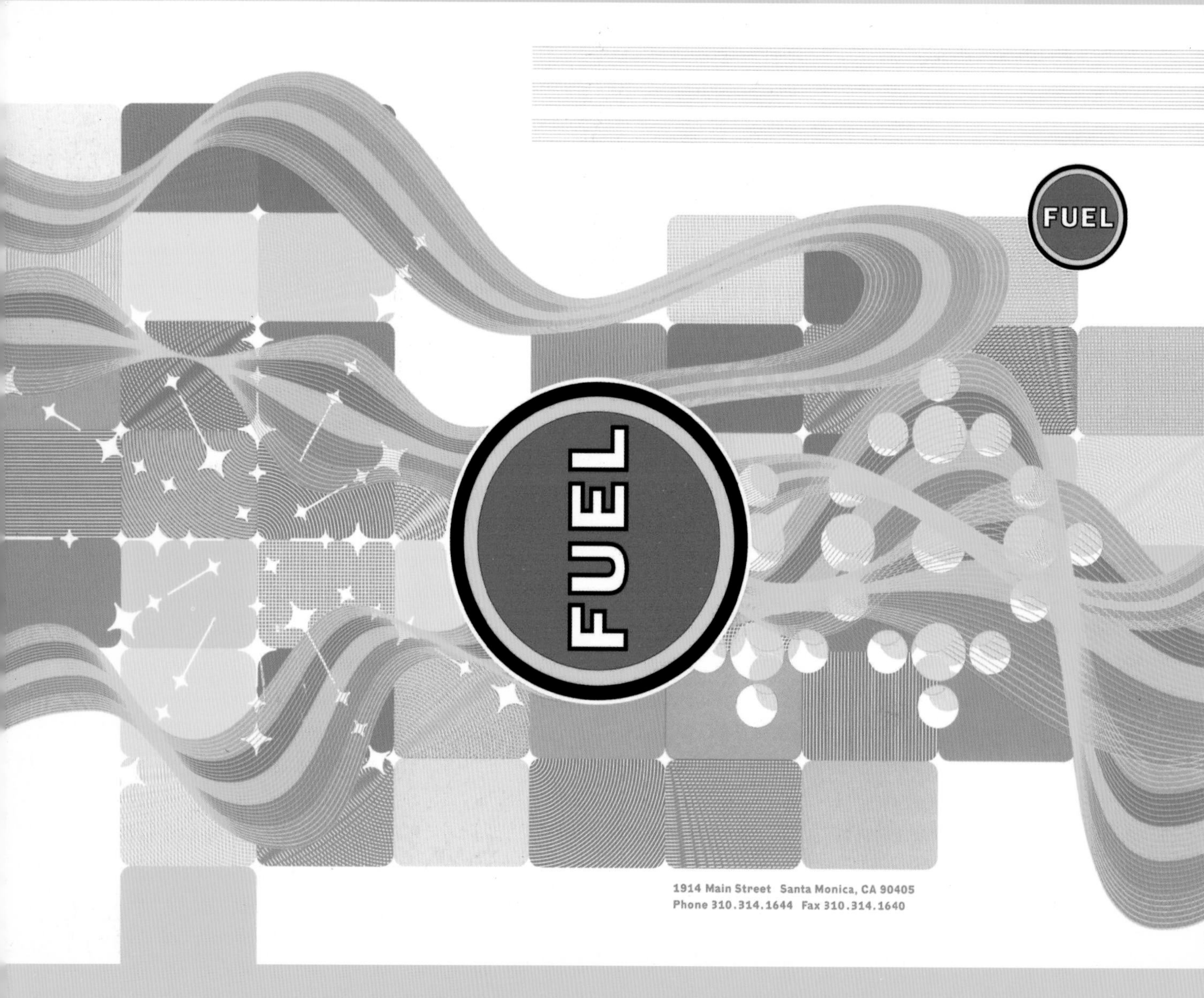

FUEL

Fuel Printed Matter

Taking its inspiration from the company's name, the designer's intention was to 'express very television-specific ideas, such as energy and motion, with very print-specific means, such as metallic inks and intaglio vector art.' The simple boldness of the logo and consistent use of color gives a strong and instantly recognizable visual identity to a wide range of stationery. The use of metallic ink enhances the visual feel by contrasting bright colors against flat metallic gray, while the 'intaglio vector art,' which hints at bank-note currency, adds a subliminal value.

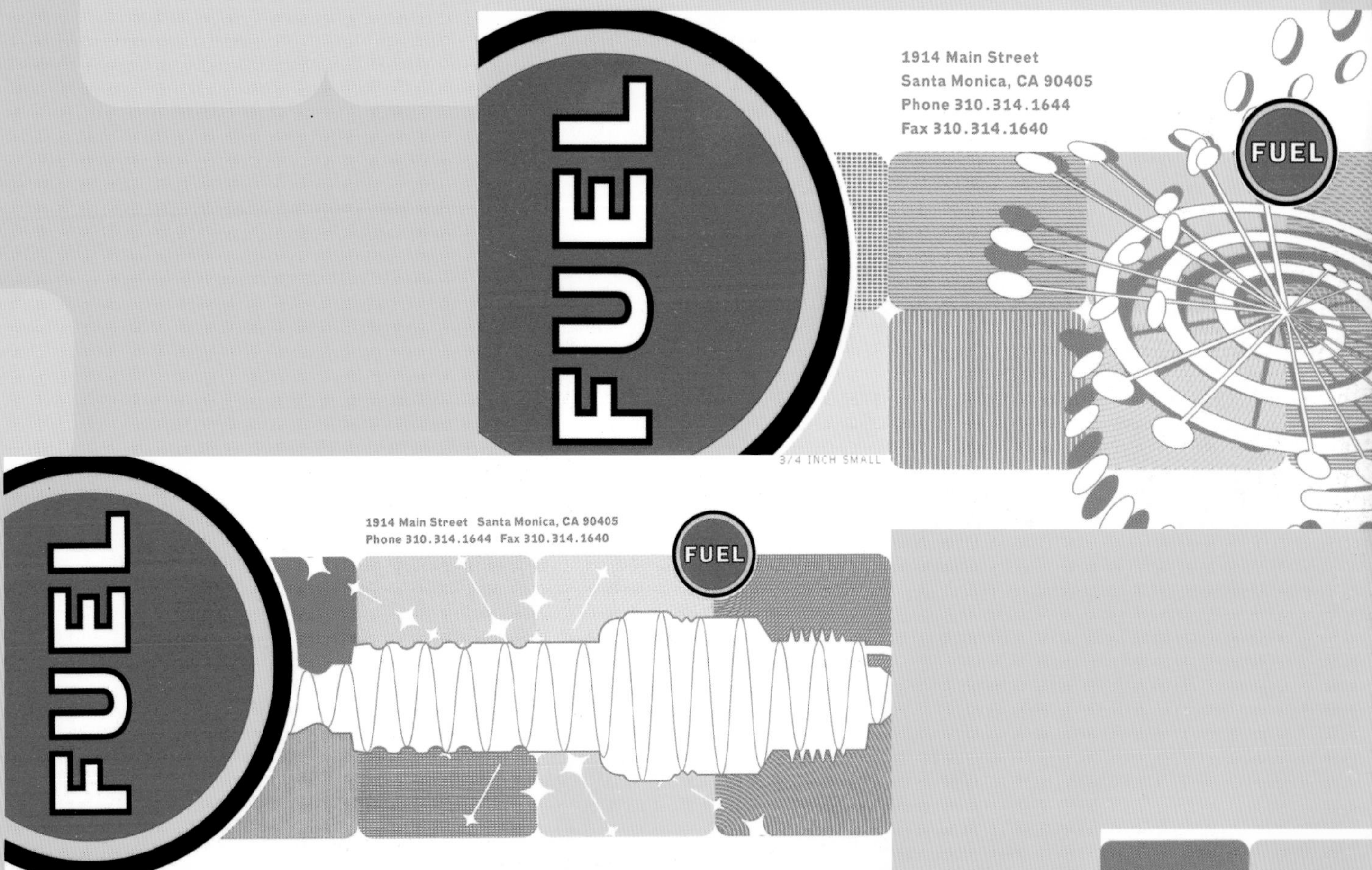

The outline of a spark plug is used to extend the analogy with engine technology and to suggest creative inspiration.

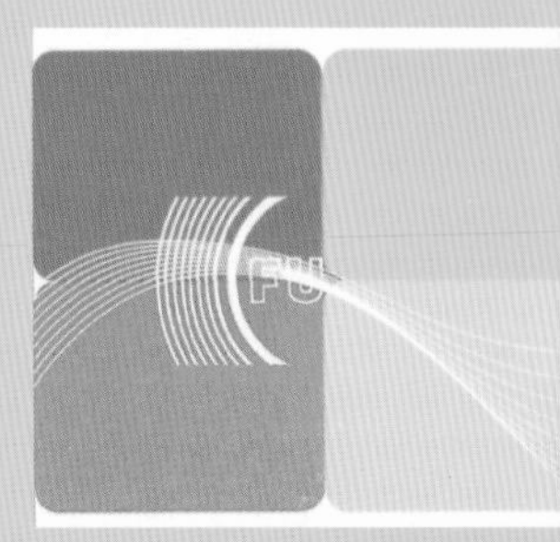

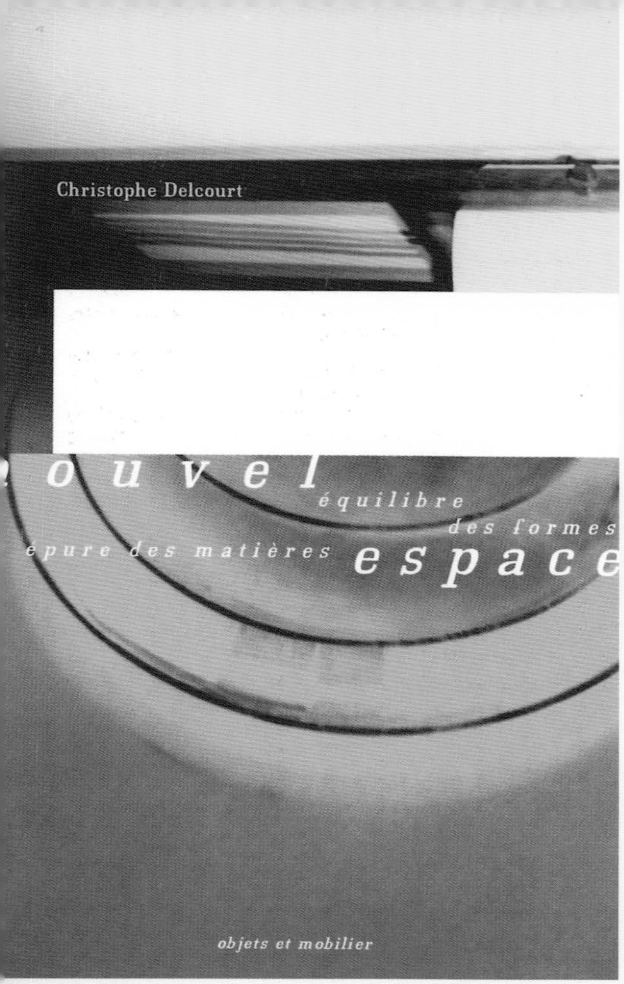

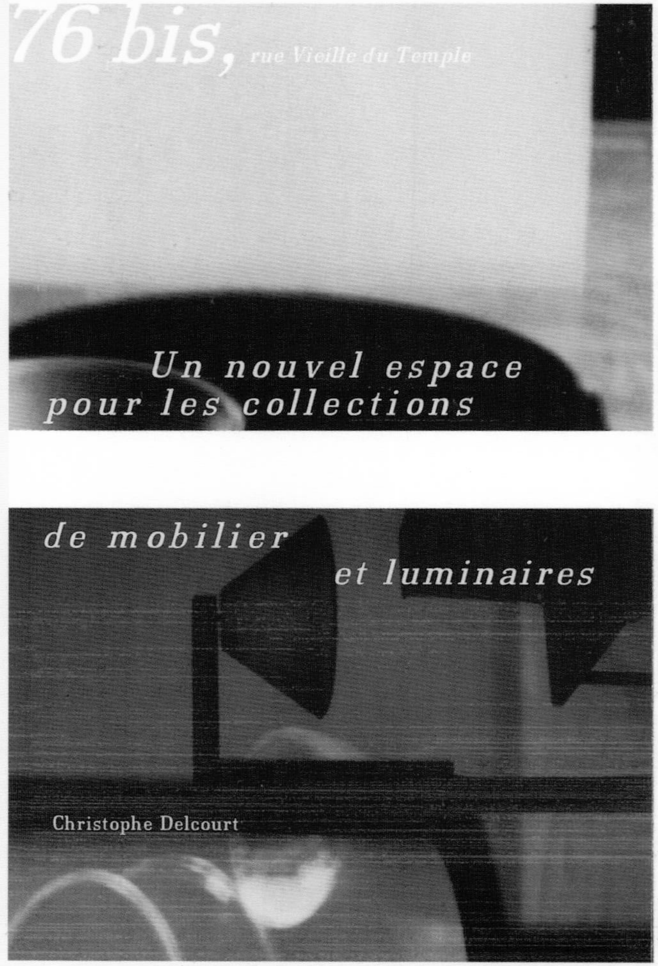

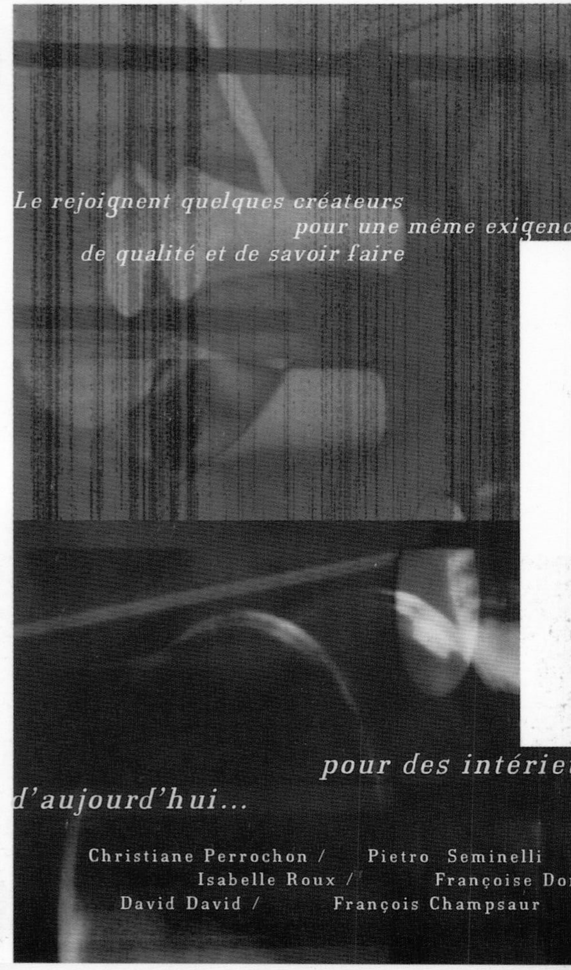

The play of forms within a space is central to this furniture designer's thinking and this is reflected in the way that the page area has been divided and intersected by areas of white.

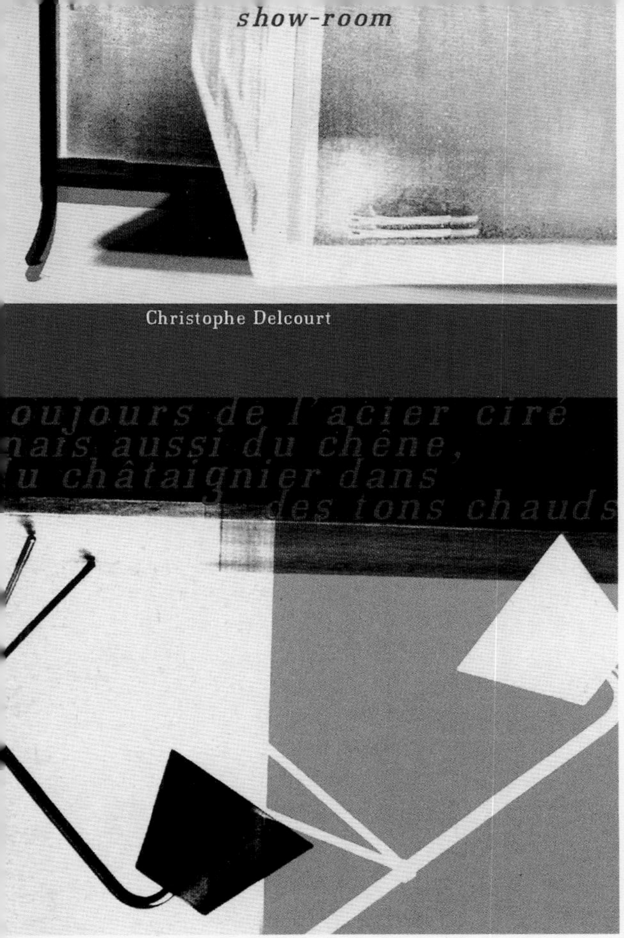

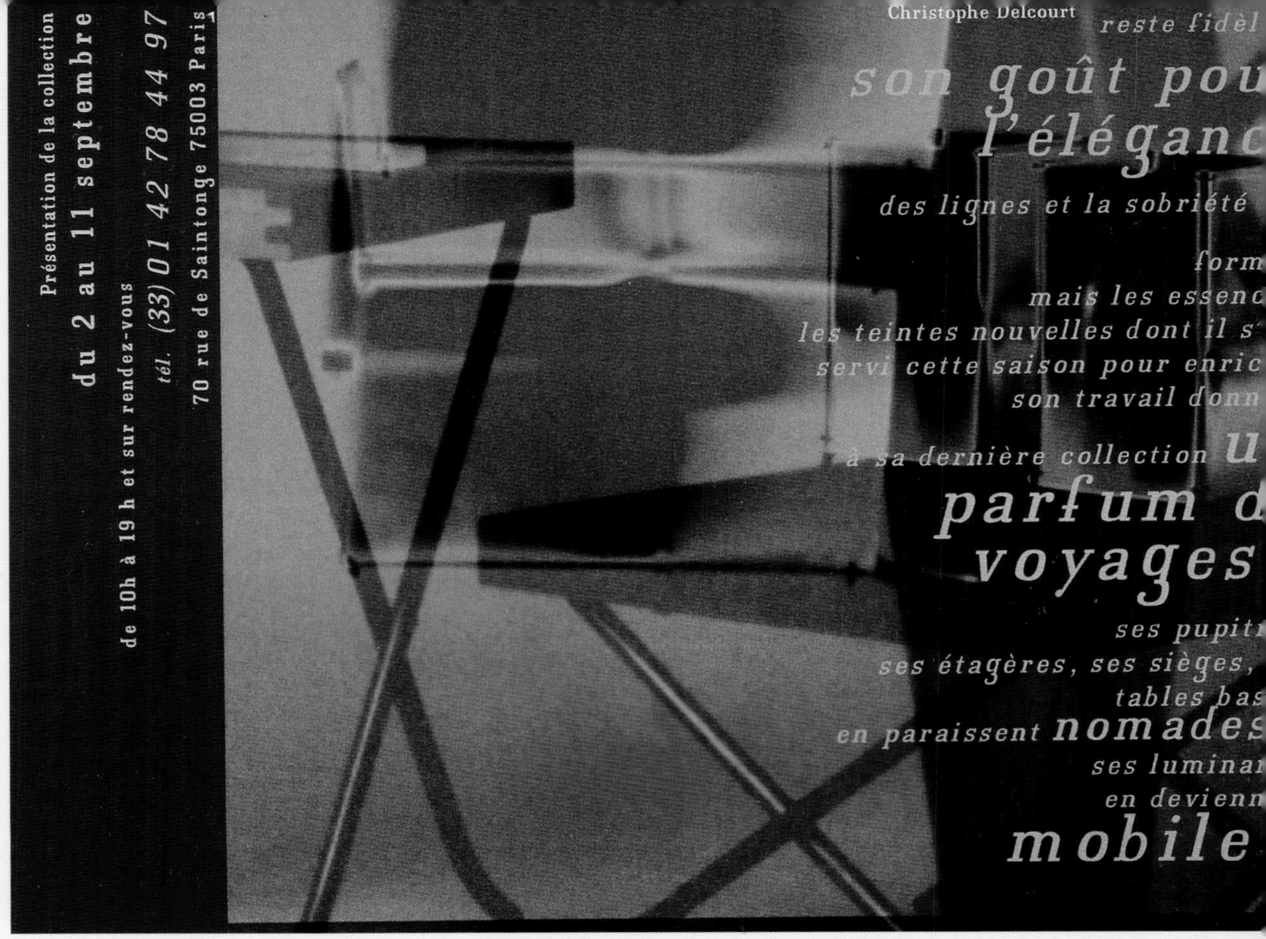

Designer
Philippe Savoir

Art Director
Philippe Savoir

Design Company
Filifox

Country of Origin
France

Description of Artwork
Invitations to view the work of furniture and lighting designer Christophe Delcourt

Page Dimensions
180 x 215 mm
7¹/₈ x 8¹/₂ in

Format
Invitation

'New Room'—Christophe Delcourt

The choice of two-color printing and the layering of abstract photographic imagery creates a subtle yet sophisticated style that matches that of the furniture and lighting on show. The delicate typography on the covers of the folded invitations (*left, above* & *opposite*) is developed inside and combined with a narrow color range that reflects the materials used by the furniture designer.

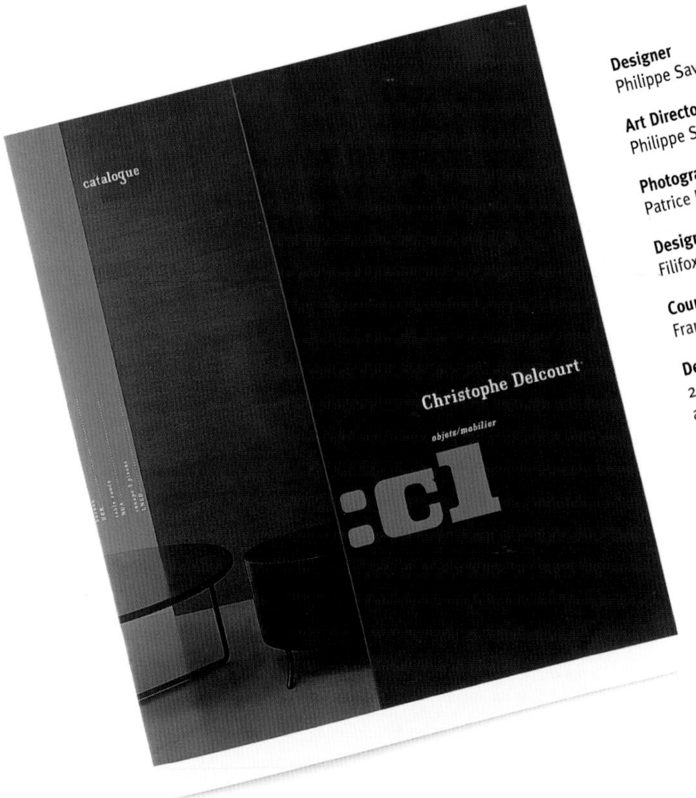

Designer
Philippe Savoir

Art Director
Philippe Savoir

Photographer
Patrice Degrandry

Design Company
Filifox

Country of Origin
France

Description of Artwork
24-page catalog of furniture and lighting design by Christophe Delcourt.

Page Dimensions
210 x 260 mm
$8^1/_4$ x $10^1/_4$ in

Format
Catalog

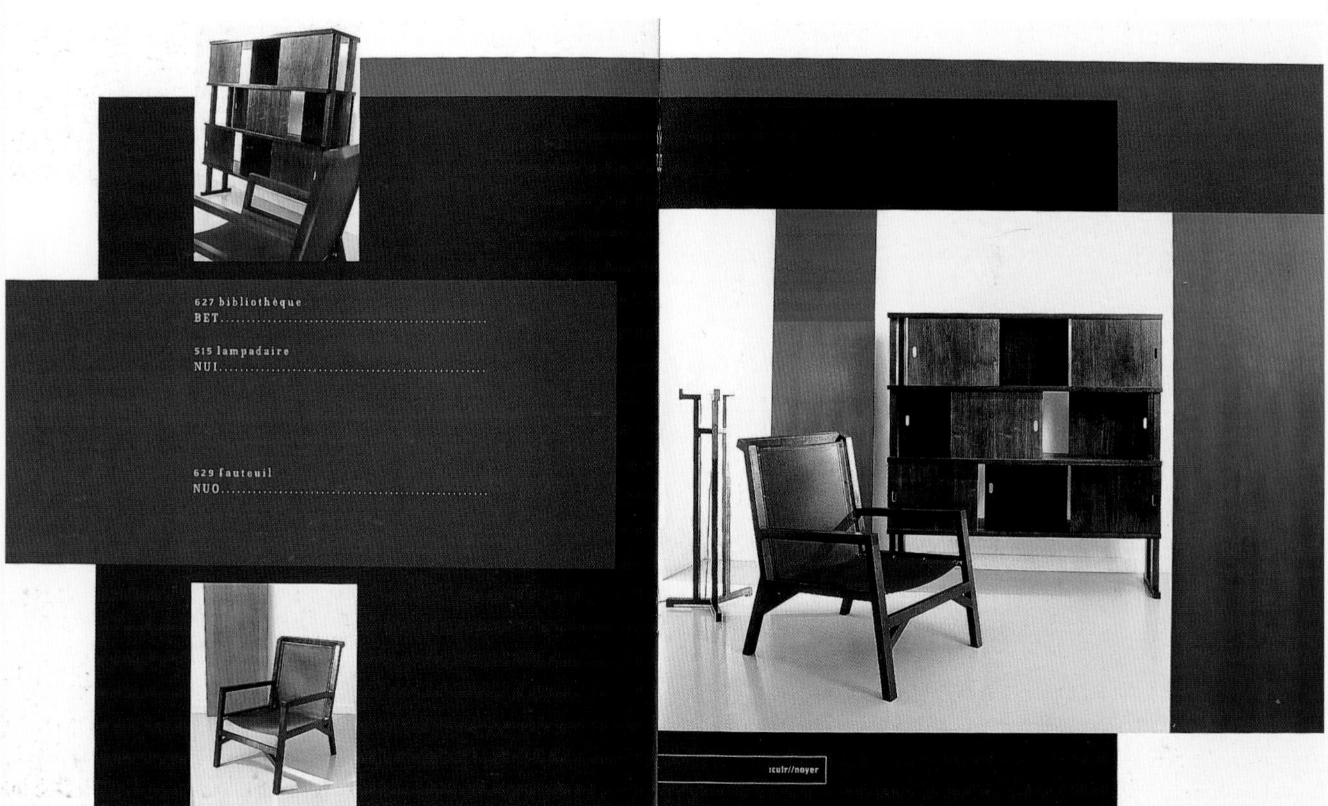

:C1—Christophe Delcourt

The clean lines and style of the furniture and lighting featured in this publication are mirrored in the clear, geometric approach taken to its layout. This aesthetic is extended to the typography which is sparse and tightly controlled. The uncluttered structure of the spreads gives prominence to the elegant richness of the dark wood and leather furniture, strikingly displayed in pristine settings.

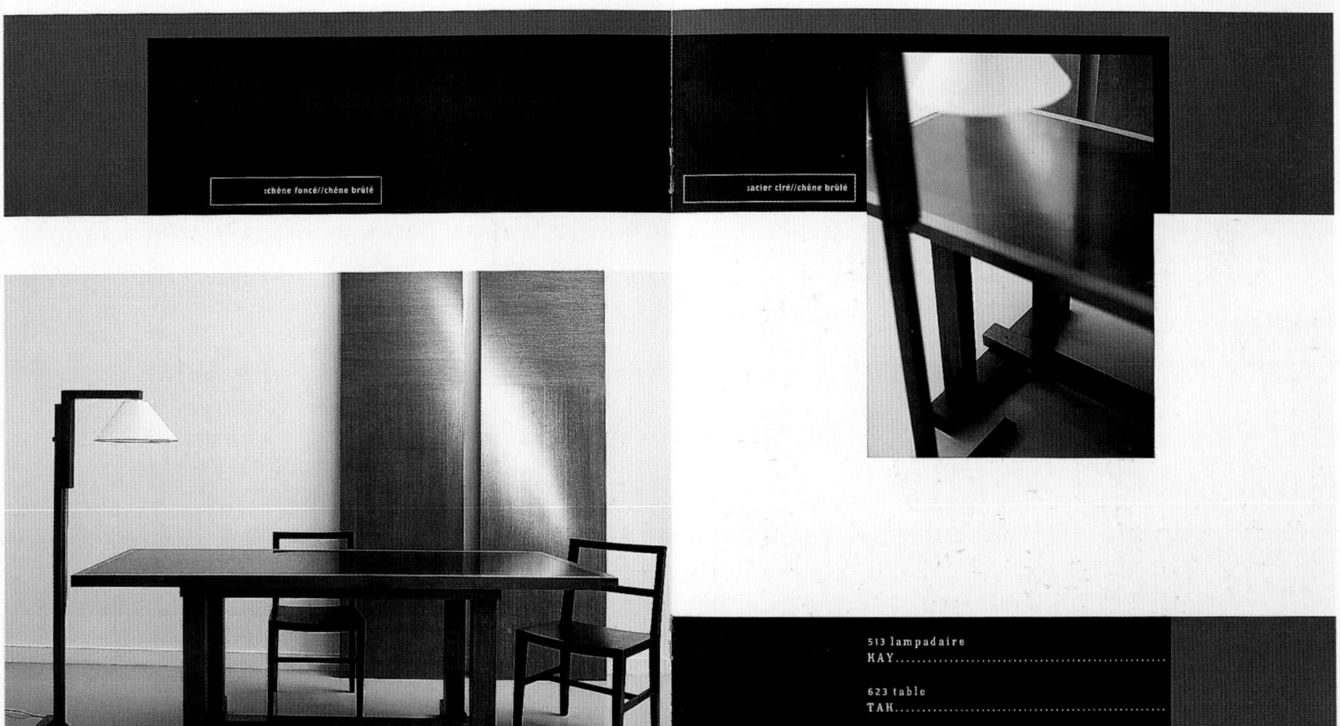

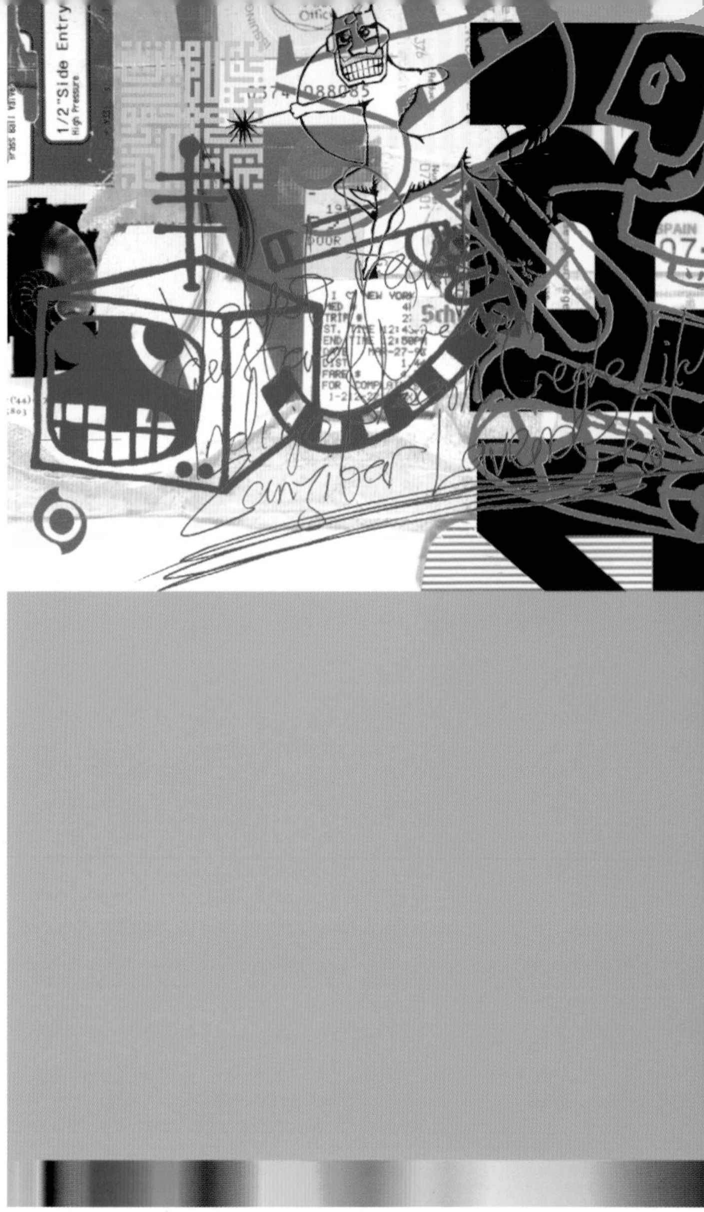

Designer
Mark Caylor

Art Directors
Rob O'Connor, Mark Caylor

Illustrator
Mark Caylor

Design Company
Stylorouge

Country of Origin
UK

Description of Artwork
Corporate identity for use on a coordinated range of stationery.

Dimensions
210 x 99 mm
$8^{1}/_{4}$ x $4^{1}/_{2}$ in

Format
Stationery

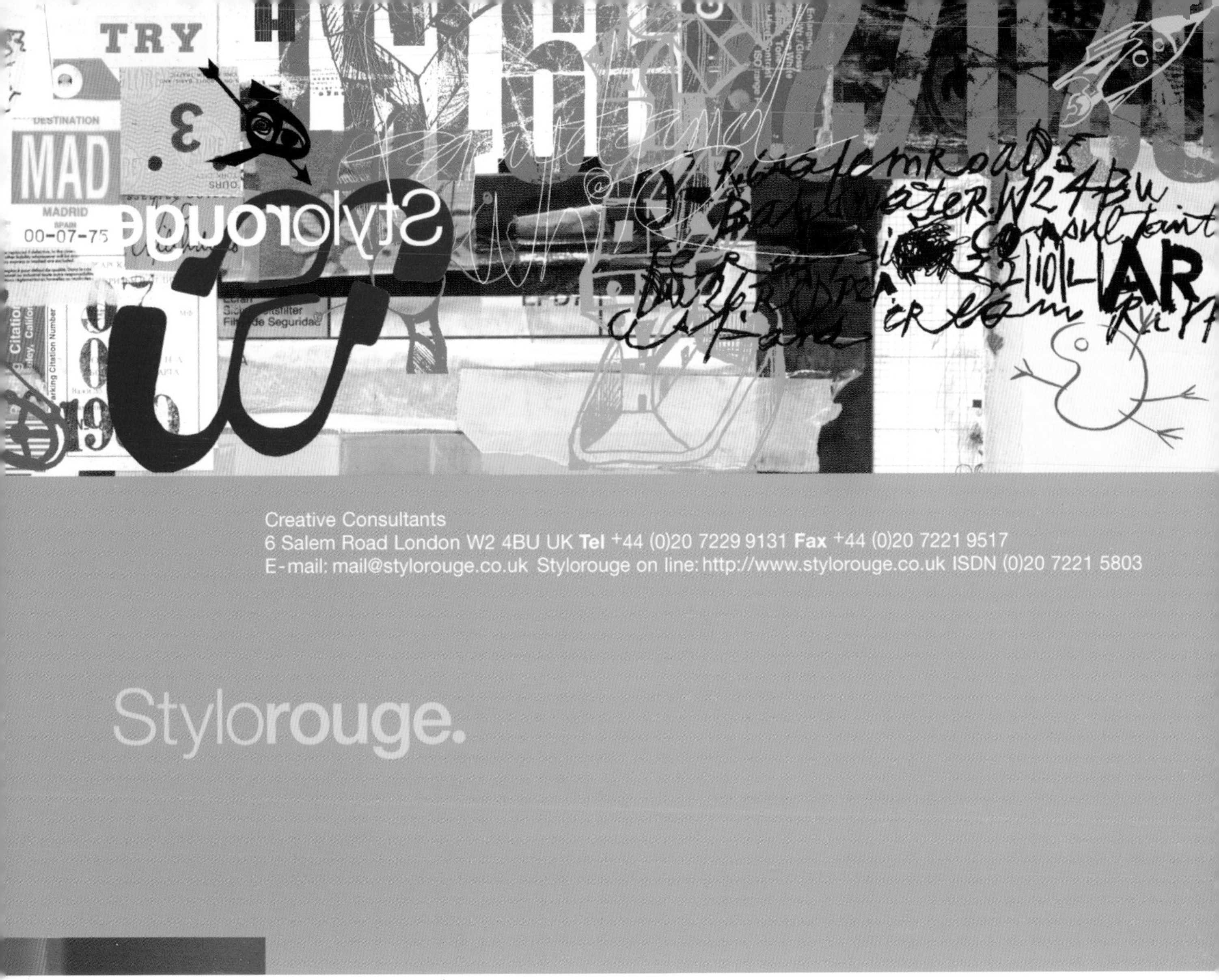

Stylorouge Corporate ID

The diverse nature of Stylorouge's work for the music industry is reflected in the component parts of the image: found typography and pictures, drawings, graffiti, labels, and tickets suggest their eclectic influences. This polyphony of visual languages, reminiscent of a flyposted city wall, stands in stark contrast to the simplicity and clarity of the logo-type and gives this self-promotional work its strong identity.

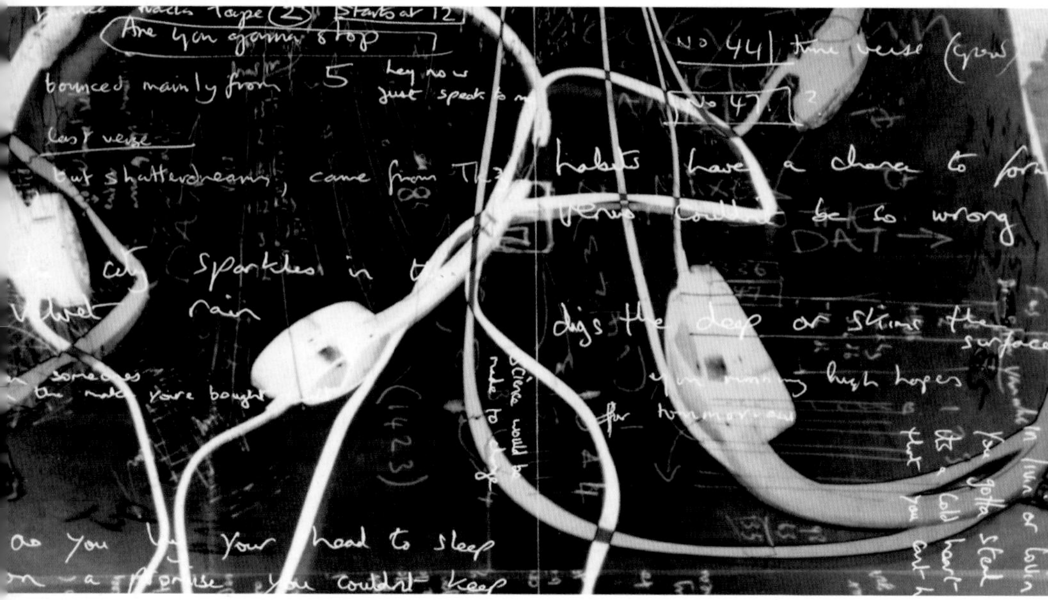

Are you gonna stop
bounced mainly from
last verse
but shatterdreams, came from The
Sparkles in the
rain
habits have a chance to form
be so wrong
digs the deep or skims the surface
high hopes
for tomorrow
your head to sleep
you couldn't keep

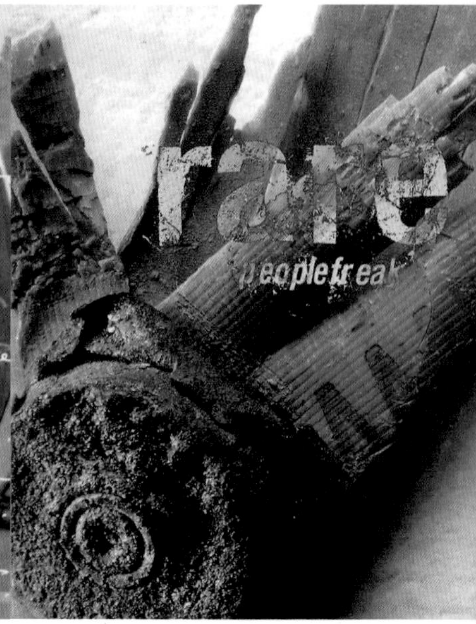

rare
peoplefreak

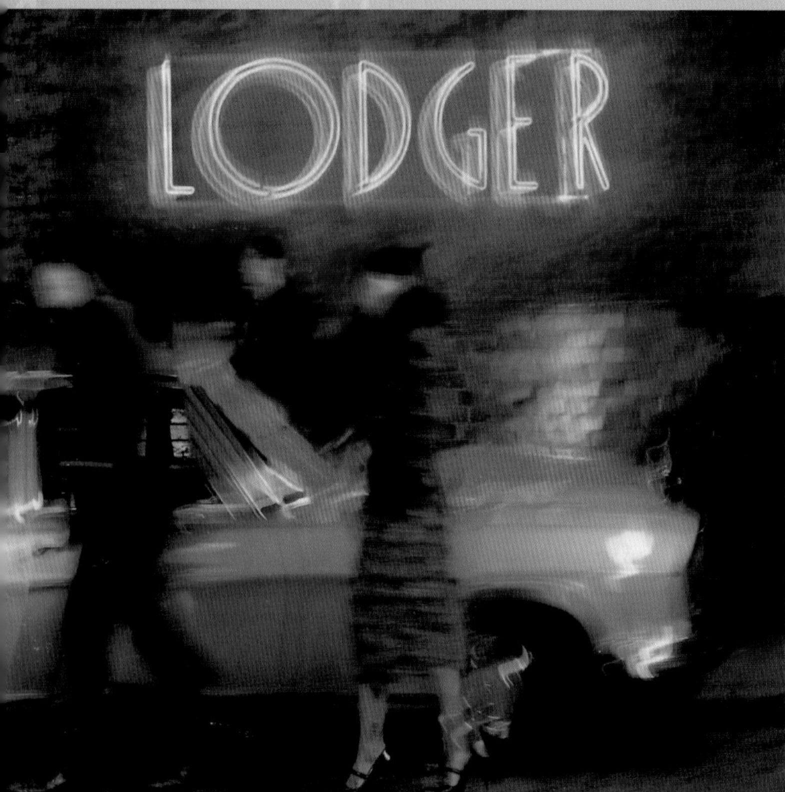

LODGER

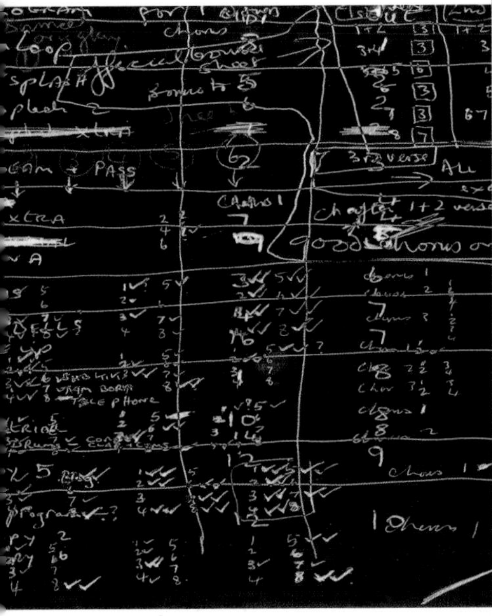

Portfolio #1

This bold presentation of design work for the music industry makes no concessions to the viewer. The abstract images are without explanation, and therefore stand or fall by their visual references and integrity. Whether the work is familiar or not, the choice of imagery suggests the theme being promoted.

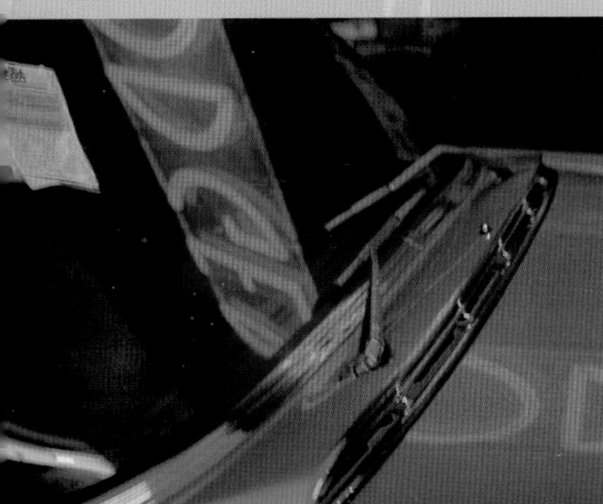

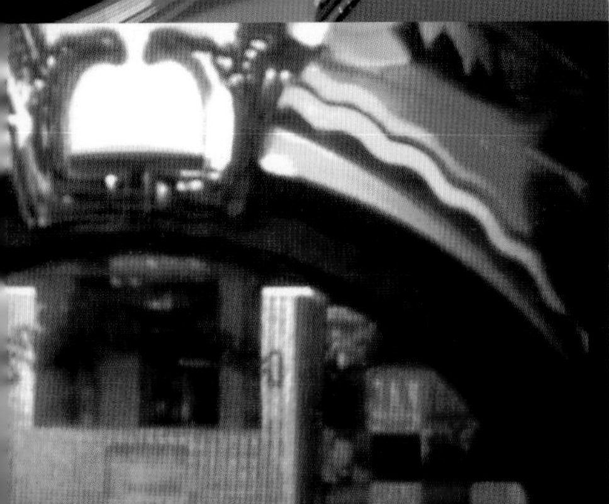

Designers
Rob Crane, Martin Yates

Art Directors
Rob Crane, Martin Yates

Photographers
Top: Alex Hanson, Lucky Morris
Bottom: Stuart Weston

Design Company
Satellite

Country of Origin
UK

Description of Artwork
A collection of design work for the music industry compiled as a promotional portfolio.

Page Dimensions
213 x 155 mm
8³/₈ x 6¹/₈ in

Format
Book

Ogier Stationery

With the type on one side and the image on the other, this slightly costly but engaging twist is an elegant solution to the job. The obscure shapes (parts used in the construction of the lighting sold in Ogier, a contemporary furniture shop) are carefully positioned on the letterhead to be the first thing seen when the envelope is opened. They not only give a feel for the products but also add an enigmatic touch that is in keeping with the whole design approach.

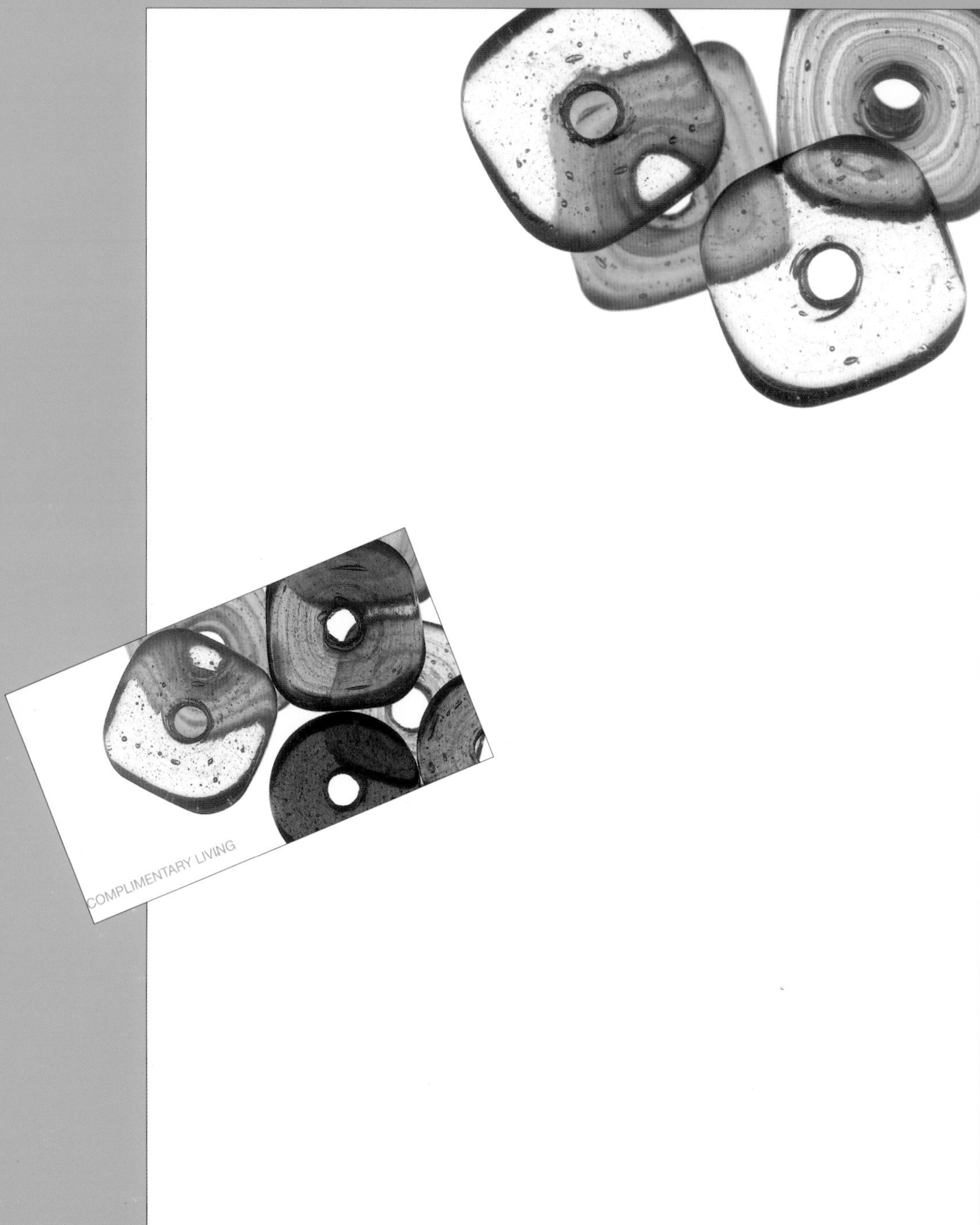

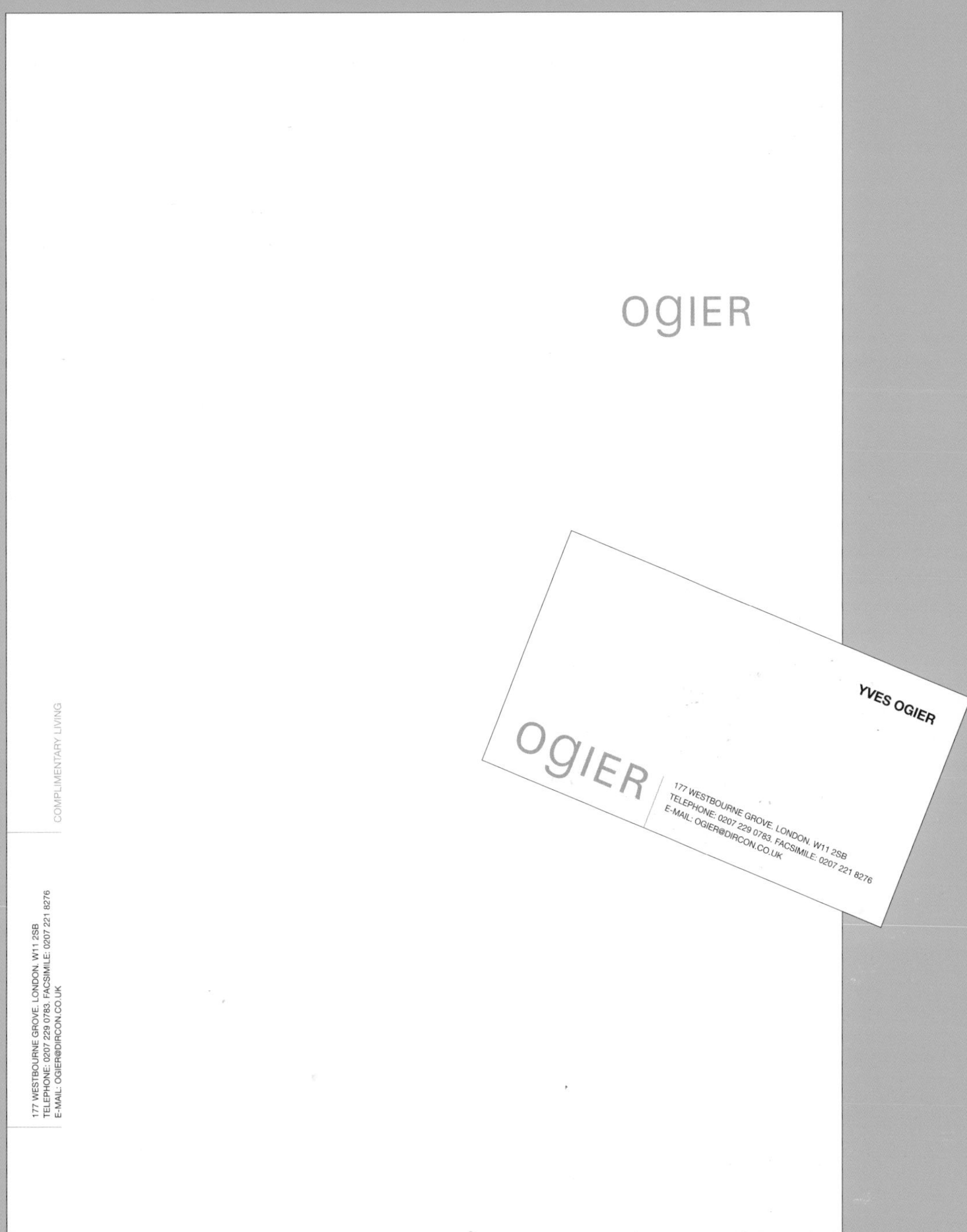

Designer
Mark Rogerson

Art Director
Mark Rogerson

Photographer
Jonathan Brade

Design Company
Mark Rogerson Associates

Country of Origin
UK

Description of Artwork
Stationery designed for Ogier, a contemporary furniture shop.

Dimensions
Letterhead: 210 x 297 mm
$8^{1}/_{4}$ x $11^{3}/_{4}$ in
Business Card: 90 x 50 mm
$3^{1}/_{2}$ x 2 in

Format
Stationery

Scintpreen/Preenscint

(See following spread for description)

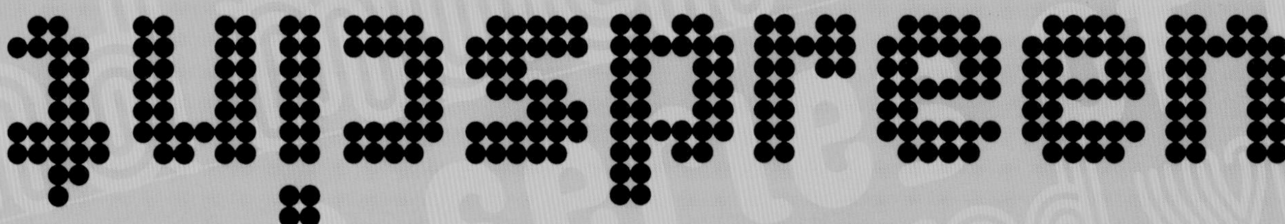

Designer
Jens Gehlhaar

Illustrator
Jens Gehlhaar

Country of Origin
USA

Description of Artwork
36-page book about the changes the graphic design profession faces with the advent of new media. Text by Jens Gehlhaar.

Page Dimensions
203 x 257 mm
8 x 10 in

Format
Book

THE VOYAGE

"[...] the process of large group or team projects in multimedia has less to do with the division of labor in print production, and is much more akin to collaborative enterprises, such as theatrical production, TV production, or movie-making in the entertainment industry. And in those enterprises, the identity and independence of individuals responsible for the visual presentation [...] are secondary in both the hierarchy of production and in the point of view of the audience to the vision or authorship of the director (and perhaps the screenwriters).

While the accomplishments of the visual collaborators may be highly celebrated and compensated, the ability to launch current and future projects rests with the authors – the directors and screenwriters."

Lorraine Wild

"That was then, and this is now: but was is next?", Emigre, № 39, 1996, p 28

26°

BEYOND THE HORIZON

Lorraine Wild

"...in new media, the connection between content and its presentation is so tight that there is barely any conceptual space in which to see a separate need for development of the visual independent from the verbal."

"That was then, and this is now: but was is next?", Emigre, № 39, 1996, p 26

"[...] at Emigre, [...] as we're trying to deal with the new technologies that surround us, we see more use for the teachings of the young Jan Tschichold: communication must appear in the briefest, simplest, most urgent form."

Rudy Vanderlans

"Graphic design and the Next Big Idea", Emigre № 39, 1996, p 11

THE PROMISED LAND

New media seems to open up a whole new set of possibilities for the design professsion on its quest for more respect. The structural aspect of design (in print: the functionality of the book format, the organization of information, the interactivity of forms) becomes more visible on the screen and is discussed by the public on a bigger scale. While in print a variety of standardized and well-tried media like brochures, flyers, folders, magazines etc. are at the designer's disposition, allowing him to take the user's familiarity with these media for granted, in interactive media with every new project a new sub-medium has to be invented. ¶ Right now, there is not much more than either a web site or a CD ROM. The web itself is just defined by – as the name suggests – its own connectedness and its boundlessness. A CD ROM is a technical term for 650 MB of data storage. As of now, neither a website nor a CD ROM is a culturally defined medium that is associated with notions of specific purposes or the amount of time it takes to go through it. As long as there are options explored that divert from the traditional personal computer interface, as long as there are no scales defined, the creation of the medium itself – manifested in its naviga-tion and the logic of its map – is a highly visible and interesting problem. ¶ If with every new digital work at the beginning the user has to learn how to navigate, then the design will never become as invisible as it is supposed to be in other traditionally structure-heavy areas like user's manuals or forms. In consequence, in new media the design becomes noticed more.

¶ Like exotic bindings, extravagant inks and technical gimmicks like punches or embossing get noticed even by non-professionals, in new media every user interface which goes beyond the traditional models of Macintosh or Windows desktops will be regarded as an innovation, an invention, as a design product – and of course gets criticized if it fails. The creation of the structure now demands a serious amount of the design process and shifts its emphasis from semantics to syntax. In print we can take the various media for granted and use them as an empty canvas we create our design on – in new media we have to create the integral functionality of the medium and run out of time when it comes to take care of the soft, intuitive aspects that enrich the meaning but don't have an impact on the function. ¶ For many designers, the option for a new level of attention makes the new media a promised land, where the graphic designer is respected as an important contributor to the finished work. At the same time, new media, with its stress on structural aspects, seems to be regarded as a place of refuge for those who have problems with contemporary degenerated or multi-layered design and are looking for an intact world to start all over ←

Maybe the boundlessness of digital media – previously regarded as its virtue – becomes its downfall. Would you pay $14.99 for a music CD if you wouldn't be sure that you are getting at least 45 minutes of music? Would you decide to watch a feature film if there would be a chance that it maybe is six hours long?

There is an interesting tension within the design profession between the notions of invention and design. The invention of folding techniques or other technical or marketing innovations in print is often seen with suspicion, because they usually are connected with high production and precious luxury products, or disregarded as a gimmick that weakens the rest of the design. At the same time, non-professionals love these things. The notion of the inventor-designer seems much more fitting to industrial design, where the invention of form often leads to a new kind of product.

A WELCOME CHA(LLE)NGE

On the other hand, those who had a share in the blame for degrading the old world, and are now bored by both the (apparent) exhaustion of possibilities and the inherent limitations of print may regard new media as a welcome change and a new challenge. Of course, they are missing that – as I mentioned above – there is a need for a re-definition of print, the working out of its integral advantages, as well as the opportunity to disprove the exhaustion theory ←

18°

19°

“The book

just doesn’t seem to have the power that it used to.

We’re persuaded much more easily and much more powerfully by a series of moving images empowered with

sound and visual imagery.

We have to understand that these new media are there and plug in.”

Mark Rattin

as quoted in: Will Novodselik: “Dumb”, Eye, № 22, Vol 6, 1996, p 67

Scintpreen/Preenscint

Using the metaphor of the discovery of the Americas, this book boldly explores the impact of new digital media on graphic design. Imaginative and complex typography has been used to great effect, overcoming the limitations of the one-color printing. Each spread holds a surprise that keeps the viewer engaged with the text, while the way in which the layout responds to the book's central metaphor sustains this typographic journey through to the end.

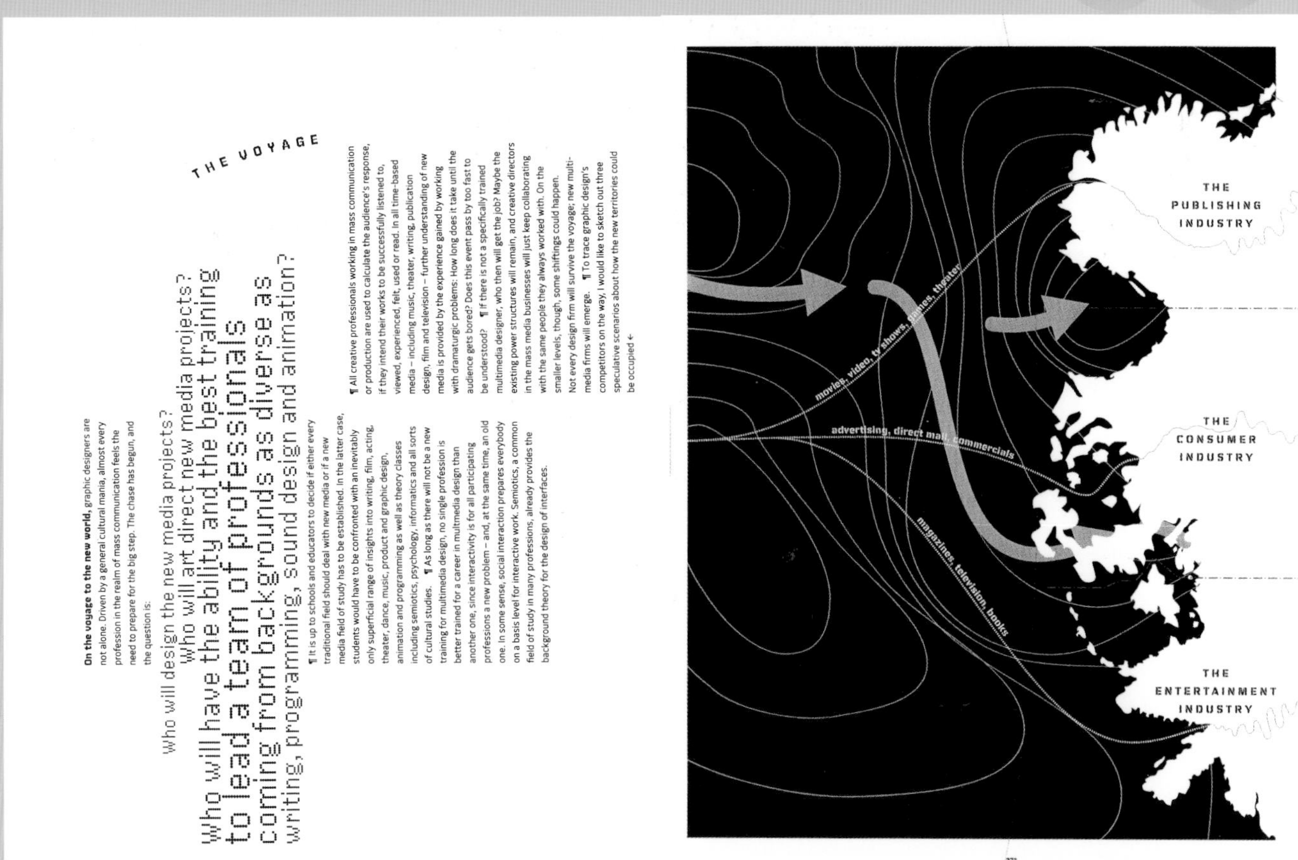

On the voyage to the new world, graphic designers are not alone. Driven by a general cultural mania, almost every profession in the realm of mass communication feels the need to prepare for the big step. The chase has begun, and the question is:

Who will design the new media projects?
Who will art direct new media projects?
Who will have the ability and the best training
to lead a team of professionals
coming from backgrounds as diverse as
writing, programming, sound design and animation?

THE VOYAGE

¶ It is up to schools and educators to decide if either every traditional field should deal with new media or if a new media field of study has to be established. In the latter case, students would have to be confronted with an inevitably only superficial range of insights into writing, film, acting, theater, dance, music, product and graphic design, animation and programming as well as theory classes including semiotics, psychology, informatics and all sorts of cultural studies. ¶ As long as there will not be a new training for multimedia design, no single profession is better trained for a career in multmedia design than another one, since interactivity is for all participating professions a new problem – and, at the same time, an old one. In some sense, social interaction prepares everybody on a basis level for interactive work. Semiotics, a common field of study in many professions, already provides the background theory for the design of interfaces.

¶ All creative professionals working in mass communication or production are used to calculate the audience's response, if they intend their works to be successfully listened to, viewed, experienced, felt, used or read. In all time-based media – including music, theater, writing, publication design, film and television – further understanding of new media is provided by the experience gained by working with dramaturgic problems: How long does it take until the audience gets bored? Does this event pass by too fast to be understood? ¶ If there is not a specifically trained multimedia designer, who then will get the job? Maybe the existing power structures will remain, and creative directors in the mass media businesses will just keep collaborating with the same people they always worked with. On the smaller levels, though, some shiftings could happen. Not every design firm will survive the voyage; new multi-media firms will emerge. ¶ To trace graphic design's competitors on the way, I would like to sketch out three speculative scenarios about how the new territories could be occupied ←

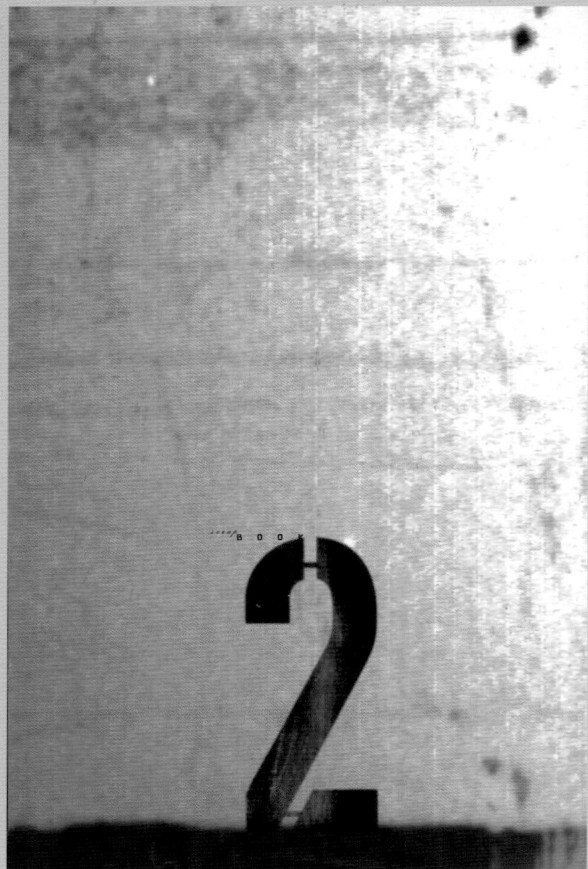

Scrapbook 2

This unashamedly personal piece of work not only gives an insight into the space the designers choose to work in, but also shows how they utilize space on the page. Although the snapshot style of photography is quite obscure, it succeeds in conveying a strong sense of the atmosphere in the building. Pleasing and quirky, the combination of informal photography and found imagery draws the reader in to this unobtrusively bilingual brochure.

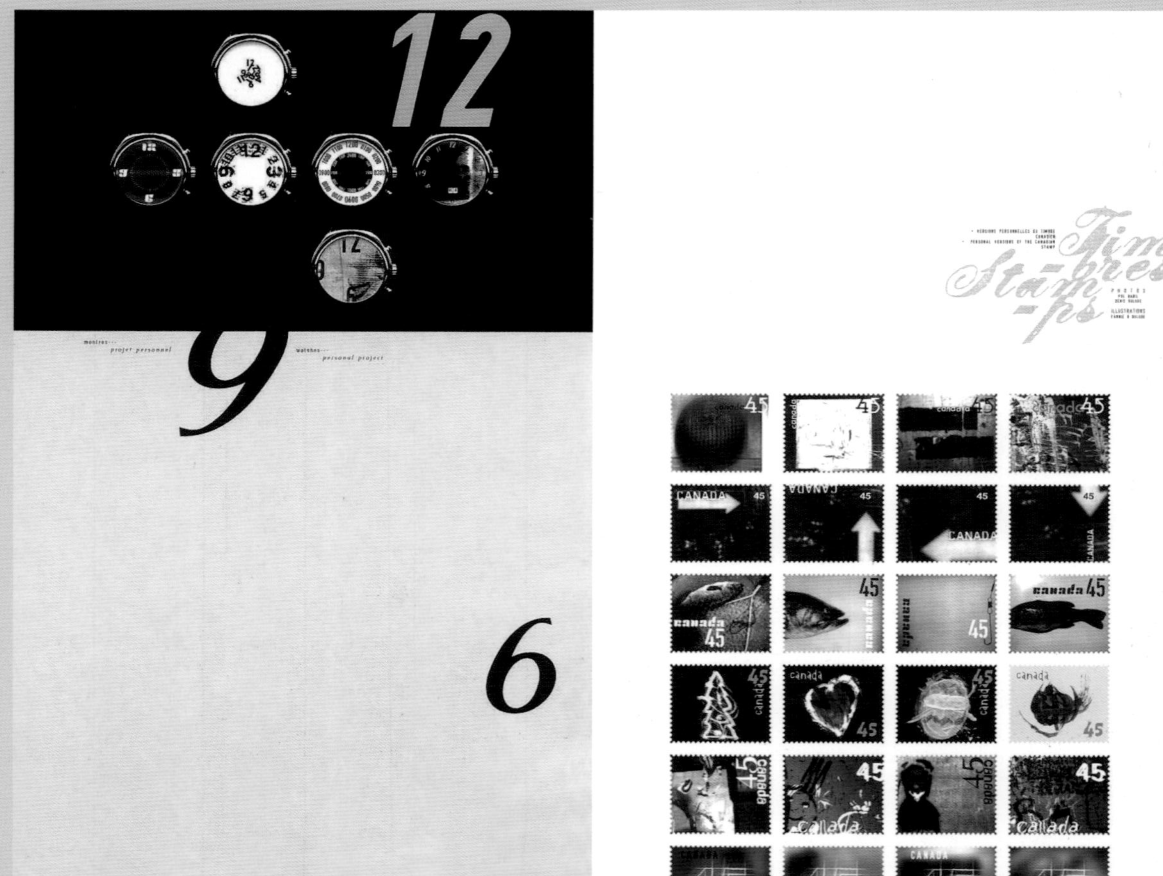

Designers
Pol Baril, Denis Dulude

Art Directors
Pol Baril, Denis Dulude

Photographers
Various

Design Company
KO Création

Country of Origin
Canada

Description of Artwork
Self-promotional brochure for KO Création, a graphic design studio.

Page Dimensions
280 x 435 mm
11 x 17 in

Format
Brochure

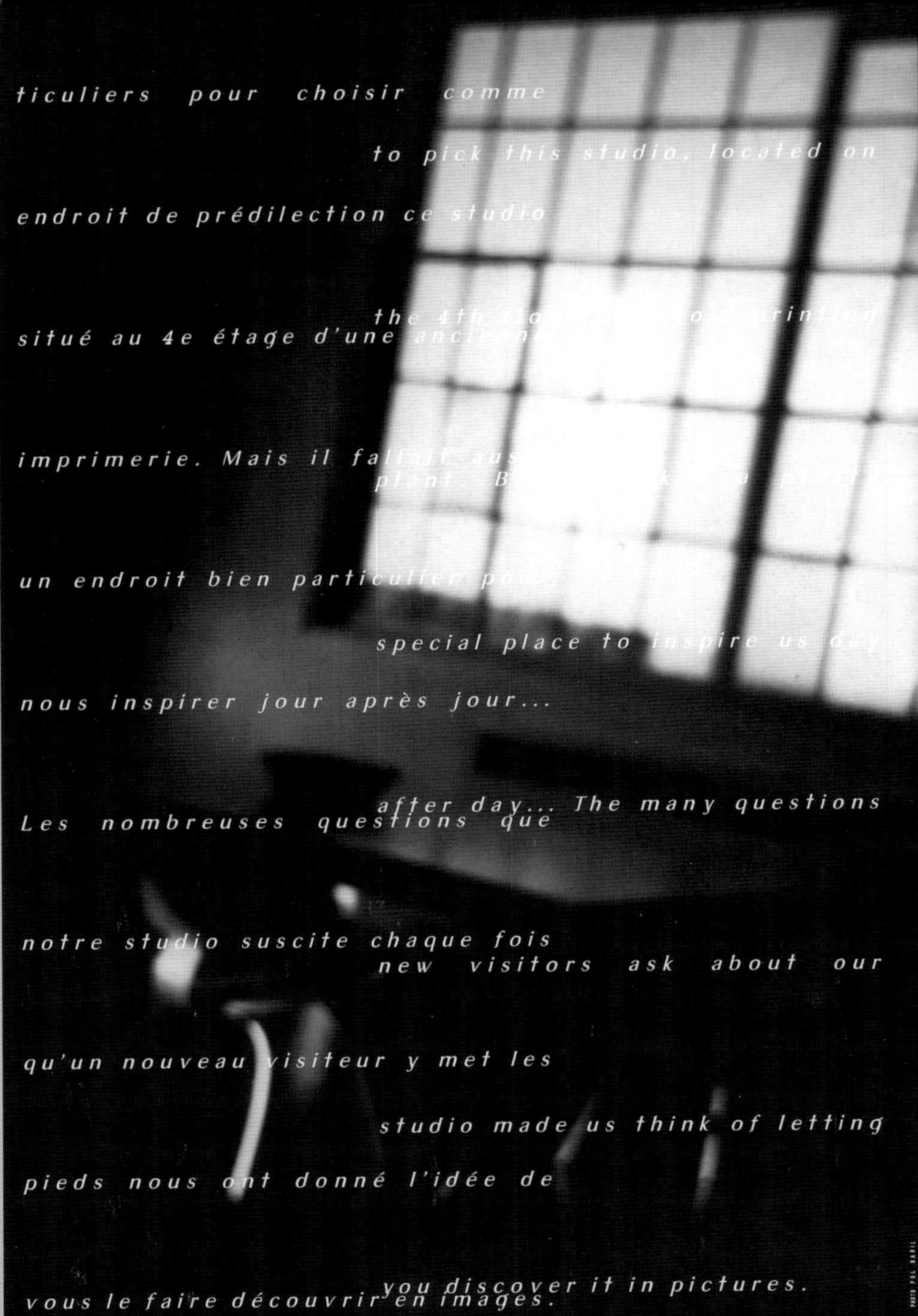

ticuliers pour choisir comme endroit de prédilection ce studio situé au 4e étage d'une ancienne imprimerie. Mais il fallait aussi un endroit bien particulier pour nous inspirer jour après jour... Les nombreuses questions que notre studio suscite chaque fois qu'un nouveau visiteur y met les pieds nous ont donné l'idée de vous le faire découvrir en images.

to pick this studio, located on the 4th [illegible] printing plant. B[illegible] special place to inspire us day after day... The many questions new visitors ask about our studio made us think of letting you discover it in pictures.

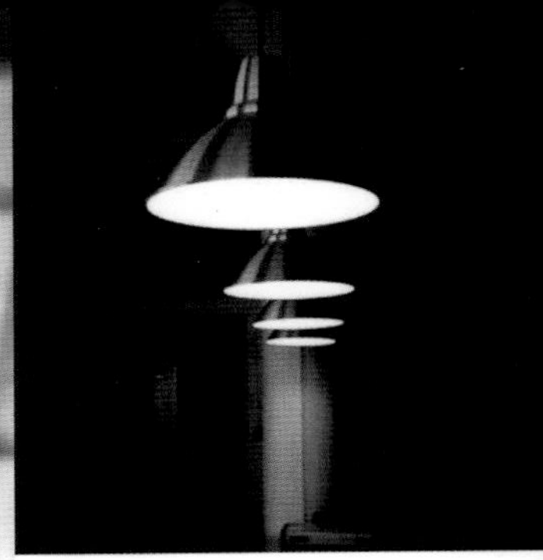

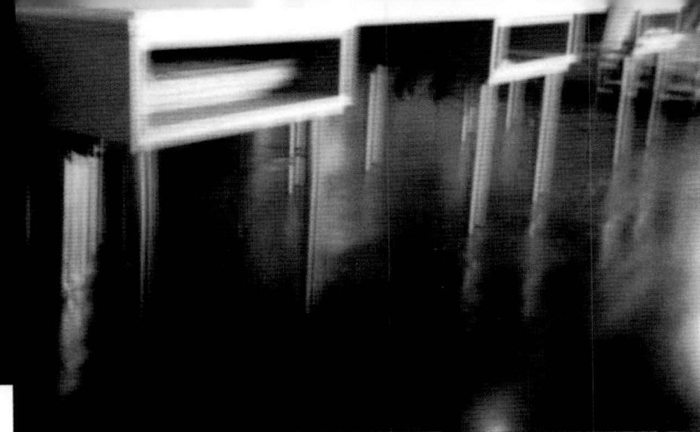

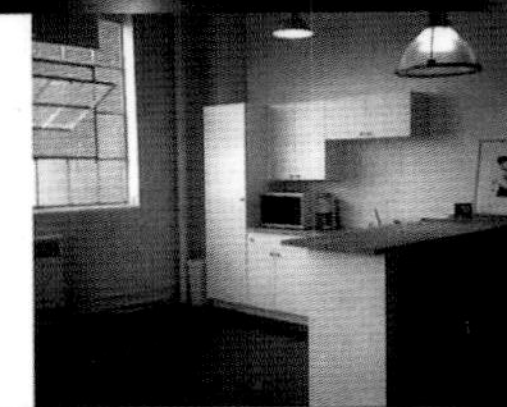

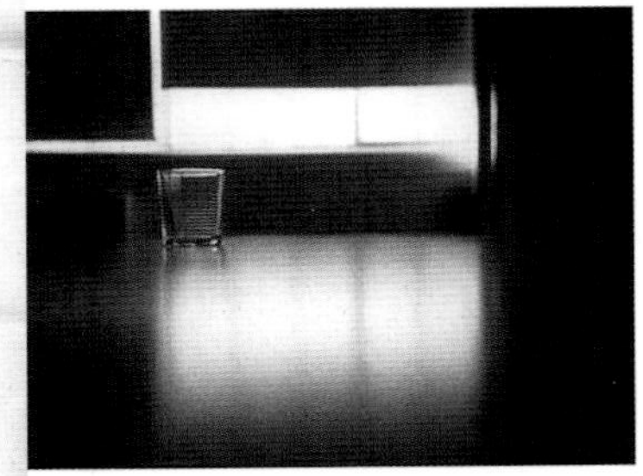

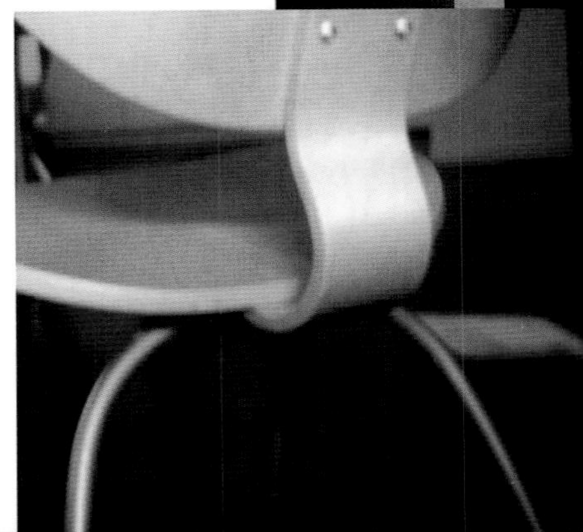

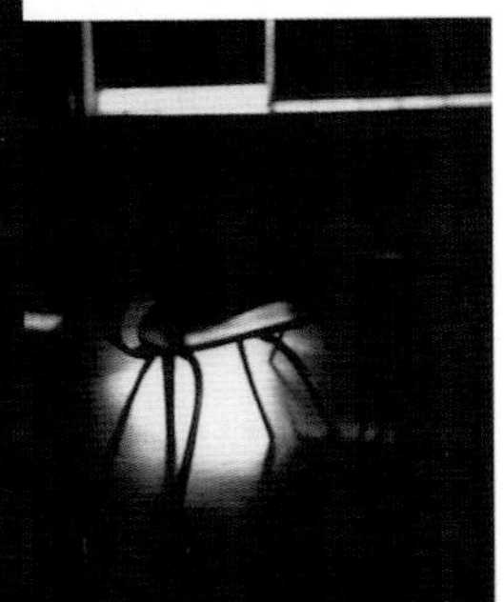

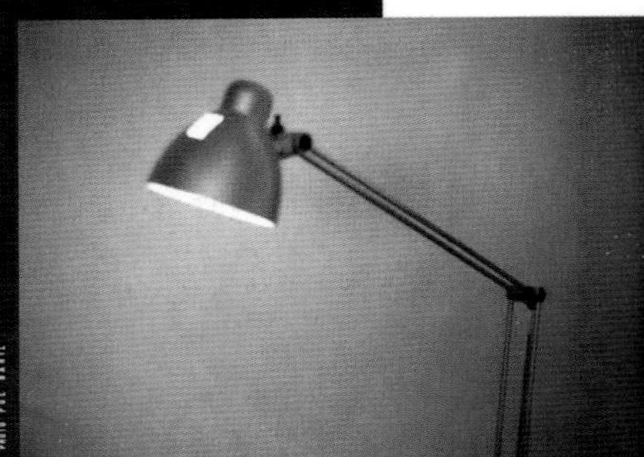

Designer
Joseph Eastwood

Art College
University of Salford

Country of Origin
UK

Description of Artwork
An experimental typographic reconstruction of the Bible.

Page Dimensions
120 x 170 mm
$4\frac{3}{4}$ x $6\frac{7}{8}$ in

Format
Book

Bible Reconstruction

The Bible must be one of the world's most printed texts, and yet this reconstruction succeeds in drawing the reader in afresh. It is particularly impressive that such an alluring and intriguing treatment should be created out of two colors and pure type—economical and a testament to the power of typography.

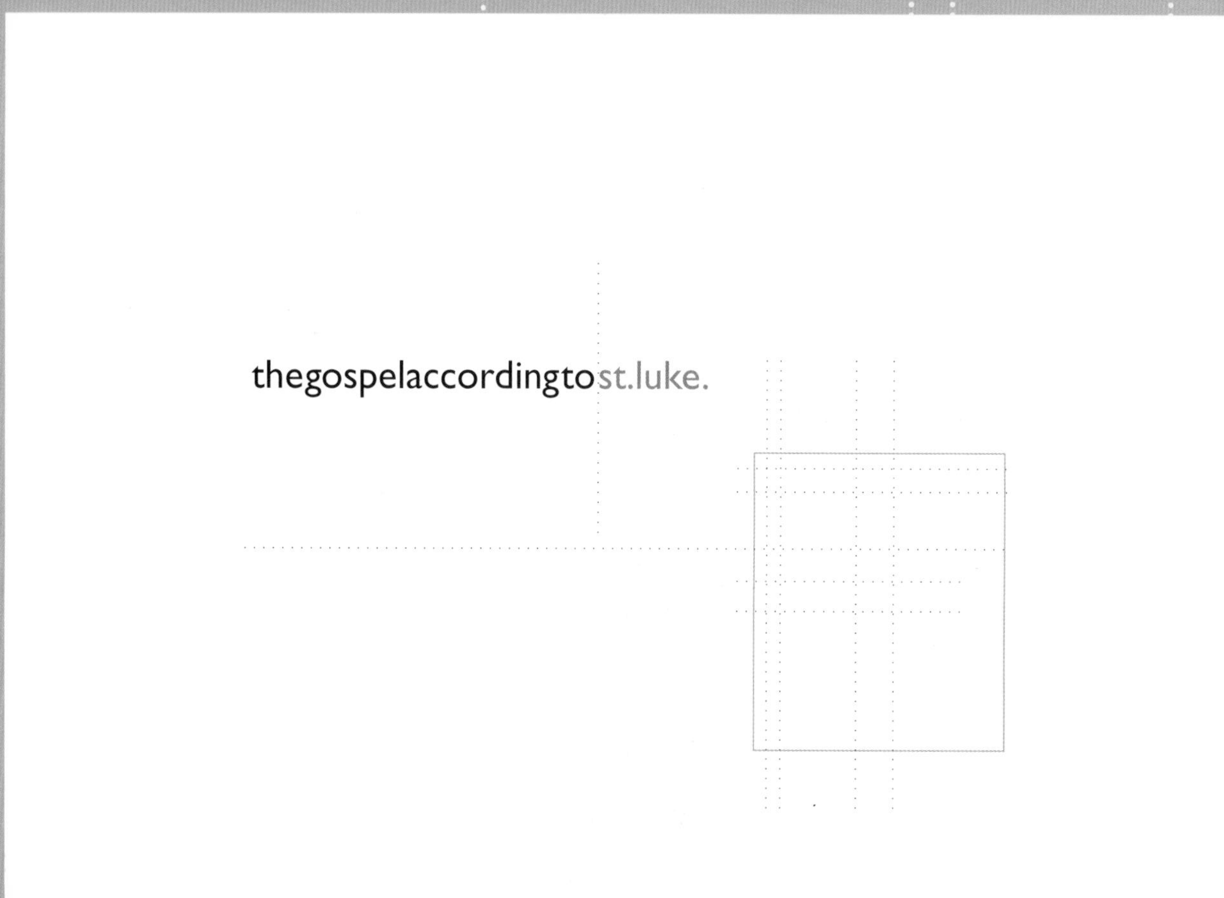

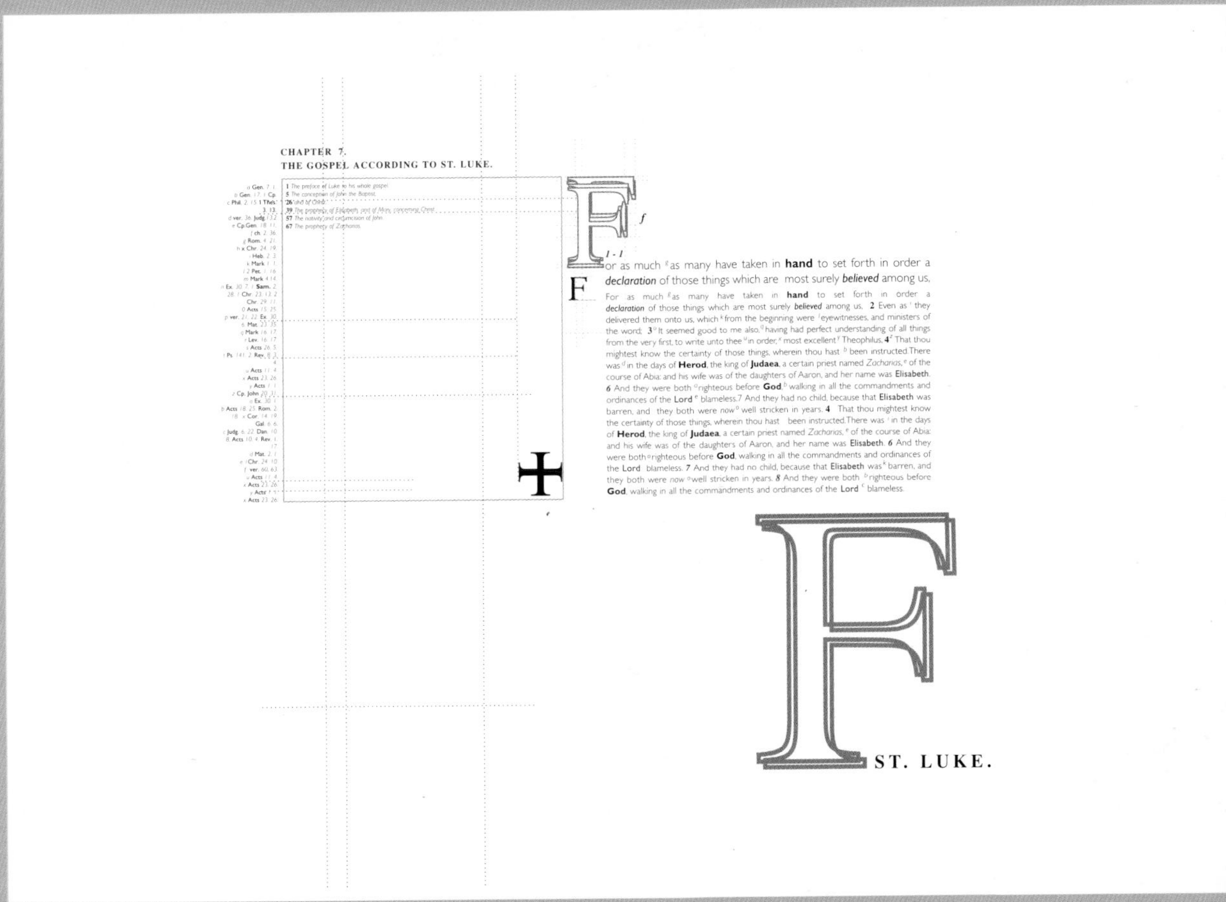
CHAPTER 7.
THE GOSPEL ACCORDING TO ST. LUKE.
F
f
1 - 1
For as much as many have taken in hand to set forth in order a declaration of those things which are most surely believed among us.
F
For as much as many have taken in hand to set forth in order a declaration of those things which are most surely believed among us. 2 Even as they delivered them onto us, which from the beginning were eyewitnesses, and ministers of the word; 3 It seemed good to me also, having had perfect understanding of all things from the very first, to write unto thee in order, most excellent Theophilus, 4 That thou mightest know the certainty of those things, wherein thou hast been instructed. There was in the days of Herod, the king of Judaea, a certain priest named Zacharias, of the course of Abia: and his wife was of the daughters of Aaron, and her name was Elisabeth. 6 And they were both righteous before God, walking in all the commandments and ordinances of the Lord blameless. 7 And they had no child, because that Elisabeth was barren, and they both were now well stricken in years. 4 That thou mightest know the certainty of those things, wherein thou hast been instructed. There was in the days of Herod, the king of Judaea, a certain priest named Zacharias, of the course of Abia: and his wife was of the daughters of Aaron, and her name was Elisabeth. 6 And they were both righteous before God, walking in all the commandments and ordinances of the Lord blameless. 7 And they had no child, because that Elisabeth was barren, and they both were now well stricken in years. 8 And they were both righteous before God, walking in all the commandments and ordinances of the Lord blameless.
F
ST. LUKE.

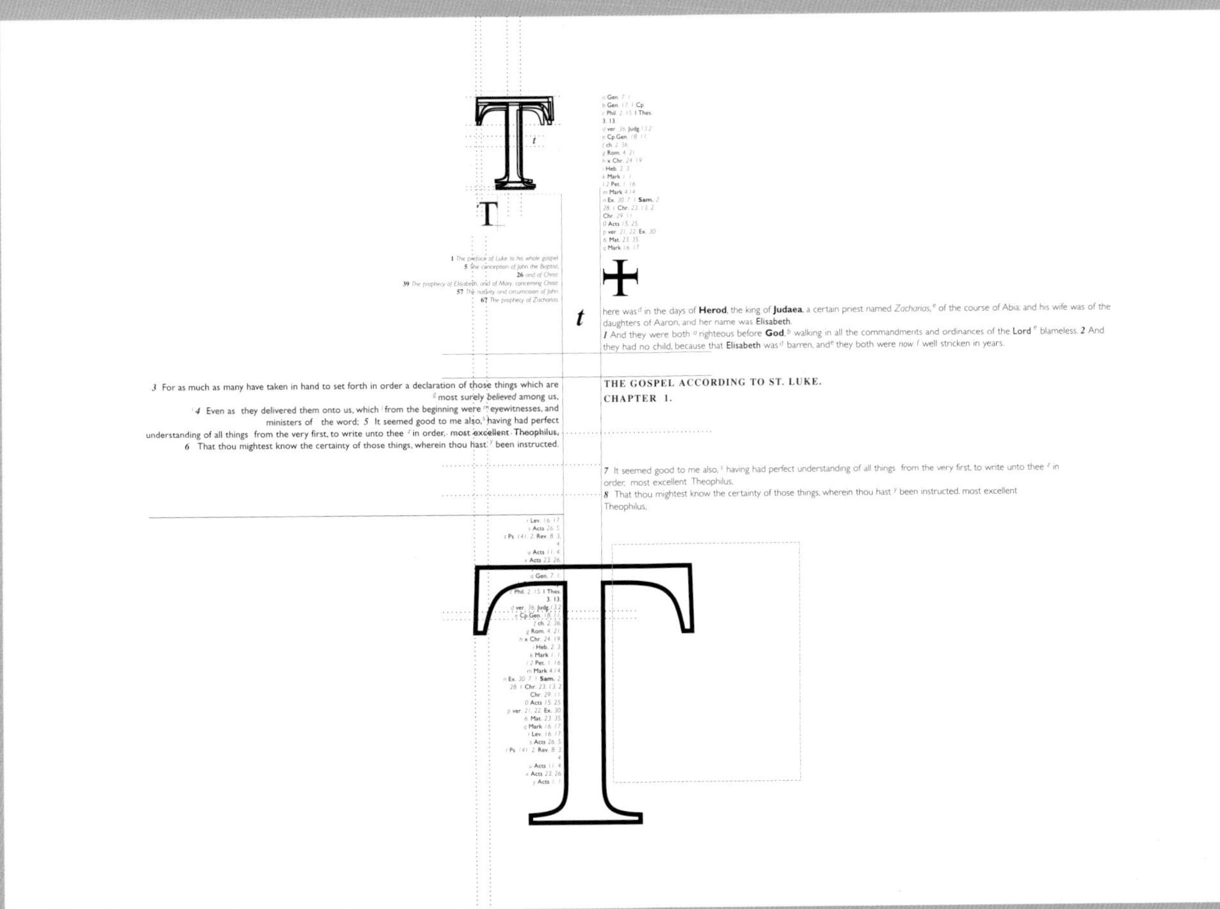
T
t
T
t
here was in the days of Herod, the king of Judaea, a certain priest named Zacharias, of the course of Abia: and his wife was of the daughters of Aaron, and her name was Elisabeth.
1 And they were both righteous before God, walking in all the commandments and ordinances of the Lord blameless. 2 And they had no child, because that Elisabeth was barren, and they both were now well stricken in years.
3 For as much as many have taken in hand to set forth in order a declaration of those things which are most surely believed among us,
4 Even as they delivered them onto us, which from the beginning were eyewitnesses, and ministers of the word; 5 It seemed good to me also, having had perfect understanding of all things from the very first, to write unto thee in order, most excellent Theophilus,
6 That thou mightest know the certainty of those things, wherein thou hast been instructed.
THE GOSPEL ACCORDING TO ST. LUKE.
CHAPTER 1.
7 It seemed good to me also, having had perfect understanding of all things from the very first, to write unto thee in order, most excellent Theophilus.
8 That thou mightest know the certainty of those things, wherein thou hast been instructed. most excellent Theophilus.
T

Designers
Esther Mildenberger,
Brian Switzer

Photographers
Esther Mildenberger,
Brian Switzer

Design Company
envision+

Country of Origin
Germany

Description of Artwork
A series of three books about our perception of cities.

Format
Book

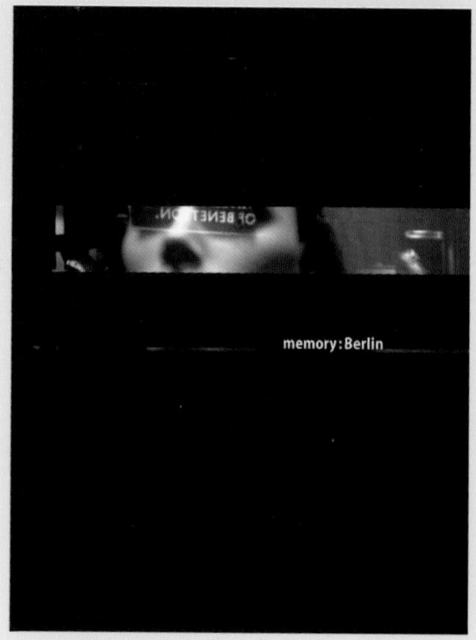

Page Dimensions (memory: Berlin)
150 x 200 mm
$5\,^{7}/_{8} \times 7\,^{7}/_{8}$ in
Opening to a maximum width of:
300 mm, $11\,^{3}/_{4}$ in

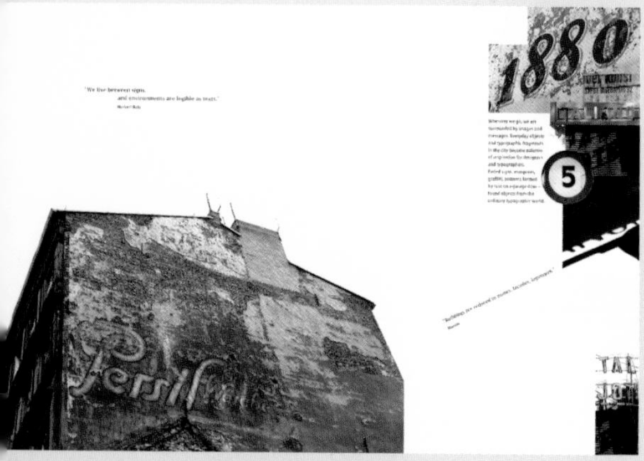

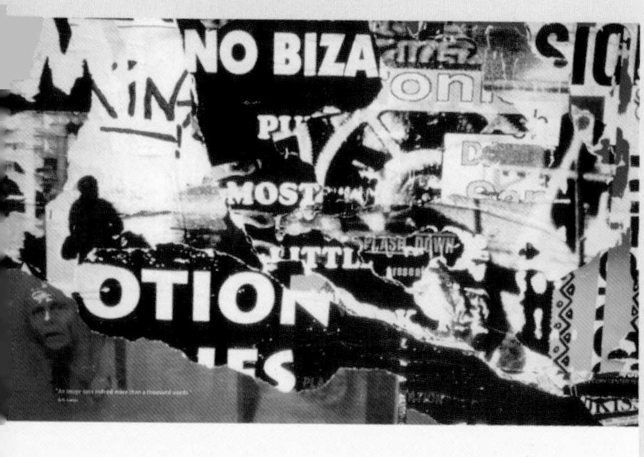

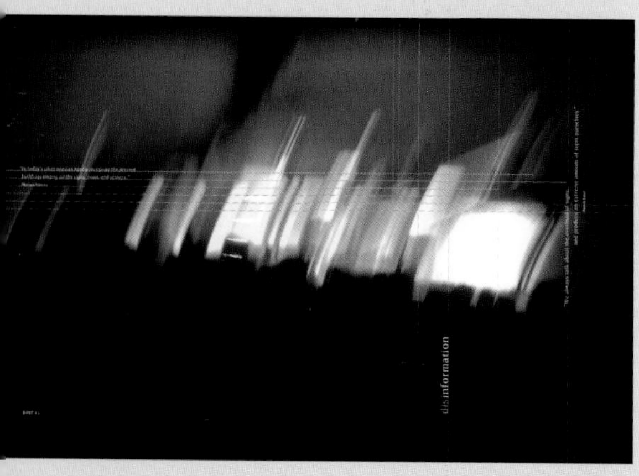

city: memory: Berlin, London, Tokyo—Book Projects, 1996–99

Part of an extensive project including videos and interactive concepts, these three books (shown on this and the following two spreads) share the same format and similar covers. Inside, the design of the books is based on a personal interpretation of the cities, and the way in which the pull-out construction and typography have been used adds to the individual flavor of each publication.

memory: Berlin

In many ways the most straightforward in its layout, this book uses abstract imagery and short texts to create a series of discrete impressions. Typography features strongly in the imagery—murals, fly posters, electronic signage—and this has been complemented by keeping the caption texts compact and unobtrusive.

"utter

Fümms bö wö tää Uu, pögiff, kwii Ee.
Dedesnn nn rrrrrr, Li Ee, mpiff tillff too, tillll, Jüü Kaa?
Rinnzekete bee bee nnz krr müü?
ziiuu ennze, ziiuu rinnzkrrmüü, rakete bee bee."

Kurt Schwitters

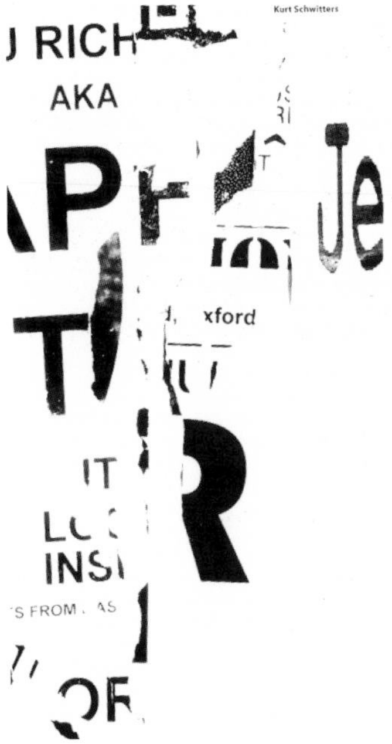

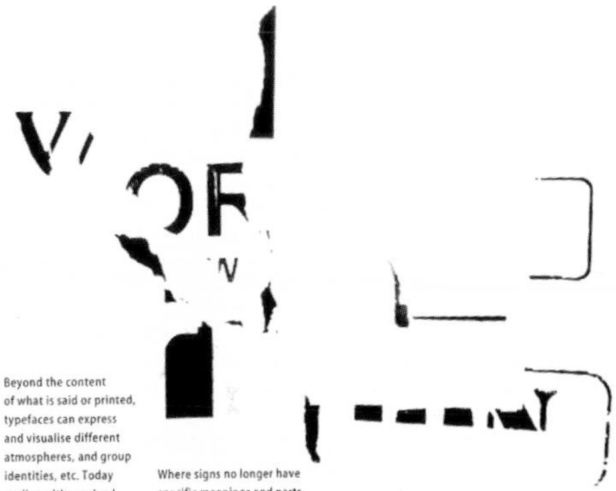

Beyond the content of what is said or printed, typefaces can express and visualise different atmospheres, and group identities, etc. Today we live with overload and clichés, with the omnipresent application of typefaces.

Where signs no longer have specific meanings and parts can no longer be assigned idiomatic expressions – then the reduction to purely visual ideas is complete. Our perception of signs and sign fragments is always based on the sum of our experience with type and language.

W O R D

Form giving and design consciously use the means of randomness and irritations to attract attention. The more cryptic a message is, the bigger its influence on the viewer can be. People are curious and try to decipher otherwise unapproachable information.

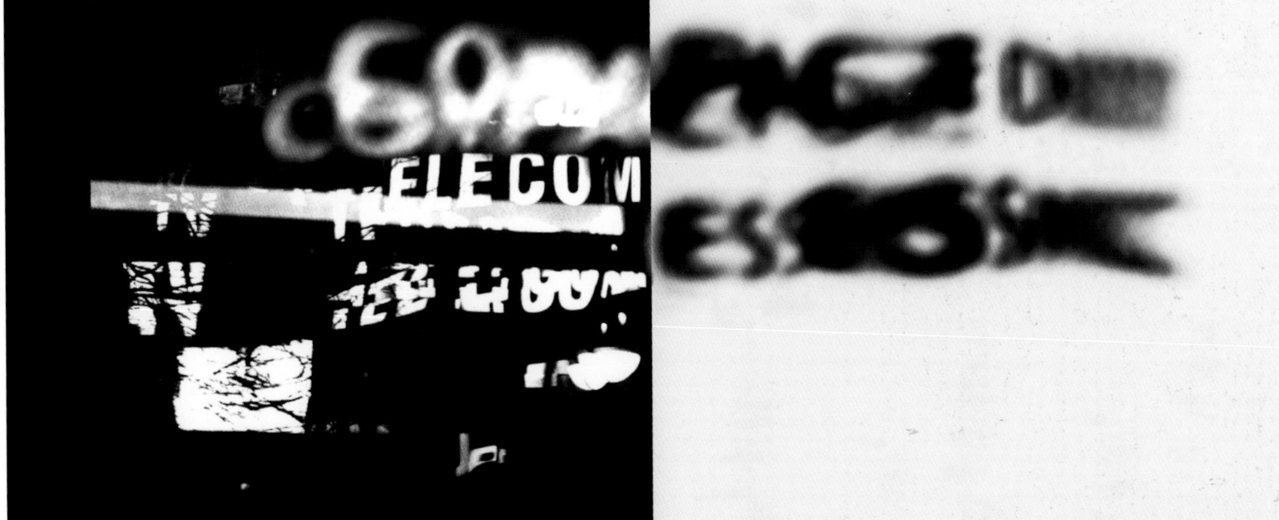

"Poetry is possible in all signs and languages."

Max Bense

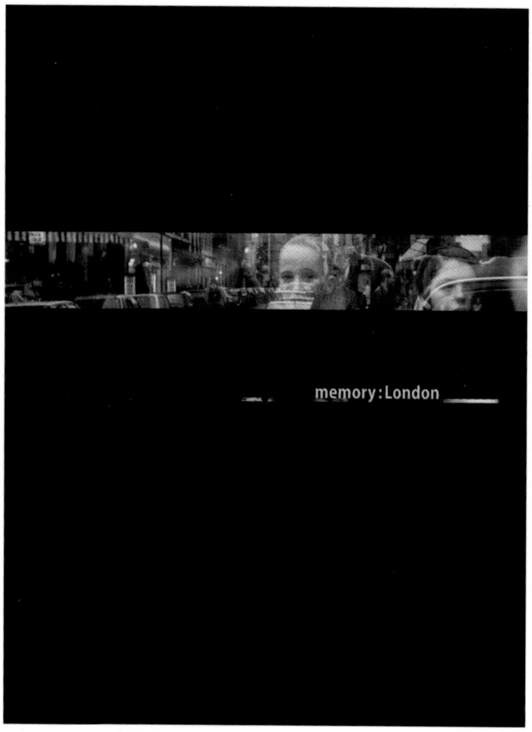

memory: London

The extended pull-out construction of this book has been used to create a sequential narrative of images and texts. Starting in restrained monochrome on the opening spreads, it progresses to the abstract, overlapping, and blurred imagery of the final color pages. The steady increase in the size of the squared-up photographs and the substantial blocks of text have been brought together into a formal yet asymmetric layout that gives a strong sense of this city.

Page Dimensions
(memory: London)
150 x 200 mm
$5^{7}/_{8}$ x $7^{7}/_{8}$ in
Opening to a maximum width of:
2,400 mm, 95 in

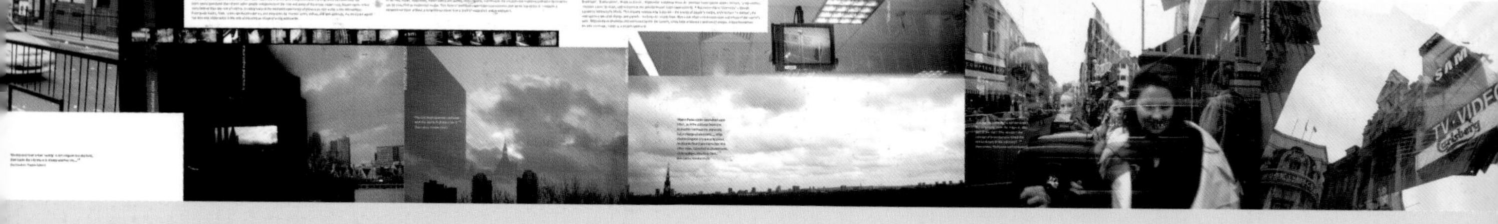

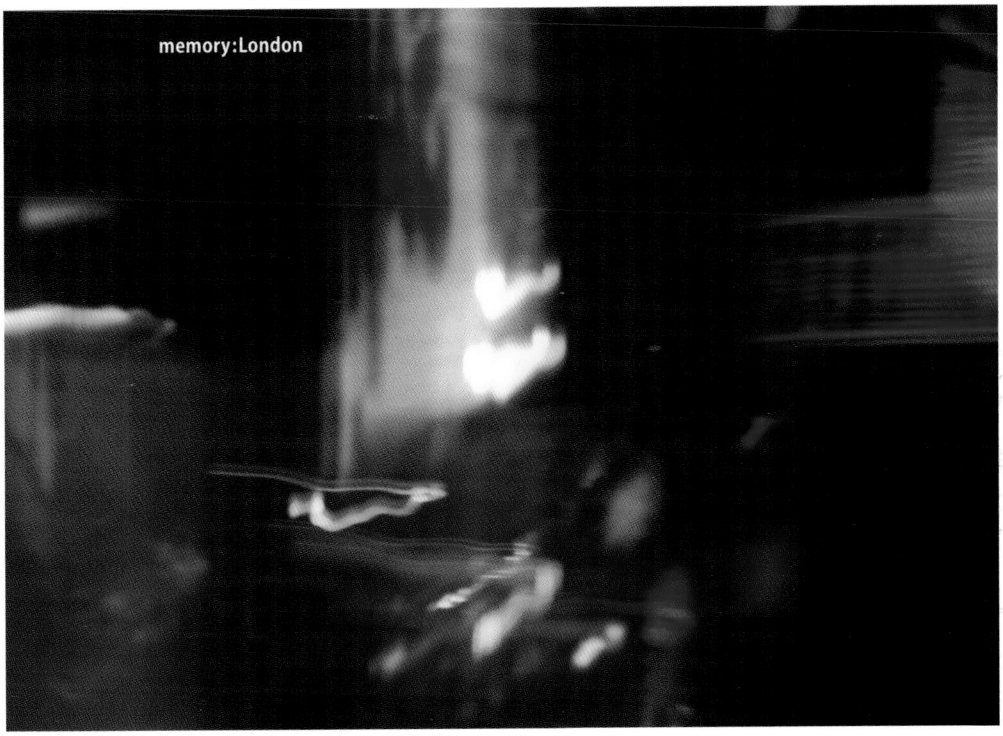

At this stage in the visual narrative, the insertion of small color images within an expanse of monochrome both surprises and hints at what is to come.

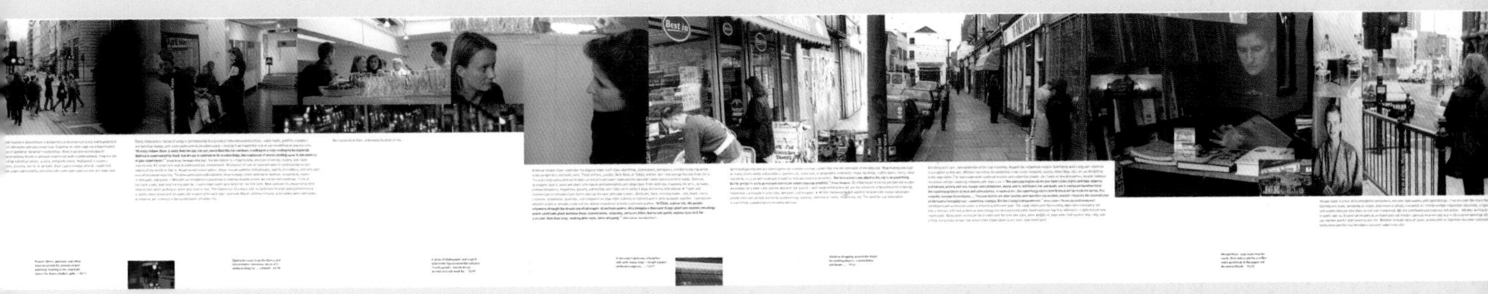

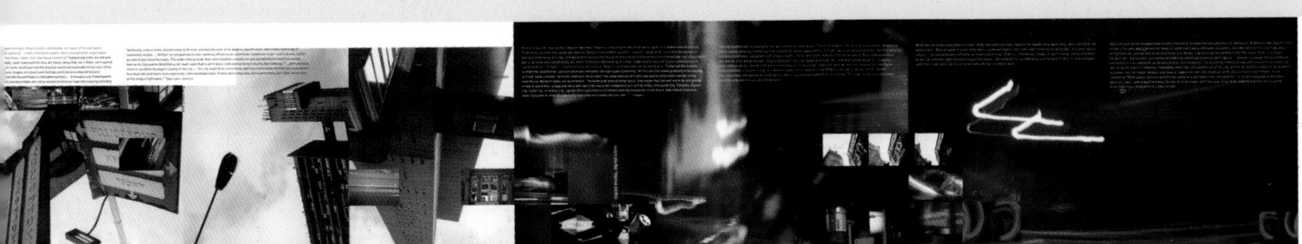

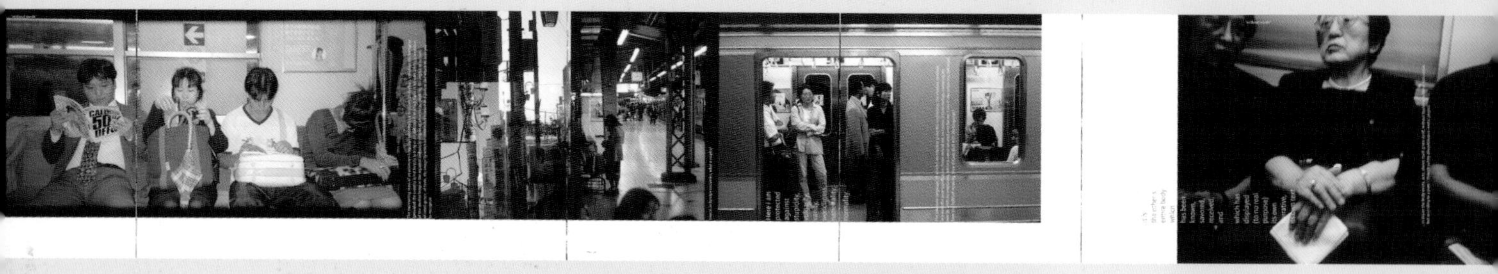

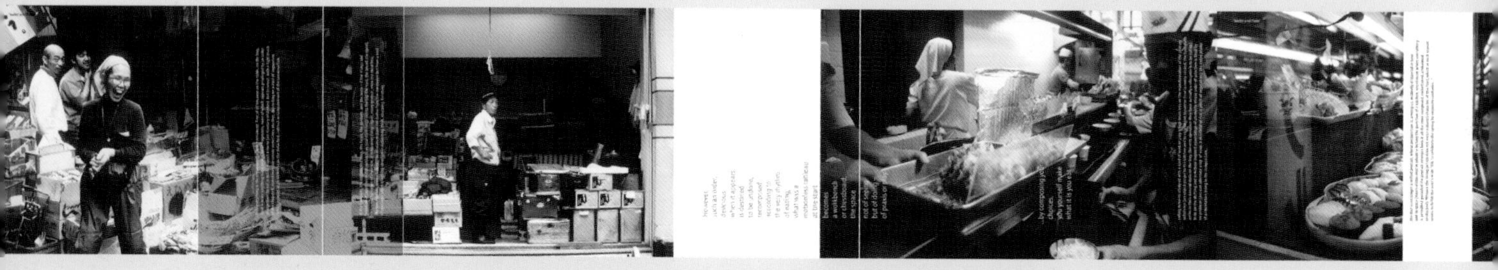

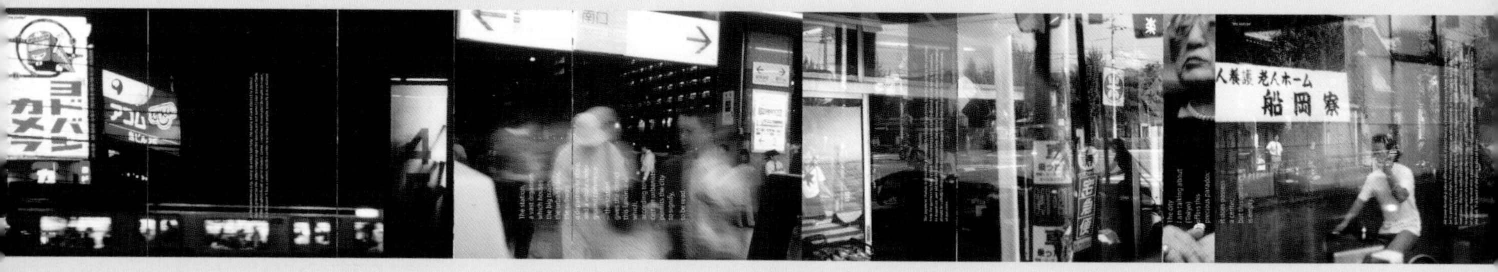
船岡寮

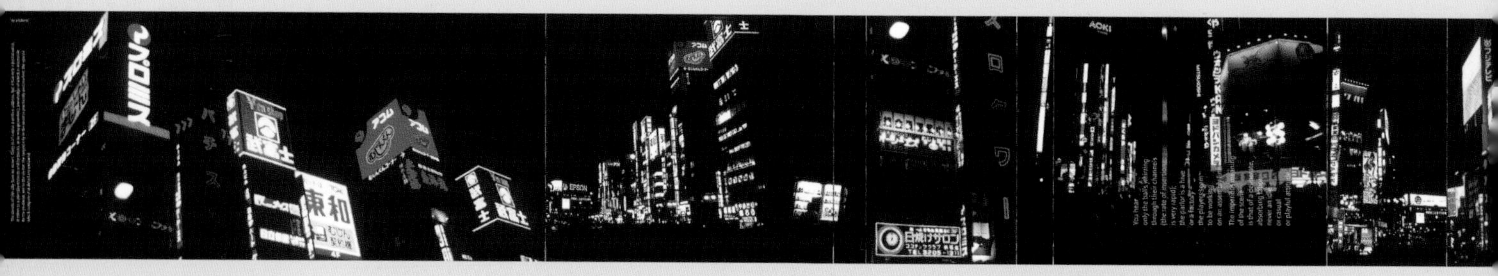

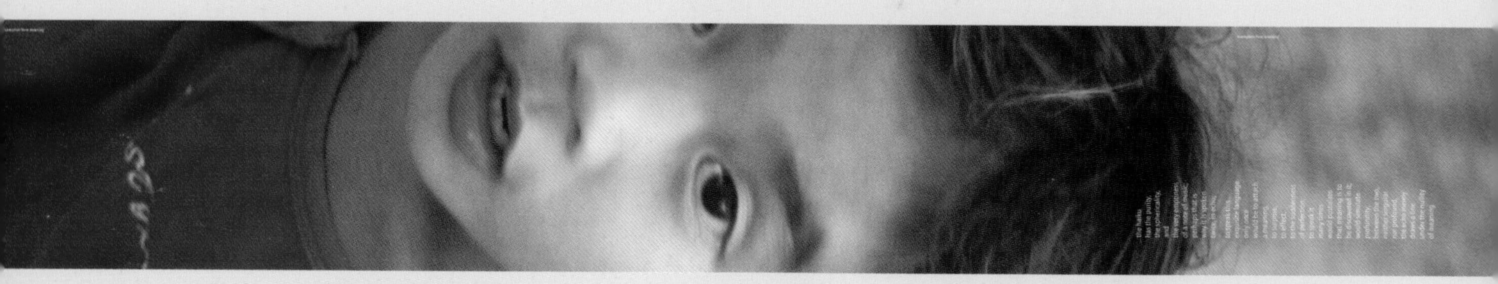

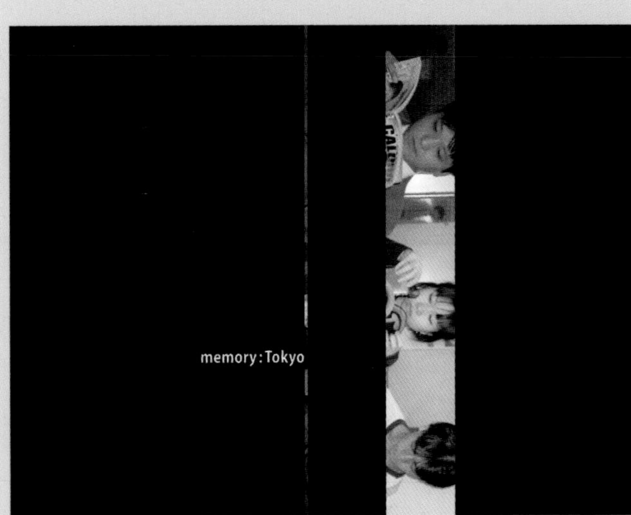

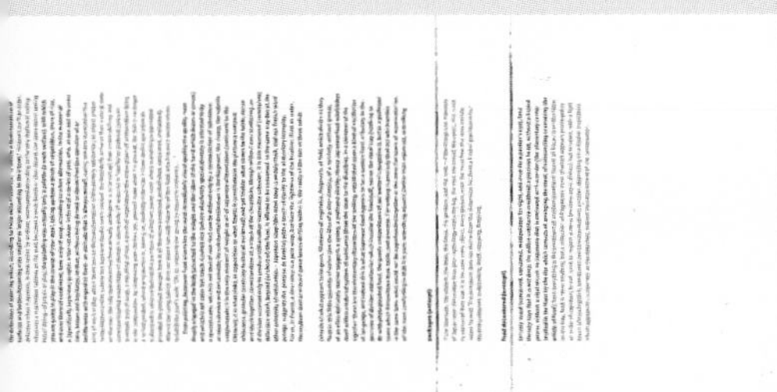

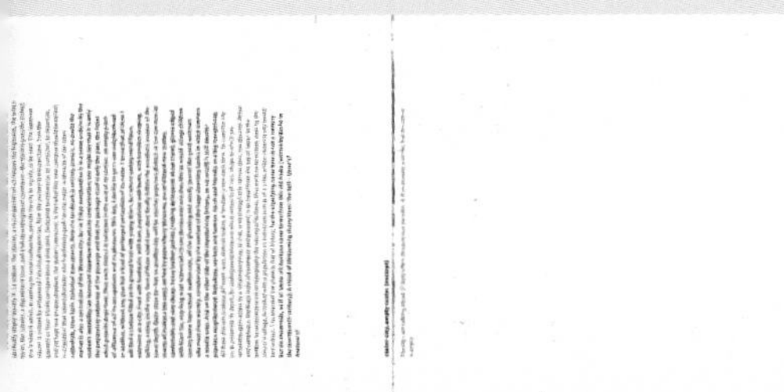

memory: Tokyo

With references to the layout of traditional Japanese calligraphic scrolls the designers have created friezes of imagery—sometimes out of separate images, sometimes one enormous picture—that play with the reader's sense of scale and intimacy. In contrast to this, the bulk of the text has been folded into the book and presented in a more formal way against the plain paper.

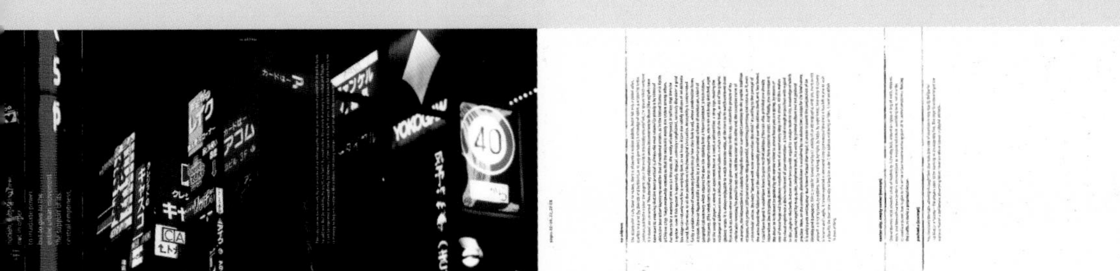

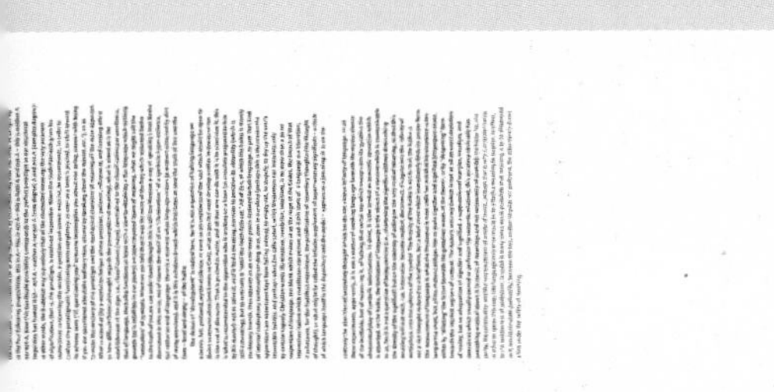

Page Dimensions
(memory: Tokyo)
150 x 200 mm
5⁷/₈ x 7⁷/₈ in
Opening to a maximum width of:
1,760 mm, 69 in

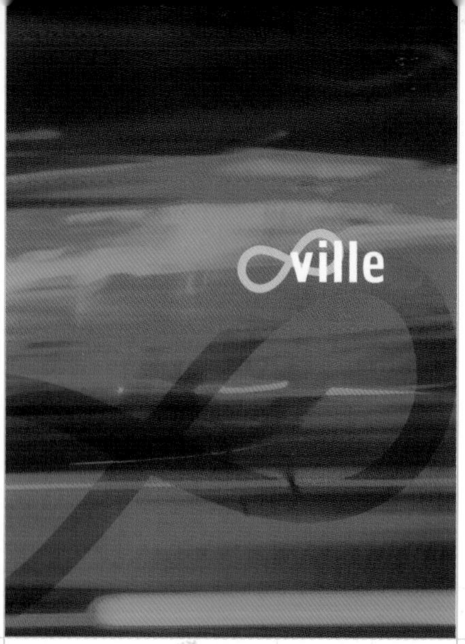

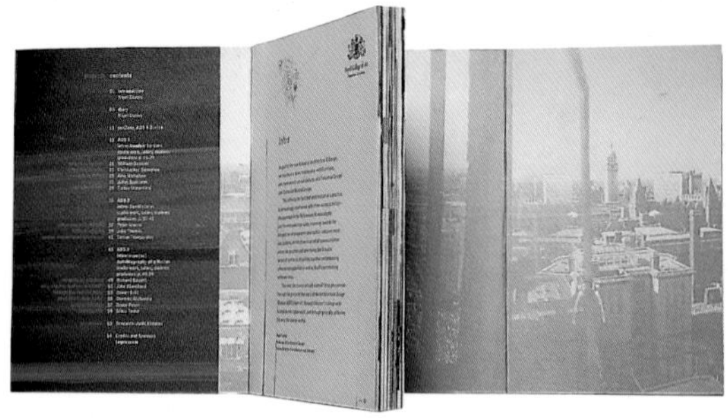

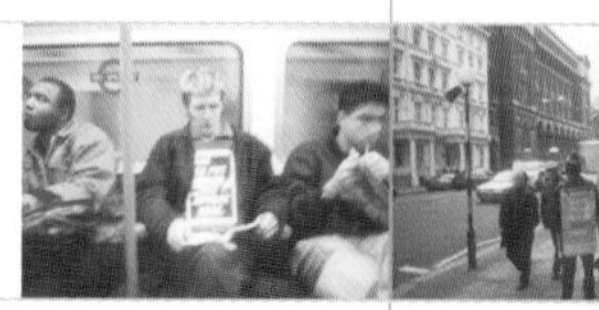

Designers
Esther Mildenberger,
Brian Switzer

Photographers
Fran Thurston, Esther Mildenberger, Brian Switzer, students

Design Company
envision+

Country of Origin
Germany

Description of Artwork
Catalog for the Architecture & Interiors Department at the Royal College of Art, London.

Page Dimensions
150 x 200 mm
5 7/8 x 7 7/8 in

Format
Catalog

8th Floor Annual 1998: Infinity-ville

Documenting projects that explore the boundaries of architecture and virtual space, this catalog reflects these concerns in its design by the use of gridlines and a strong structural band across each spread. The bold use of a second color adds real power to the look of the spreads. The cover, on the other hand, takes its cue from the title and uses the two colors to create a more abstract and endless feel.

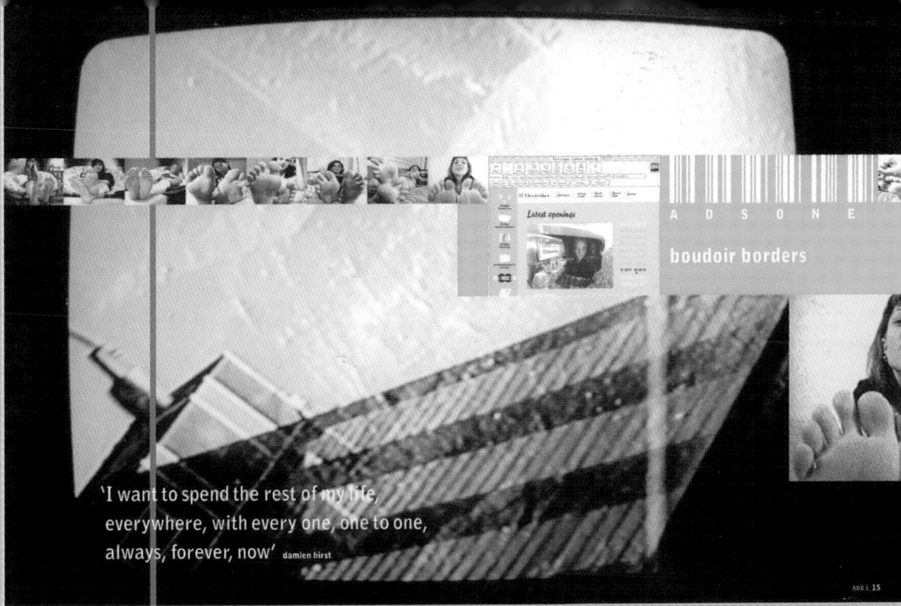

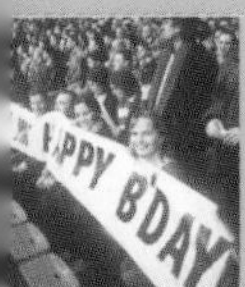

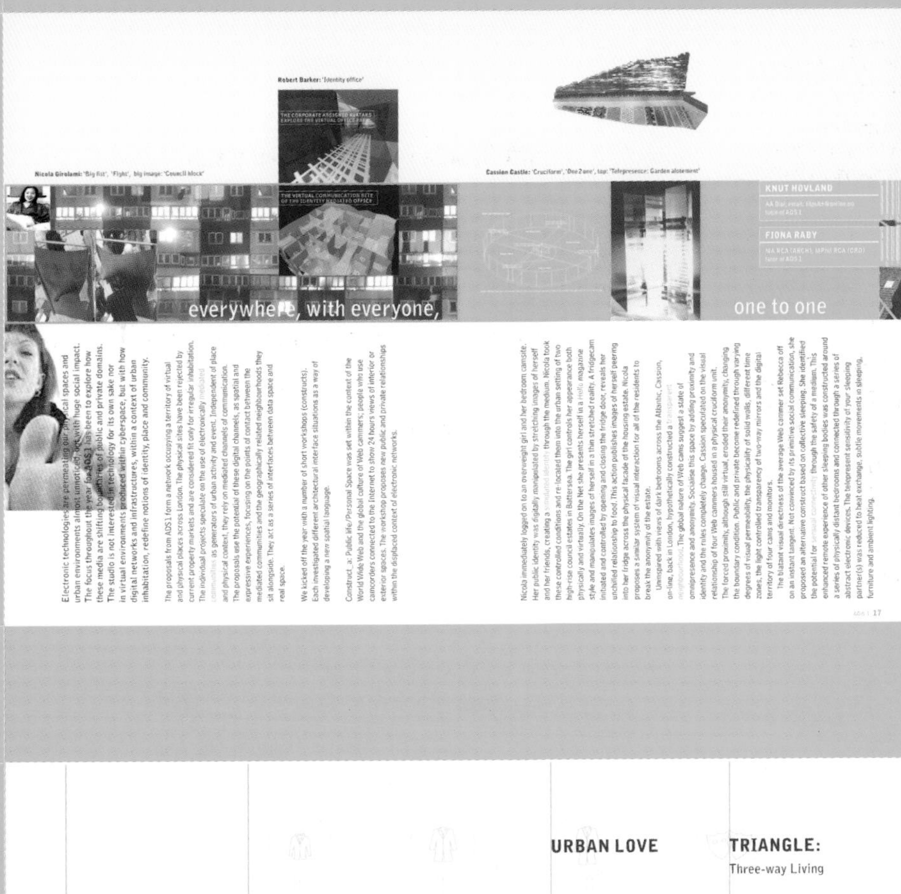

Robert Barker: 'Identity office'

Nicola Girolami: 'Big Fist', 'Fight', big image: 'Council block'

Cassion Castle: 'Cruciform', 'Duo Zone', top: 'Telepresence: Garden allotment'

KNUT HOVLAND

FIONA RABY

everywhere, with everyone,

one to one

Electronic technologies are permeating our physical spaces and urban environments almost unnoticed, but with huge social impact. The focus throughout the year for ADS 1 has been to explore how these media are shifting boundaries of public and private domains. The studio is not interested in technology for its own sake nor in virtual environments produced within cyberspace, but with how digital networks and infrastructures, within a context of urban inhabitation, redefine notions of identity, place and community.

The proposals from ADS 1 form a network occupying a territory of virtual and physical places across London. The physical sites have been rejected by current property markets and are considered fit only for irregular inhabitation. The individual projects speculate on the use of electronically mediated communities as generators of urban activity and event. Independent of place and physical context, they rely on mediated channels of communication. The proposals use the potential of these digital channels, as spatial and expressive experiences, focusing on the points of contact between the mediated communities and the geographically related neighbourhoods they sit alongside. They act as a series of interfaces between data space and real space.

We kicked off the year with a number of short workshops (constructs). Each investigated different architectural interface situations as a way of developing a new spatial language.

Construct_a: Public life/Personal Space was set within the context of the World Wide Web and the global culture of Web cammers; people who use camcorders connected to the Internet to show 24 hours views of interior or exterior spaces. The workshop proposes new public and private relationships within the displaced context of electronic networks.

Nicola immediately logged on to an overweight girl and her bedroom camsite. Her public identity was digitally manipulated by stretching images of herself and her friends, creating a simulated identity through the medium. Nicola took these controlled conditions and re-located them into the urban setting of two high-rise council estates in Battersea. The girl controls her appearance both physically and virtually. On the Net she presents herself in a Hello magazine style and manipulates images of herself in a thin stretched reality. A fridgecam initiated and controlled by opening and closing the fridge door, reveals her unchiffed relationship to food. This action publishes images of herself peering into her fridge across the physical facade of the housing estate. Nicola proposes a similar system of visual interaction for all of the residents to break the anonymity of the estate.

Uninspired with views of dark bedrooms across the Atlantic, Cassion, on-line, back in London, hypothetically constructed a transparent neighbourhood. The global nature of Web cams suggest a state of omnipresence and anonymity. Socialise this space by adding proximity and identity and the rules completely change. Cassion speculated on the visual relationship of four Web cammers housed in a physical cruciform unit. The forced proximity, although still virtual, eroded their anonymity, changing the boundary condition. Public and private become redefined through varying degrees of visual permeability, the physicality of solid walls, different time zones, the light controlled transparency of two-way mirrors and the digital territory of four cams and monitors.

The blatant visual directness of the average Web cammer set Rebecca off on an instant tangent. Not convinced by its primitive social communication, she proposed an alternative construct based on collective sleeping. She identified the potential for sensual connectivity through the safety of a medium. This enhanced remote experience of other sleeping bodies was constructed around a series of physically distant bedrooms and connected through a series of abstract electronic devices. The telepresent sensitivity of your sleeping partner(s) was reduced to heat exchange, subtle movements in sleeping, furniture and ambient lighting.

ADS 1 17

URBAN LOVE TRIANGLE:

Three-way Living

Christopher Donoghue

MA in Architecture and Interiors: RCA
BA in AR: Kingston University

The aim of my project is to translate the ever flourishing virtual network between 'Web cam' users across the globe into a physical relationship. The resultant physical spaces will speculate on the potential interface between the public and private domain, utilising controlling devices implemented by the Internet for 'Web cam' browsers.

The project began with a story of three characters; the Husband, the Wife and the Mistress. Each character occupied their own 'boudoir' which either physically or virtually overlapped the others. These relationships set out a series of new physical spaces which would function as a network within an urban context, but at a virtual scale. The Apartment for 'three-way' Living explores this reality of experiencing private space whilst occupying communal space simultaneously.

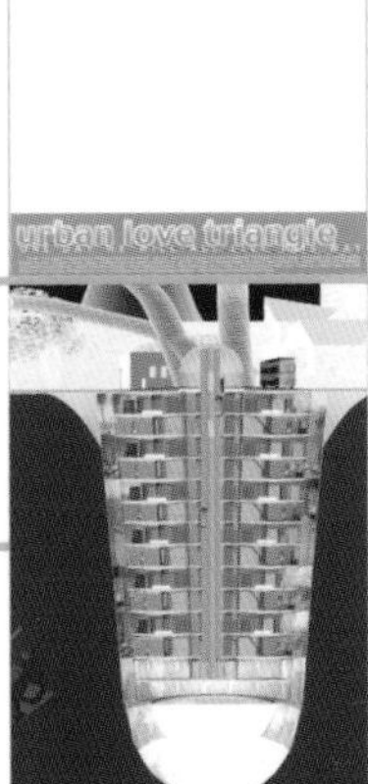

'Apartment for "three-way" living'

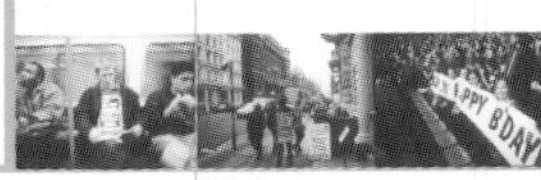

Hijacking the system
'Chest ad', 'Full sandwich', 'Double Whammy'

boudoir ('bu:dwa:, -dwc:) n.
a woman's bedroom or a private sitting room.
The Collins Paperback English Dictionary - 1996

Web cam ('survi:an-ce, ca|mera:) n.
1) an electronic camera connected to the World Wide Web
2) a device to relay 'Live' images taken from the source camera to the screen of any Internet browser
Still to be officially defined - 1998

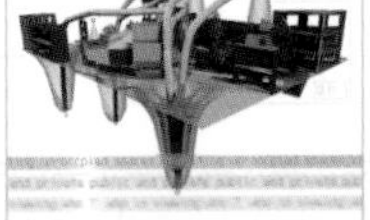

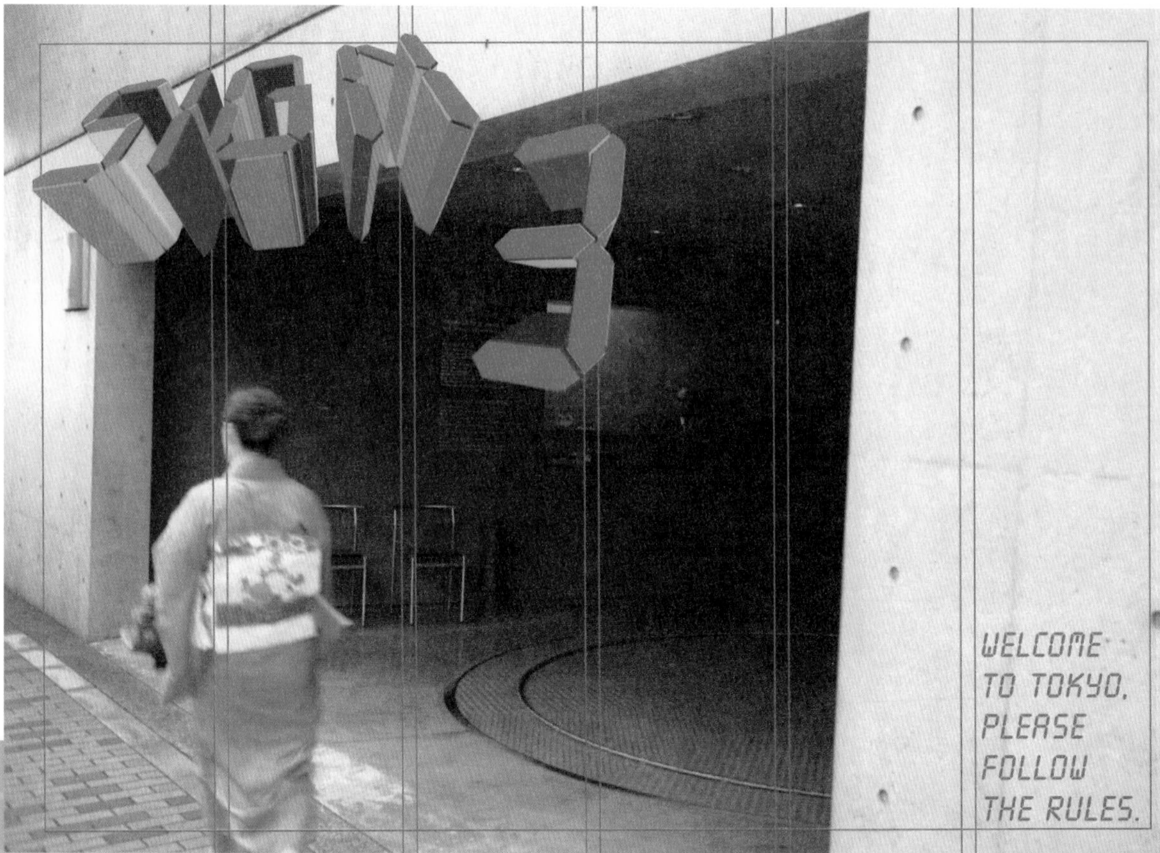
WELCOME
TO TOKYO.
PLEASE
FOLLOW
THE RULES.

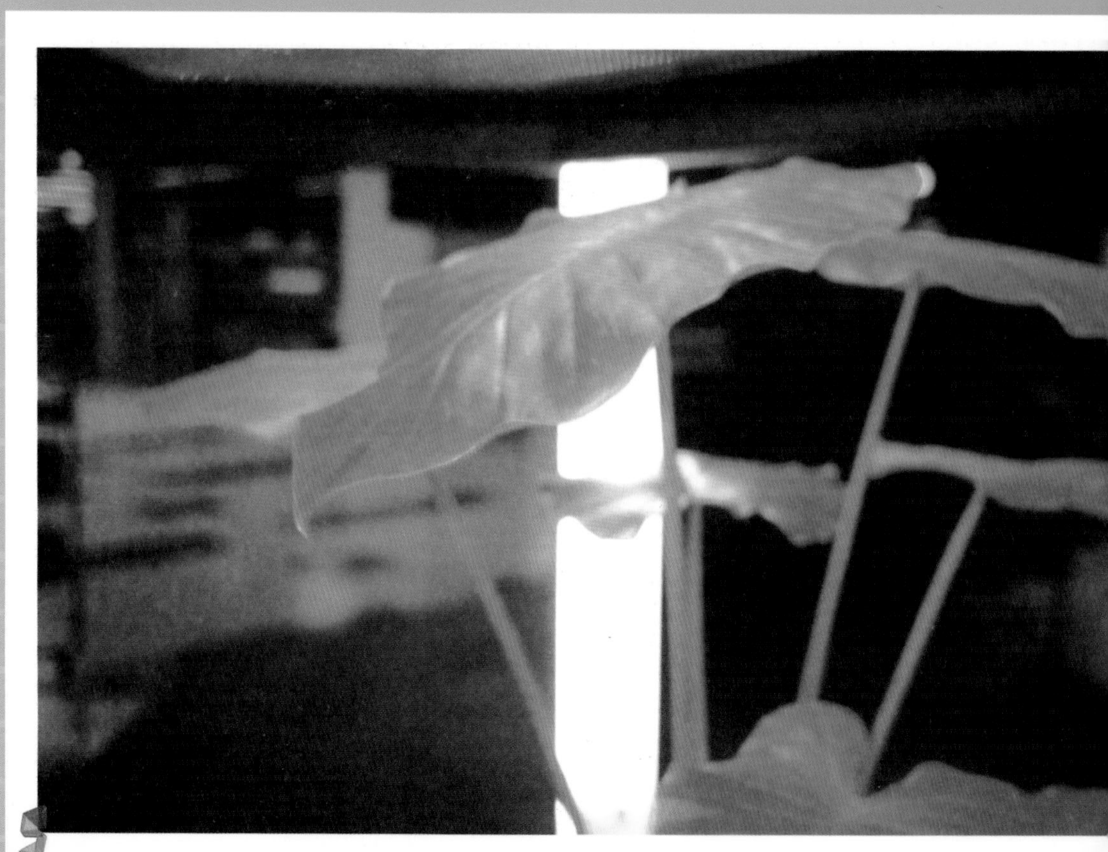

Sign 3, Welcome to Tokyo

This promotional book takes the form of a short trip to Tokyo. At first sight this is an unlikely starting point from which to promote a design company. The informal nature of the photography creates the illusion of familiarity with the circumstance. This is set against the device of a superimposed text grid which refers to the subtitle on the front cover (*left*): Please Follow the Rules. The pictures themselves also reveal the rules and signage of everyday life in Tokyo. Taken as a whole, this distinctive publication explores the possibilities of working imaginatively within a set structure. The highly designed and eccentric page numbers add a quirky and surreal touch.

Special Production Techniques

The book is constructed in the traditional Japanese manner (with spine to the right) so that the sequence of pages runs from right to left.

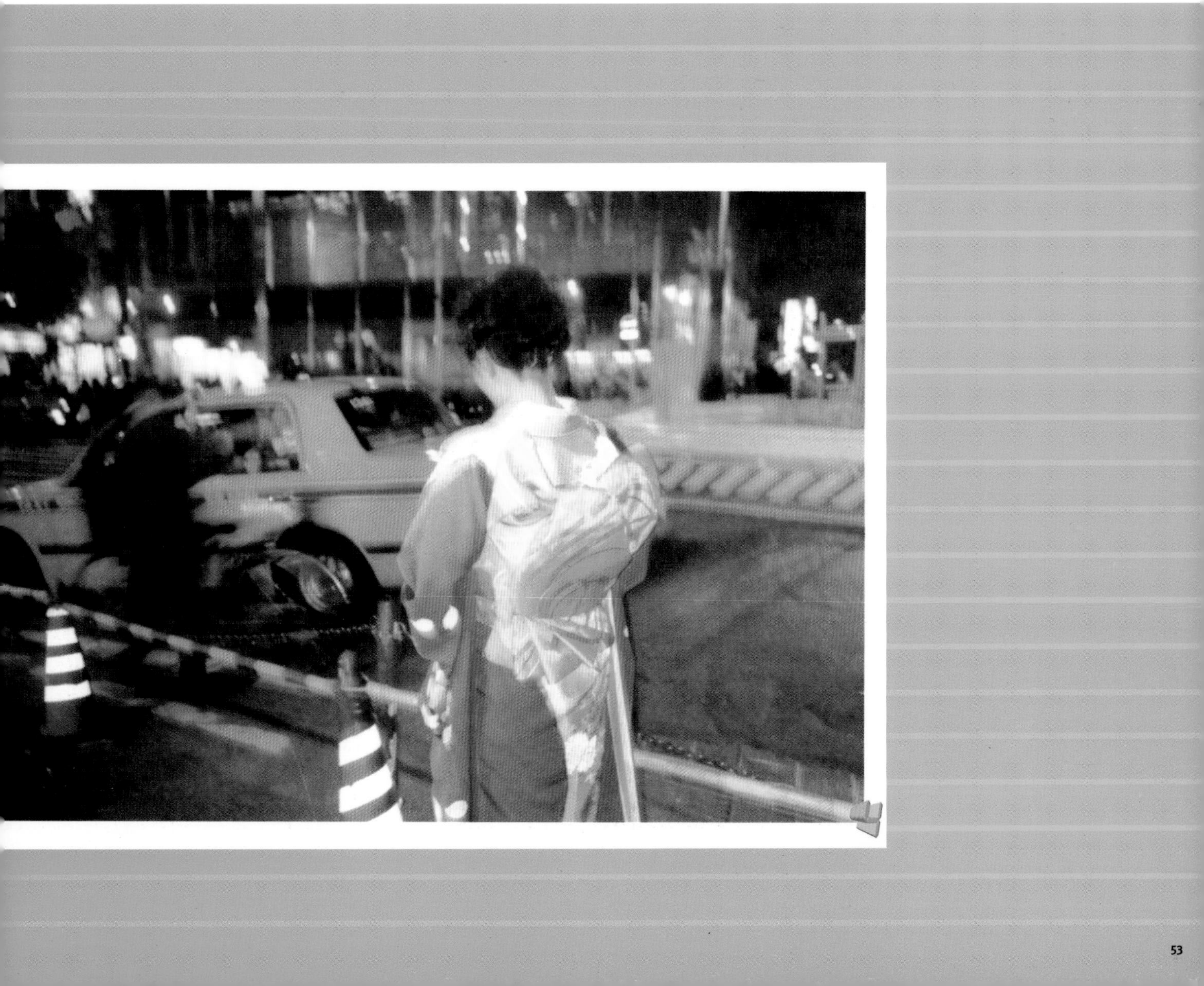

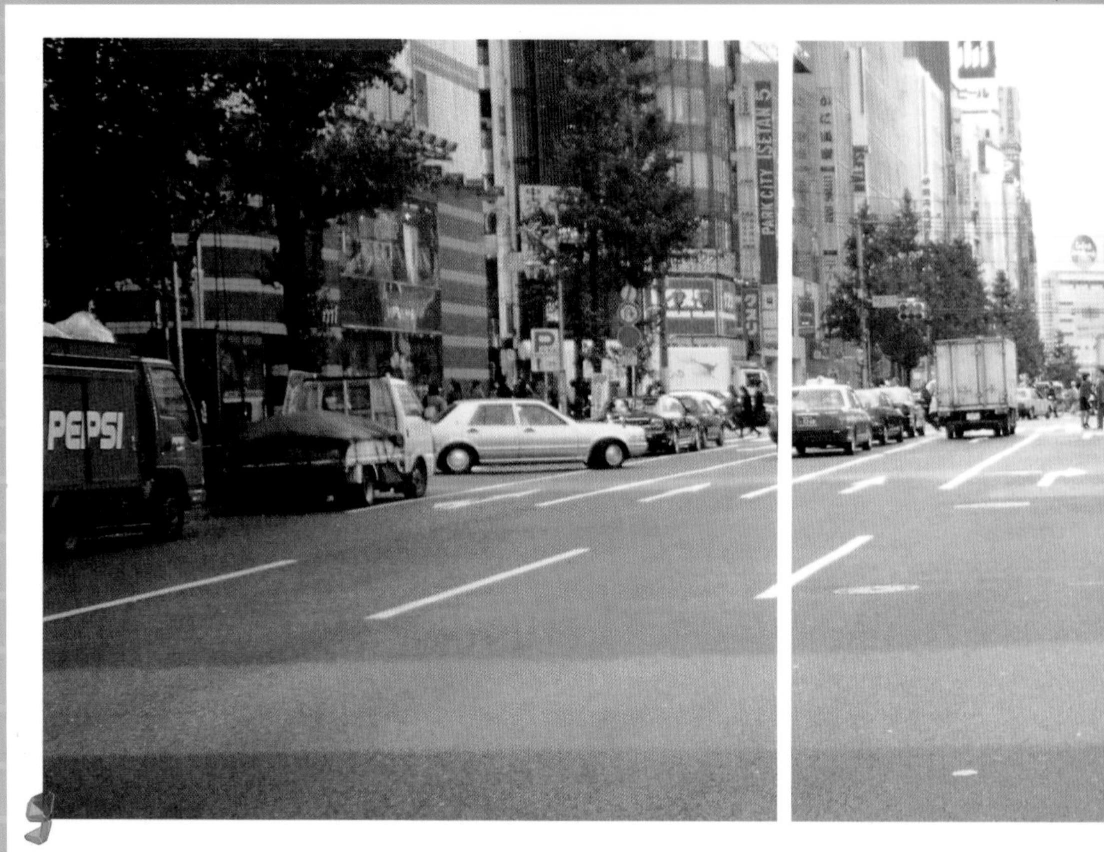
PEPSI
PARK CITY
ISETAN 5

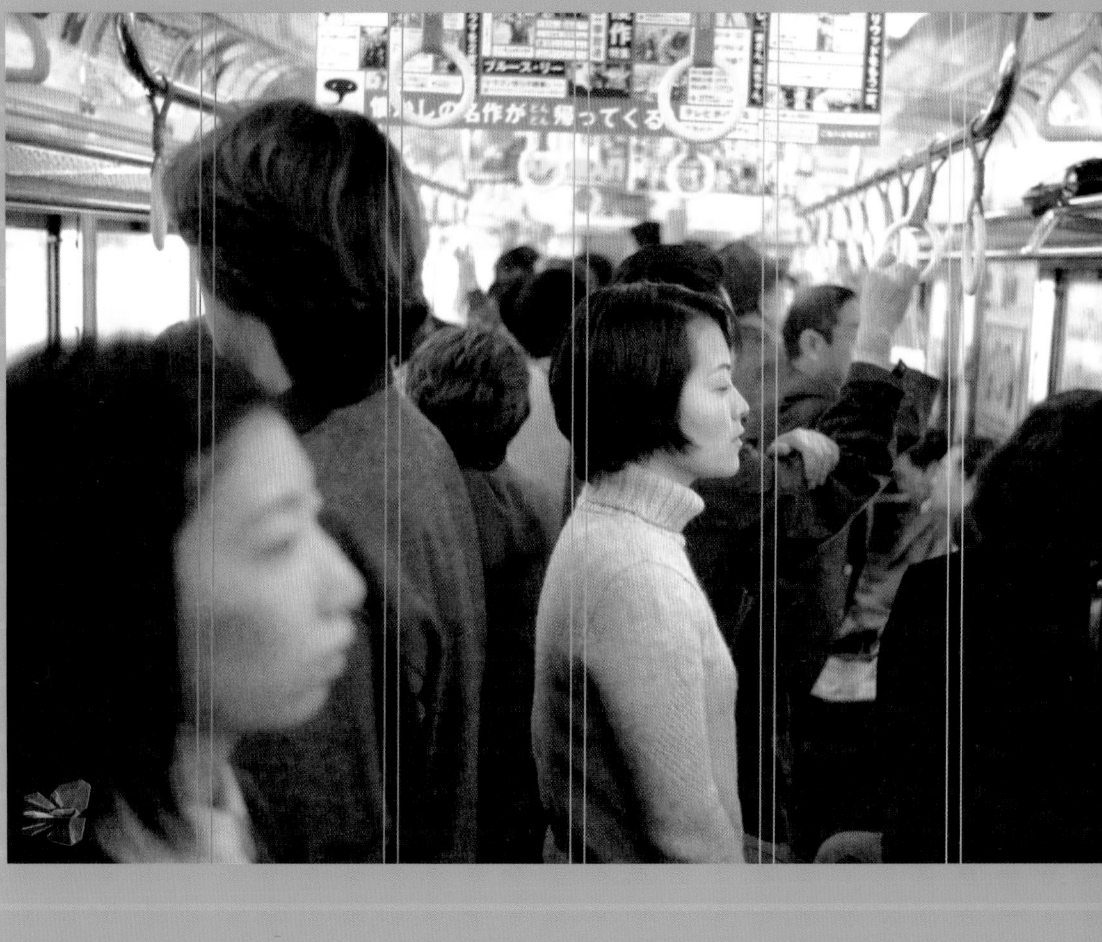
ブルース・リー

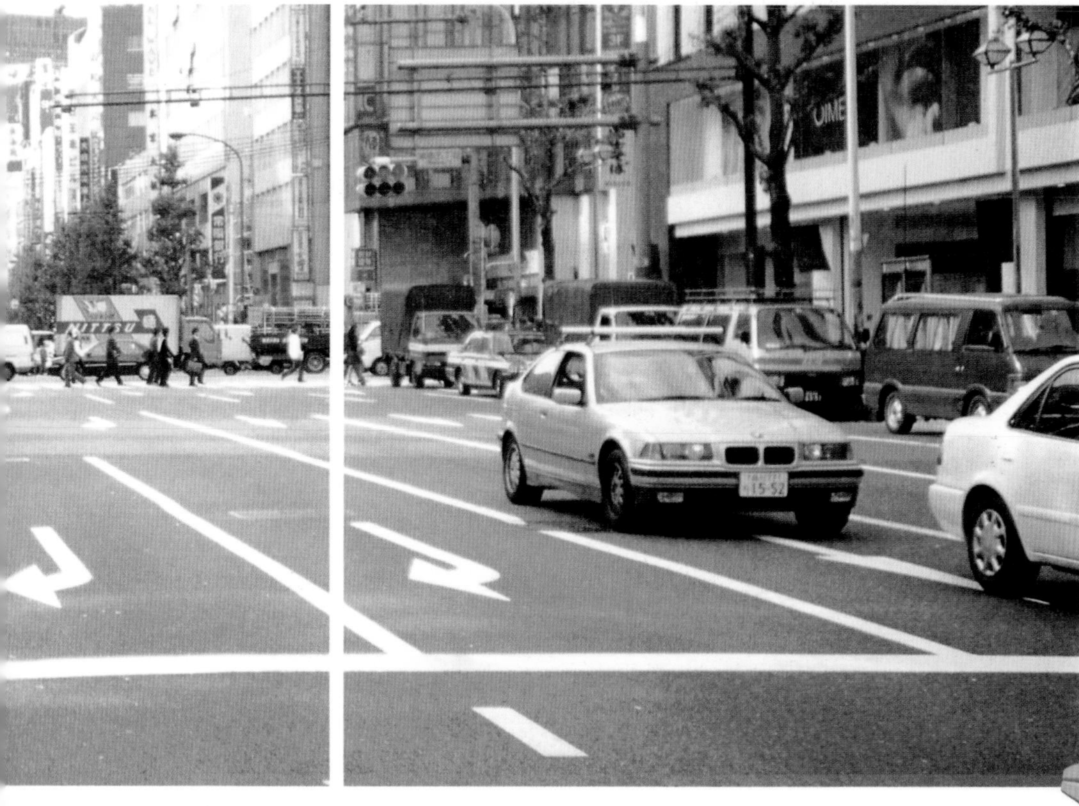

WIE TANAKA VON „FANTASTIC PLASTIC MACHINE" SCHEREN SICH UM KEINE GRENZEN: ENGLISCHE DRUM & BASS-MAXIS WERDEN IN SCHLAGER VON MARY
S UND VERGESSENE HITS VON A-HA GEMIXT. UND ALLES TOBT UND TANZT. OHNE DROGEN UND MIT WENIG ALKOHOL DAUERT JEDE NACHT BIS ZUM
HEN MORGEN. UM FÜNF UHR NIMMT DIE U-BAHN DEN BETRIEB WIEDER AUF.

, 21, IST SO EINER, DER JEDE NACHT DURCHHÄLT UND DOCH JEDEN MORGEN UM ZEHN UHR IN EINER DER SECOND-HAND-BOUTIQUEN SEINES VATERS
RITT, UM SELTENE LEVIS-JEANS UND ANDERE MODE-RARITÄTEN ZU VERKAUFEN. ER TRÄGT JEANS AUS PAPAS LADEN, EIN HAWAII-HEMD („SEHR GÜN-
I") UND NIKE-TURNSCHUHE, VON DENEN ER BEHAUPTET, DASS ES SIE NUR EINEN TAG ZU KAUFEN GAB. DIE GELDSCHEINE, DIE ER AUS DER TASCHE ZIEHT,
EN FRISCH GEDRUCKT AUS. UND OB NUN DIE TOURISTEN AUS GERMANY ODER DOCH AUS JAMAIKA KOMMEN, DAS IST EGAL. WICHTIG IST IHM NUR, WAS
MARKEN SIE TRAGEN. UND DIE KRISE? HITO STUTZT EINEN KLEINEN AUGENBLICK. „WELCHE KRISE?" FRAGT ER SCHLIESSLICH. OHNE GELD ABER WIRD
UYA ZU EINEM TRAURIGEN ORT. EINZIG IM YOYOGI PARK, ABSEITS DER LÄRMENDEN EINKAUFSSTRASSEN, FINDET EIN LEBEN STATT, DAS NICHT IN YEN
ESSEN WIRD. DRAG QUEENS STELLEN SICH ZUR SCHAU, SCHULMÄDCHEN FÜHREN AKROBATISCHE TÄNZE VOR, UND AMATEURBANDS LÄRMEN UM DIE WETTE.
PULSIERT DER ENERGIESTROM, DER SHIBUYA DURCHZIEHT, EIN WENIG LANGSAMER.

BÖCKEM UND CHRISTOPH DALLACH
T ERSCHIENEN IN SPIEGEL KULTUR EXTRA, HEFT 7/1998

Designer
Antonia Henschel

Art Director
Antonia Henschel

Photographers
Antonia Henschel, Ingmar Kurth

Country of Origin
Germany

Description of Artwork
A 62-page book, third in a series promoting the German design company Sign Kommunikation GmbH.

Page Dimensions
297 x 210 mm
$11^3/_4$ x $8^1/_4$ in

Format
Book

DESIGN FOR BUSINESS

Businesses from across the whole commercial spectrum rely on fresh, imaginative design to differentiate themselves from their competitors. The work presented here—calendars, websites, brochures, and catalogs—has been commissioned by companies as diverse as the *International Herald Tribune* and Ultramagic, a Spanish hot-air balloon manufacturer.

SECTION TWO

Designer
Mark Rogerson

Art Director
Mark Rogerson

Photographer
International Herald Tribune archive

Design Company
Mark Rogerson Associates

Country of Origin
UK

Description of Artwork
Calendar for the *International Herald Tribune* newspaper.

Dimensions
180 x 180 mm
7[1]/8 x 7[1]/8 in

Format
Calendar

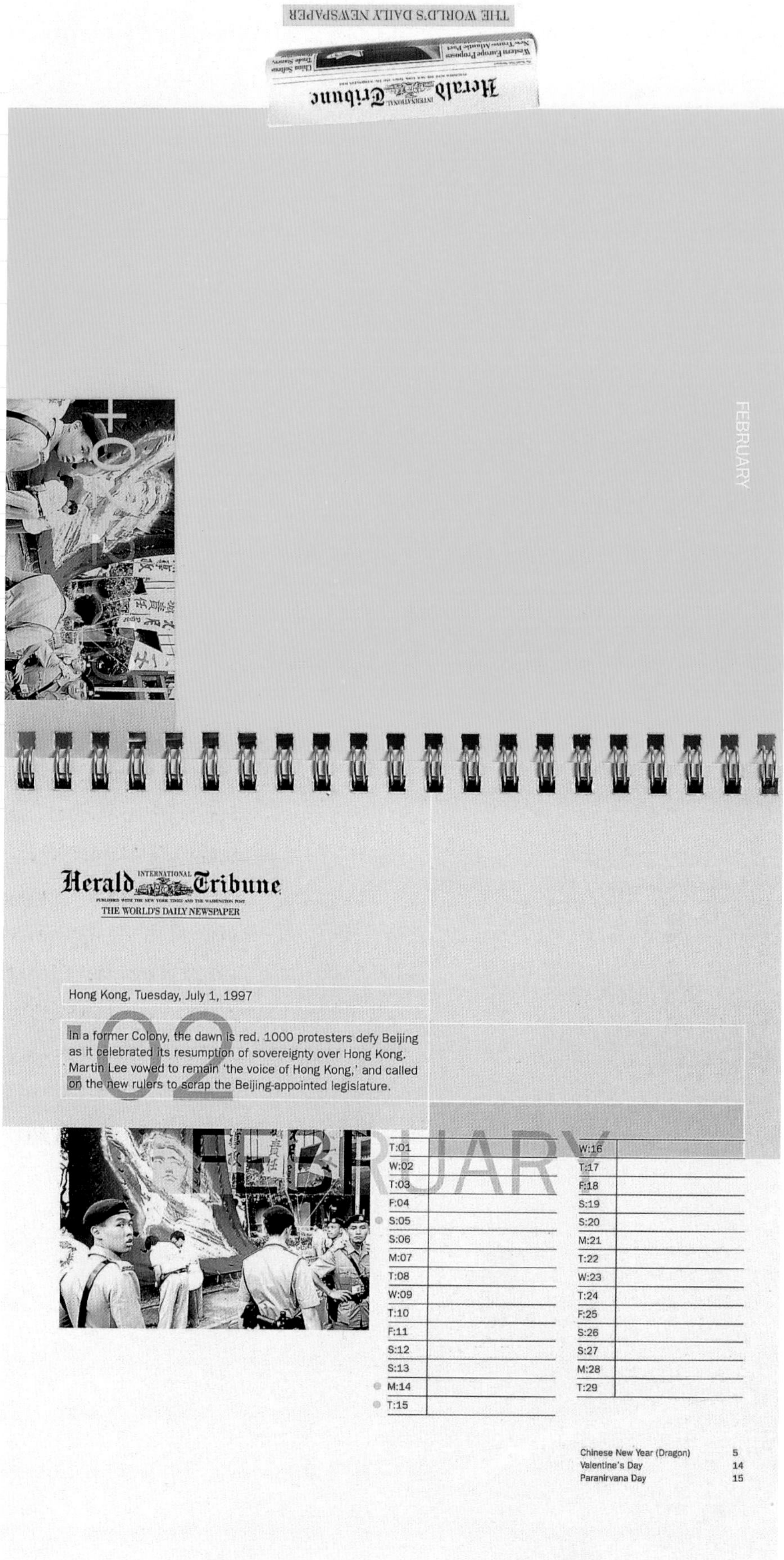

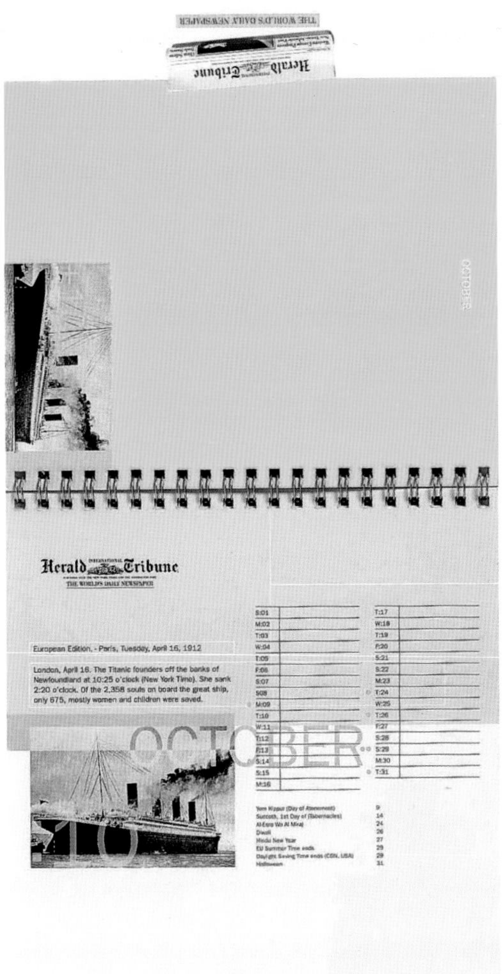

International Herald Tribune 2000 Calendar

This strong design for the *International Herald Tribune*, a traditionally monochrome newspaper, celebrates a century of news reporting by using text quotes and photographs from the paper's archives. The layout is based on a simple structure of four blocks: the large area of yellow; the position of the picture within that color area; the dark gray area on the other side; and the position of the second photographic image. The fixed position of the logo and rolled-up newspaper is orientated for when the calendar is stood up. The well-considered clarity of the typography in a sans serif typeface and the clever way its positioning is varied for each month, makes this apparently simple solution satisfying and fresh for each month of the year.

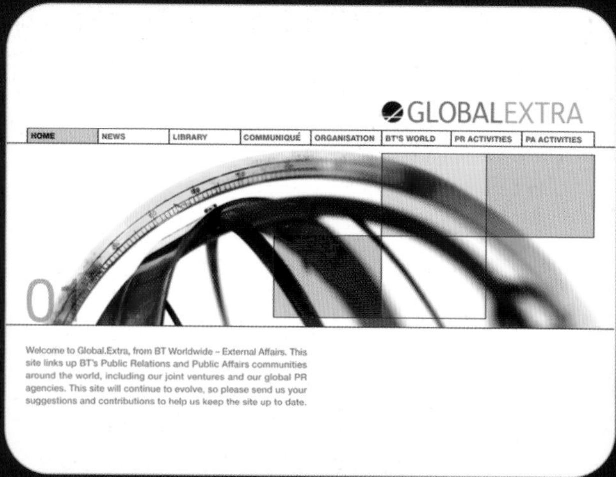
GLOBALEXTRA
HOME NEWS LIBRARY COMMUNIQUÉ ORGANISATION BT'S WORLD PR ACTIVITIES PA ACTIVITIES
01
Welcome to Global.Extra, from BT Worldwide – External Affairs. This site links up BT's Public Relations and Public Affairs communities around the world, including our joint ventures and our global PR agencies. This site will continue to evolve, so please send us your suggestions and contributions to help us keep the site up to date.

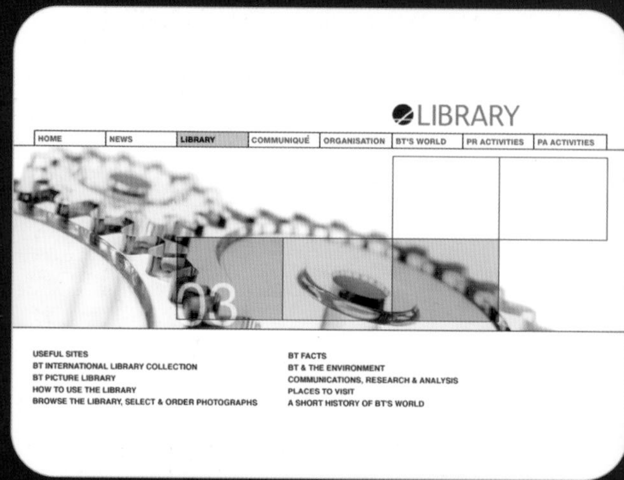
LIBRARY
HOME NEWS LIBRARY COMMUNIQUÉ ORGANISATION BT'S WORLD PR ACTIVITIES PA ACTIVITIES
03
USEFUL SITES
BT INTERNATIONAL LIBRARY COLLECTION
BT PICTURE LIBRARY
HOW TO USE THE LIBRARY
BROWSE THE LIBRARY, SELECT & ORDER PHOTOGRAPHS
BT FACTS
BT & THE ENVIRONMENT
COMMUNICATIONS, RESEARCH & ANALYSIS
PLACES TO VISIT
A SHORT HISTORY OF BT'S WORLD

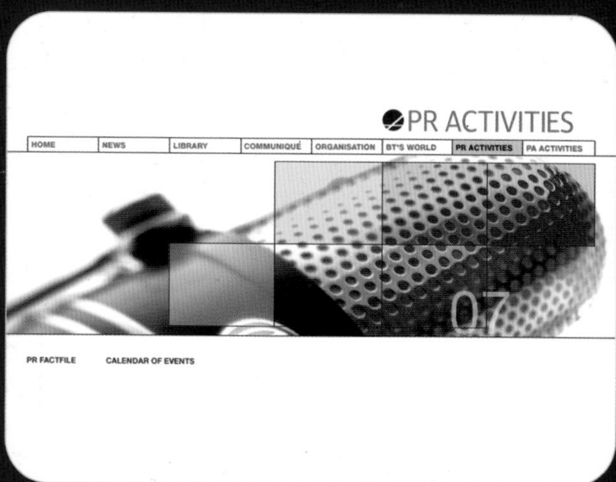
PR ACTIVITIES
HOME NEWS LIBRARY COMMUNIQUÉ ORGANISATION BT'S WORLD PR ACTIVITIES PA ACTIVITIES
07
PR FACTFILE
CALENDAR OF EVENTS

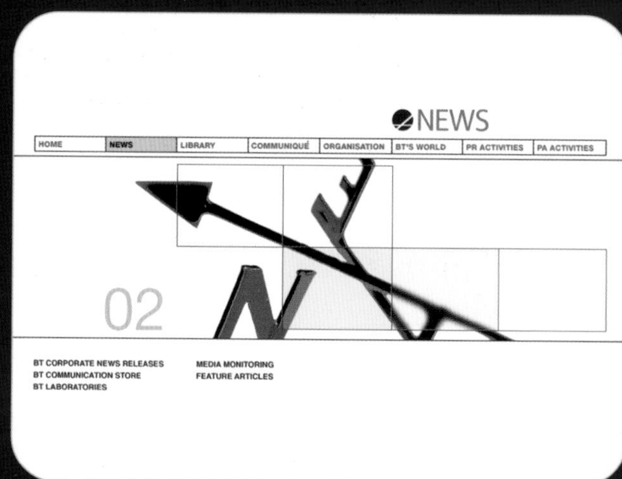
NEWS
HOME NEWS LIBRARY COMMUNIQUÉ ORGANISATION BT'S WORLD PR ACTIVITIES PA ACTIVITIES
02
BT CORPORATE NEWS RELEASES
BT COMMUNICATION STORE
BT LABORATORIES
MEDIA MONITORING
FEATURE ARTICLES

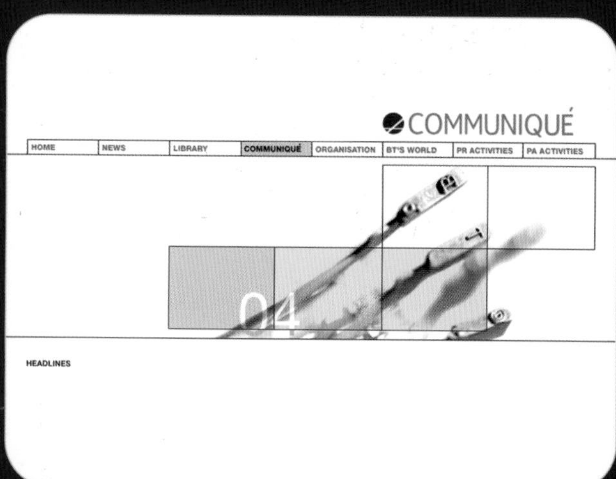
COMMUNIQUÉ
HOME NEWS LIBRARY COMMUNIQUÉ ORGANISATION BT'S WORLD PR ACTIVITIES PA ACTIVITIES
04
HEADLINES

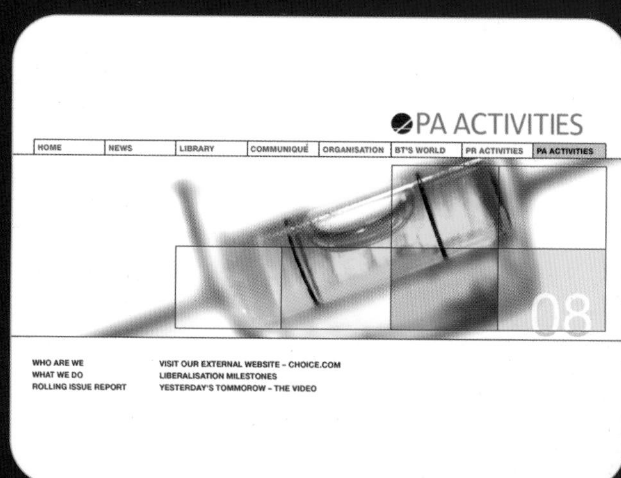
PA ACTIVITIES
HOME NEWS LIBRARY COMMUNIQUÉ ORGANISATION BT'S WORLD PR ACTIVITIES PA ACTIVITIES
08
WHO ARE WE
WHAT WE DO
ROLLING ISSUE REPORT
VISIT OUR EXTERNAL WEBSITE – CHOICE.COM
LIBERALISATION MILESTONES
YESTERDAY'S TOMMOROW – THE VIDEO

BT Global Extra Intranet Site

Simply using the logo and web-page title in a set position above the navigation bar, over similarly treated abstract imagery, gives this site a clean, stylish, and consistent appearance. The strong typographic framework provides a corporate look to a site which contains much diverse information. The regularity of the design also makes it easy for users to familiarize themselves with the site layout and enables them to find relevant information quickly.

Designer
Mark Rogerson

Art Directors
Mark Rogerson, Jonathan Brade

Photographer
Jonathan Brade

Design Company
Mark Rogerson Associates

Country of Origin
UK

Description of Artwork
Intranet site for British Telecom Worldwide External Affairs used by BT's advertising agencies and PR companies to source BT information including the latest news, logos, corporate guidelines, and stock photography.

Dimensions
Varies to screen size

Format
Website

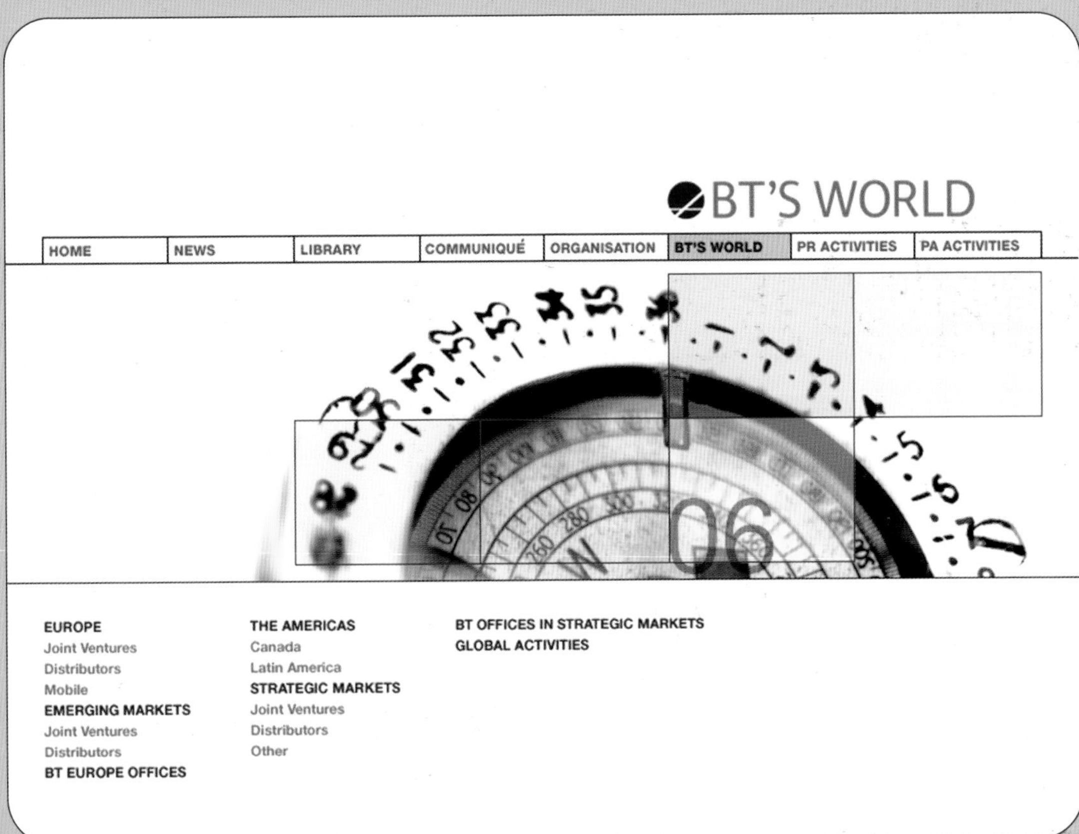

Designer
Martin Brown

Art Directors
Jim Sutherland, Pierre Vermeir

Photographer
Phil Starling

Design Company
HGV Design

Country of Origin
UK

Description of Artwork
Spiral-bound direct mail brochure for a rail-based parcel-courier company.

Dimensions (Main Page)
297 x 210 mm
$11^{3}/_{4}$ x $8^{1}/_{4}$ in

Format
Brochure

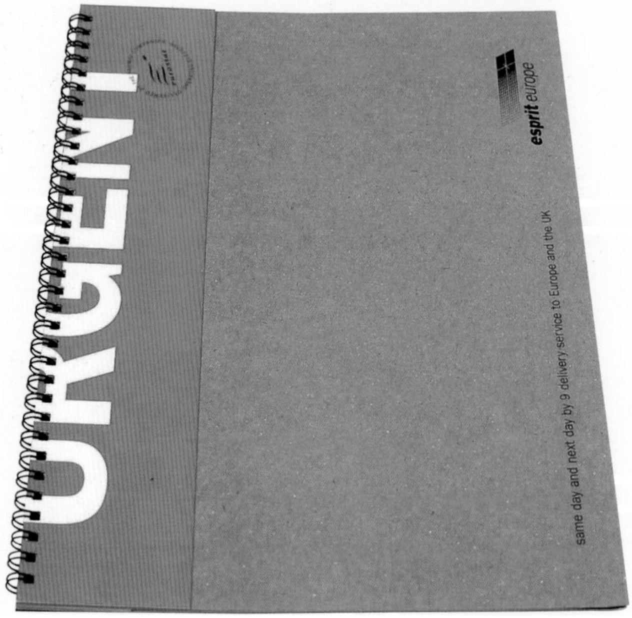

Esprit Europe Brochure

This imaginative brochure combines high-quality photography, railway-inspired graphics, and an ingenious use of spiral binding to produce a very effective promotional publication that works on many different levels. The photography evokes the romance and speed of the train, while the text is presented in ways that directly connect with the graphic devices employed at railroad stations. For example, the clever use of spiral binding and alternate thin 'flip' pages mimics the rollerdeck-style of announcement board used in many station terminuses.

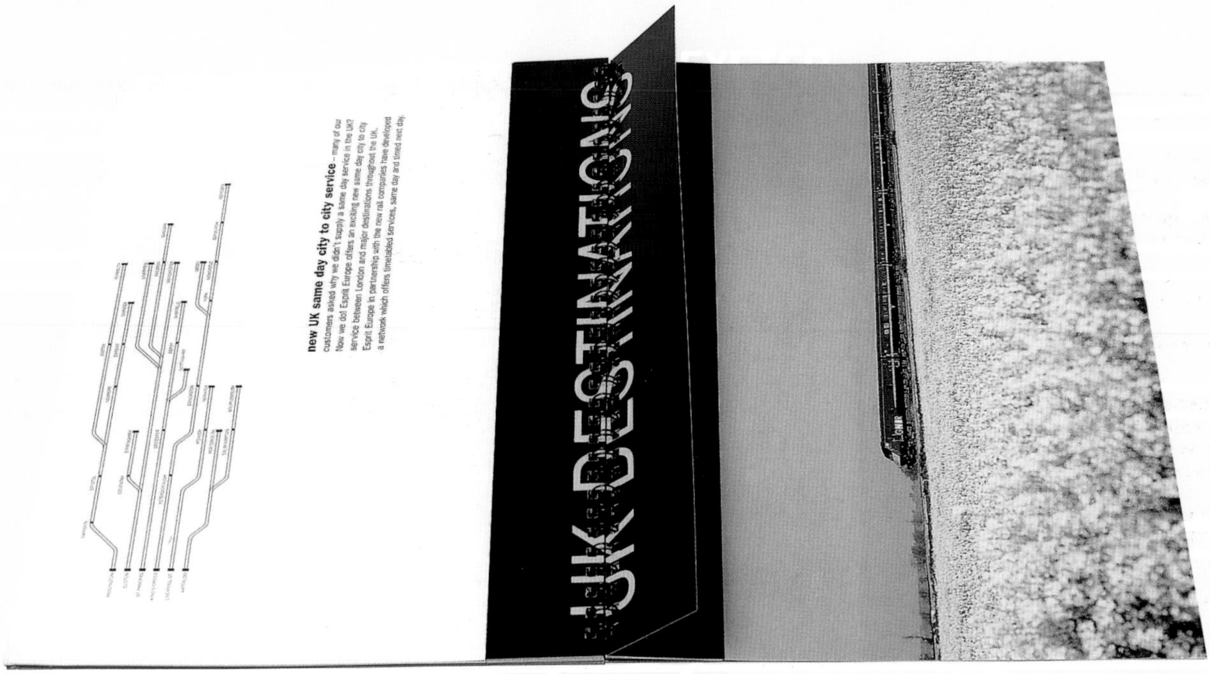

Visual references to the railroad are used to enliven the text. Here, the information is presented in the form of a railroad network diagram.

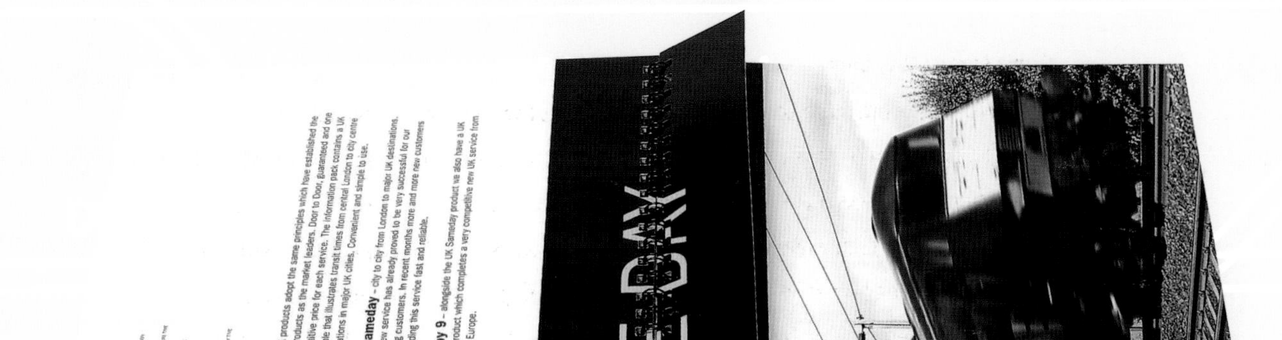

The thin 'flip' page not only allows two different messages to be presented on the same spread, but also involves the reader in flipping the page to find out what is hidden beneath.

Immortality Poster

Created as part of a promotion for paper, the designer has chosen images 'to depict the immortal quality' of the medium. The juxtaposition of images and text draws the reader in and creates a beguiling atmosphere; while the treatment of the typography (different typefaces used in a variety of colors, sizes, and states of legibility) adds texture to the overall composition.

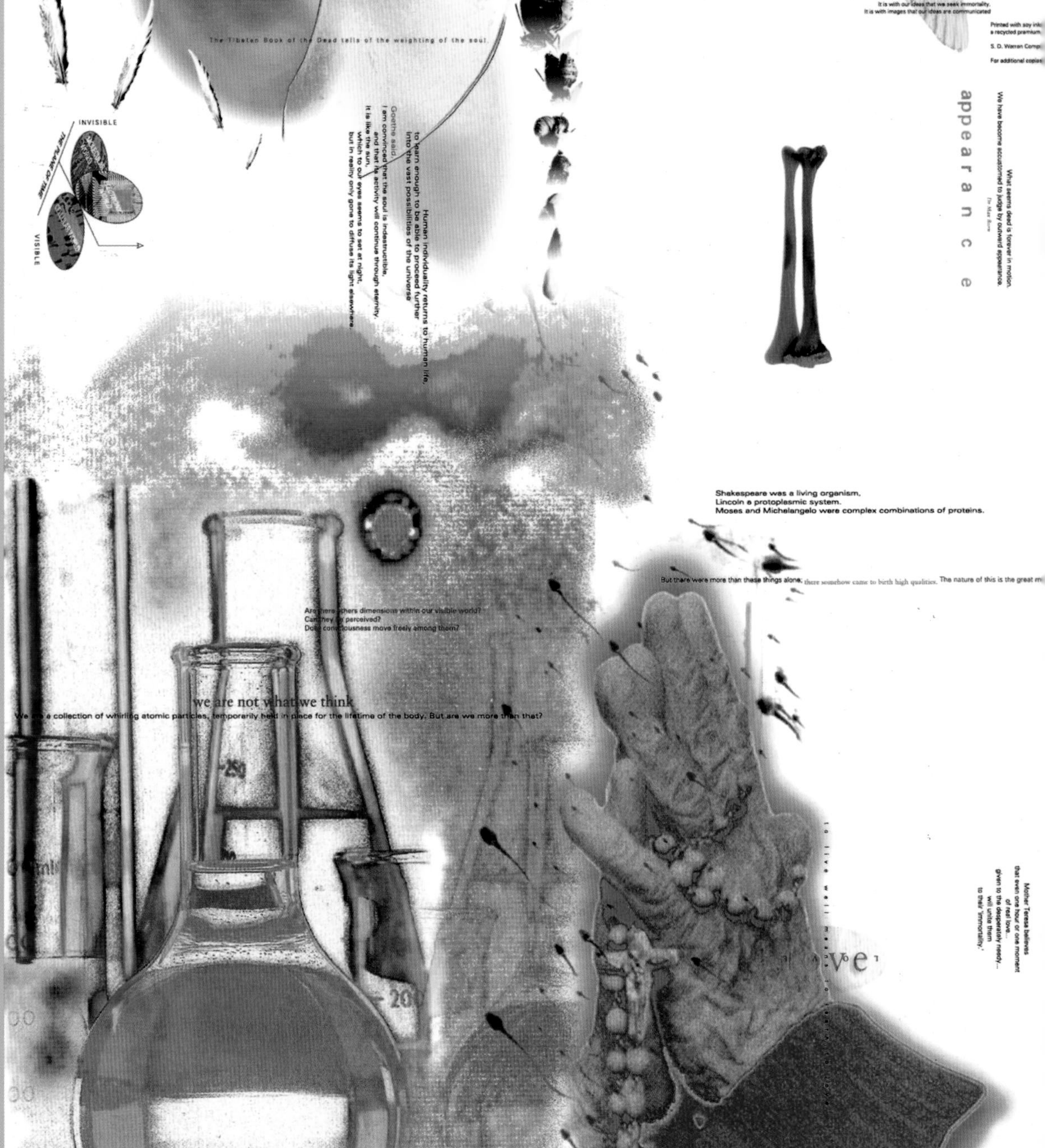

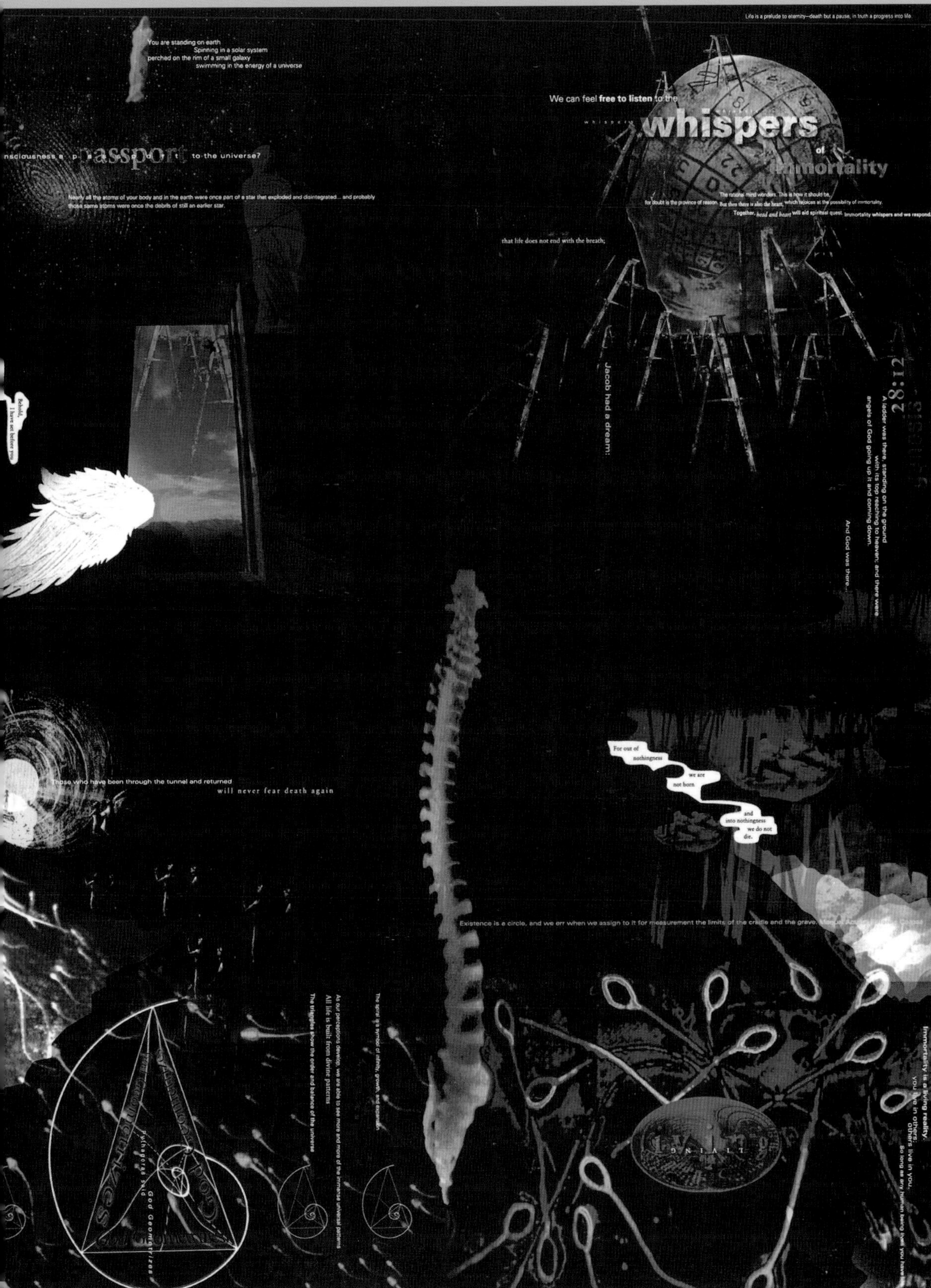

Designer
Rafael Esquer

Art Director
Rafael Esquer

Instructor
Steve Madden

Art College
Art Center College of Design

Country of Origin
USA

Description of Artwork
Double-sided concept poster designed to promote the use of paper.

Dimensions
550 x 710 mm
$21^3/_4$ x $28^3/_8$ in

Format
Poster

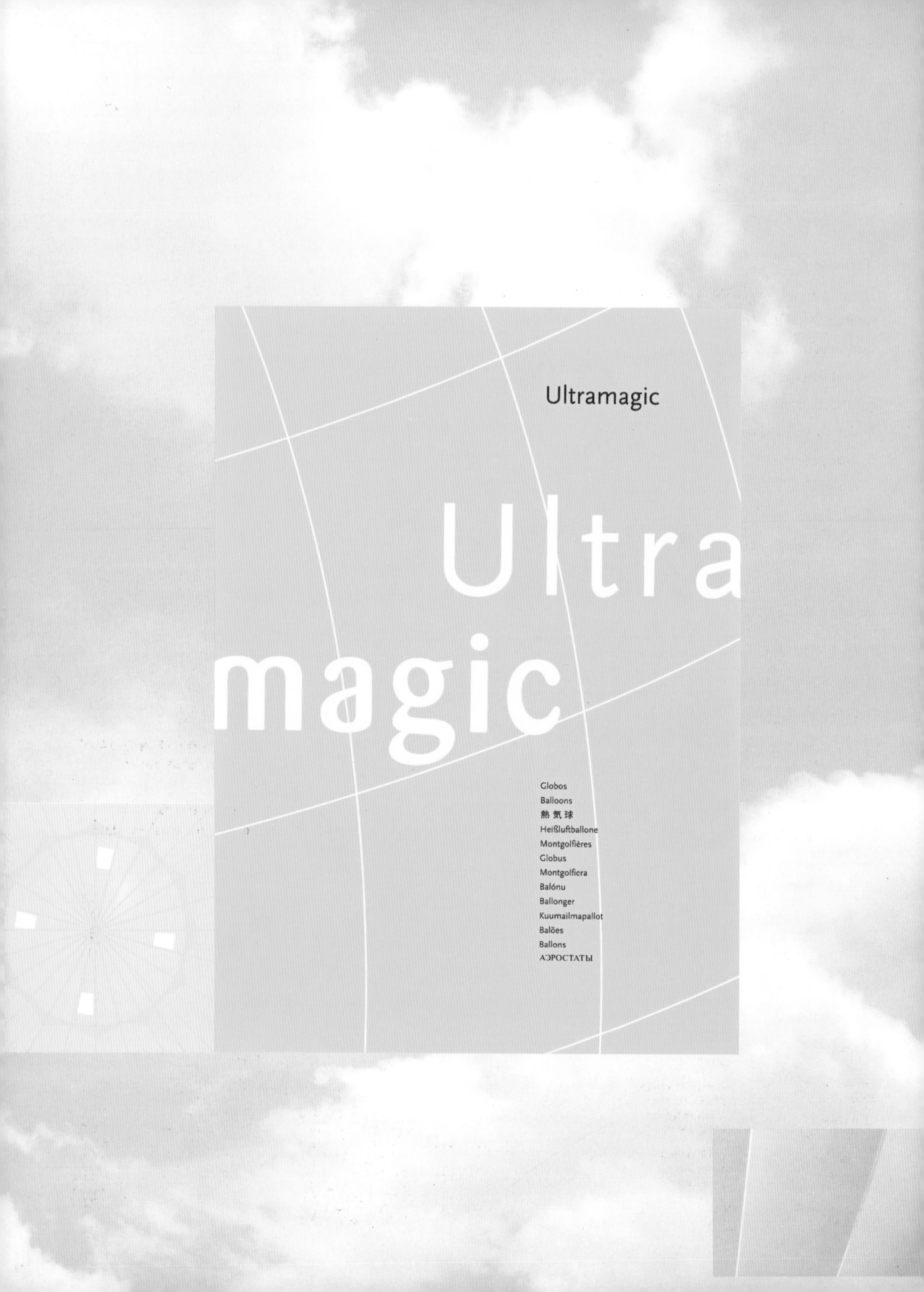
Ultramagic
Ultra
magic
Globos
Balloons
熱 気 球
Heißluftballone
Montgolfières
Globus
Montgolfiera
Balónu
Ballonger
Kuumailmapallot
Balões
Ballons
АЭРОСТАТЫ

Ultramagic

The simple line-and-flat-color cover (*opposite*) gives little away about what to expect inside this multilingual catalog. Once inside, images and text seem to float across the page, creating a sense of space and freedom. The catalog has been used to promote the bespoke nature of balloon construction and to encourage the reader to start imagining their own design by the inclusion of color swatches down the side of one spread (*bottom, right*).

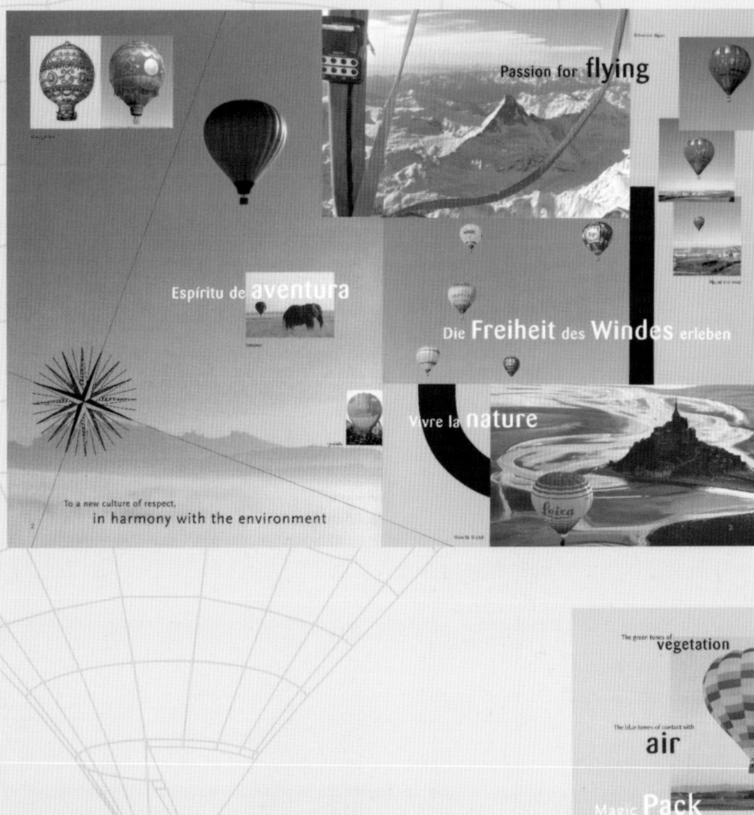

Left: the inclusion of historical imagery sets up a contrast that emphasizes the modern nature of ballooning.

Below: the images of a balloon under construction illustrate the high degree of care and attention to detail offered by the company.

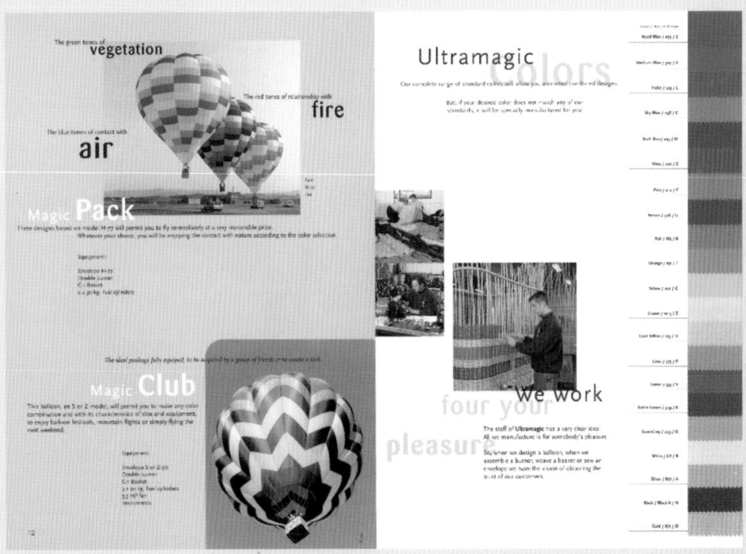

Designer
Lluis Jubert

Art Director
Ramon Enrich

Illustrations
Ultramagic Archive

Photographers
Roger Velazquez and various

Design Company
Espai Grafic

Country of Origin
Spain

Description of Artwork
Promotional catalog for a balloon factory near Barcelona.

Page Dimensions
210 x 295 mm
$8^1/_4$ x $11^5/_8$ in

Format
Catalog

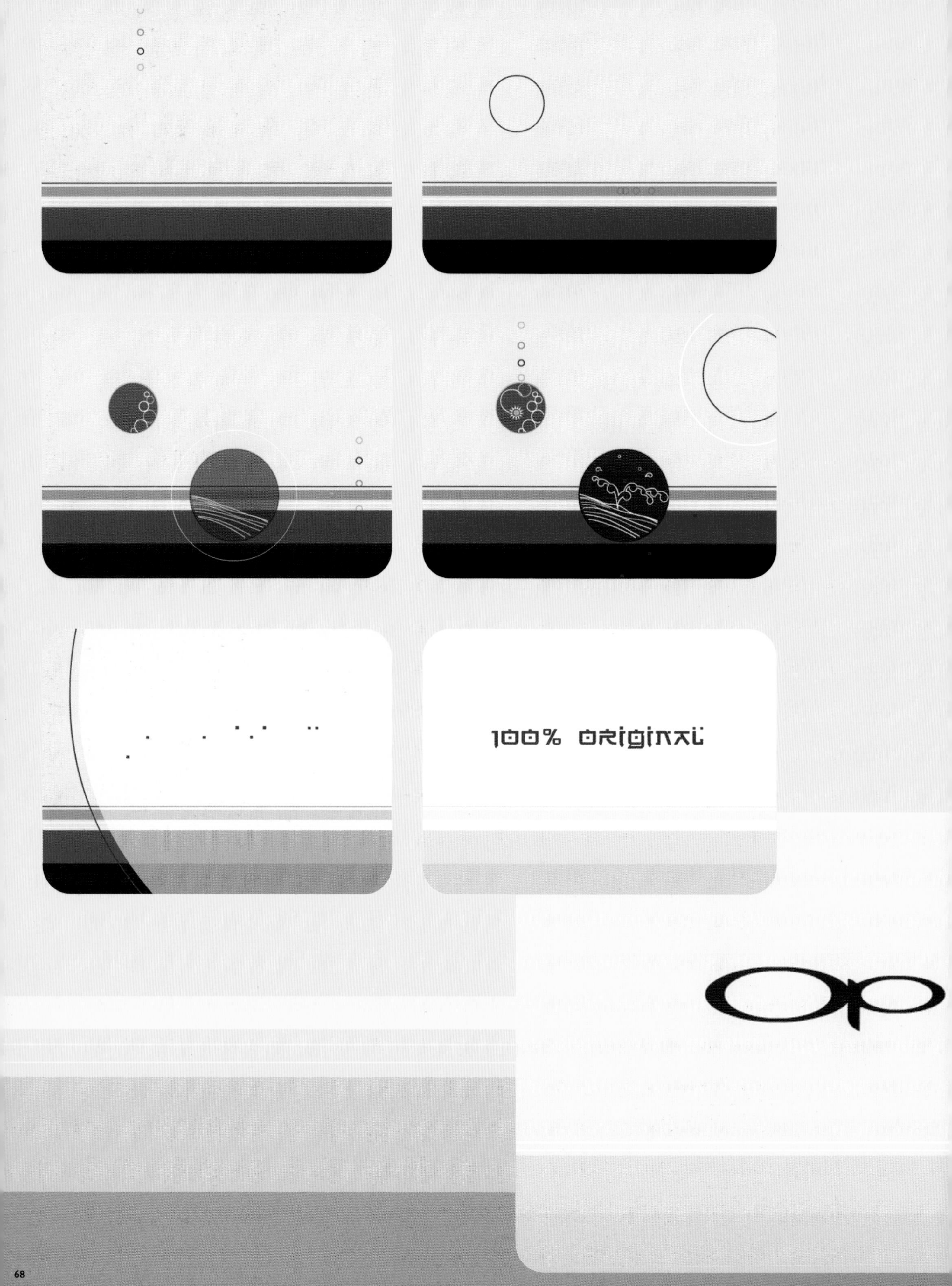
100% ORIGINAL
Op

Ocean Pacific

The opening animated sequence (*opposite*) establishes a visual style within which different types of information can be presented while maintaining the overall identity of the company Ocean Pacific. This complex site combines text, still images, and short animations in a highly appealing and accessible format.

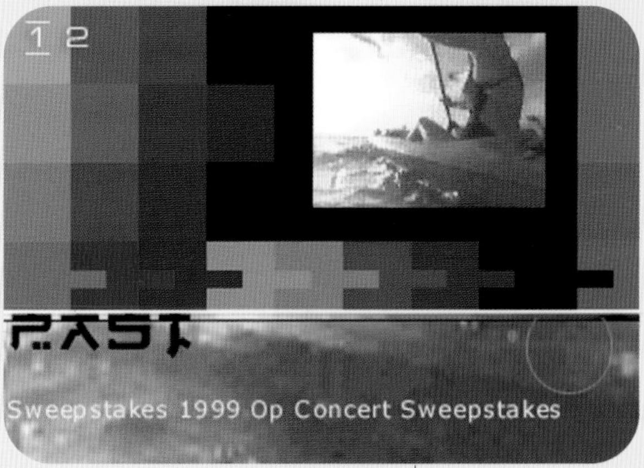

Opposite: the motif of rising bubbles, first seen in the opening sequence, is subsequently used as a device to access information. When the cursor is placed over the word LIFESTYLE, bubbles rise from behind it to reveal two options: 'boys' or 'girls.'

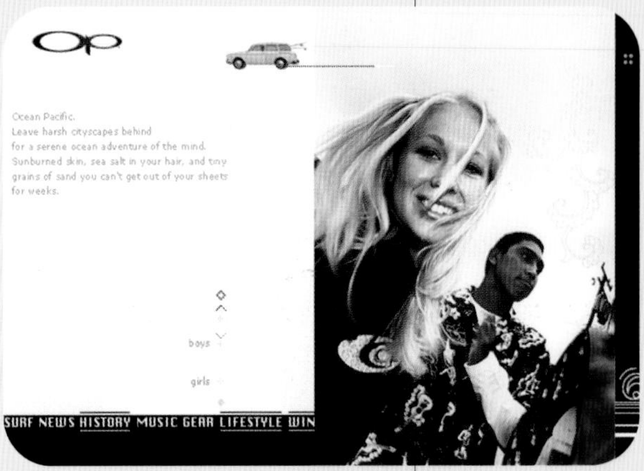

Right: two main graphic devices are employed to help separate different types of information—the division of the screen 75:25 (*top*), and a black rim along the bottom and right-hand side (*center and bottom*).

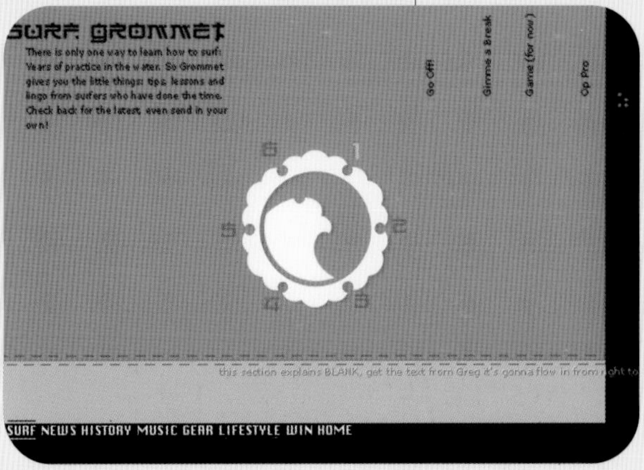

Designers
Mark Allen, Adrianne De Loia, Alejandra Jarabo, Chris Martinez

Art Director
Adrianne De Loia

Illustrators
Adrianne De Loia, Alejandra Jarabo

Photographer
Adrianne De Loia

Design Company
Kick Media

Country of Origin
USA

Description of Artwork
Website for Ocean Pacific, showcasing clothing, lifestyles, games, surf pro, and the surf dance.

Dimensions
640 x 480 pixels

Format
Website

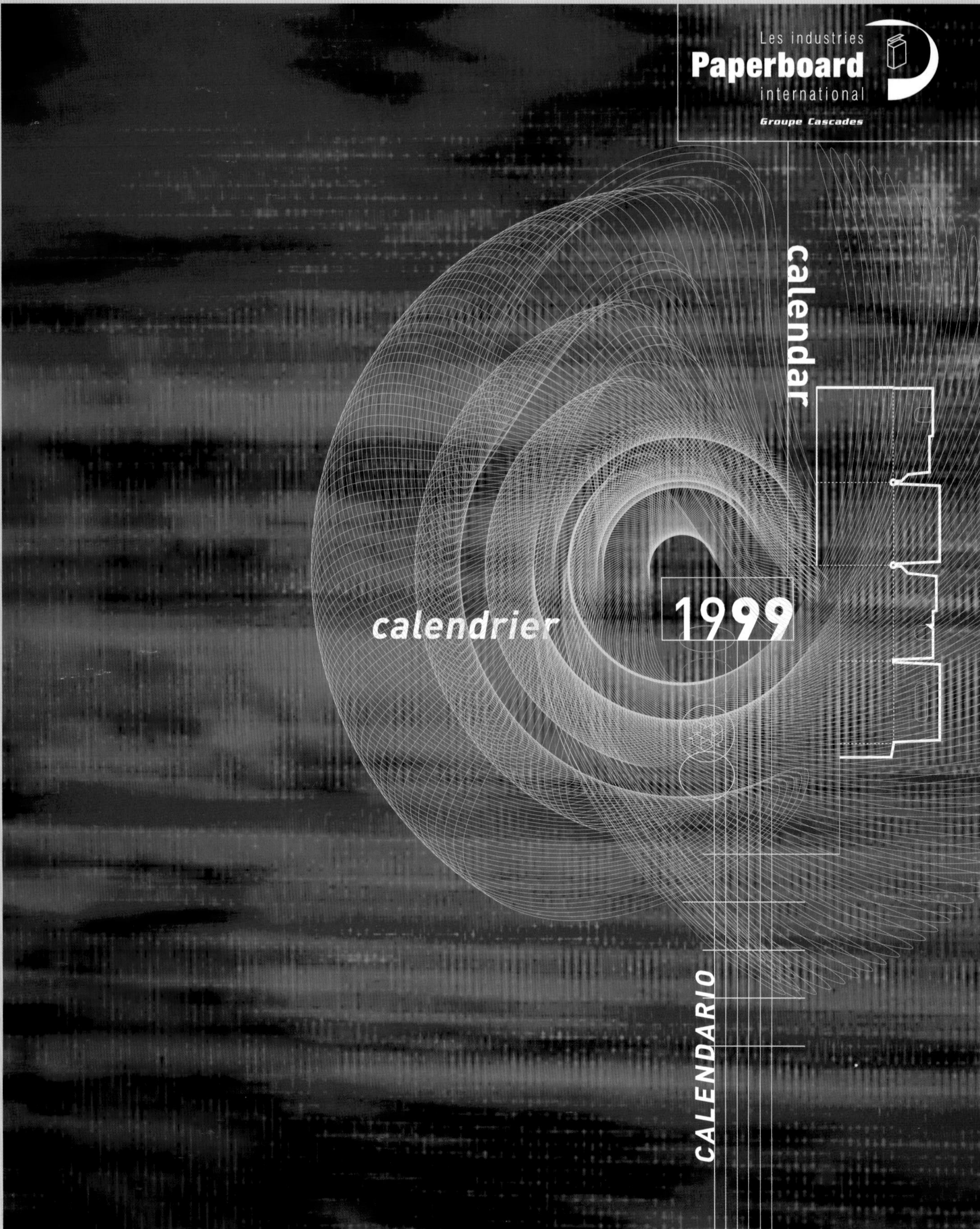
Les industries
Paperboard
international
Groupe Cascades
calendar
calendrier
1999
CALENDARIO

Les Industries Paperboard International **Calendar 1999**

The brief was to promote the equipment used in the production of paperboard. The designers have taken images which are in themselves descriptive rather than inspirational and have used the design to suggest the advanced nature of the technology. The use of geometric patterns and a consistent style of type and color panels draws together the different qualities of the photographs, presenting them in a fresh and dynamic way.

Designer
Catherine Petter

Creative Directors
Daniel Fortin, George Fok

Art Director
Catherine Petter

Illustrator
Catherine Petter

Photographer
Jean-François Gratton

Design Company
Époxy

Country of Origin
Canada

Description of Artwork
Trilingual calendar designed to showcase the high-tech equipment of Les Industries Paperboard International.

Dimensions
406 x 507 mm
16 x 20 in

Format
Calendar

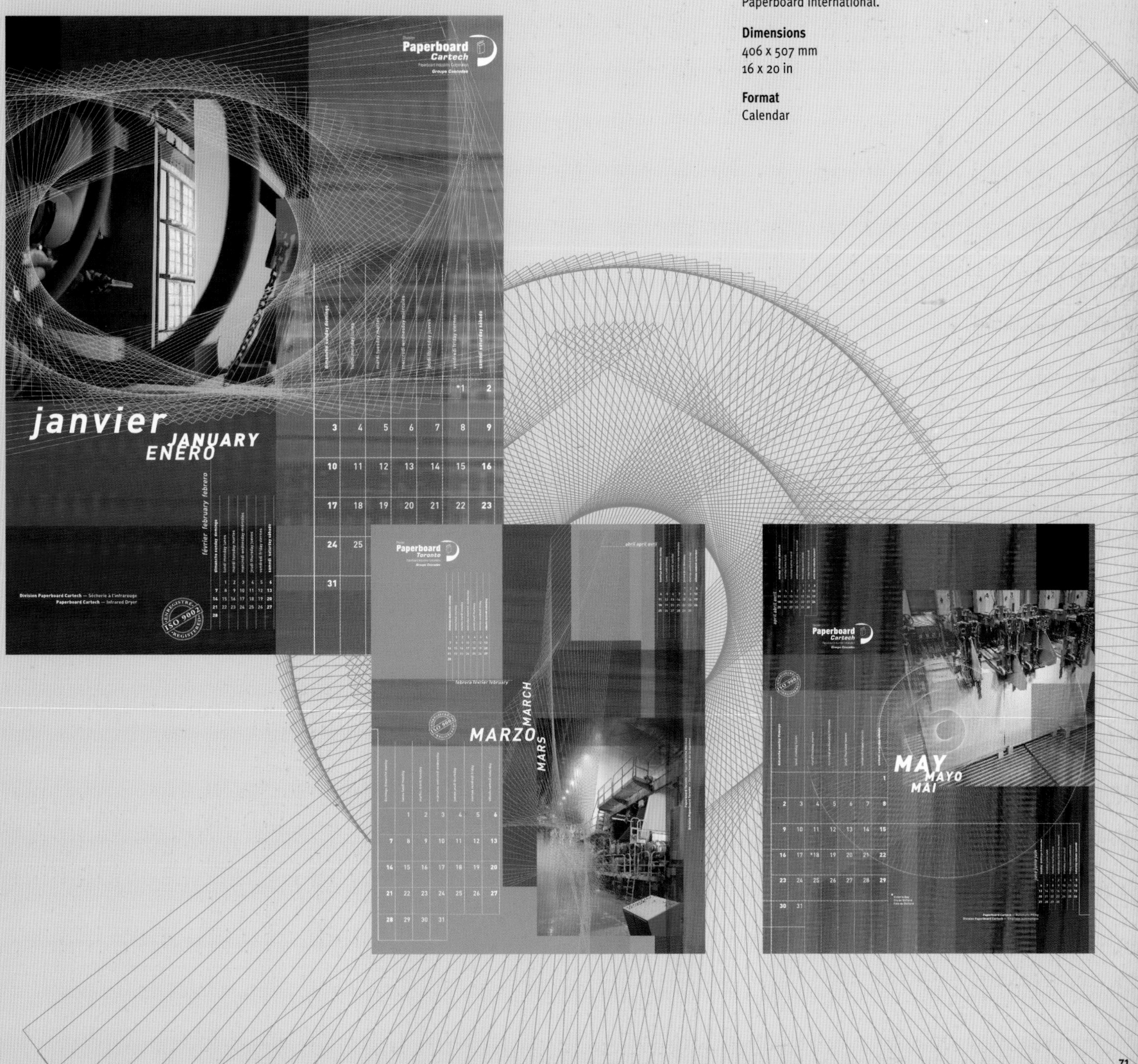

october octobre octubre

sunday domingo dimanche	monday lunes lundi	tuesday martes mardi	wednesday miércoles mercredi	thursday jueves jeudi	friday viernes vendredi	saturday sábado samedi
					1	**2**
3	4	5	6	7	8	**9**
10	11	12	13	14	15	**16**
17	18	19	20	21	22	**23**
24	25	26	27	28	29	**30**
31						

Division
Paperboard
Jonquière
Paperboard Industries Corporation
Groupe Cascades

NOVEMBER
NOVIEMBRE
NOVEMBRE

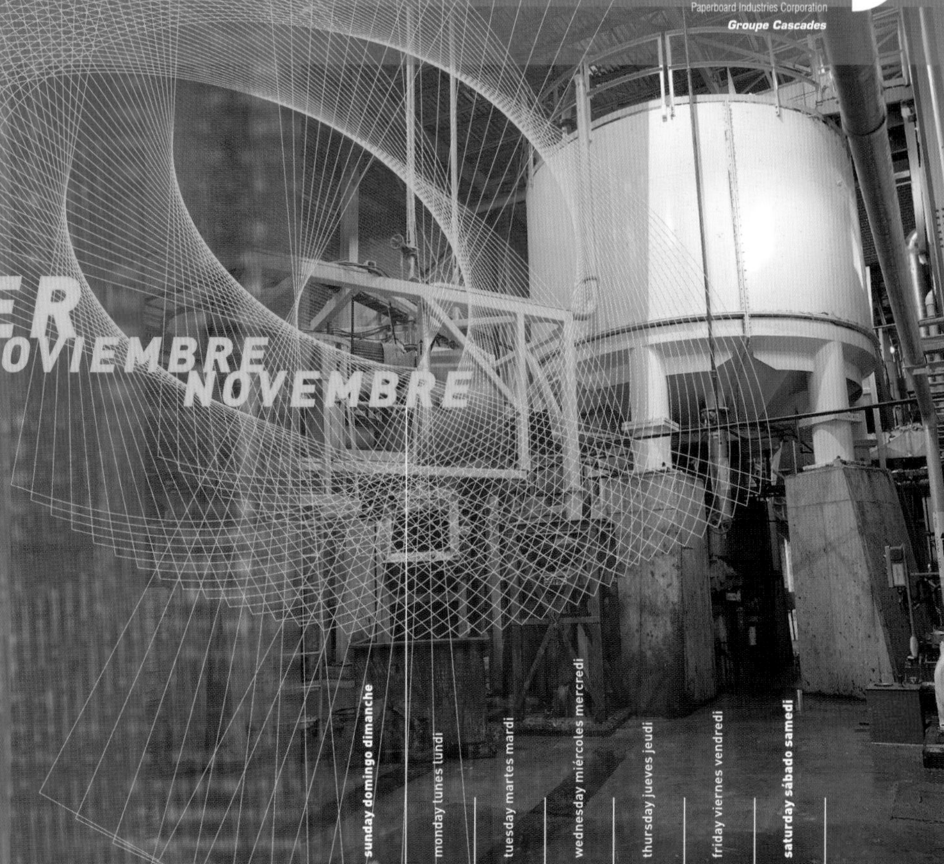

december diciembre décembre

sunday domingo dimanche	monday lunes lundi	tuesday martes mardi	wednesday miércoles mercredi	thursday jueves jeudi	friday viernes vendredi	saturday sábado samedi
			1	2	3	**4**
5	6	7	8	9	10	**11**
12	13	14	15	16	17	**18**
19	20	21	22	23	24	**25**
26	27	28	29	30	31	

sunday domingo dimanche	monday lunes lundi	tuesday martes mardi	wednesday miércoles mercredi	thursday jueves jeudi	friday viernes vendredi	**saturday sábado samedi**
	1	2	3	4	5	**6**
7	8	9	10	*11	12	**13**
14	15	16	17	18	19	**20**
21	22	23	24	25	26	**27**
28	29	30				

* Remembrance Day
Jour du souvenir
Día del recuerdo

ENREGISTRÉ · ISO 9002 · REGISTERED

Paperboard Jonquière — Pulper
Division Paperboard Jonquière — Triturateur

diciembre
DÉCEMBRE
DECEMBER

noviembre novembre november

domingo dimanche sunday	lunes lundi monday	martes mardi tuesday	miércoles mercredi wednesday	jueves jeudi thursday	viernes vendredi friday	sábado samedi saturday
	1	2	3	4	5	6
7	8	9	10	11	12	13
14	15	16	17	18	19	20
21	22	23	24	25	26	27
28	29	30				

domingo dimanche sunday	lunes lundi monday	martes mardi tuesday	miércoles mercredi wednesday	jueves jeudi thursday	viernes vendredi friday	sábado samedi saturday
			1	2	3	4
5	6	7	8	9	10	11
12	13	14	15	16	17	18
19	20	21	22	23	24	25
26	27	28	29	30	31	

* Navidad Noël Christmas Day

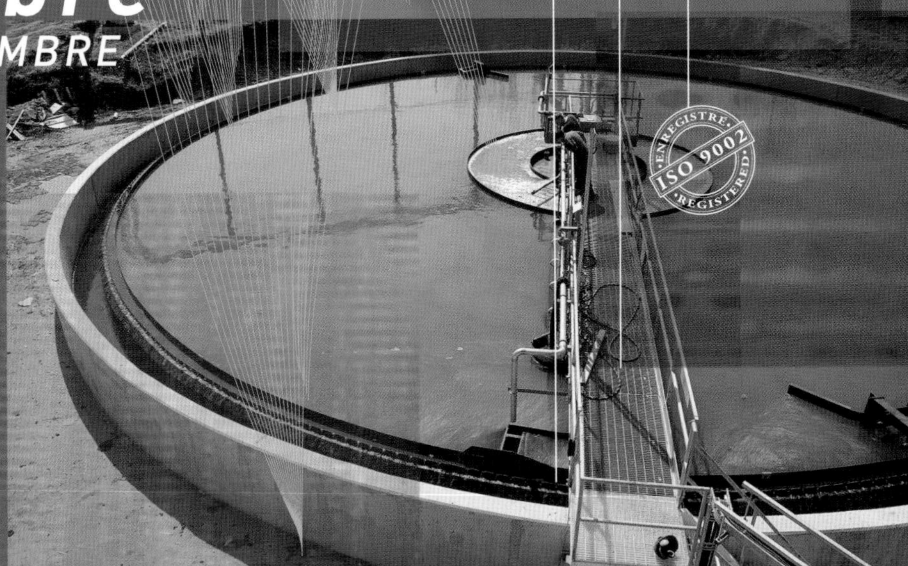

Division Paperboard Jonquière — Traitement des eaux usées
Paperboard Jonquière — Waste Water Treatment

Division **Paperboard Jonquière**
Paperboard Industries Corporation
Groupe Cascades

DESIGN FOR EDUCATION AND THE ARTS

The pieces shown in this final section are centered around the worlds of education and the arts. Cultural websites, university-faculty brochures, CD packaging, invitations to art exhibitions—a wide range of design projects, demonstrating an equally wide range of approaches and solutions.

SECTION THREE

Archi
tecture
Must
Burn

manifesto for an architecture beyond building

Aaron Betsky + Erik Adigard

Thames & Hudson

Designers
Erik Adigard, Patricia McShane

Art Director
Erik Adigard

Illustrator
Erik Adigard

Design Company
M.A.D.

Country of Origin
USA

Description of Artwork
144-page book that examines possible strategies for living in an electronic age. Text by Aaron Betsky and Erik Adigard.

Page Dimensions
229 x 279 mm
9 x 11 in

Format
Book

Architecture Must Burn

Bold type and simple flat color give the provocative title (*left*) a powerful presence, while the device of turning parts of the title upside-down suggests the subversive and surprising nature of the book's content. The design inside (*see next page*) contrasts the layered styling of the typography with enigmatic imagery—sometimes bold, sometimes complex and abstract—underlying the atmosphere of architectural chaos and 'sprawl' which is the subject of the text.

The central generator of sprawl is the road. Over a quarter of our urbanized areas are covered with collections of empty arteries that represent no more and no less than potential: places always prepared for movement but in themselves no-place. The road always leads somewhere else, carving out a void and eviscerating everything around it. These days we try to contain **highways** with walls, embankments and regulations, turning them into surreally invisible slashes across our land. As soon as the road slows down, it re-enters the fabric of sprawl, eating out more space for itself with intersections and the I-, U- and L-shaped constructions that allow parking in front of stores and businesses. The road, in other words, seeps out to flatten everything around it to make room for the highest value in our society: not freedom or money, but access.

The road is thus the human-made equivalent of the river that shaped so much of the land we inhabit. It creates connections and barriers, cuts into the land to create breaks in the undulating terrain and generates activity on its banks. The road and the river are metaphors of movement and change, but also very real places where one can float, isolated from the city's grids and laws of nature, creating a freer culture: the world of riverboat gamblers, truckers and the Snowbirding tribes in their RVs.

Up above, skyways course around the globe. They are meta-roads that leave far behind the railroad and shipping lanes that once symbolized the freedom and vast expanses to which the road could only aspire. Their physical manifestation are airport runways. They are small segments of road that show us only the beginning and the end of a journey that is completely divorced from geography. They eat up huge amounts of space, making us realize how great the emptiness caused by the road causes really is. Even inside the adjacent airports, empty transience pervades and eats out buildings that are places for limbo; jet-lag carries the road's vacant nature into our own bodies.

We have long romanticized the road. It is the way to freedom, the act of moving beyond Eden into an untamed nature. The first humans were nomads, and in some ways we memorialized their peregrinations in the earliest roads (such as the Road of the Kings that traced the Fertile Crescent). The road is also the way to power, the path of conquest that, at crossings, at the bottom of mountains or at springs, turns into what the Romans called the *cardo*, engendering the very urban civilization of which we are so proud. Their needs framed an entire empire by proliferating crossroads that connected regions, blocks, houses and rooms, all making abstract geometry real.

In the United States, the road embodies our manifest destiny. It is the line of escape that accommodates ever more immigrants in search of a New Eden. That perfect place is always located somewhere that is not now and here. It is just beyond the place where the perspectival edges of the road out of town converge into infinity. It is a place of economic and physical escape, along which we can move into the future and a better life by gobbling up rocks and trees on the way and turning them into usable resources.

In our current culture the road is in many ways more important than the town. If the road once disappeared into a metropolitan maze as soon as it entered through the city gates, today it has become the city walls, in the form of beltways that encircle most of our metropolises. <u>In many cities, there is no longer a central urban core, only the "strip": the elongation of commercial and sometimes civic development along paths leading somewhere else.</u> "Houston is a city running away from itself, always further west," says architect and critic Lars Lerup of his own town. On a smaller scale, neighborhoods have disappeared into planned enclaves or gridded developments that expose the geometry and sheer presence of the road as the most significant aspect of the landscape. <u>We travel from entry to entry, or along a rhythm of intersections with a monotonous predictability. At a smaller scale still, roads turn into the driveways that dominate our houses' front façades.</u> We try to curb the creation of more roads, blaming not their presence but the vehicles that relentlessly use them for the corrosion of our landscape. <u>We think that by limiting the presence of cars, hiding them behind buildings and pooling them in parking garages at the periphery of pedestrian zones, we can defeat the road.</u> But the road is more essential and can never be marginalized. It just becomes the route of the light-rail system, the void of the shopping street, the outdoor mall that takes over the city. <u>To many, the road is therefore the great destroyer.</u> It replaces certainty and place with movement and space. Yet it is also the great fulfillment of modern culture's dream, our manifest destiny to keep moving as the new nomads who have freed themselves from the constraints of place and history. It is the ultimate modernist space, where movement, speed and change disintegrate all fixed forms into abstraction. <u>The road is a collage generator that mixes and matches the real world into a continually changing composition, leaving us to be the deracinated interpreters who make sense of it all.</u> The artery of sprawl might unleash us to the wonder of discovery, even as it seems to destroy all that we hold dear.

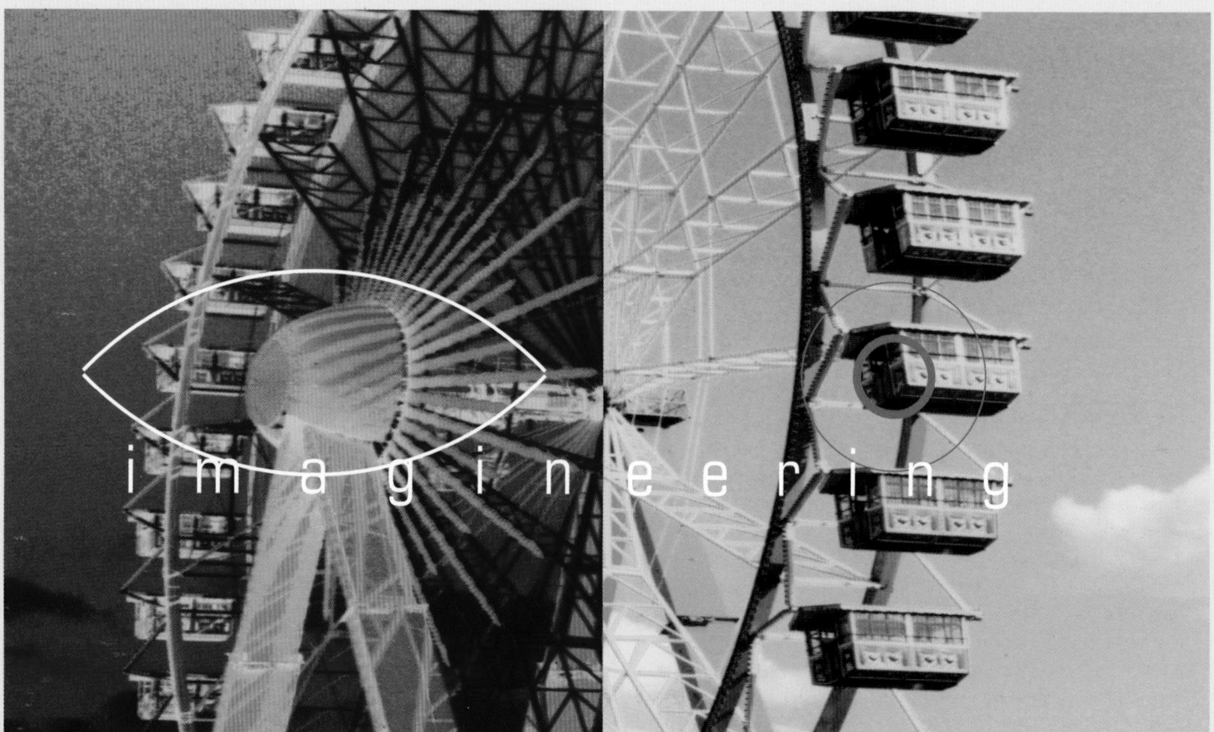

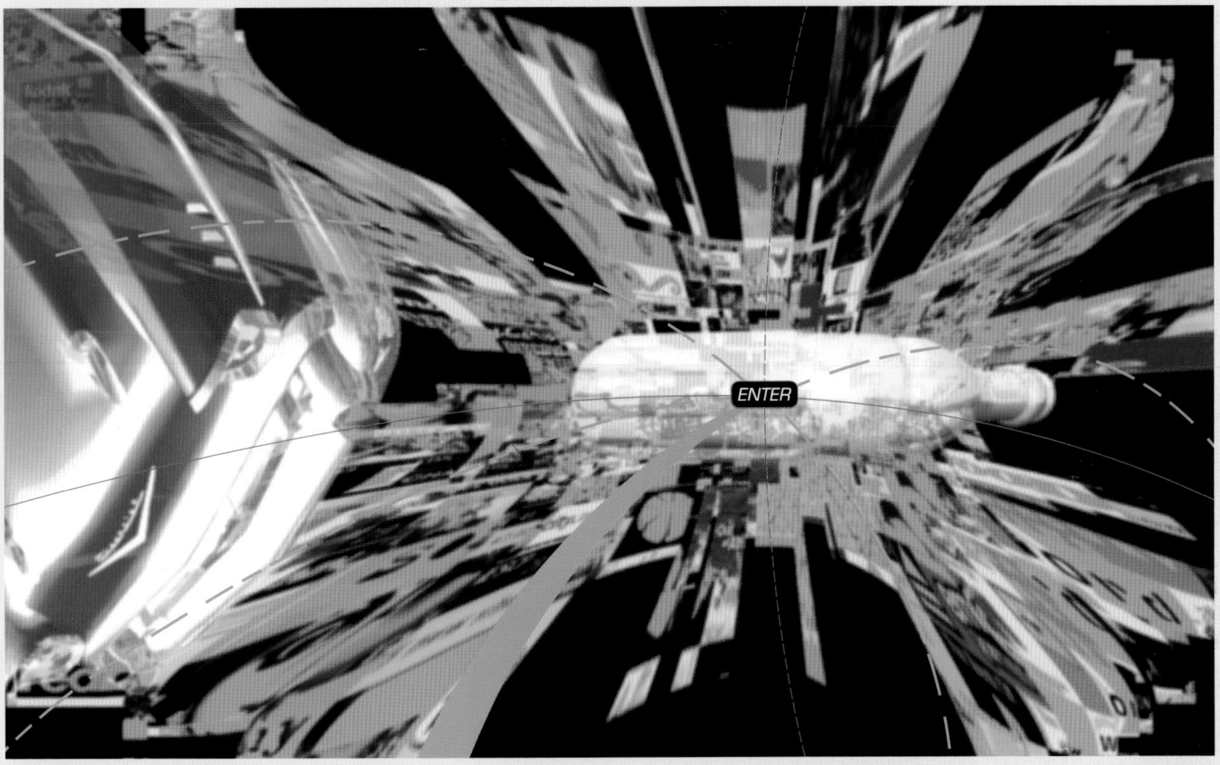

What makes sprawl work are its magnets of meaning: objects and spaces that provide focus in a disparate world. They can be as big as a football stadium or as small as a pair of blue jeans. The "attractors" catch our attention in the field through which we move every day. They also capture our investments of time and money. Their scale, form and composition are both molded by sprawl and give it definition. Attractors make some sort of sense in the realm of sprawl.

Attractors are what stabilize emergent, entropic systems. Since the advent of chaos theory in science, experts in disciplines as far apart as biology and astrophysics have become interested in how smooth, undifferentiated space begins to differentiate itself into a self-forming, or "epigenetic," landscape around one or more centers of attraction. Systems gyrate in wild loops among these attractors, until they fall into repetitive rhythms and finally freeze into place. It is in the tenuous state between chaos and order that the greatest energy exists in a system. In human terms, such a state might be called creativity, which can occur at times of crisis. Sprawl is also such a state. It used to be that cities coalesced around natural features: the places where it was easy to cross a river, a natural harbor, a spring or a high, defensible point. Humans civilized these features with structures of resistance (castles), the domiciles of those who controlled the feature (traders, warlords) and with expressions of wealth extracted from the surrounding countryside and transformed into symbolic artifacts (cathedrals, mosques).

Over time, cities became their own landscapes, thrusting up skyscraper ridges and forests of housing blocks. Cities assumed their own topographies; nowadays we navigate through them by landmarks, at major intersections or in the middle of large clearings. The institutions of culture and finance, the monuments to our past achievements or the moments where movement becomes visible – railroad stations or freeway overpasses – are today's equivalent to the river crossing, Mount Fuji or New York harbor.

As capital has been disseminated throughout our landscape, new landmarks have appeared. Some sprout up like little pieces of the city from which they have fled. Freeway intersections are marked by shopping malls, office compounds and dense housing arrangements. But a strange inversion takes place: the point of crossing does not lead to a landmark; instead it becomes the empty core of one. Similarly, large buildings no longer focus on a plaza or square, but on an often unpassable barrier of movement.

The largest structures one finds in such places are even stranger. Like castles, they have a closed appearance with only a few entrances; they are surrounded by an easily defensible space; their riches are inside, where they are laid out in a labyrinth whose ultimate focal points are places of entertainment and dining. These monoliths are, of course, shopping malls. Bland on the outside, they look out over seas of parking that let people get as close to the keep as possible without having to contend with weather or undesirable sorts. Inside, the visitor meanders through our culture's treasury on route to the food court or multiplex.

Even stranger are the largest attractors that rise out of the world of sprawl. There are three kinds: back-office blocks, places of transportation or trans-shipping, and stadia and convention centers. The first kind crop up like Edge City crystals, rising up around road intersections, sheered off into blocks of air-conditioned ice that sit in the middle of nowhere. Inside, thousands of phone operators or data clerks toil away in oceans of anonymity. These blocks could be anywhere. They are abstract fragments of a world made real.

The second type of these attractors are the airports, truck stops and regional warehouses that move people or material goods. Despite some attempts to make airports into places of beauty, the effects of structural exhilaration and vast scale are as fleeting as the planes they house. On the outside, airports are spiders' webs of terminals, parking garages, service spaces, ramps and gates that spread out through seas of tarmac. They have no recognizable form or relationship to human experience.

Stadia and convention centers, the third great attractors, do. These large blobs proudly display the mammoth structure it takes to accommodate tens of thousands. Each city has its own signature form, but they are all designed by a handful of firms whose primary concern is to maximize space usage in a manner that differentiates among pay scales and uses. These structures are about booth rentals and skyboxes, not about the communal experience of a place. After a period of quiet, they are again appearing in traditional cities, and although they might cloak themselves in a thin veneer of local color, they now bring sprawling scale into spectatorship, transfering the environment and the factory aesthetic to the heart of the urban experience.

The strangest aspect of such attractors is that they have taken a world focused on places of power and replaced them with realms of leisure. The promenades through shopping arcades and the gathering around conventionalized violence in the stadium stand in for the great palaces and factories that used be our daily destinations. Monuments of movement have replaced points of destination. Even the back-office space has become a holding pen for activities that take place not in this world but in cyberspace, tethered only to an external reality by phone cords and the rituals of selling. There is no there there, anywhere, only a suggestion of somewhere else around which we circulate.

These attractors attract investment, are the largest things on the landscape and are our navigational focal points. They are, however, profoundly empty. They are warehouses devoid of meaning: No sense or product is made there. We can find no certainty there, no place to gather and define ourselves as a culture. These attractors are mute enigmas that absorb energy and money and give nothing back. The empty football field symbolizes their moment of tr

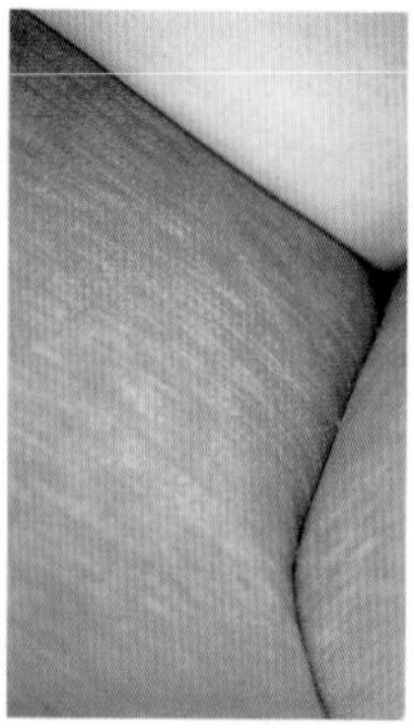

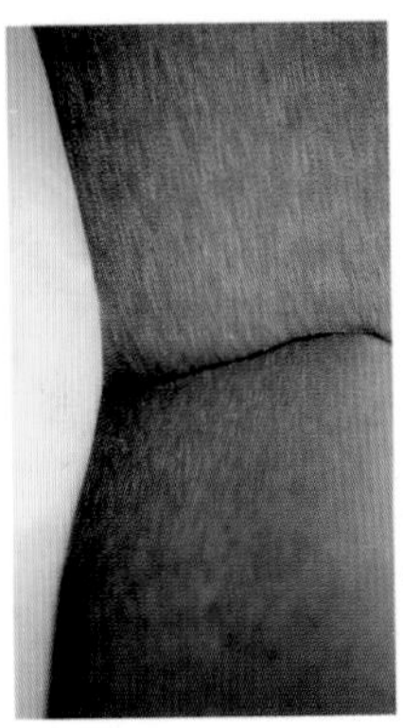

Simone Cobbold

10 Butts Road, Stanford-Le-Hope, Essex SS17 0JH

(01375) 404 287

"Harry" 1997

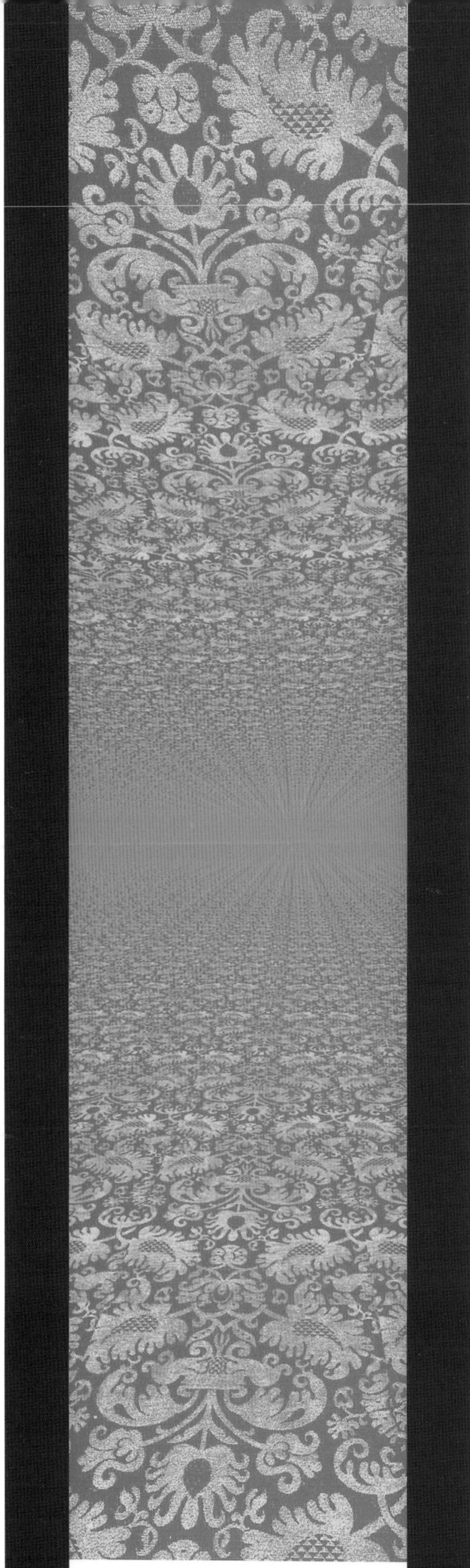

Tracey Vane

2 May Court, Little Thurrock, Essex RM17 6UB

(01375) 384 042

"Damask!" 1998

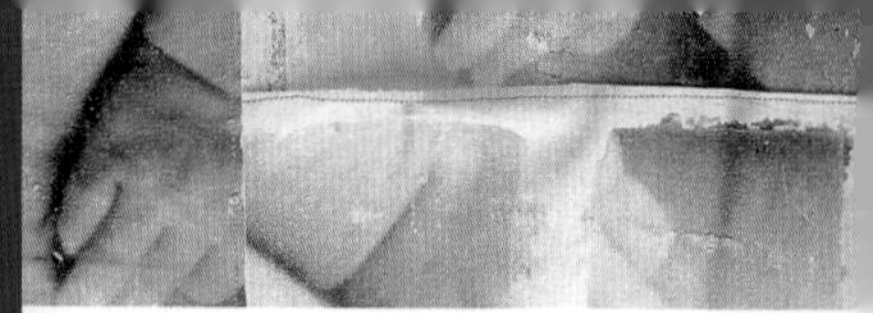

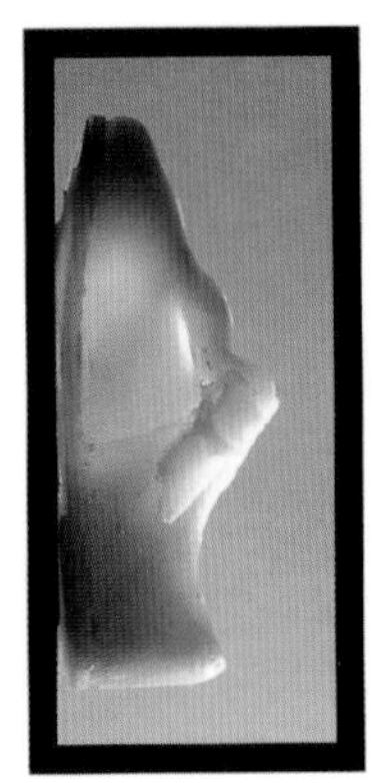

Beverley Holgate

Coggeshall Hall, Coggeshall Road, Kelvedon, Colchester, CO5 9PH

(01376) 570 394

"Untitled" 1998

Stretched

The layout of each double-page spread in this college catalog has been individually designed to present the featured artist's work in the best light. The use of the 'check book' format, with its subliminal allusion to the relationship between art and commerce, is a striking way to display the wide range of work on show.

Second from left: with the gutter as a horizon, the layout for Tracey Vane's *Damask!* utilizes the long format brilliantly to create the illusion of a limitless expanse.

Third from left: by leaving as much blank space as possible between the images, the designer has set up an ambiguous, questioning relationship between the two pages of Beverley Holgate's *Untitled* giving a delicate feel to this spread.

Designer
Gavin Ambrose

Art Director
Gavin Ambrose

Photographer
Arnold Borgerth

Design Company
Mono

Country of Origin
UK

Description of Artwork
48-page brochure for the 1998 graduation exhibition of the BA Textiles degree course at Goldsmiths' College, London.

Page Dimensions
210 x 85 mm
8¹/₄ x 3¹/₄ in

Format
Brochure

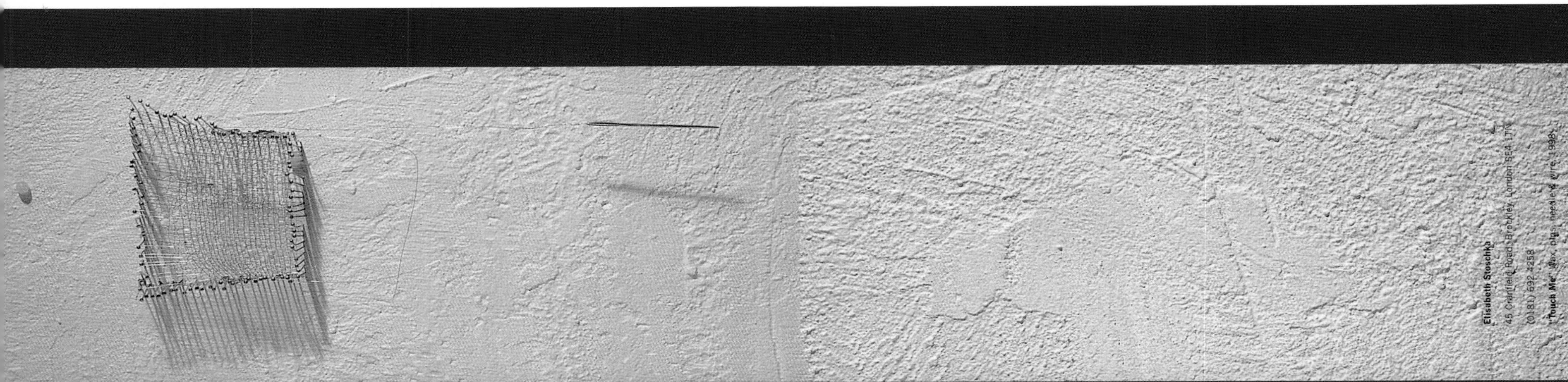

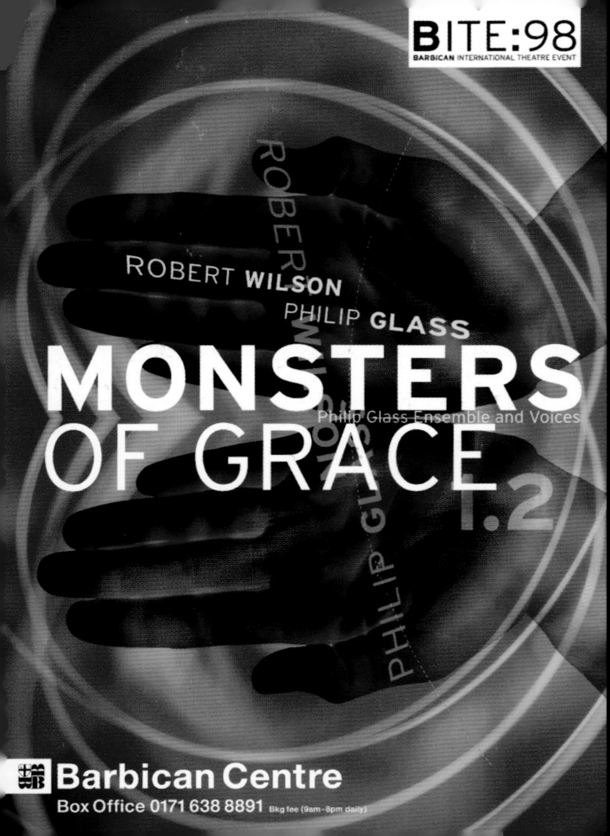
BITE:98
BARBICAN INTERNATIONAL THEATRE EVENT
ROBERT WILSON
PHILIP GLASS
MONSTERS OF GRACE 1.2
Philip Glass Ensemble and Voices
Barbican Centre
Box Office 0171 638 8891 Bkg fee (9am - 8pm daily)

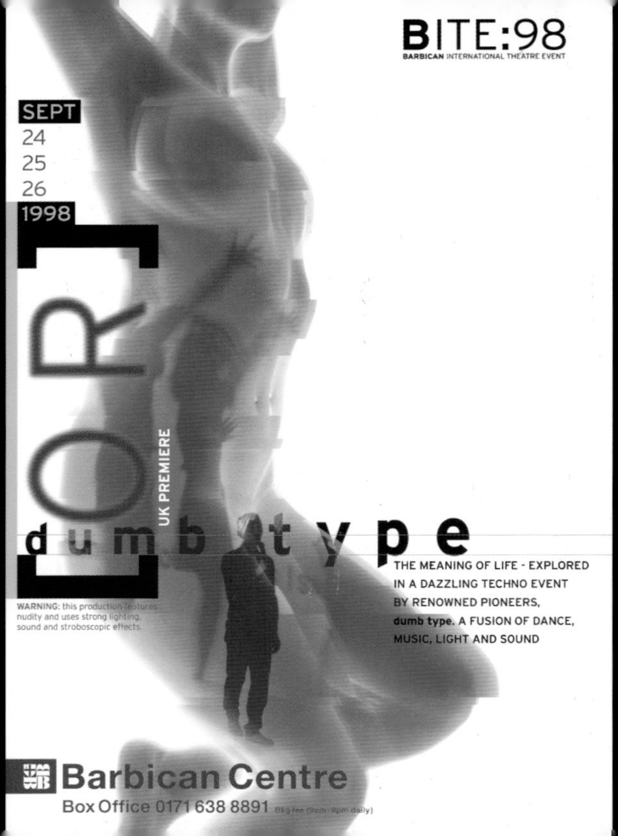
BITE:98
BARBICAN INTERNATIONAL THEATRE EVENT
SEPT
24
25
26
1998
[OR]
UK PREMIERE
dumb type
WARNING: this production features nudity and uses strong lighting, sound and stroboscopic effects.
THE MEANING OF LIFE - EXPLORED IN A DAZZLING TECHNO EVENT BY RENOWNED PIONEERS, dumb type. A FUSION OF DANCE, MUSIC, LIGHT AND SOUND
Barbican Centre
Box Office 0171 638 8891

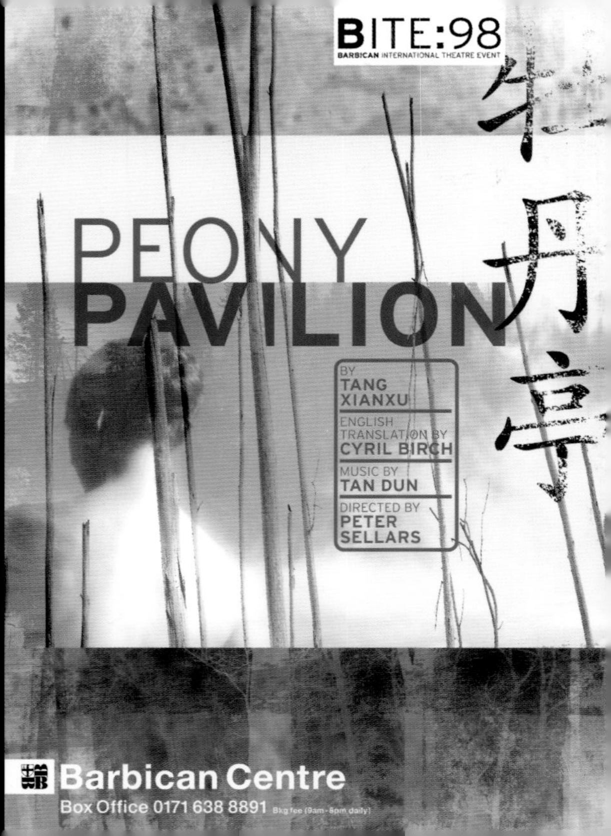
BITE:98
BARBICAN INTERNATIONAL THEATRE EVENT
牡丹亭
PEONY PAVILION
BY TANG XIANXU
ENGLISH TRANSLATION BY CYRIL BIRCH
MUSIC BY TAN DUN
DIRECTED BY PETER SELLARS
Barbican Centre
Box Office 0171 638 8891 Bkg fee (9am - 8pm daily)

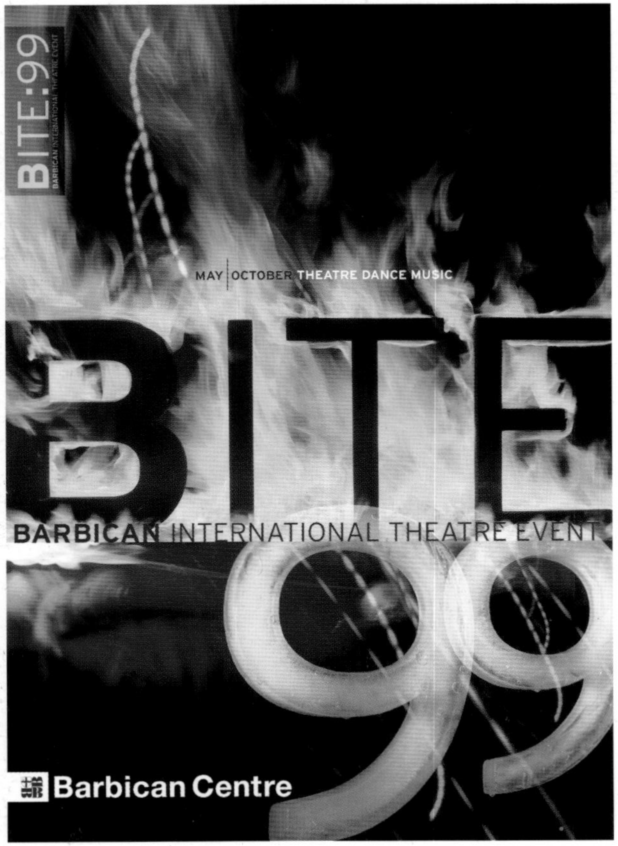

Barbican Centre BITE:98 and BITE:99

The diversity of the events within the 1998 season of this international theater festival is reflected in the promotional leaflets (*above*). One of the few constant elements on them is the festival logotype and its position. This is enough to indicate that all three events belong under the BITE umbrella. For the 1999 season, the logotype was further developed to become the central point of the dramatic and surreal imagery used on the cover of the festival brochure (*left*). This fiery treatment has been carried through to the inside (*below*) where it is contrasted, very effectively, with the clean, asymmetric typography.

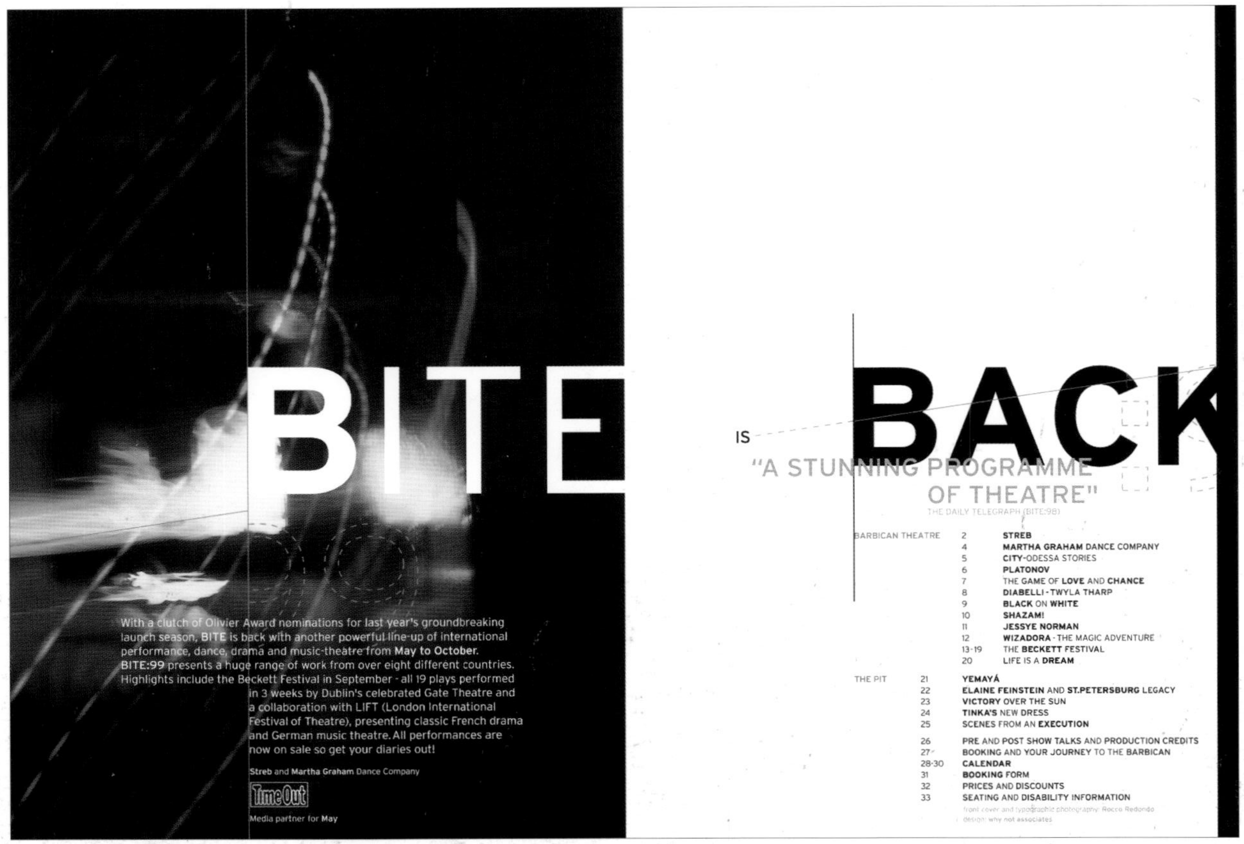

Designers
Why Not Associates

Design Company
Why Not Associates

Photographers
Photodisc (BITE:98 Monsters of Grace and Peony Pavilion), E. Valette and Rocco Redondo (BITE:98 OR), Rocco Redondo (BITE:99 Brochure)

Country of Origin
UK

Description of Artwork
Promotional leaflets (*opposite page*) and brochure (*above and right*) for the Barbican Centre BITE Festival, 1998 and 1999.

Dimensions
148 x 210 mm
$5^{7}/_{8}$ x $8^{1}/_{4}$ in

Formats
Leaflets and brochure

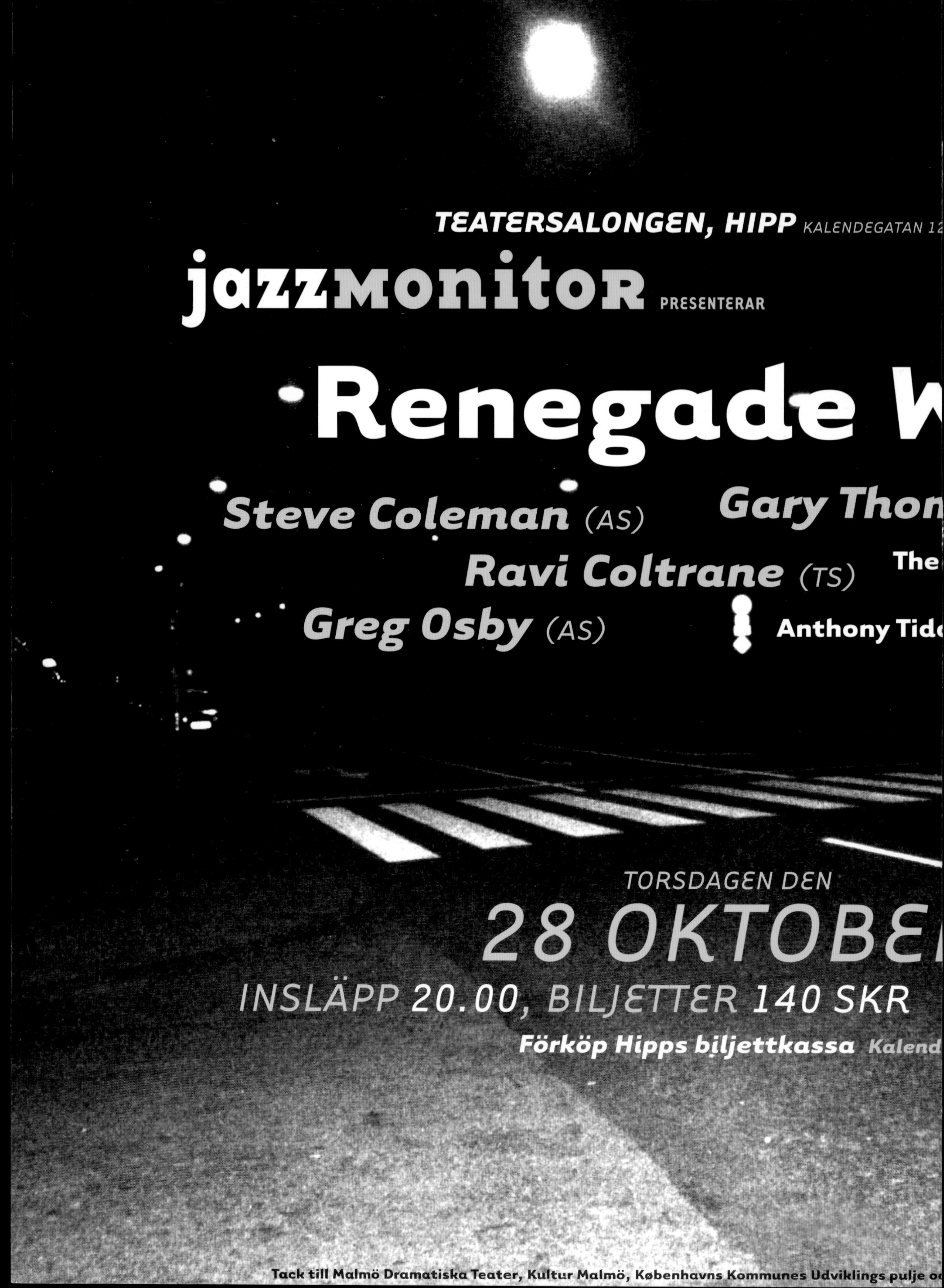
TEATERSALONGEN, HIPP KALENDEGATAN 1
jazzmonitor PRESENTERAR
Renegade
Steve Coleman (AS)
Gary Thon
Ravi Coltrane (TS)
The
Greg Osby (AS)
Anthony Tid
TORSDAGEN DEN
28 OKTOBE
INSLÄPP 20.00, BILJETTER 140 SKR
Förköp Hipps biljettkassa Kalend
Tack till Malmö Dramatiska Teater, Kultur Malmö, Københavns Kommunes Udviklings pulje o

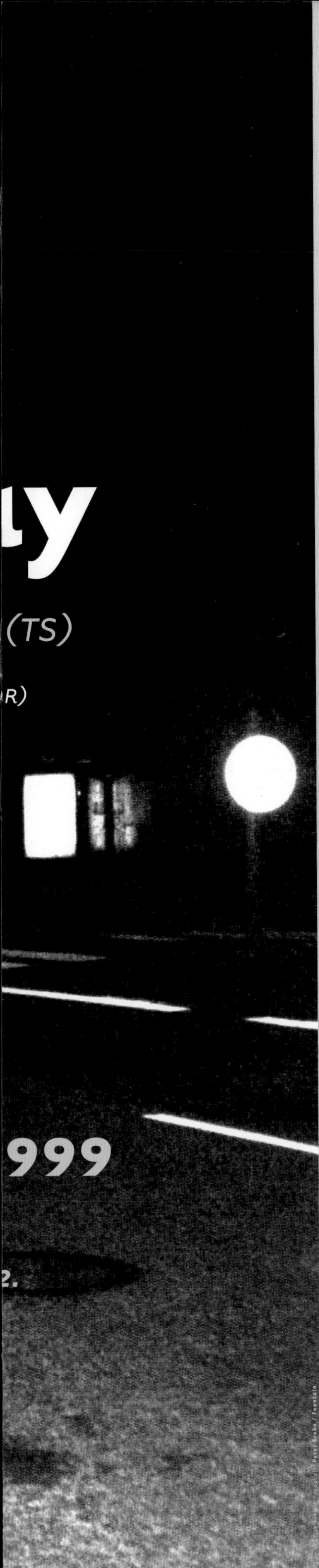

Graphic Identity for Jazzmonitor

Enigmatic photography, bold typography, the controlled use of flat color, and a careful choice of color palette all combine here to produce a very effective and strong visual identity. This solution is flexible and distinctive enough to work at different scales, ranging from a small business card to the size of a poster (*left*). The slightly abstract hard-edged style of imagery adds to the urban mystique of this club event.

Designer
Peter Bruhn

Art Director
Peter Bruhn

Photographer
Peter Bruhn

Design Company
Fountain-Bruhn

Country of Origin
Sweden

Description of Artwork
Poster (*left*) and flier (*following spread*), as part of a package including letterhead, logo, business card, and labels, for the ambient club event Jazzmonitor.

Dimensions
Poster: 500 x 500 mm
$19^{3}/_{4}$ x $19^{3}/_{4}$ in
Flier: 286 x 95 mm
$11^{1}/_{4}$ x $3^{3}/_{4}$ in

Formats
Poster and flier

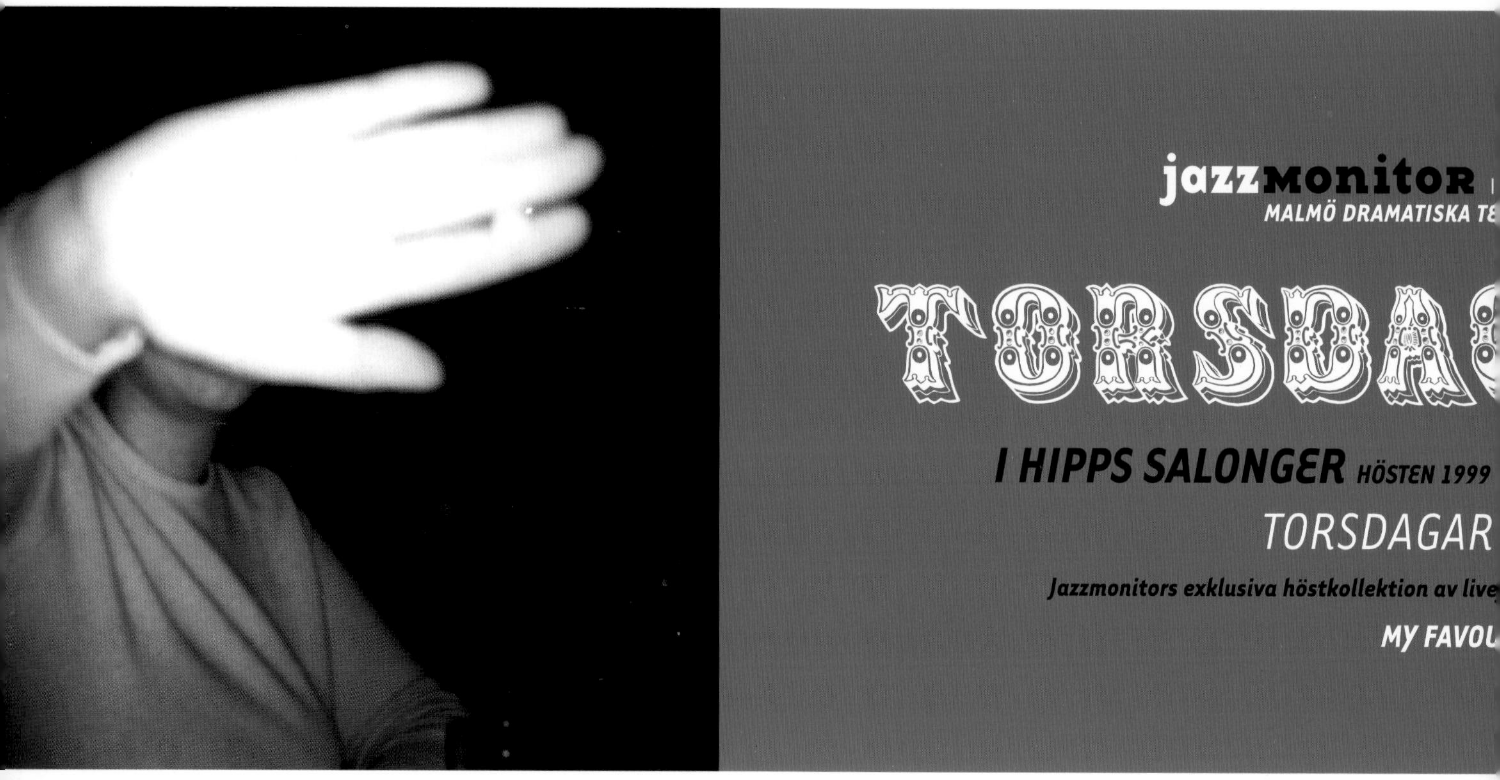

This dramatic image gives the impression that this club event is not for the uninitiated.

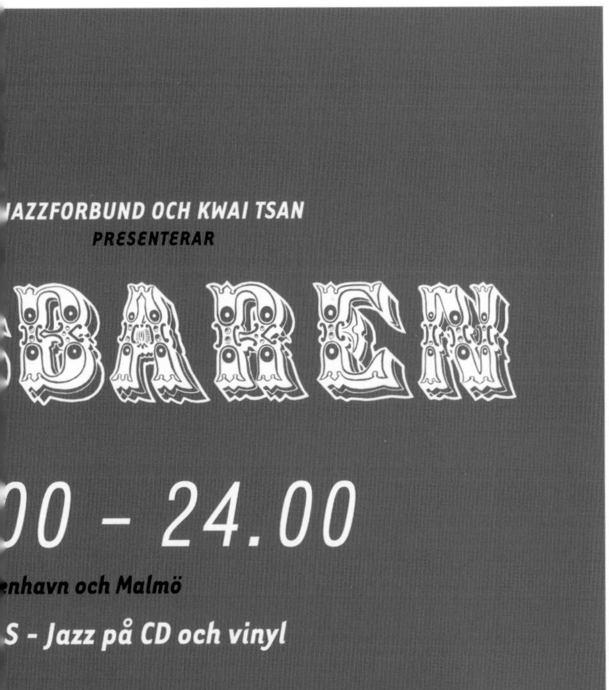

Left & below: the consistent use of carefully chosen colors and the repetition of the same photograph on both the poster (*see previous spread*) and flier (*below*) set up a series of visual connections that serve to strengthen the Jazzmonitor identity.

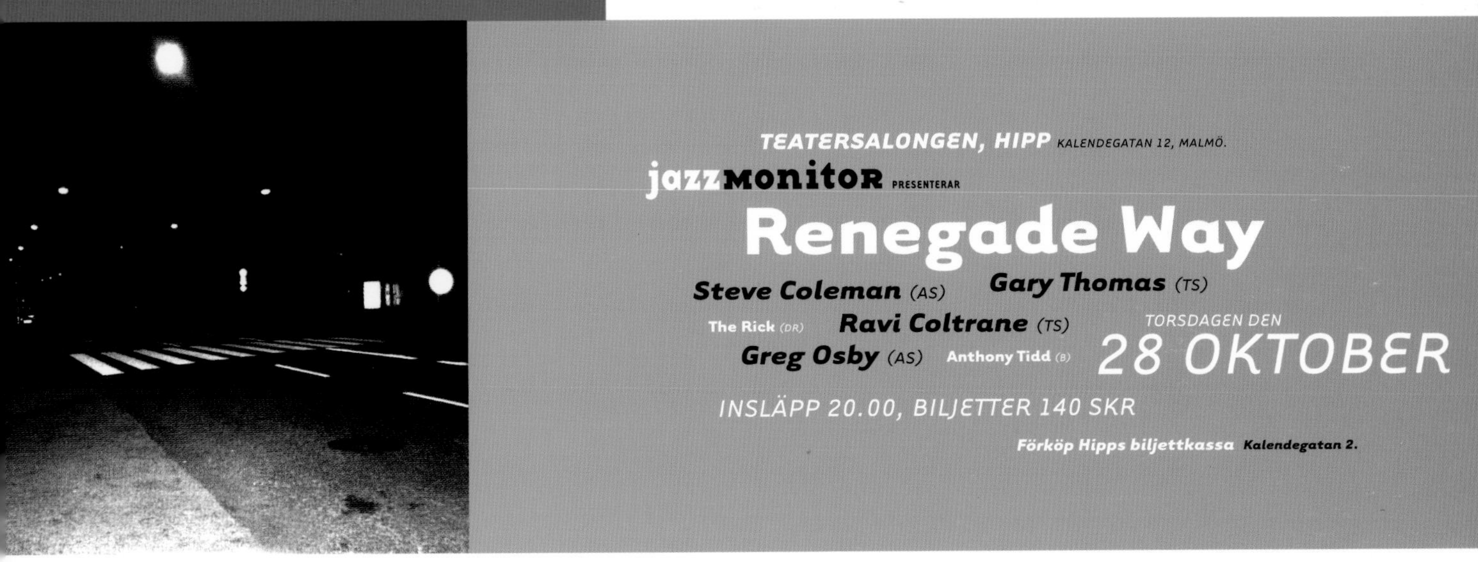

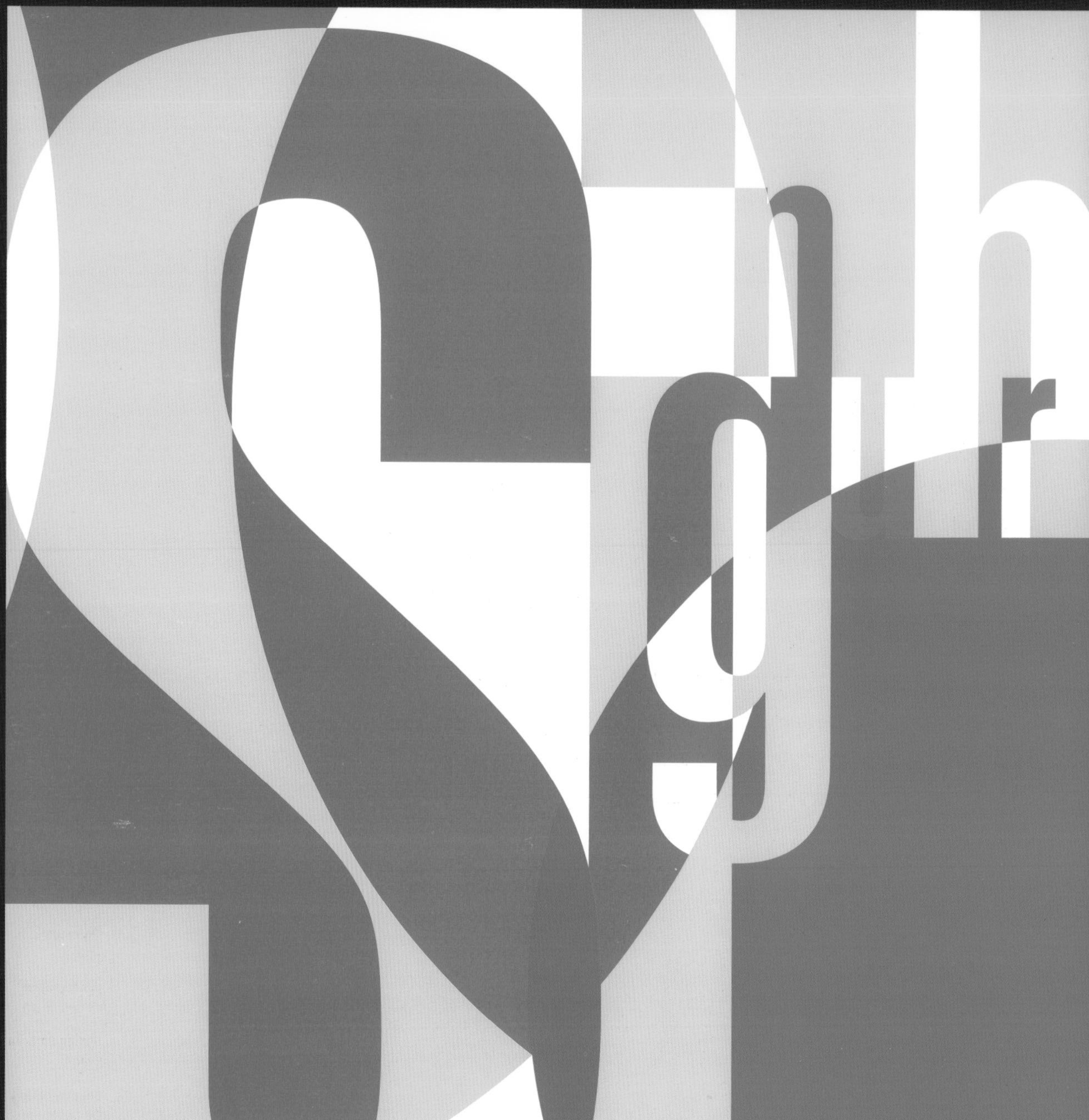

Singuhr Klangkunst

The abstract concept of a sound-art gallery is, by its very nature, hard to visualize. Faced with this challenge, the designers chose simplicity and a bold abstract approach to create an intriguing visual analogy for the events at the gallery. The cover typography (*opposite*) makes clever use of three colors to suggest overlapping circular ripples of spreading sound. Inside, this mental image extends to the display of photographic imagery (*below*). On the typographic pages (*shown on the following spread*), the blocks of text have been sculpted to suggest the nature of the aural experience, with curved margins and text blocks 'bouncing' off each other like echoes. The use of monochrome adds a starkness to each composition.

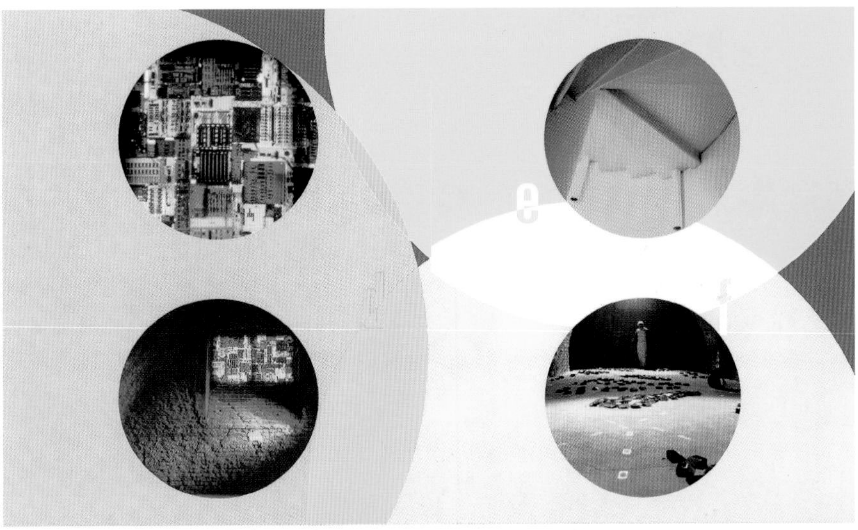

Designers
Cyan

Photographer
Roland Maerz

Design Company
Cyan

Country of Origin
Germany

Description of Artwork
120-page catalog documenting the activities of the sound-art gallery Singuhr from 1996–98.

Page Dimensions
200 x 233 mm
$7^7/_8$ x $9^1/_8$ in

Format
Catalog

ben von Jacobis Glocken urteilte dieser, daß die verwendete Legierung nicht für Spielglocken geeignet sei. Gleichzeitig bot er ein neues Carillon an. Im August 1716 starb Weiß und im März 1717 wurde der Niederländer Arnoldus Carsseboom als sein Nachfolger eingestellt, allerdings gab es kein vollständiges Instrument mehr. Zwei Jahre nach der enttäuschenden Einweihung des Carillons schrieb König Friedrich Wilhelm I. u. a. an den Kirchenrat der Parochialkirche: Vornach Ihr Euch also gehorsamst zu achten, ... und zwar bey Verlust der von Uns Euch hierunter zugewendeten Gnade zu sehen habt, daß binnen Jahresfrist ein anderes tüchtiges und vollkommenes Glocken-Spiel aus Holland angeschaffet und an der jetzigen Stelle wieder aufgesetzet werde.[6] Daraufhin wandte sich das Presbyterium im April 1717 an den Glockengießer de Grave mit der Bitte um einen neuen Glockenchor. Bereits am 4. Oktober 1717 wurde das neue Carillon, versehen mit einem hervorragenden Gutachten, auf dem Schiffsweg von Amsterdam nach Berlin geschickt. Carillonneur Carsseboom übernahm die sofortige Installation und schon im November 1717 erklang das zweite Berliner Carillon (Abb. 6). Es bestand aus den 35 Glocken von de Grave mit einem Gesamtgewicht von 7,3 Tonnen. Die Herkunft der zwei kleinsten Glocken (36. und 37.) ist nicht nachweisbar. Wahrscheinlich sind sie erst 1797 oder 1838 bei den Generalüberholungen hinzugefügt worden. Auch der Stockspieltisch besaß nach einem 1764 erschienenen Bericht von Johann Samuel Halle nur 35 Tastenstöcke (22 sogenannte weiße und 13 sogenannte schwarze). Erst ein weiterer Bericht aus dem Jahre 1846 spricht von 37 Glocken. Die Aufhängung der Glocken in der Glockenkammer war symmetrisch (Abb. 7), die fünf größten Glocken hingen in der Mitte und um diese ordneten sich die restlichen Glocken in Reihen im West-, Nord- und Südfenster des Turms. Der Stockspieltisch war in einer hölzernen Spielkabine auf dem Boden des Glockengeschosses untergebracht und über ein mechanisches System mit den Glockenklöppeln verbunden. Er wurde per Hand gespielt. Eine automatische Vorrichtung verkoppelte das Carillon über eine Eisenwalze mit der Turmuhr (Abb. 2). Bei dem Uhrglockenspiel erfolgte der Glockenanschlag über zusätzlich montierte Glockenhämmer auf den Glockenaußenseiten, die von der Automatik in Gang gesetzt wurden. Die Walze der Automatik besaß für den Melodienwechsel auswechselbare Metallstifte, deren Länge und Anordnung Tonhöhe und Anschlagzeitpunkt bestimmten. Alle siebeneinhalb Minuten erklang ein Zeitsignal, viertelstündlich ein kurzer und halbstündlich ein längerer Choral, immer mit Vor- und Nachspiel. Die Melodien, z.B. kleine Fugen, verzierte Psalmenmelodien und Choräle, wurden 14-15 mal im Jahr gewechselt: zu Advent, Weihnachten, Neujahr, zur Passionszeit, zu Ostern, Himmelfahrt, Pfingsten, zum Reformationsfest und zu den Monatsanfängen von Februar, Juli, August, September und Oktober. Auf dem Carillon der Parochialkirche gab es von Beginn an eine rege Konzerttätigkeit. Siebzehn Carillonneure waren hier tätig. Sie hatten die Aufgabe, die Walze des Glockenspiels mit den entsprechenden Melodien zu bestiften und Carillon-Konzerte zu spielen. Gespielt wurde auf dem Carillon an Festtagen, bei Hochzeiten und Begräbnissen. Zu den Geburtstagen des Herrscherhauses erklang noch bis 1918 stets ein Sonderkonzert zur Mittagszeit. Ebenso boten Kriegssiege und hohe Staatsbesuche Anlaß zu Sonderkonzerten.

6 ibid. S.69

Regelmäßige Konzerte erklangen zwischen 1717 und 1782 an drei Tagen in der Woche (Sonntag, Mittwoch und Freitag), im Sommer von 5-6 Uhr nachmittags, ansonsten von 11-12 Uhr morgens. Von 1782-1839 wurde das Carillon zweimal wöchentlich (Sonntag, Mittwoch) ca. eine Stunde gespielt. Zwischen 1839 und 1848 war dem Carillonneur Ludwig Thiele nur ein Konzert wöchentlich erlaubt, Sonntags von 12-13 Uhr. Sein Nachfolger durfte nur noch halbstündige Konzerte einmal wöchentlich geben. Diese Entwicklung mit immer deutlicheren Einschnitten in die Konzerttätigkeit ist eng verbunden mit dem im 19. Jahrhundert wachsenden Bedeutungsverlust der Carillonkunst in Europa. 1891/92 wurden Turm und Carillon generalüberholt, und der Posten des Carillonneurs blieb unbesetzt. 1893 übernahm Richard Thiele das Amt und übergab es 1903 seinem Sohn Eugen Thiele. Beide spielten zu den Gottesdiensten und gaben wöchentlich ein halbstündiges Sonntagskonzert. Das Repertoire der Konzerte umfaßte geistliche und weltliche Musik, größtenteils Bearbeitungen der jeweiligen Carillonneure für das Instrument. Hauptsächlich waren dies Choräle, geistliche Lieder, Arien und Volkslieder. Seit 1921 gab es unter Hans Siepert wieder wöchentlich 2 Konzerte, das traditionelle Sonntagskonzert nach dem Gottesdienst und die sogenannten Vorträge auf dem Glockenspiele am Mittwoch. Die Mittwochsprogramme enthielten sechs bis vierzehn Stücke, die sich nach den wiederkehrenden Ereignissen des Jahres und des Kirchenkalenders richteten. Siepert füllte drei Hefte mit über vierhundert kurzen, auf einem Notensystem geschriebenen Bearbeitungen. Den Hauptteil der ‹Vortragsstücke› bildeten Kirchenchoräle: Wie schön leuchtet der Morgenstern, Christ ist erstanden, Komm heiliger Geist und Volkslieder: Blaue Luft – Blumenduft, Es war ein König in Thule, Mein Vater war ein Wandersmann. Zum Repertoire gehörten ebenfalls einige Märsche: Der Torgauer, Der Hohenfriedberger und Bearbeitungen klassischer Werke: Largo aus der Oper Xerxes von Händel, Andante aus der Klaviersonate op. 14 Nr. 2 von Beethoven, Pilgerchor aus der Oper Tannhäuser von Wagner, das Lied O Täler weit, o Höhen von Mendelssohn. Wie seine Vorgänger kannte Siepert allerdings weder Originalwerke für Carillon, noch verfaßte er selbst welche.[7] Ab 1922 wurden regelmäßig Turmmusiken mit dem Carillon und Bläsern gegeben. Siepert warb regelmäßig mit ca. 200 gedruckten Programmzetteln für seine Konzerte,[8] zu denen teilweise tausende Besucher die Straßen um die Kirche belagerten (Abb. 1). Allerdings findet sich im Archiv der Parochialkirche auch eine Reihe von Beschwerdebriefen, z. B. schreibt Herr

7 ibid. S.85 8 vgl. Heinz Siepert Das Glockenspiel der Evangelischen Parochialkirche zu Berlin Typoskript, 1940 dem Archiv der Parochialkirche gestiftet S.69

Klangkunst im Berliner Kulturbetrieb – die singuhr – hœrgalerie in parochial

Susanne Binas

... ich bin ein Propagandist des Anti-Institutionellen, des nicht-gattungsmäßigen Begrenzens oder Definierens, ... Klangkunst ist für mich ein mehr oder weniger brauchbarer beschreibender Sammelbegriff für ein Bündel von künstlerischen Erscheinungs- und Arbeitsformen. ... Typisch dabei ist, daß die beteiligten Künstler aus den allerunterschiedlichsten Ecken kommen. Beteiligte Künstler sind nicht nur Musiker, da sind bildende Künstler, Filmemacher, Videokünstler, Mediakünstler, wer auch immer. Es sind Künstler, die sich in der Form grenzüberschreitend oder intermedial äußern und dabei Klang konstitutiv mitbenutzen. Klangkunst sollte nicht reduziert sein auf Klanginstallationen, Klang-Environments, Klang-Skulptur oder womöglich Klangkunst am Bau, sondern sollte sehr wohl temporäre, eventhafte, performancehafte Formen mit einbeziehen, d.h. netzwerkartig gedachte Formen medienkünstlerischer Art etc. ...

Matthias Osterwold*

I. Es fällt außerordentlich schwer, Klangkunst auf einen bestimmten musikalischen Gattungszusammenhang zu projizieren. Keiner der Gesichtspunkte, die einen ‹klassischen› Gattungszusammenhang konstituieren, macht im Angesicht der vielgestaltigen künstlerischen Konzepte und Formen, die sich hinter dem Begriff Klangkunst verbergen, eigentlich Sinn: Besetzung, Text, Funktion, Aufführungsort etc.. Hier scheinen sämtliche Ordnungssysteme der europäischen Tradition artifizieller Musik außer Kraft gesetzt. Was Klangkunst ist, ... wissen immer nur jene, die sie ausschließen, sei dies bei Ausstellungen oder aber der Verteilung von Tantiemen. Ausgrenzungen sind möglich, aber keine Eingrenzungen.[1] Das allerdings dürfte auf sehr viele musikalischen Formen der ‹Neuzeit› zutreffen. Der Kanon künstlerischer Arbeitsweisen und Produktion hat im 20. Jahrhundert einen atemberaubenden Prozeß der Öffnung in jeder Hinsicht (Material, Orte der Präsentation, Verhältnis von Künstlern und Publikum, Verflüchtigung des Kunstgegenstandes) durchlaufen. Was Kunst sei und was nicht, entzieht sich dabei zunehmend der Definitionsmacht akademischer Kunst- und Musikwissenschaften, die in ihrem latenten Traditionsbewußtsein einst normierende Funktion hatten und kulturelle und künstlerische Formen hierarchisch geordnet wissen wollten. Warum aber finden Begriffe – wie der der Klangkunst – so vehement Eingang in den Sprachgebrauch entsprechender Diskurse? Sie besetzen künstlerisches Terrain, fungieren bisweilen gar als ‹Kampfbegriffe› gegen vermeintlich überkommene Formen oder werden erstmals als Schwerpunkte in die Vergaberichtlinien ‹öffentlicher Kunstförderung[2] aufgenommen. Warum beflügeln sie akademisches Interesse und Forschungen, geben Festivals, Symposien, Fachzeitschriften oder Radiosendungen Anlaß zur Präsentation und Diskussion? Dieses Bündel von Fragen ist sicherlich kaum zufriedenstellend zu beantworten. Zu viele Dimensionen des aktuellen Kunstprozesses wären angesprochen. Interessant scheint es aber allemal, weil eine Fragerichtung avisiert ist, die latent den vielfältigen Diskussionen um ‹Klangkunst› zwar inhärent ist, aber nie eigentlich ausgesprochen wird: Klangkunst im Kunst- bzw. Kulturbetrieb. Die weiter oben genannten Tendenzen zeugen in der Konsequenz vom Wunsch einer wie auch immer gestalteten Institutionalisierung dessen, was notdürftig mit dem Begriff Klangkunst umrissen ist; die Gründung und Unterhaltung spezieller Einrichtungen bzw. Fonds, Etats, Sendestrukturen, Lehrstühle etc. – die gesellschaftliche Anerkennung eines vagen, sich eigentlich permanent verändernden künstlerischen Feldes, das im Kanon der etablierten Zusammenhänge beargwöhnt und gleichsam von magnetischer Anziehungskraft ist, weil eigentlich nicht faßbar, aber als Indiz des dynamisch sich verändernden Kunstprozesses von den Platzhaltern des traditionellen Kulturbetriebes keinesfalls zu vernachlässigen.

1 Helga de la Motte-Haber Klangkunst. Alternative oder Ergänzung zur traditionellen Präsentationsform von Kunst In: Alternativen Veröffentlichungen des Institutes für Neue Musik und Musikerziehung Darmstadt Bd. 38 hrsg. v. Johannes Fritsch (Schott) 1998 S.55 2 Seit 1997 hat die Berliner Senatsverwaltung für Wissenschaft, Forschung und Kultur den Begriff Klangkunst als Schwerpunkt in den Katalog ihrer Förderrichtlinien im Bereich Ernste Musik für die sogenannte Freie Musikszene aufgenommen.

* Podiumsdiskussion Klangkunst institutionalisieren? Symposium Klang-Kunst-Räume am 10.10.1998 Alle weiteren Statements im Text entstammen ebenfalls dieser Diskussion.

Wohin zieht es Klangkünstler auf der Suche nach Räumen zur Produktion und Präsentation ihrer Arbeiten?

Jutta Ravenna

Symposium Klang-Kunst-Räume 10.10.1998

Man müßte eine Musique d'ameublement produzieren, genauer gesagt, eine Musik, die an den Geräuschen
der Umgebung teilhat und auf diese Rücksicht nimmt. Ich stelle sie mir folgendermaßen vor:
melodiös, die Geräusche der Gabeln
und Messer abschwächend,
sie jedoch nicht dominierend.
Erik Satie, 1920

Warum sollte man Rücksicht auf die Geräusche von Messern und Gabeln nehmen?
Satie behauptet das.
Und er hat Recht.
Andernfalls würde die Musik Mauern errichten müssen, um sich selbst zu verteidigen.
Mauern, die beständig instandgesetzt werden müßten, und über die man sich, selbst um ein Glas Wasser trinken zu können,
die Katastrophe herausfordernd, hinwegsetzen müßte.
Es ist offensichtlich eine Frage,
ob intendierte Handlungen
von jemandem in Relation zu den nichtintendierten der Umgebung gebracht werden.
John Cage, 1961

Kontextbezogenheit In einigen meiner Arbeiten geht es darum, Musik in einen bestimmten Kontext zu stellen. In der Suche nach Räumen manifestiert sich die Suche nach einem Kontext, d.h. einem realen Bezugssystem, in welches die Arbeit gestellt werden kann. Hierbei unterscheide ich zwischen Räumen mit einem intakten funktionalen Innenleben und funktionsfreien Orten. Mit musikalisch nicht besetzten, funktionsfreien Räumen wie z.B. dem natürlichen Ambiente oder einer zum Großstadtidyll gewordenen Stadtbrache, Baulücken, verwilderten Bahngeländen, stillgelegten Schwimmhallen, leerstehenden Fabrikgebäuden, Bau- und Kriegsruinen bieten sich Spielräume für die ungestörte ästhetische Praxis. Manchmal ist es eine bestimmte akustische Geräuschsphäre, manchmal hingegen die Ruhe, die mich an einem Ort anzieht. Auch ein in regelmäßigen Abständen über einen Ort hereinbrechender Lärm hat mich schon fasziniert. Auf der optischen Ebene sind es andere Merkmale: Die infolge von Witterungseinflüssen entstandene Patina auf der Fassade, das Bröckeln des Gesteins von der architektonischen Form und das mit voranschreitender Zeit zunehmende Verwildern und Überwuchern durch zufällig herbeigeflogene Pflanzensamen, die sich zu Gräsern, Ranken und Büschen an funktionslos gewordenen Orten entwickeln, lösen Erinnerungen aus und wirken zunächst als Inspiration. Später werden sie als räumlicher und akustischer Kontext zum wichtigen Bestandteil bei der Inszenierung einer künstlerischen Idee. (Das ist natürlich nicht zwangsläufig der Fall: Es gibt auch Klangskulpturen, die souverän sind. Diese funktionieren fast überall, egal in welchem Kontext sie präsentiert werden.) Andererseits ermöglichen Klangskulpturen an intakten und belebten Orten wie Brücken, Parks, öffentlichen Plätzen, Bahnhofshallen, in S-Bahnen, Shopping Malls, Universitätsgeländen, Krankenhäusern und Schulen die spannende Integration in Alltagsprozesse. Der alltägliche Lärm der Geräusche vor Ort bildet den akustischen Kontext, zu dem kritisch Stellung bezogen werden kann, in den es einzudringen oder den es zu überlagern gilt. Zunächst erfordert dies eine akustische Bestandsaufnahme, um die Voraussetzung dafür zu schaffen, – im Sinne John Cages – ‹intendierte Handlungen in Relation zu den nichtintendierten der Umgebung zu bringen›. Deswegen ist auch der soziale Kontext als außermusikalischer Faktor – wie zum Beispiel die Arbeits-, Bildungs- oder Erholungszusammenhänge in Büros, an Universitäten oder in Parks – für mich von immenser Bedeutung. Dieser wird zum zusätzlichen Steuerelement für die musikalischen Parameter meiner Musik. Bestimmte soziale Vorgänge erfordern beispielsweise leise Klänge, andere das Gegenteil. Manche Situationen erfordern Klangprozesse mit vielen Pausen, um das akustische Umfeld durchscheinen zu lassen, andere andauernde Schallfelder. Darauf werde ich später noch genauer eingehen.

Mit dem Einbrechen von Klangkunst in Alltagszusammenhänge verbindet sich ganz konkret die Auseinandersetzung mit der Sozialstruktur des Ortes: Hausmeister, Sicherheitsangestellte für den zivilen Wachschutz, BibliothekarInnen, Bootsverleiher, LehrerInnen, Geistliche und Ordnungsbeamte werden zum Dialogpartner oder zu Gegnern des eigenen Engagements. Meine Sensibilität als Klangkünstlerin für die ortsgegebenen Sozial- und Funktionsstrukturen bildet die Voraussetzung dafür, in solchen ungewohnten Zusammenhängen überhaupt arbeiten zu können. Die entscheidende Frage

ist jedoch, ob es mir darum geht, soziale Abläufe zu berücksichtigen, mit einzubinden, abzubilden, zu unterlaufen oder zu stören. Eine gesellschaftliche Einbindung von Kunst erfolgt oft um den Preis ihrer Störqualität. Oft ist die künstlerische Idee im öffentlichen Raum nur in abgeschwächter Form realisierbar. Die Rolle der Klangkunst sehe ich trotzdem als kritischen Kommentar künstlerischer Reflexion innerhalb eines sozialen, architektonischen und akustischen Kontextes und nicht in der Funktion, die Kunst im öffentlichen Raum oft erhält: nämlich der eines gefälligen, geistreichen Aperçus. Ich fühle mich eben nicht einer Ästhetik des ‹schönen Scheins› verpflichtet. Die Geräusche sowie das optische Erscheinungsbild meiner Klangskulpturen sollten keinesfalls das akustische Kompensat mißglückter Stadtarchitektur und konfliktreicher Soziostrukturen bilden, sondern vielmehr die Realität eines spezifischen Ortes, so wie er ist, mit neuen künstlerischen Mitteln sinnlich erfahrbar machen.

Status Quo Die Mauern zwischen einer für den abgeschirmten Konzertsaal konzipierten Musik und der Geräuschsphäre des Alltags existieren jedoch im allgemeinen auch heute noch. Abgesehen von der nichtssagenden Dauerberieselung durch Muzak in Shopping Malls, Restaurants, Wartehallen und Aufzügen, treffen Klänge und Geräusche des äußeren akustischen Umfelds sowie des akustischen Designs der Gebrauchsgegenstände meist ganz unvermittelt auf unser Ohr. Will man eine Hörsituation schaffen, welche die Geräusche der Umgebung miteinbezieht, so ist es heute technisch ohne weiteres möglich, ein spezifisches akustisches Material zu generieren, das als Klanginstallation in den öffentlichen Raum implantiert wird. Im urbanen Rauschen verbirgt sich hierfür eine Vielzahl von Anknüpfungsmöglichkeiten. Dies erzeugt eine auditive Wahrnehmungsdichte aus Hintergrundgeräuschen wie Straßenlärm, Baulärm, Stimmengewirr und unzähligen anderen Quellen, die nur mit viel Geduld überhaupt differenzierbar sind. In meinen Klanginstallationen versuche ich das hörbar zu machen, was das selektive Hören gewöhnlich ausblendet. Die Geräusche der Umgebung werden hierbei ebenso wichtig wie die Eigengeräusche meiner Klangskulpturen. Der Begriff ‹Feld› bezieht sich in meiner Arbeit auf ebendiesen akustischen Kontext. Fernab von den zu verteidigenden Mauern, von denen bei Cage die Rede ist, möchte ich eine Musik schaffen, welche ihr Umfeld nicht dominiert, sondern miteinbezieht. Intentionslos, bar jeder ästhetischen Gelüste, fließt ein Strom zufälliger Passanten an meiner Klanginstallation vorbei: ein Zufallspublikum aus unterschiedlichsten Bevölkerungsschichten und Altersgruppen. Jenseits von Erklärungen hat hier die Unmittelbarkeit das Wort.

Temporär – Stationär oder: Ein Hördenkmal? Ich spreche hier besonders von Klanginstallationen für den Außenraum. Die Inbesitznahme des öffentlichen Raumes durch die Klangkunst kann sowohl temporär als auch stationär – als permanente Installation – erfolgen. Oftmals ist Klangkunst lediglich als temporäres, akustisches Ereignis vorhanden. Die akustische Intervention mit Hilfe einer temporären Installation von Geräuschen im öffentlichen Raum folgt der kritischen Selbsterkenntnis einer Kunst, die den Ewigkeitsmythos hinter sich gelassen hat. In der Vorläufigkeit und Vergänglichkeit erzeugt sie lediglich das Übergangsstadium eines Ortes von einem Zustand in den nächsten. Ihr Erscheinen erfolgt unter dem Vorbehalt, bald wieder zu verschwinden. Zugrundegelegt ist hier ein ganz einfaches Wahrnehmungsgesetz: sich bewegen zu müssen, um wahrgenommen zu werden. Ihre historischen Wurzeln hat die temporäre Klanginstallation oder Klang-Inter-Vention mit ihrem Impetus des Sich-dazwischen-Schaltens oder Sich-Einmischens in gesellschaftliche Zusammenhänge in den Formen der Events, Happenings und Aktionen der Sechziger Jahre. Der Handlungscharakter wandte sich damals – abgesehen von der Auflösung des traditionellen Werkbegriffs – gegen das Vermarkten von Kunstwerken als Ware auf dem Kunstmarkt. Die dauerhafte Inbesitznahme eines Ortes durch eine variabel programmierte Klangskulptur würde anfangs vielleicht zur Irritation der alten und zum Einschleifen neuer Hörgewohnheiten führen. Umbrandet von einer permanent sich wandelnden realen Umgebung, könnte sie jedoch bald selbst Gewohnheit werden. Hier stellt sich mir die Frage: Wie lange dauert es, bis eine permanent installierte Klangskulptur – auch wenn sie so programmiert ist, daß sie immer wieder anders klingt – im öffentlichen Raum überhört wird? Im Gegensatz zum ‹Eingesperrtsein› im Konzertsaal kann der Hörer in der Wildnis der Großstadt, befreit von Zwängen des Anstands, jederzeit der Musik entfliehen: Die Ströme von Passanten und Verkehr, ihre Verdichtungen, Stauungen und Auflösungen, ihre Tempi und Zeitnester sind für die Wahrnehmungssituation der Klanginstallation von immenser Bedeutung. Wird sie, eingebettet in Alltagszusammenhänge, zur ‹musique d'ameublement› – zum klingenden Großstadtmobiliar?

Hörsituation: einige Beispiele aus meiner künstlerischen Arbeit Die Wahrnehmungssituation vor Ort ist von unterschiedlichen Faktoren geprägt: ein bestimmtes Licht, ein besonderer Duft oder Geruch, Temperatur und Luftfeuchtigkeit, mein eigenes Befinden, die Geräusche. Bevor ich mich auf die Suche nach einem bestimmten Klangmaterial für den entsprechenden Raum mache, inspiziere ich den Ort und die Menschen. Der architektonische, soziale und akustische Kontext, in den meine Klangskulptur eingebettet werden soll, bildet das wesentliche Ausgangsmaterial für meine Klänge und für die Art und Weise, wie sie gehört werden können. Bedingt durch architektonische und funktionelle Setzungen herrscht eine Situation des Verweilens,

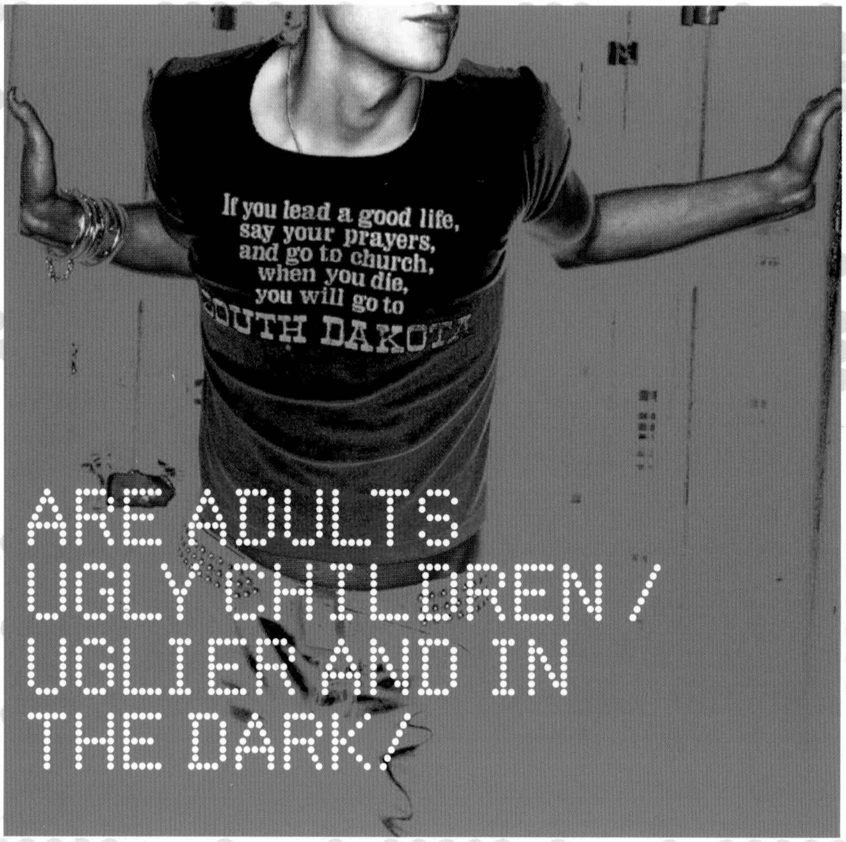

Subcircus—60 Second Love Affair

The packaging for this CD single works simply and effectively. The manipulation of the two photographs to produce large areas of flat, strong background color, which tonally complement the figure, has added to the images' graphic impact. The device of cropping both images through the head of the subject creates a further startling visual link between the two. The computer-till-receipt/neon-newsflash style of the typeface used—Dot Matrix—also gives a subliminal immediacy to the lyrics printed on the sleeve to underline the fleeting nature of the song's theme.

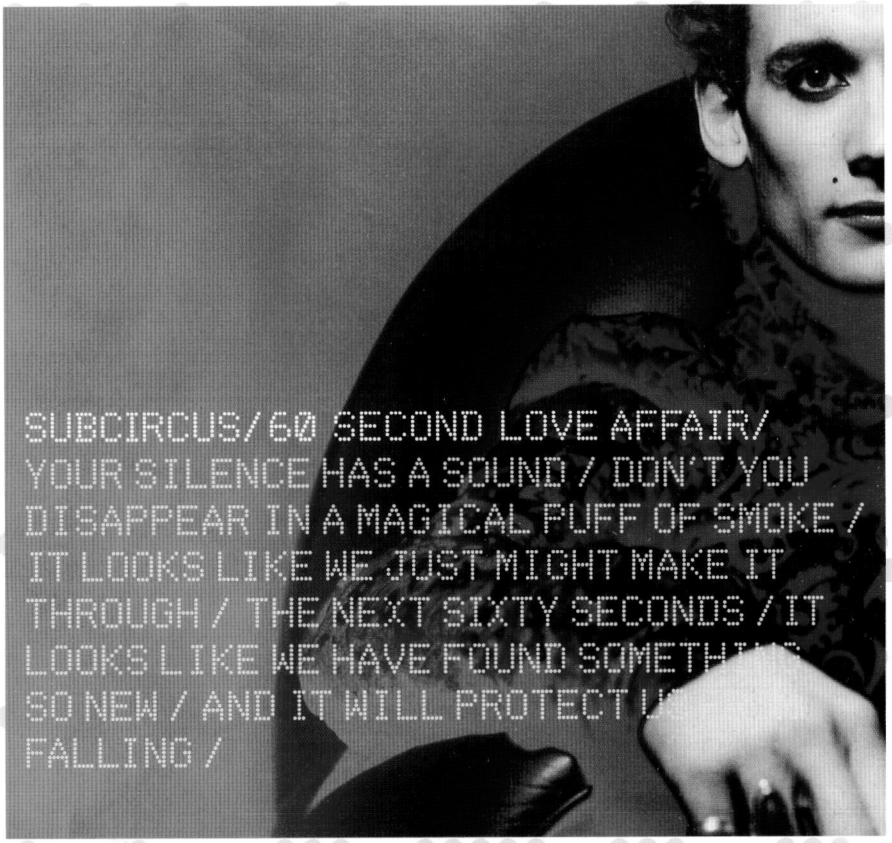

Designer
Rob Chenery

Art Director
Rob O'Connor

Photographer
Michele Turriani

Design Company
Stylorouge

Country of Origin
UK

Description of Artwork
Packaging for the CD single of *60 Second Love Affair* by Subcircus.

Dimensions
120 x 120 mm
4 3/4 x 4 3/4 in

Format
CD single

Designer
Dom Raban

Design Company
Eg.G

Country of Origin
UK

Description of Artwork
24-page color brochure overprinted with opaque white ink on 230 micron Colourmaster Grey paper.

Page Dimensions
205 x 205 mm
8 x 8 in

Format
Brochure

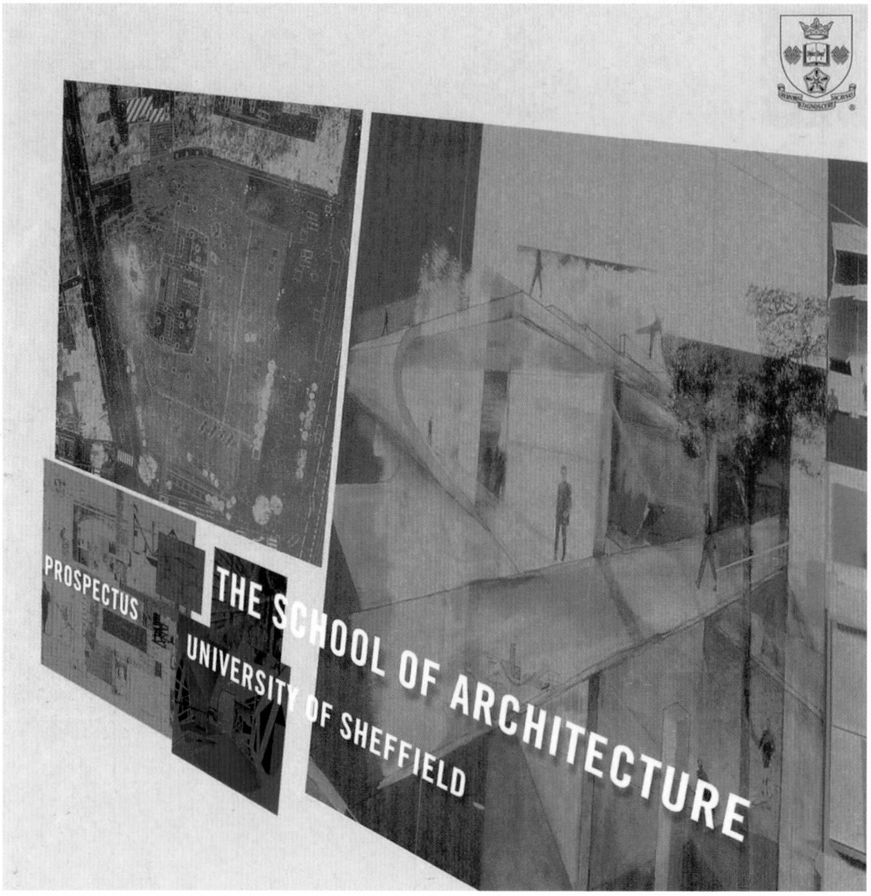

University of Sheffield School of Architecture

The layout for this brochure has been developed from the proportions of the golden section, an appropriate starting point considering its architectural theme. Blocks of strong color have been used to enliven technical imagery, such as site overview drawings, aerial photographs, and cross-sections. This, combined with the use of white text, gives the work consistency even though the shapes and layouts are irregular.

Special Production Techniques

The brochure has been printed in four colors, overprinted with an opaque white ink that unites the different aspects of the design. This and the subtle contrast of white ink on off-white paper gives this publication a strong visual and tactile presence.

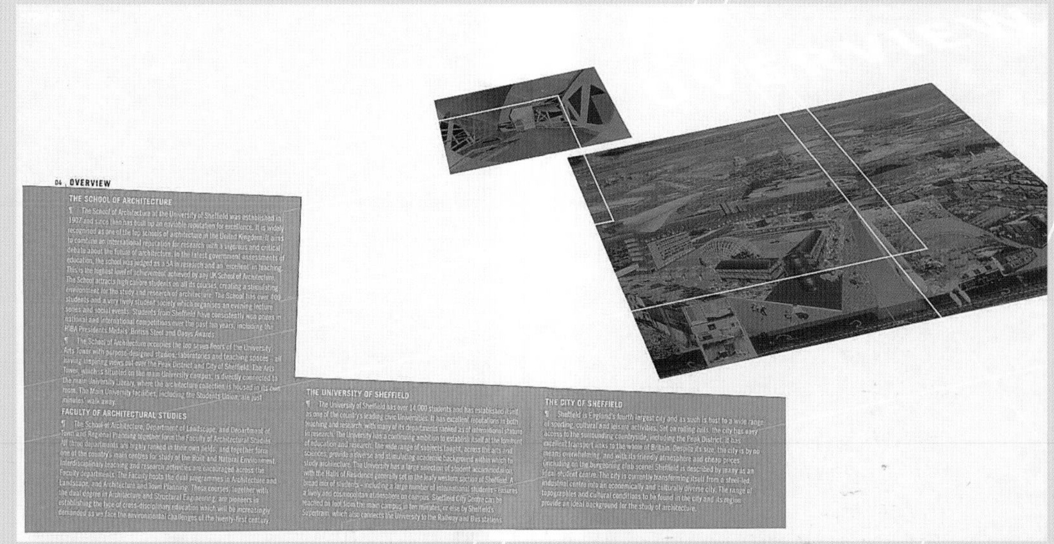

PP04-05

04 . OVERVIEW

THE SCHOOL OF ARCHITECTURE

¶ The School of Architecture at the University of Sheffield was established in 1907 and since then has built up an enviable reputation for excellence. It is widely recognised as one of the top schools of architecture in the United Kingdom. It aims to combine an international reputation for research with a vigorous and critical debate about the future of architecture. In the latest government assessments of education, the school was judged as a 5A in research and an 'excellent' in teaching. This is the highest level of achievement achieved by any UK School of Architecture. The School attracts high calibre students on all its courses, creating a stimulating environment for the study and research of architecture. The School has over 400 students and a very lively student society which organises an evening lecture series and social events. Students from Sheffield have consistently won prizes in national and international competitions over the past ten years, including the RIBA Presidents Medals, British Steel and Oasys Awards.

¶ The School of Architecture occupies the top seven floors of the University Arts Tower with purpose-designed studios, laboratories and teaching spaces - all having inspiring views out over the Peak District and City of Sheffield. The Arts Tower, which is situated on the main University campus, is directly connected to the main University Library, where the architecture collection is housed in its own room. The Main University facilities, including the Students Union, are just minutes' walk away.

FACULTY OF ARCHITECTURAL STUDIES

¶ The School of Architecture, Department of Landscape, and Department of Town and Regional Planning together form the Faculty of Architectural Studies. All three departments are highly ranked in their own fields, and together form one of the country's main centres for study of the Built and Natural Environment. Interdisciplinary teaching and research activities are encouraged across the Faculty departments. The Faculty hosts the dual programmes in Architecture and Landscape, and Architecture and Town Planning. These courses, together with the dual degree in Architecture and Structural Engineering, are pioneers in establishing the type of cross-disciplinary education which will be increasingly demanded as we face the environmental challenges of the twenty-first century.

THE UNIVERSITY OF SHEFFIELD

¶ The University of Sheffield has over 14 000 students and has established itself as one of the country's leading civic Universities. It has excellent reputations in both teaching and research, with many of its departments ranked as of international stature in research. The University has a continuing ambition to establish itself at the forefront of education and research. The wide range of subjects taught, across the arts and sciences, provide a diverse and stimulating academic background within which to study architecture. The University has a large selection of student accommodation with the Halls of Residence generally set in the leafy western section of Sheffield. A broad mix of students - including a large number of international students - ensures a lively and cosmopolitan atmosphere on campus. Sheffield City Centre can be reached on foot from the main campus in ten minutes, or else by Sheffield's Supertram, which also connects the University to the Railway and Bus stations.

THE CITY OF SHEFFIELD

¶ Sheffield is England's fourth largest city and as such is host to a wide range of sporting, cultural and leisure activities. Set on rolling hills, the city has easy access to the surrounding countryside, including the Peak District. It has excellent transport links to the whole of Britain. Despite its size, the city is by no means overwhelming, and with its friendly atmosphere and cheap prices (including on the burgeoning club scene) Sheffield is described by many as an ideal student centre. The city is currently transforming itself from a steel-led industrial centre into an economically and culturally diverse city. The range of topographies and cultural conditions to be found in the city and its region provide an ideal background for the study of architecture.

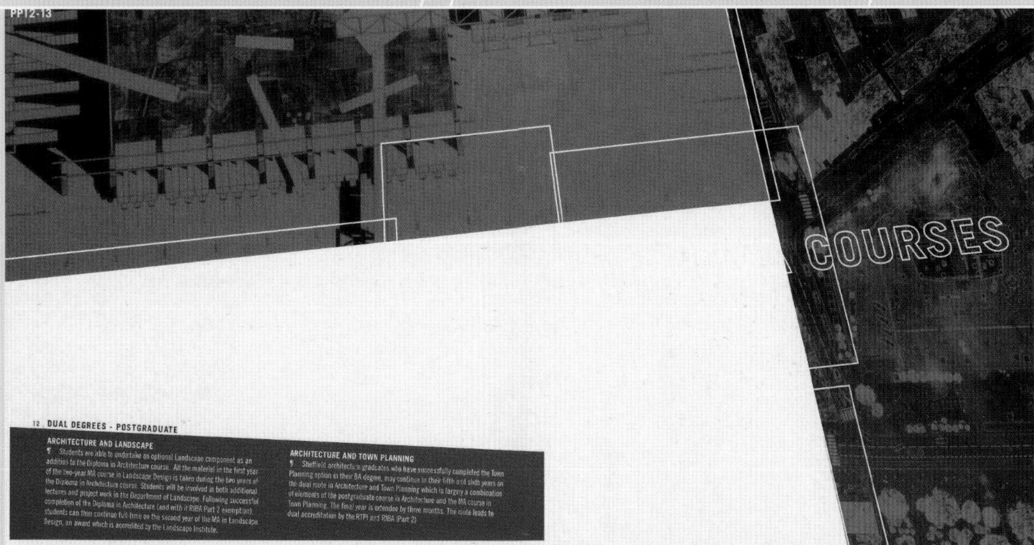

PP12-13

12 . DUAL DEGREES - POSTGRADUATE

ARCHITECTURE AND LANDSCAPE

¶ Students are able to undertake an optional Landscape component as an addition to the Diploma in Architecture course. All the material in the first year of the two-year MA course in Landscape Design is taken during the two years of the Diploma in Architecture course. Students will be involved in both additional lectures and project work in the Department of Landscape. Following successful completion of the Diploma in Architecture (and with it RIBA Part 2 exemption), students can then continue full-time on the second year of the MA in Landscape Design, an award which is accredited by the Landscape Institute.

ARCHITECTURE AND TOWN PLANNING

¶ Sheffield architecture graduates who have successfully completed the Town Planning option in their BA degree, may continue in their fifth and sixth years on the dual route in Architecture and Town Planning which is largely a combination of elements of the postgraduate course in Architecture and the MA course in Town Planning. The final year is extended by three months. The route leads to dual accreditation by the RTPI and RIBA (Part 2).

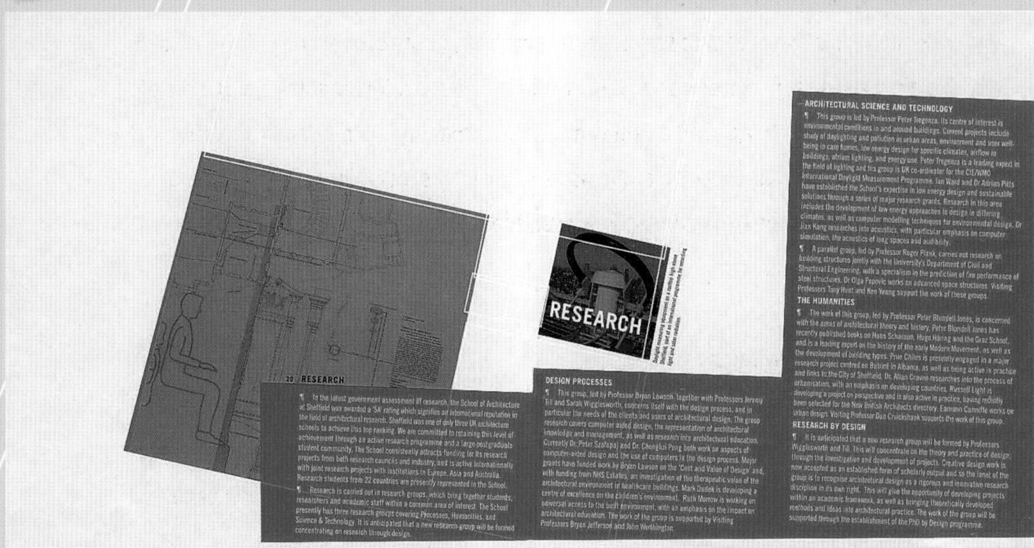

20 . RESEARCH

¶ In the latest government assessment of research, the School of Architecture at Sheffield was awarded a '5A' rating which signifies an international reputation in the field of architectural research. Sheffield was one of only three UK architecture schools to achieve this top ranking. We are committed to retaining this level of achievement through an active research programme and a large postgraduate student community. The School consistently attracts funding for its research projects from both research councils and industry, and is active internationally with joint research projects with institutions in Europe, Asia and Australia. Research students from 22 countries are presently represented in the School.

¶ Research is carried out in research groups, which bring together students, researchers and academic staff within a common area of interest. The School presently has three research groups covering Processes, Humanities, and Science & Technology. It is anticipated that a new research group will be formed concentrating on research through design.

DESIGN PROCESSES

¶ This group, led by Professor Bryan Lawson, together with Professors Jeremy Till and Sarah Wigglesworth, concerns itself with the design process, and in particular the needs of the clients and users of architectural design. The group research covers computer aided design, the representation of architectural knowledge and management, as well as research into architectural education. Currently Dr. Peter Szalapaj and Dr. Chengzhi Peng both work on aspects of computer-aided design and the use of computers in the design process. Major grants have funded work by Bryan Lawson on the 'Cost and Value of Design' and, with funding from NHS Estates, an investigation of the therapeutic value of the architectural environment in healthcare buildings. Mark Dudek is developing a centre of excellence on the children's environment. Ruth Morrow is working on universal access to the built environment, with an emphasis on the impact on architectural education. The work of the group is supported by Visiting Professors Bryan Jefferson and John Worthington.

ARCHITECTURAL SCIENCE AND TECHNOLOGY

¶ This group is led by Professor Peter Tregenza. Its centre of interest is environmental conditions in and around buildings. Current projects include study of daylighting and pollution in urban areas, environment and user well-being in care homes, low energy design for specific climates, airflow in buildings, atrium lighting, and energy use. Peter Tregenza is a leading expert in the field of lighting and his group is UK co-ordinator for the CIE/WMO International Daylight Measurement Programme. Ian Ward and Dr Adrian Pitts have established the School's expertise in low energy design and sustainable solutions through a series of major research grants. Research in this area includes the development of low energy approaches to design in differing climates, as well as computer modelling techniques for environmental design. Dr Jian Kang researches into acoustics, with particular emphasis on computer simulation, the acoustics of long spaces and audibility.

¶ A parallel group, led by Professor Roger Plank, carries out research on building structures jointly with the University's Department of Civil and Structural Engineering, with a specialism in the prediction of fire performance of steel structures. Dr Olga Popovic works on advanced space structures. Visiting Professors Tony Hunt and Ken Yeang support the work of these groups.

THE HUMANITIES

¶ The work of this group, led by Professor Peter Blundell Jones, is concerned with the areas of architectural theory and history. Peter Blundell Jones has recently published books on Hans Scharoun, Hugo Häring and the Graz School, and is a leading expert on the history of the early Modern Movement, as well as the development of building types. Prue Chiles is presently engaged in a major research project centred on Butrint in Albania, as well as being active in practice and links to the City of Sheffield. Dr. Allan Craven researches into the process of urbanisation, with an emphasis on developing countries. Russell Light is developing a project on perspective and is also active in practice, having recently been selected for the New British Architects directory. Eamonn Canniffe works on urban design. Visiting Professor Dan Cruickshank supports the work of this group.

RESEARCH BY DESIGN

¶ It is anticipated that a new research group will be formed by Professors Wigglesworth and Till. This will concentrate on the theory and practice of design through the investigation and development of projects. Creative design work is now accepted as an established form of scholarly output and so the tenet of the group is to recognise architectural design as a rigorous and innovative research discipline in its own right. This will give the opportunity of developing projects within an academic framework, as well as bringing theoretically developed methods and ideas into architectural practice. The work of the group will be supported through the establishment of the PhD by Design programme.

Artur — Forum für Kunst und Kultur
(see following spread for description)

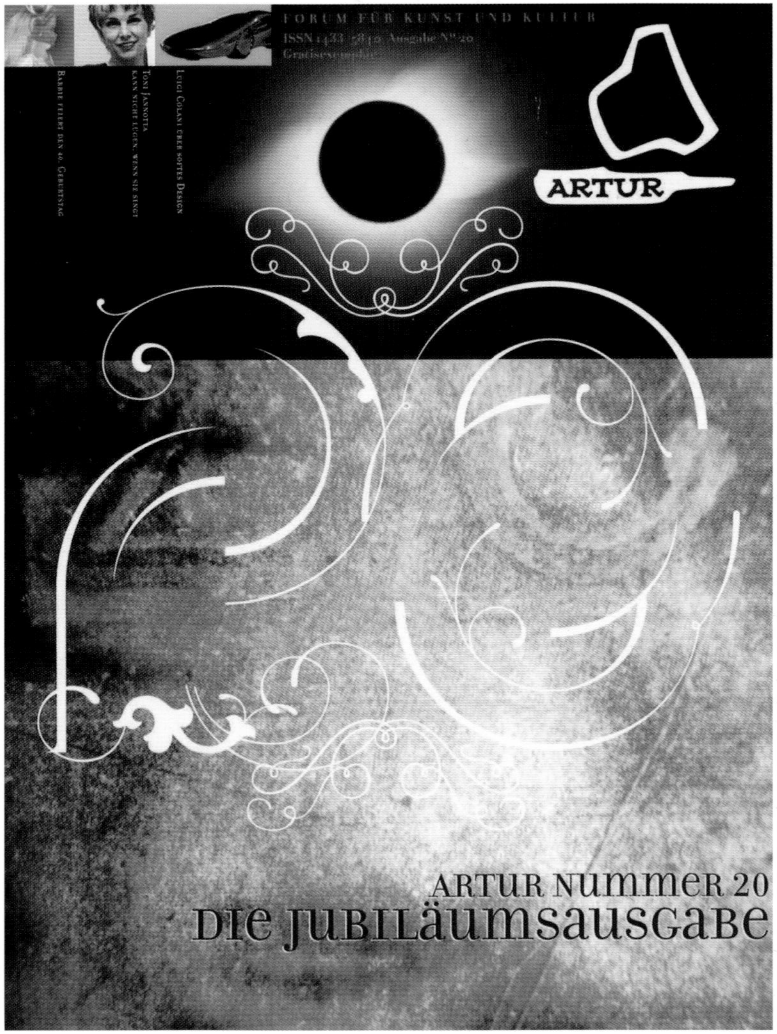

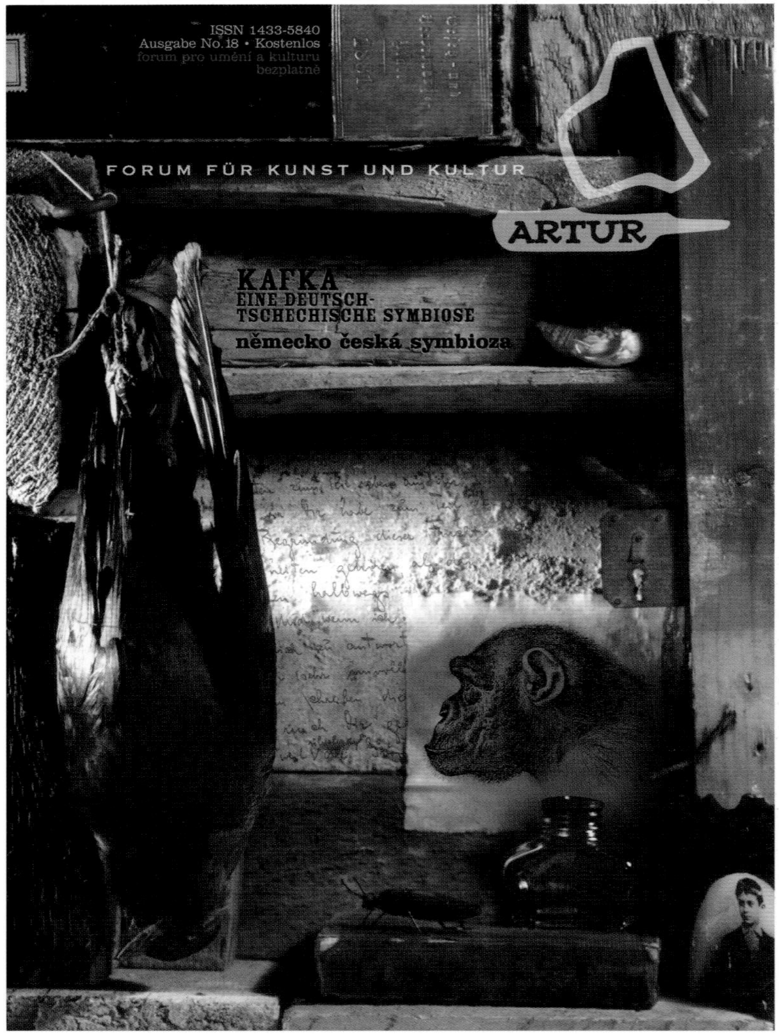

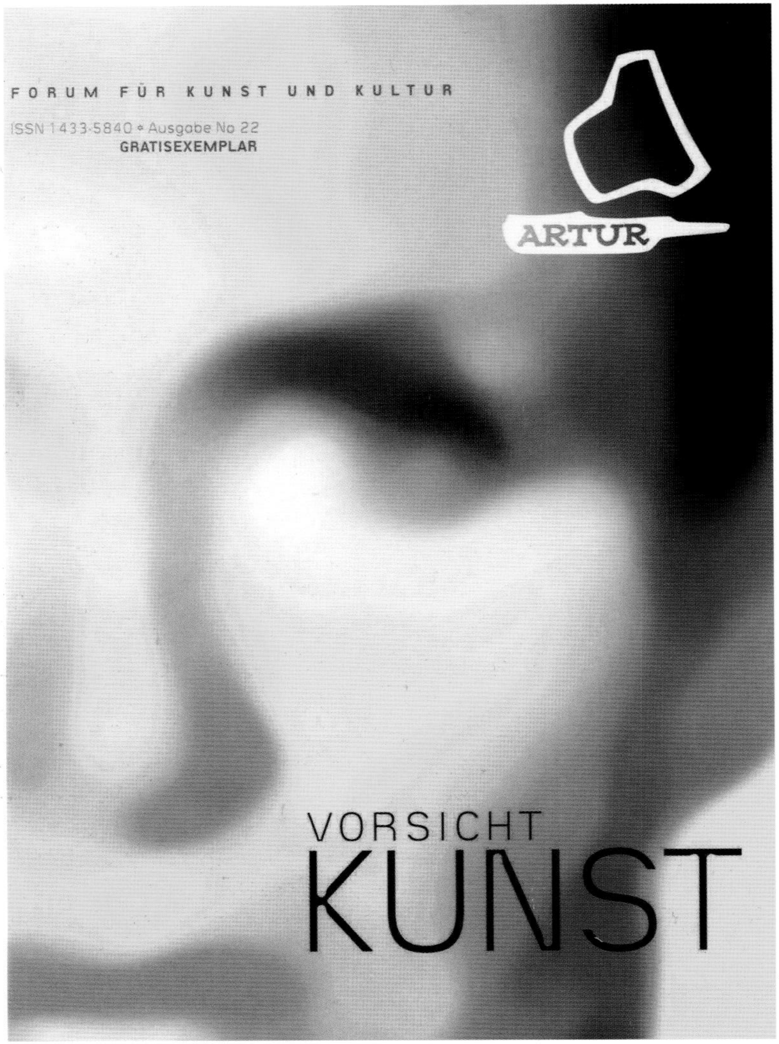
FORUM FÜR KUNST UND KULTUR
ISSN 1433-5840 • Ausgabe No 22
GRATISEXEMPLAR
ARTUR
VORSICHT
KUNST

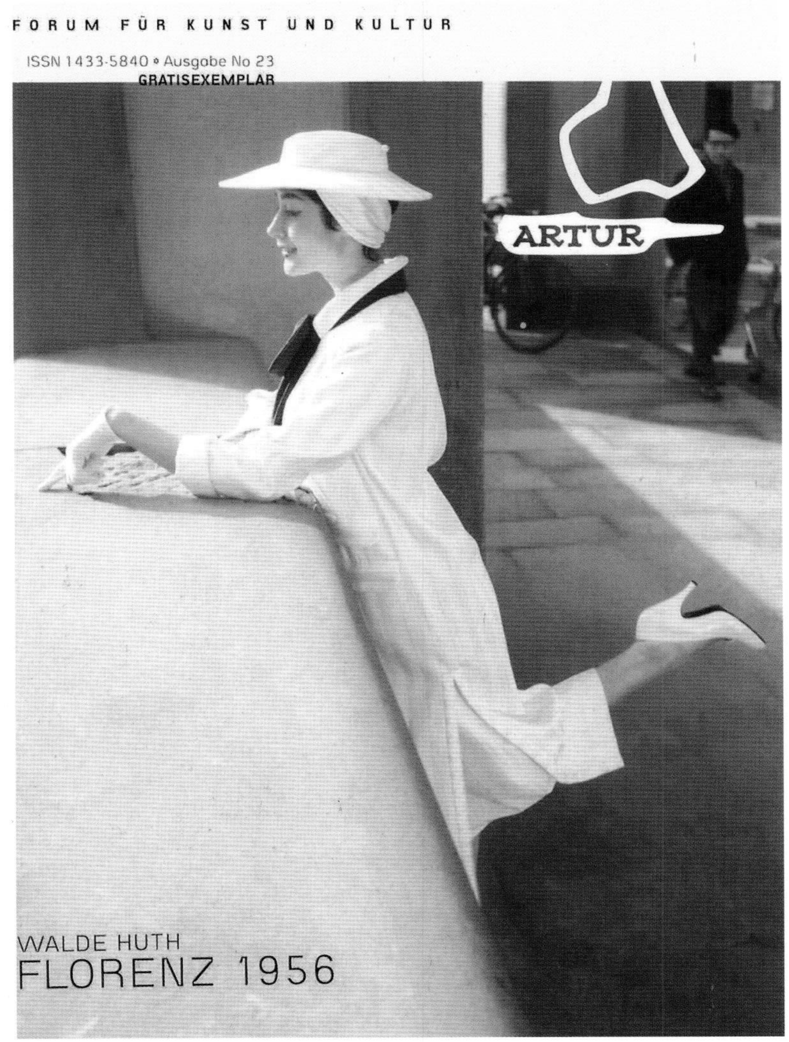
FORUM FÜR KUNST UND KULTUR
ISSN 1433-5840 • Ausgabe No 23
GRATISEXEMPLAR
ARTUR
WALDE HUTH
FLORENZ 1956

Designers
Ilja Sallacz, Carina Orschulko (issue 19)

Art Director
Ilja Sallacz

Illustrators
Ilja Sallacz, Carina Orschulko (issue 19)

Photographers
Bernd Hohlen, Walde Huth (issue 23)

Editor
Sonja Hefele

Design Company
LIQUID Agentur für Gestaltung

Publisher
Thomas H. Rossmann

Country of Origin
Germany

Description of Artwork
A quarterly magazine about art and culture published in southern Germany. Previous spread: covers from issues 18, 20, 22, 23. This spread: cover and inside pages from issue 19.

Page Dimensions
210 x 292 mm
8¼ x 11½ in
Opening to a maximum width of: 840 mm, 33 in

Format
Magazine

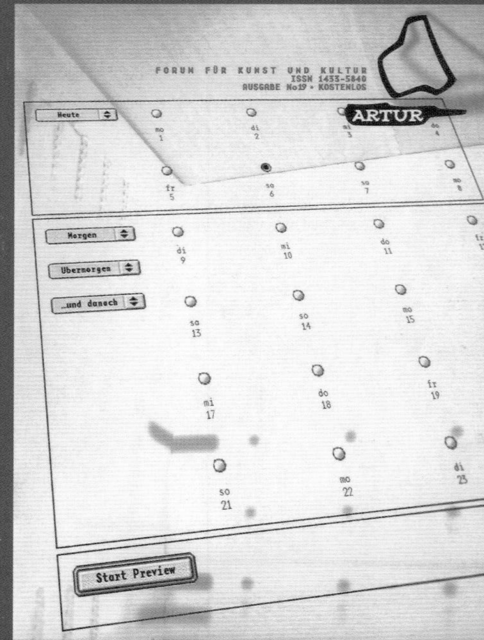

The way the logo casts a shadow on the page signals one of the concerns of this issue: the representation of three dimensions on a two-dimensional surface.

The application of perspective to this type extends the 3D theme begun with the logo on the cover.

Artur—Forum für Kunst und Kultur

No two issues of this magazine are alike; the content, design, number of colors printed, and paper, all change each time. Sometimes in four-color, sometimes in monochrome, this open-ended brief allows the designer free rein to make each issue as exciting and provocative as possible. It also gives the magazine visual and textural diversity. Set against this freedom is the magazine logo, its constancy identifying the magazine and highlighting the variety in the rest of the publication. Its unusual and obscure shape is strong enough to transcend the subtle changes it undergoes from issue to issue.

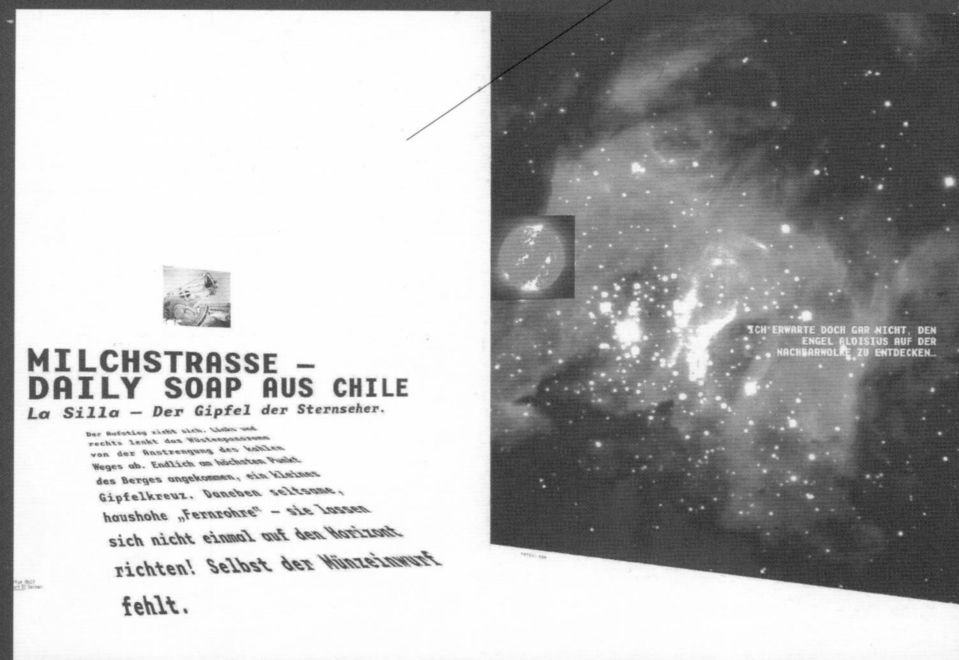

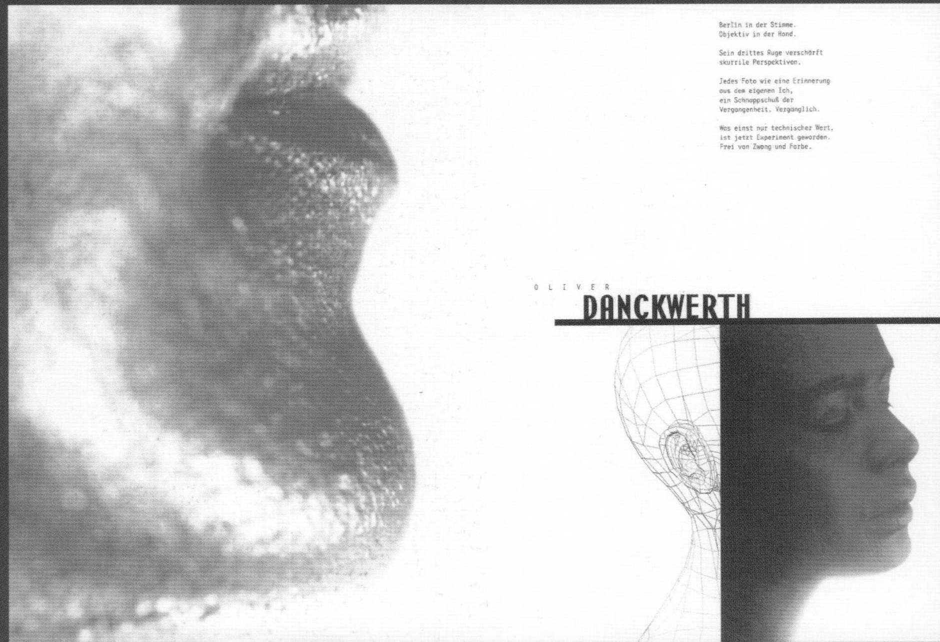

The use of line drawing to 'map' the human body (*head, left and stretching figure, below*) shows another approach to the way three dimensions can be visualized on the page.

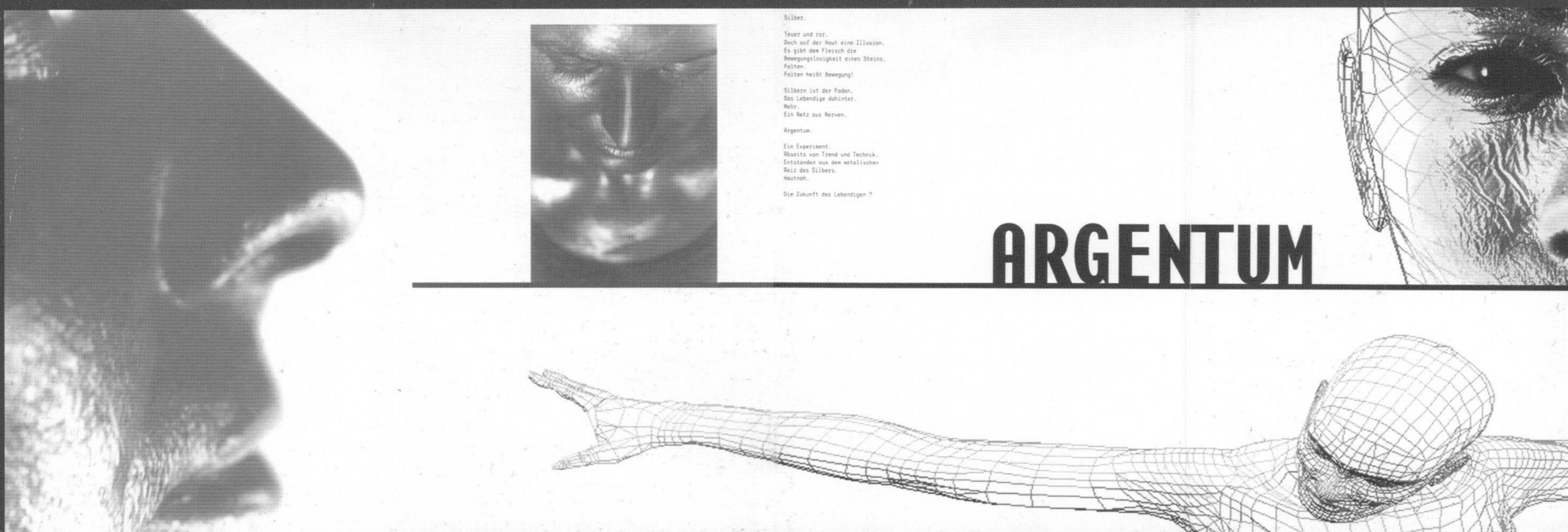

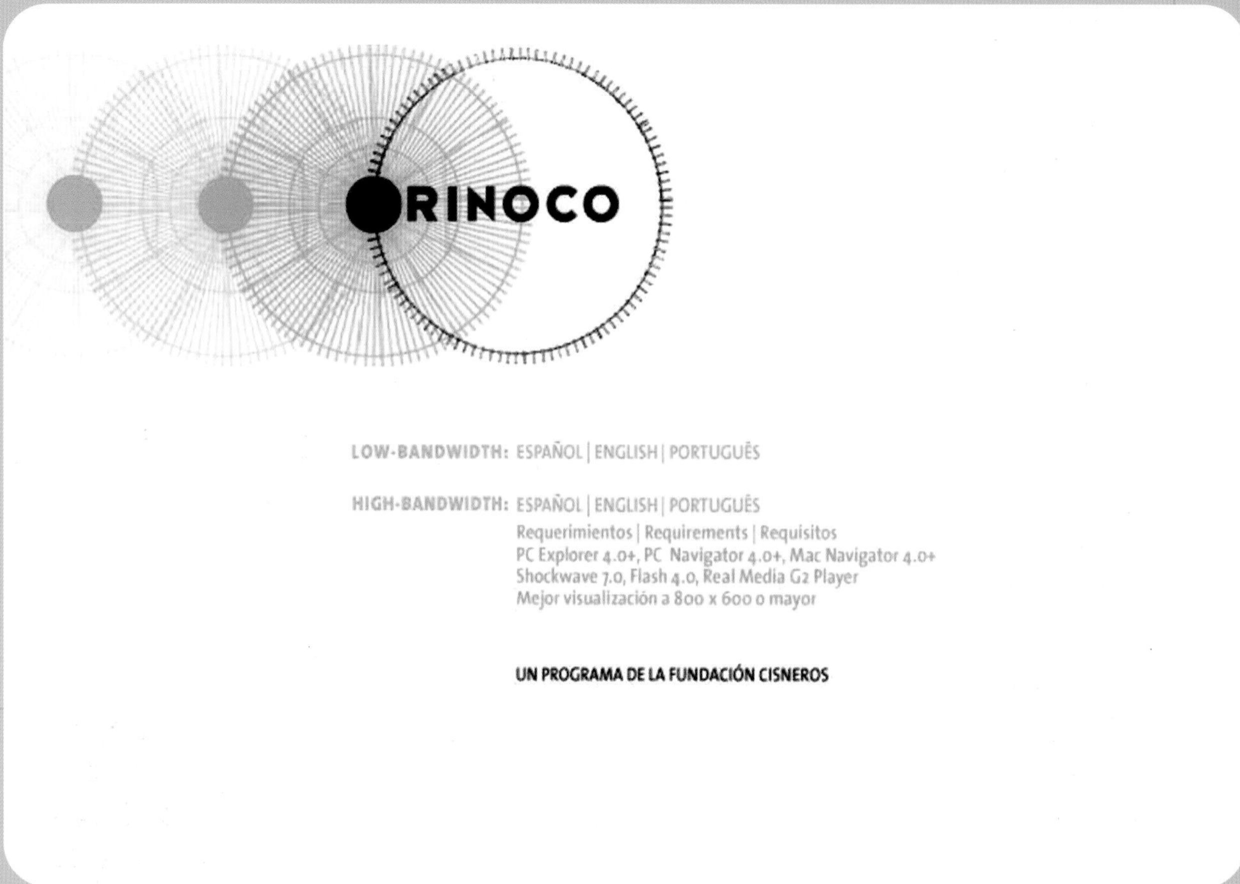

Orinoco Online

In this website design, the consistent graphic presentation of diverse images and cultures brings them together with a clear and pleasing aesthetic. It succeeds in making relatively obscure information both appealing and accessible. The non-linear structure of the site, with information grouped in constellations rather than hierarchically, is derived from the way in which the indigenous cultures conceptualize the universe. This integrated approach extends to the color palettes and other design elements, all of which were inspired by different aspects of the cultures featured.

The circular navigation graphic is intended to encourage a more intuitive exploration of the site. At first a little unfamiliar, this device mediates the way in which the site is viewed, allowing each visitor to find their own route between the different cultures.

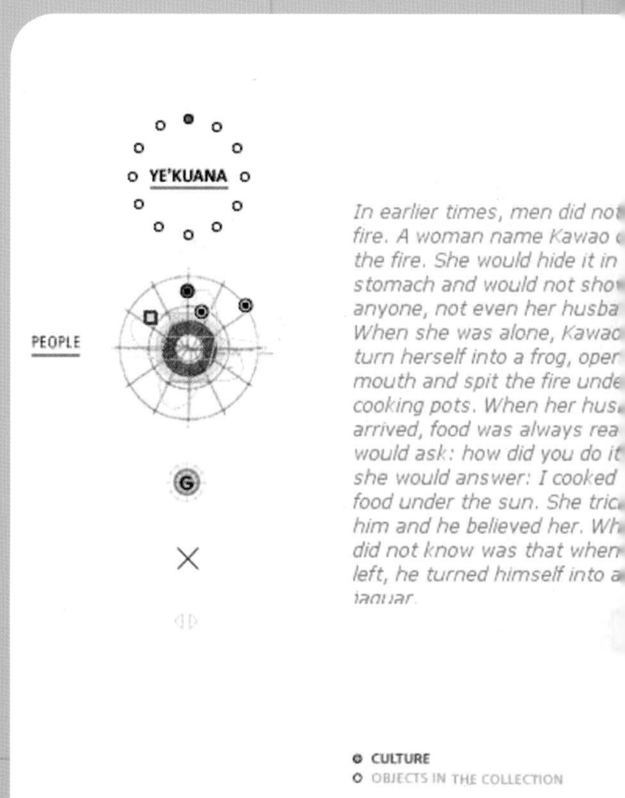

Designers
Rafael Esquer, Mariana Saddakni, Chakaras Johnson

Creative and Art Direction
Rafael Esquer

Creative and Project Management
Angela Fung

Programmers
Harsha Kalidindi, Valerie Valoueva, Stephen Chu

Audio/Video Editor
Paul Bozymowski

Executive Producer
Hillary Leone

Editorial Director
Lelia Delgado

Design Company
@radical.media

Country of Origin
USA

Description of Artwork
A website (www.orinoco.org) for the Fundación Cisneros to help promote interest, knowledge, and support for the indigenous populations of southern Venezuela.

Dimensions
800 x 550 pixels

Format
Website

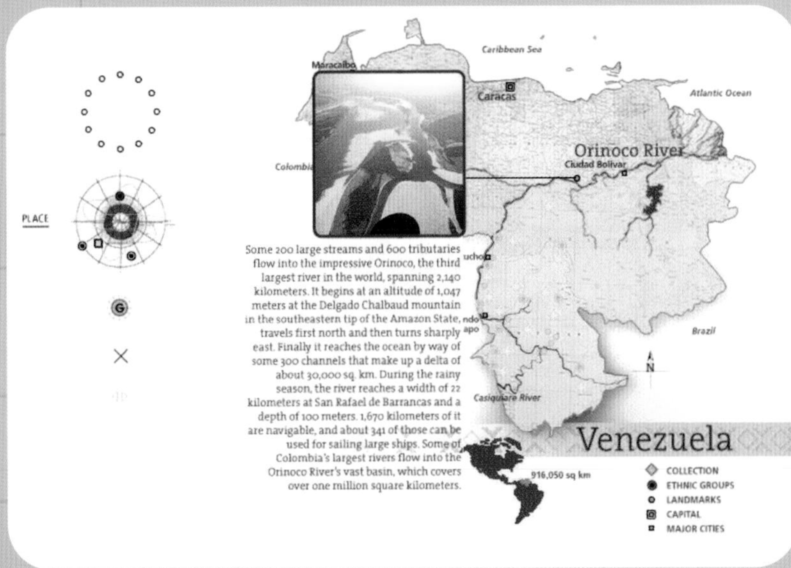

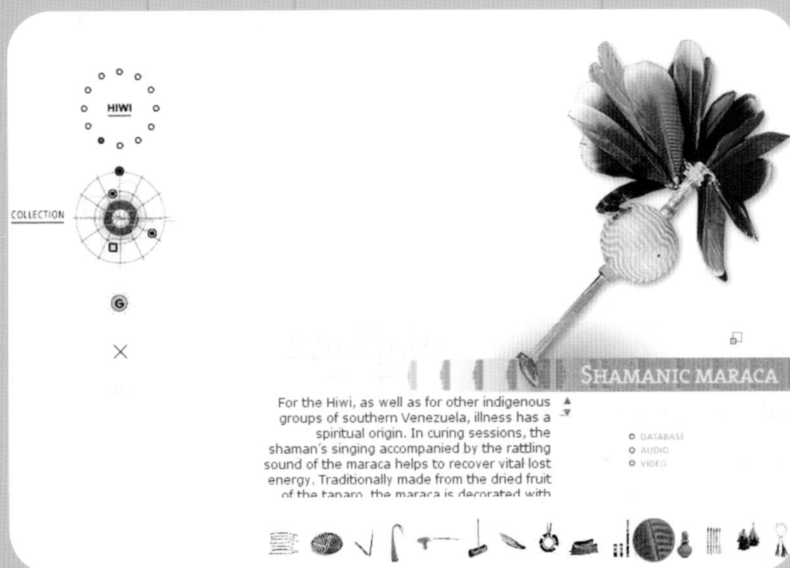

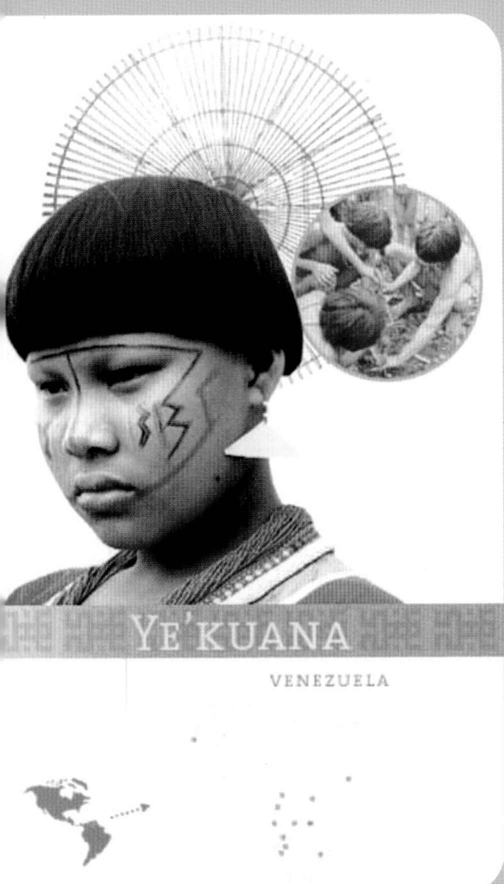

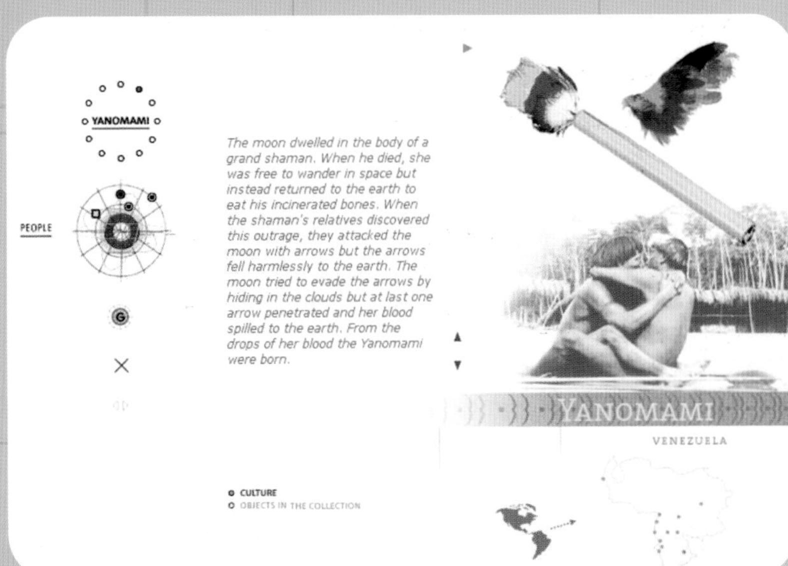

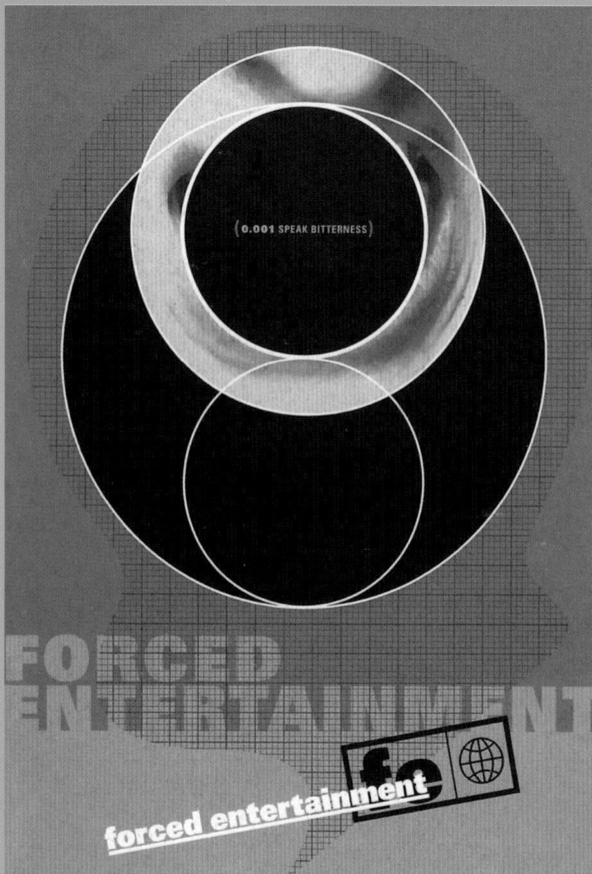

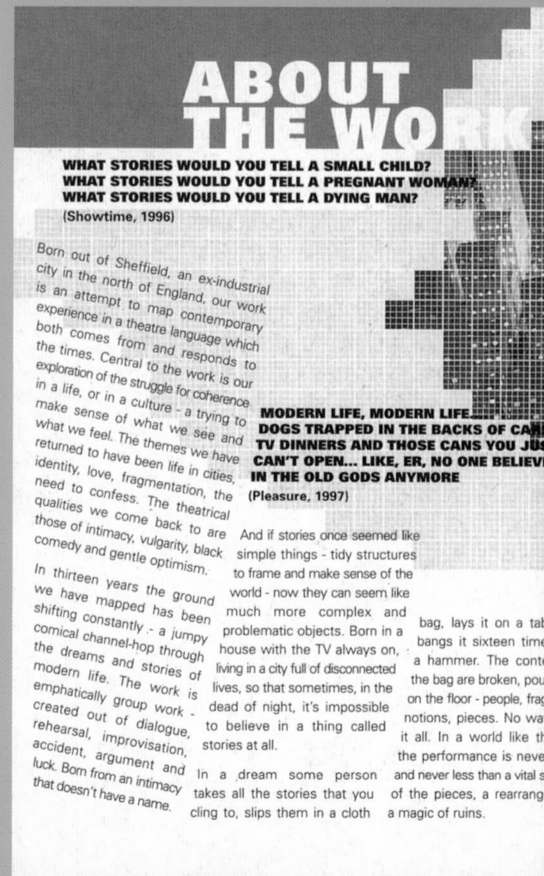

ABOUT
THE WO

WHAT STORIES WOULD YOU TELL A SMALL CHILD?
WHAT STORIES WOULD YOU TELL A PREGNANT WOMAN?
WHAT STORIES WOULD YOU TELL A DYING MAN?
(Showtime, 1996)

Born out of Sheffield, an ex-industrial city in the north of England, our work is an attempt to map contemporary experience in a theatre language which both comes from and responds to the times. Central to the work is our exploration of the struggle for coherence in a life, or in a culture - a trying to make sense of what we see and what we feel. The themes we have returned to have been life in cities, identity, love, fragmentation, the need to confess. The theatrical qualities we come back to are those of intimacy, vulgarity, black comedy and gentle optimism.

In thirteen years the ground we have mapped has been shifting constantly - a jumpy comical channel-hop through the dreams and stories of modern life. The work is emphatically group work - created out of dialogue, rehearsal, improvisation, accident, argument and luck. Born from an intimacy that doesn't have a name.

MODERN LIFE, MODERN LIFE... DOGS TRAPPED IN THE BACKS OF CA TV DINNERS AND THOSE CANS YOU JU CAN'T OPEN... LIKE, ER, NO ONE BELIEV IN THE OLD GODS ANYMORE
(Pleasure, 1997)

And if stories once seemed like simple things - tidy structures to frame and make sense of the world - now they can seem like much more complex and problematic objects. Born in a house with the TV always on, living in a city full of disconnected lives, so that sometimes, in the dead of night, it's impossible to believe in a thing called stories at all.

In a dream some person takes all the stories that you cling to, slips them in a cloth bag, lays it on a tab bangs it sixteen time a hammer. The conte the bag are broken, pou on the floor - people, frag notions, pieces. No way it all. In a world like th the performance is never and never less than a vital s of the pieces, a rearrange a magic of ruins.

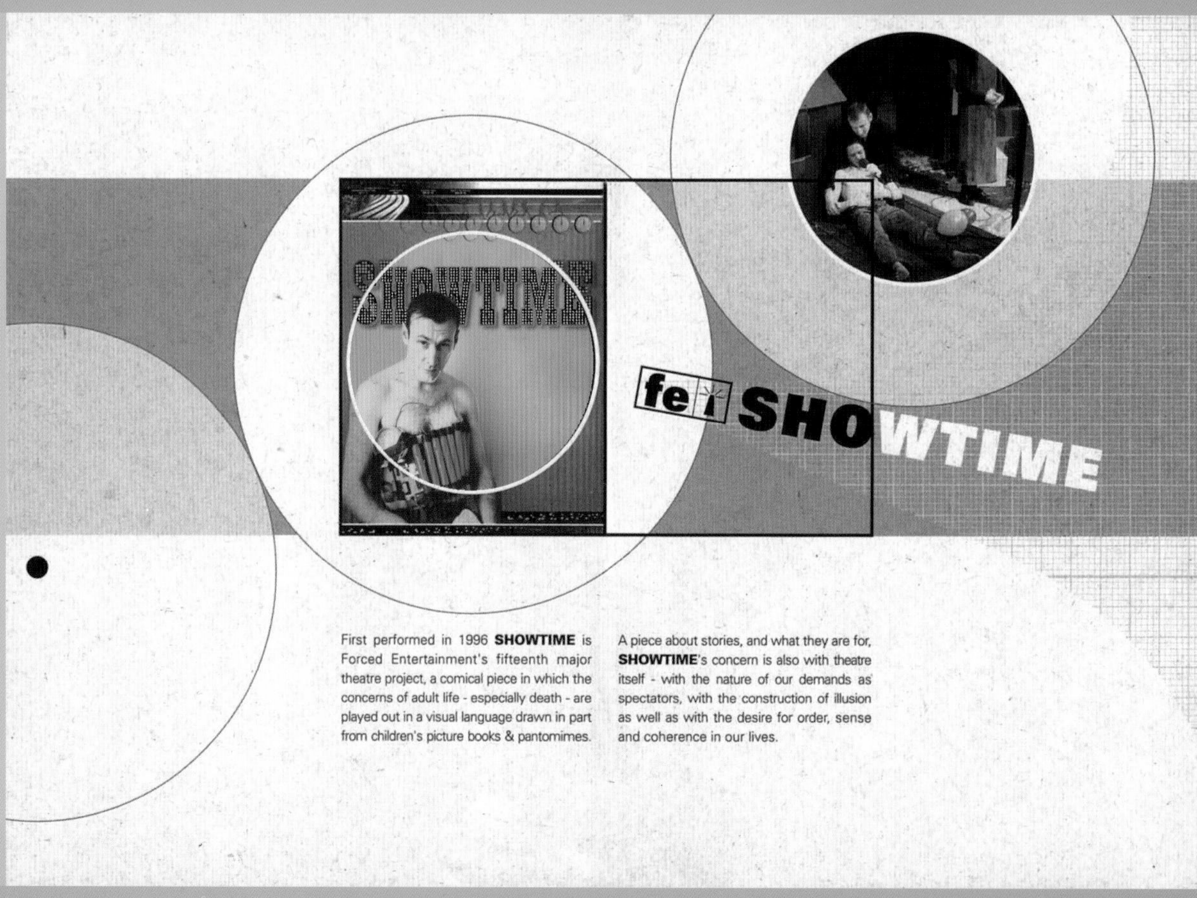

First performed in 1996 **SHOWTIME** is Forced Entertainment's fifteenth major theatre project, a comical piece in which the concerns of adult life - especially death - are played out in a visual language drawn in part from children's picture books & pantomimes.

A piece about stories, and what they are for, **SHOWTIME**'s concern is also with theatre itself - with the nature of our demands as spectators, with the construction of illusion as well as with the desire for order, sense and coherence in our lives.

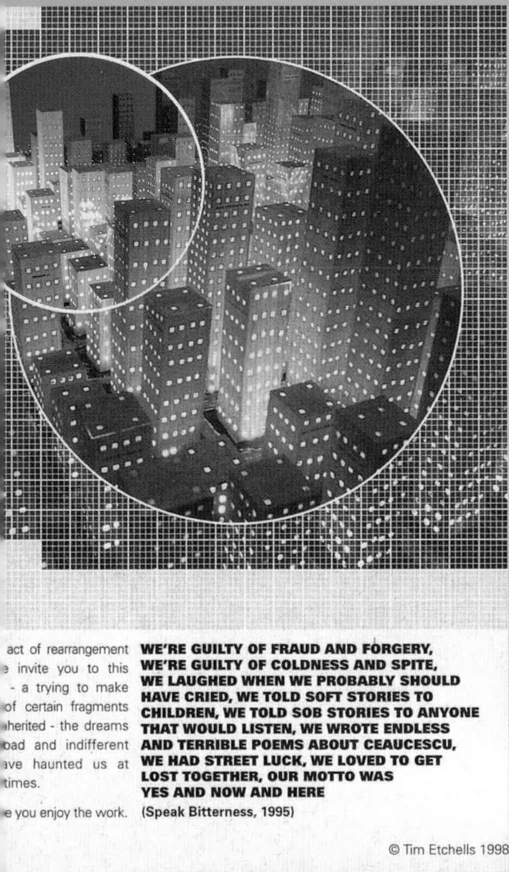

Designer
Dom Raban

Photographer
Hugo Glendinning

Design Company
Eg.G

Country of Origin
UK

Description of Artwork
12-page mono brochure supplied with 6 do-it-yourself color stickers.

Page Dimensions
105 x 148 mm
4¹/₄ x 6³/₄ in

Format
Brochure

Forced Entertainment

This witty and imaginative retrospective brochure for an innovative theater company succeeds in both entertaining and intriguing, all within a tight budget. A spirit of experimentation is encouraged through the use of cost-effective one-color printing combined with the inclusion of six colored stickers for the reader to add to the design. The do-it-yourself nature of the brochure makes it a memorable publication.

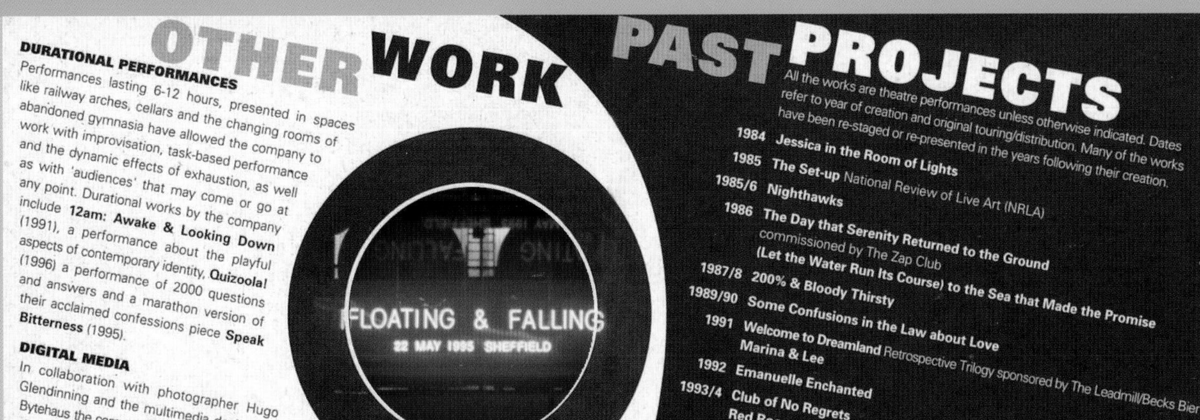

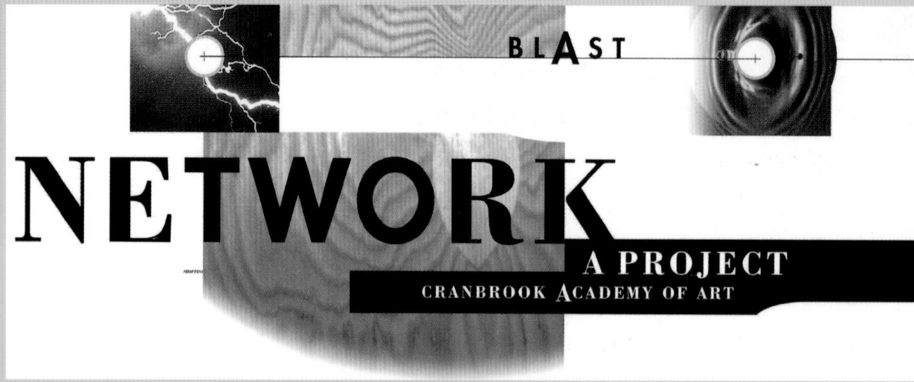

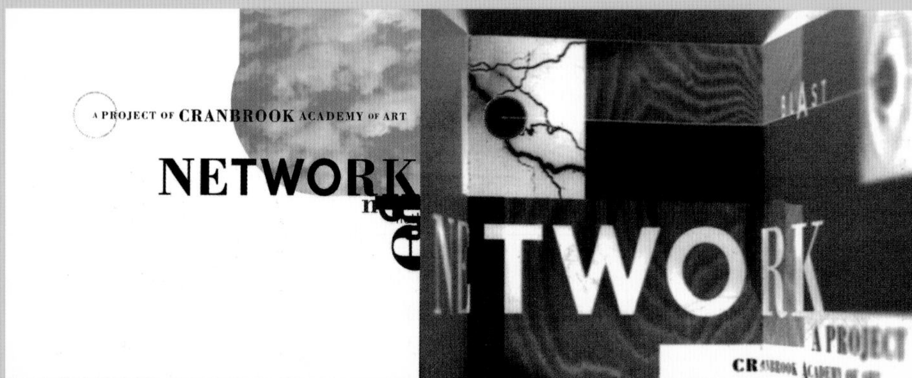

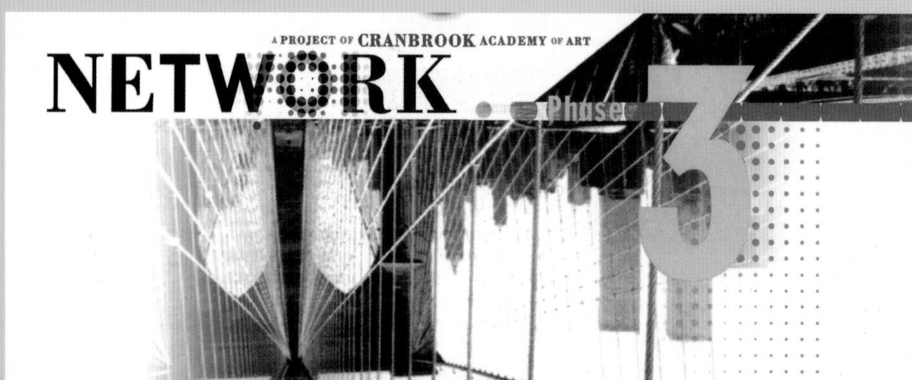

At first glance deceptively simple, the logotype is in fact composed of various typefaces.

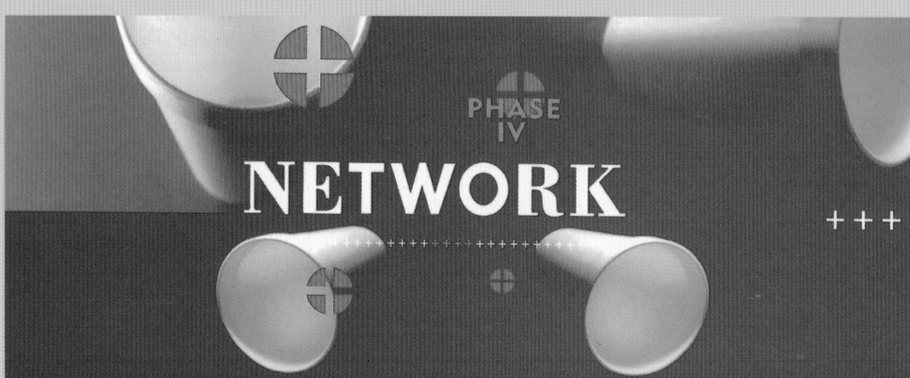

Network Gallery

The distinctive logotype allows the designer to present many of the different visual aspects of the gallery on each card while maintaining a sense of continuity. The success of this strategy can be seen, in particular, in the fifth card (*below*) where a strikingly different approach to the photography and a change in format have been successfully accommodated. All these two-color cards effectively and economically promote the gallery and reflect the fact that it shows a wide range of work.

Designer
Brad Bartlett

Art Director
Brad Bartlett

Photographer
Brad Bartlett

Art College
Cranbrook Academy of Art

Country of Origin
USA

Description of Artwork
Series of cards to announce the opening of the Network Gallery, Cranbrook Academy of Art.

Dimensions
Phases 1–4 (*opposite*):
254 x 101 mm
10 x 4 in
Phase 5 (*right*):
140 x 197 mm
$5^1/_2$ x $7^3/_4$ in

Format
Cards

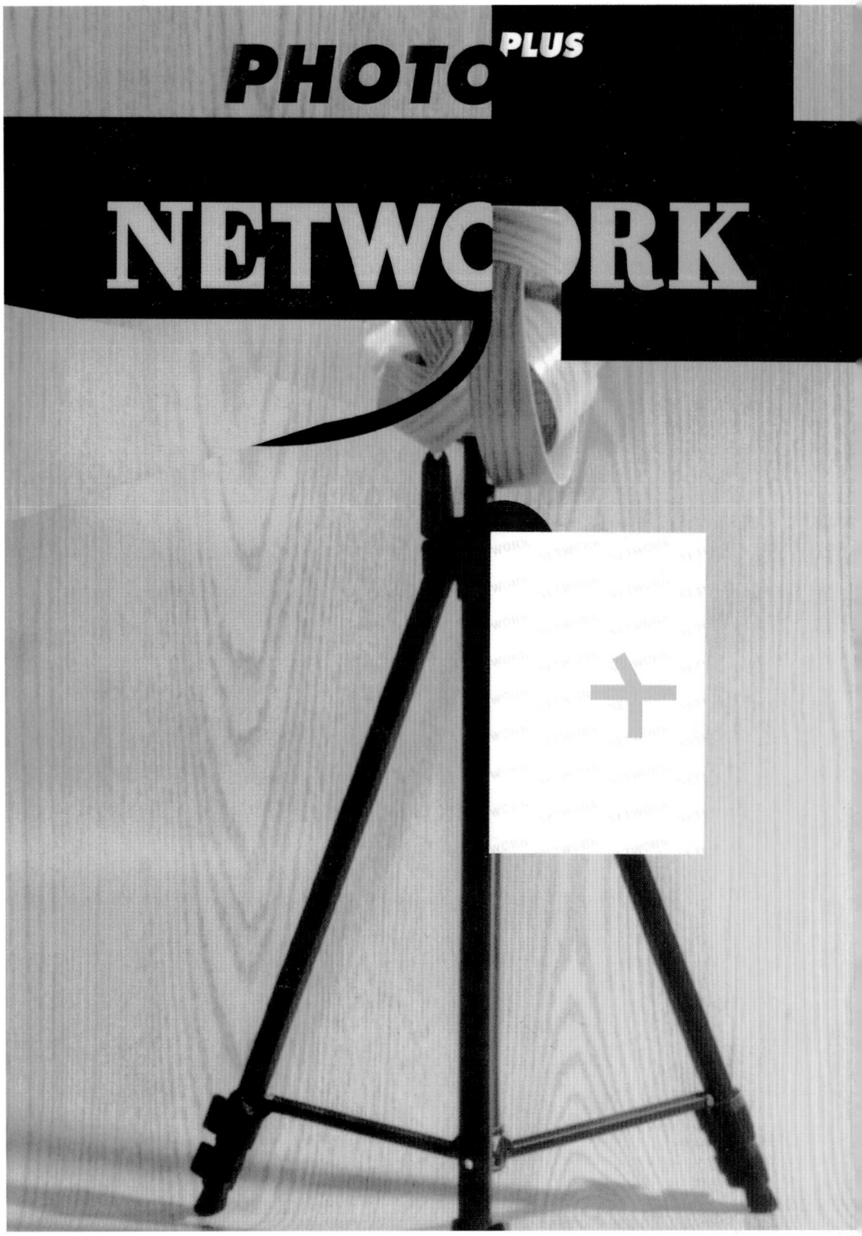

Designer
Danielle Foushee

Art Director
Danielle Foushee

Country of Origin
USA

Description of Artwork
A series of Family Gallery Guides for the Museum of Contemporary Art, Los Angeles.

Page Dimensions
254 x 305 mm
10 x 12 in

Format
Museum Gallery Guide

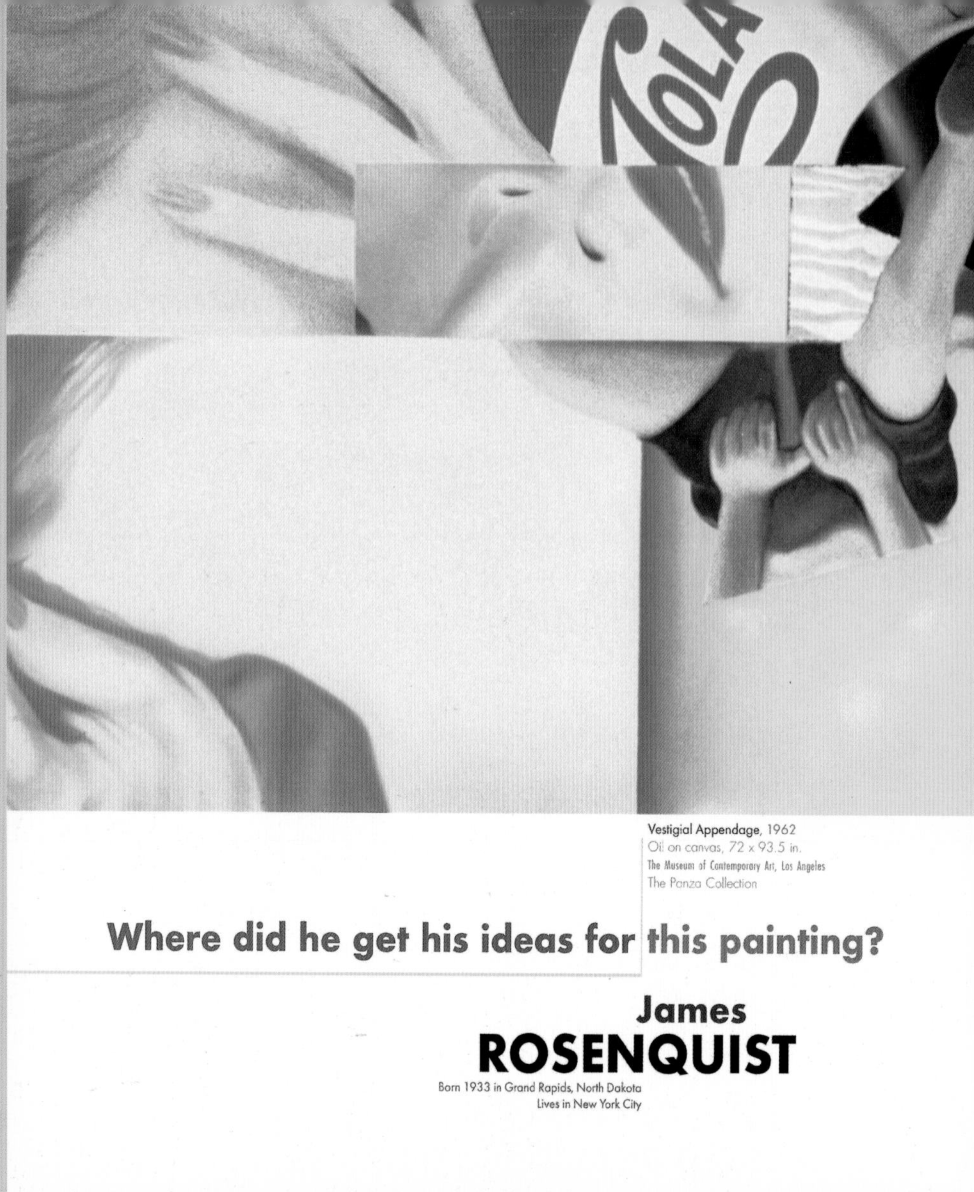

MOCA Family Gallery Guides

The bold setting of each artist's work and the accompanying typography against a white ground draws together image and text in this distinctive series. An uncomplicated device, but it allows the designers to sustain a stylish solution throughout a large number of titles. The skill in creating eye-catching typography out of a small amount of information and subtle color combinations shows that often simple solutions are the most flexible.

Below and opposite: printing type in colors drawn from the artwork places the emphasis on the artist, rather than the design, and gives each guide an individual feel.

Map, 1962
Encaustic and collage on canvas, 60 x 93 in.
The Museum of Contemporary Art, Los Angeles
Gift of Marcia Simon Weisman

WHAT MAKES THIS A WORK OF ART ?

Jasper JOHNS

born 1930 in Augusta, Georgia
lives in New York City

Haarlem Goes Missing

The style of illustration, the simple integration of typography and images, and the physical construction of this joyous project all imbue it with immense charm. The pages can be viewed as a sequence of double-page spreads or, as the book concertinas out into a long frieze, as a series of connected images on a single surface charting the character's progress through the story. Apparently a children's story, it is also a witty allegory for adults.

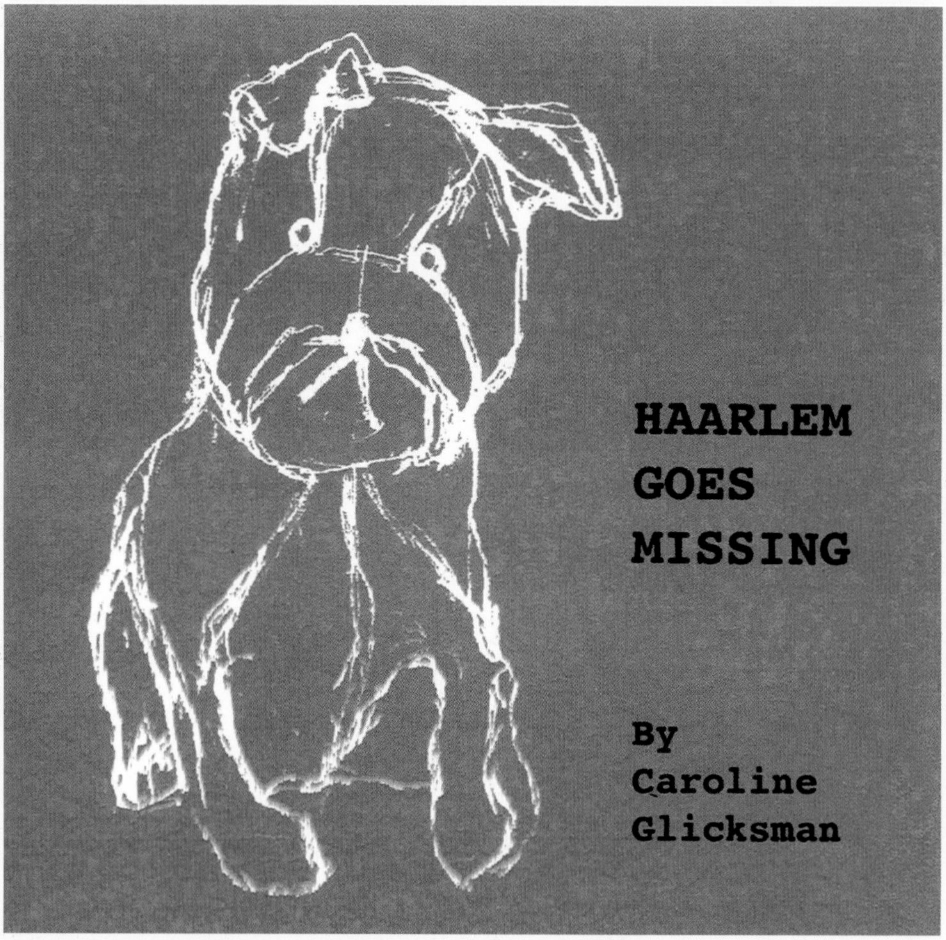

Special Production Techniques

Silkscreen printing, as used in this work, involves the application of different colored inks which build up, layer by layer, into the complete image. The inks may be opaque or translucent, allowing the colors beneath to show through.

Haarlem was a little brown and white dog... ...who secretly longed for a more colourful existence, so...

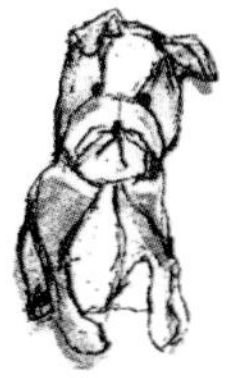

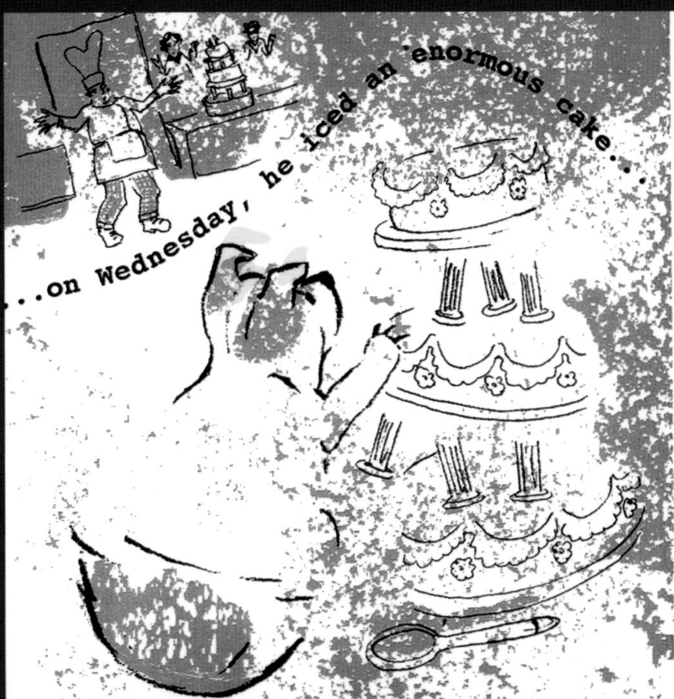

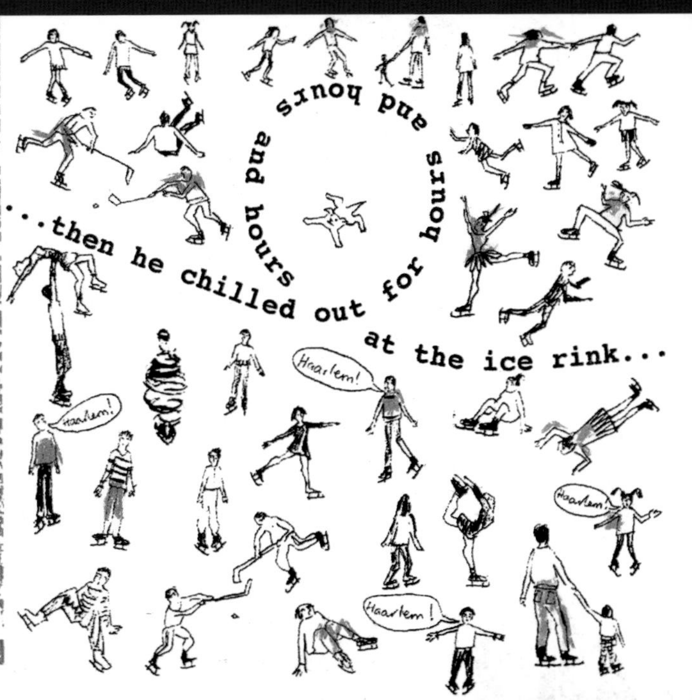

Designer
Caroline Glicksman

Illustrator
Caroline Glicksman

Art College
University of Brighton

Country of Origin
UK

Description of Artwork
Screenprinted concertina-bound artist's book

Page Dimensions
150 x 150 mm
5⁷/₈ x 5⁷/₈ in

Format
Limited edition artist's book

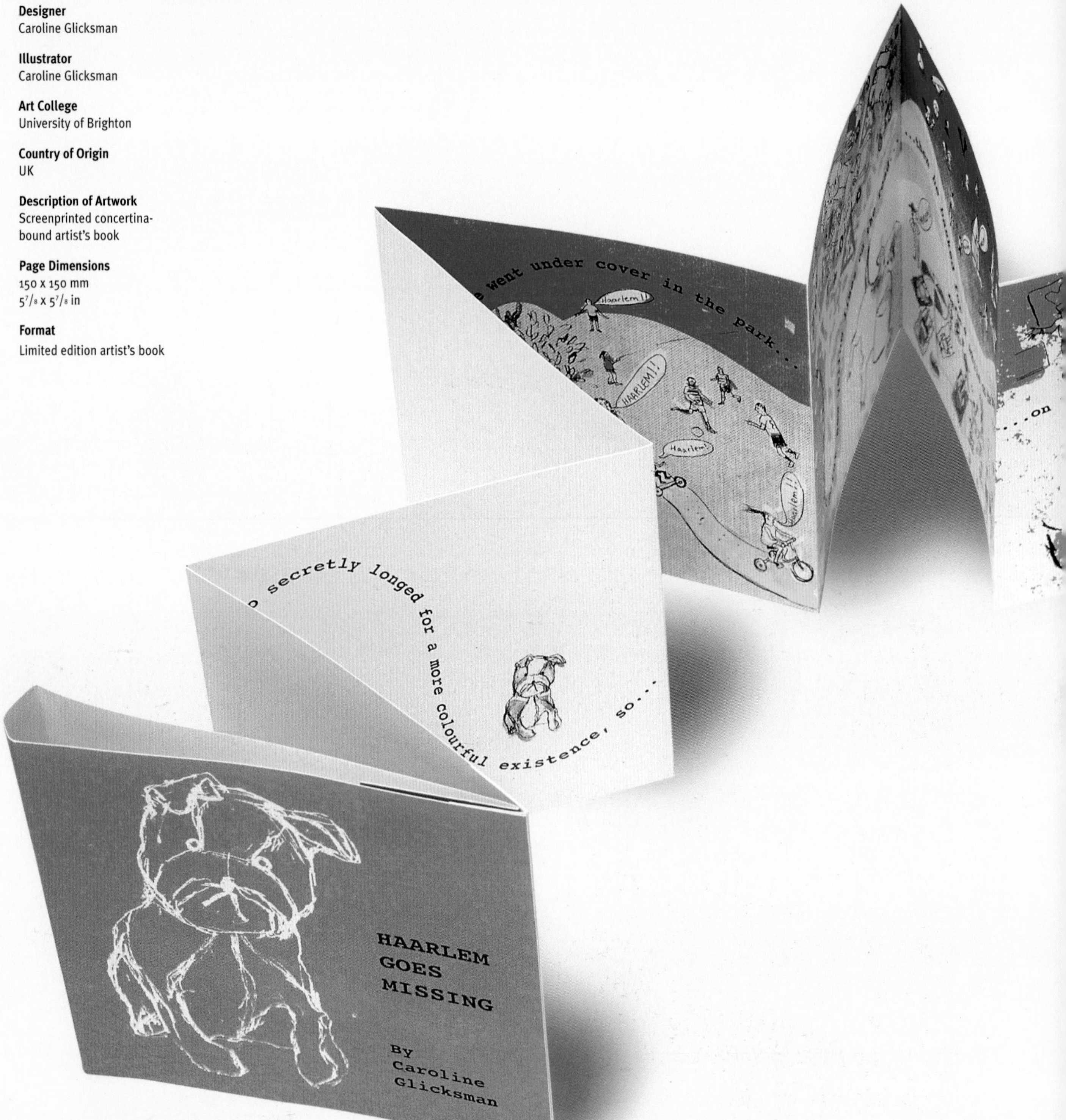

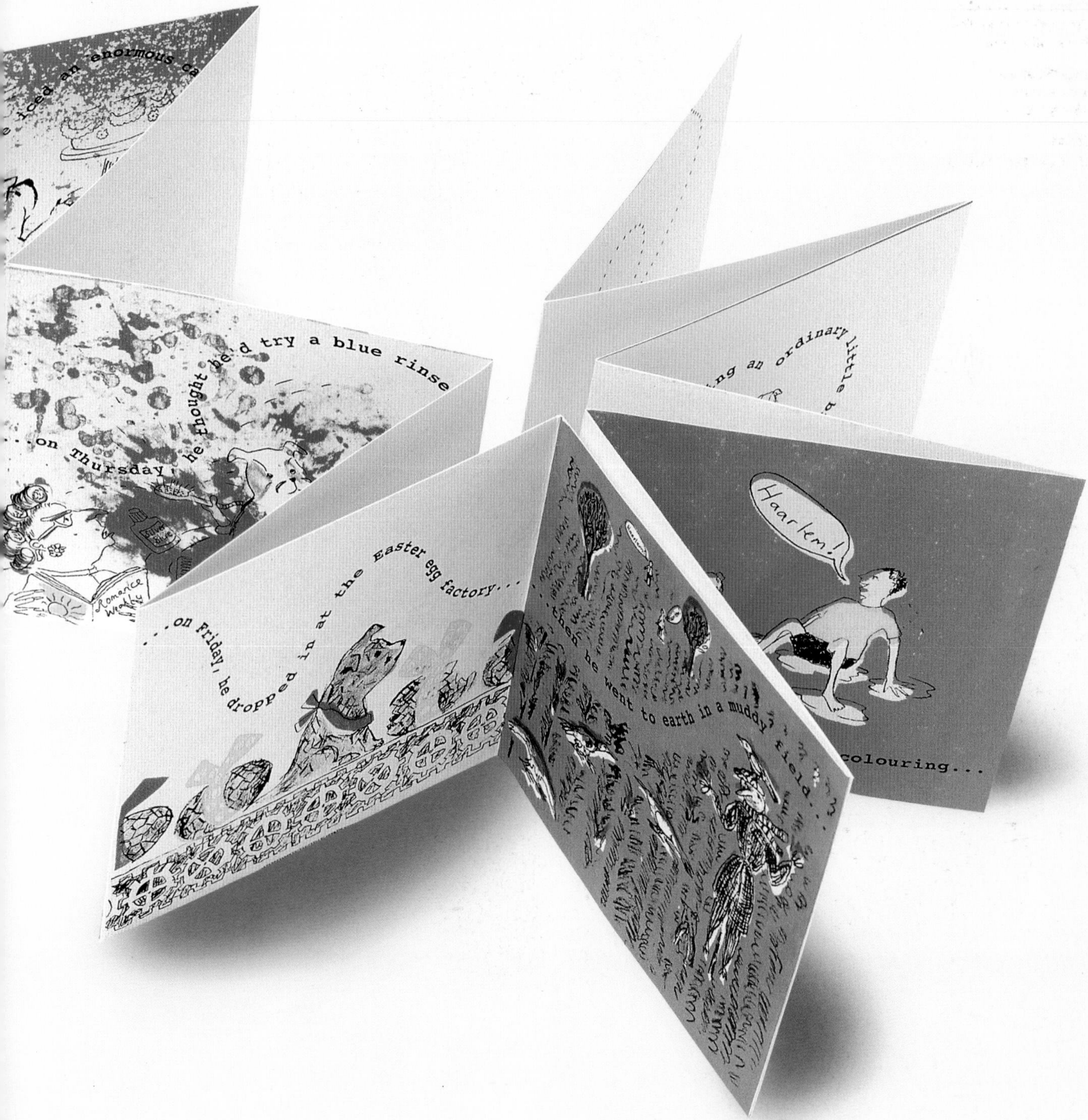
iced an enormous ca
...on Thursday, he thought he'd try a blue rinse
Romance Weekly
ng an ordinary little
Haarlem!
colouring...
...on Friday, he dropped in at the Easter egg factory...
...then he went to earth in a muddy field...

Crossing Boundaries: Jamex and Einar de la Torre, Steven La Ponsie, Ronald Gonzalez

Crossing Boundaries: Jamex and Einar de la Torre, Steven La Ponsie, and Ronald Gonzalez Crossing
Jamex and Einar de la Torre, Steven La Ponsie, and Ronald Gonzalez Crossing Boundaries: Jamex and Einar de la Torre, Steven La Ponsie, and
Crossing Boundaries: Jamex and Einar de la Torre, Steven La Ponsie, and Ronald Gonzalez Crossing Boundaries: Jamex and

Crossing Boundaries:

Designer
Sibylle Hagmann

Art Director
Sibylle Hagmann

Design Company
TypoStudio

Country of Origin
USA

Description of Artwork
Catalog and invitation for a fine-art exhibition entitled 'Crossing Boundaries.' The invitation includes the program of events scheduled during the show.

Page Dimensions
Catalog: 216 x 241 mm
$8^1/_8$ x $9^1/_2$ in
Invitation: 142 x 159 mm
$5^5/_8$ x $6^1/_4$ in

Formats
Catalog and invitation

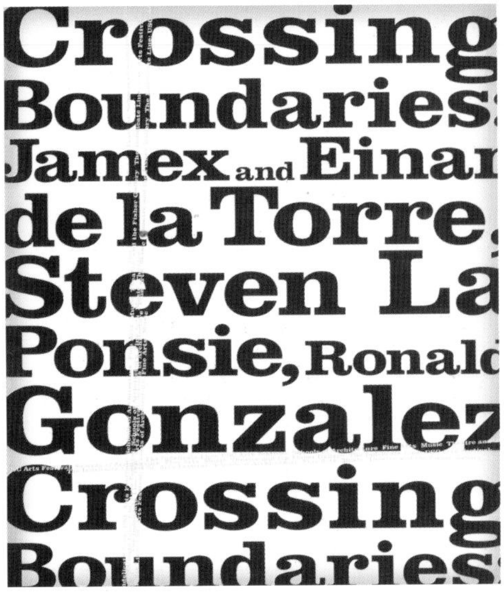

Crossing Boundaries

The bold use of a slab serif typeface combined with subtle color fades around the edges of the catalog cover (*opposite*) and on the front of the invitation (*left*) clearly identifies this event—a simple and effective solution. The use of faded color is picked up on the inside of the invitation (*below*), in which the unusual and irregular positioning of the text in and over the edges of the white cutouts brings a distinctive quality to the list of exhibition talks and workshops.

Special Production Techniques

The design of the invitation has been achieved with minimal use of color: the outside is printed using three colors and the inside two.

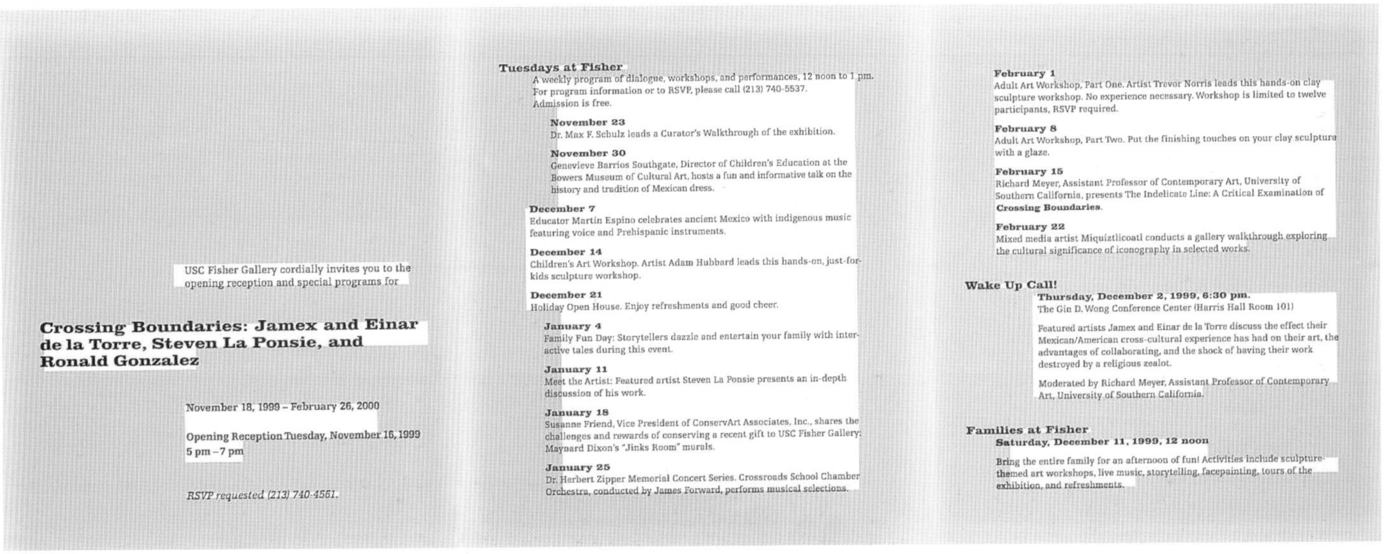

Designer
Christina Glahr

Art Director
Simon Schmidt

Illustrator
Christina Glahr

Photographer
Frank Voth

Design Company
Lorem Ipsum, Büro Für Konzeption & Gestaltung

Country of Origin
Germany

Description of Artwork
Brochure to promote surfing at Klitmoeller Beach on the North Sea coast of Denmark.

Page Dimensions
250 x 200 mm
9⅞ x 7⅞ in

Format
Brochure

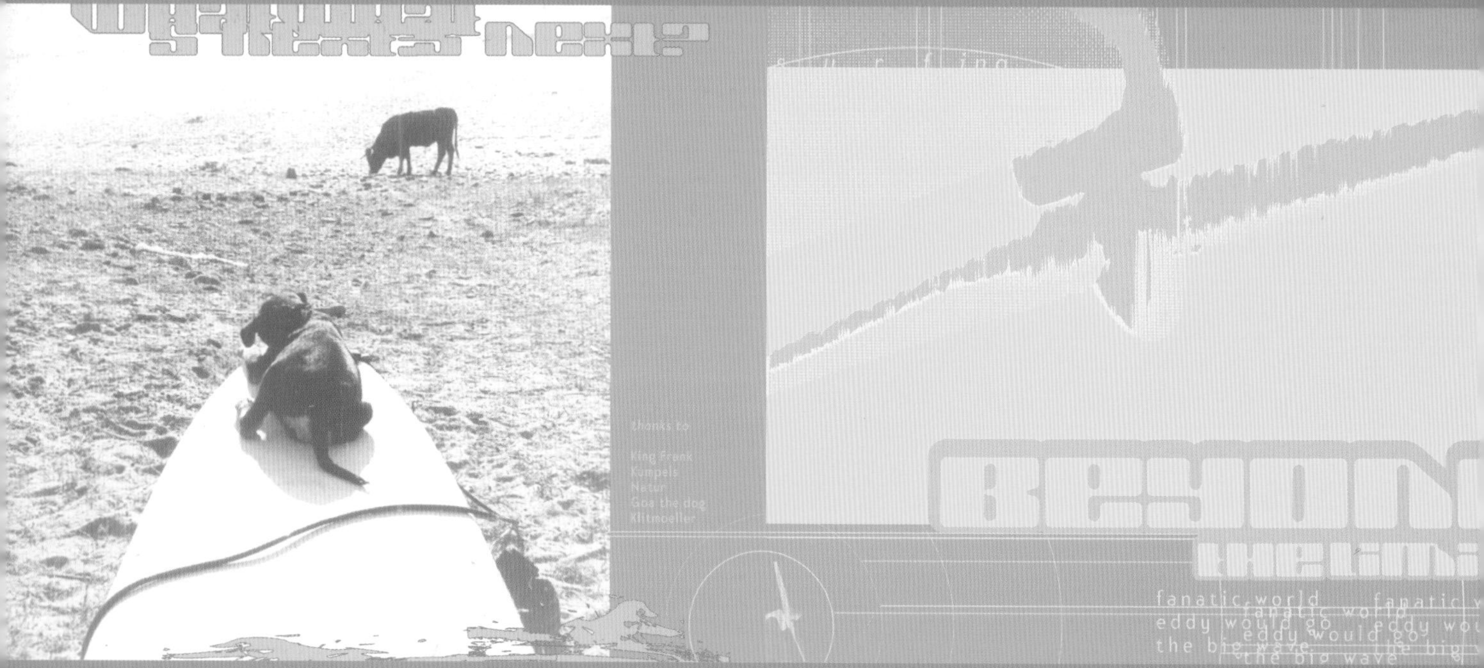

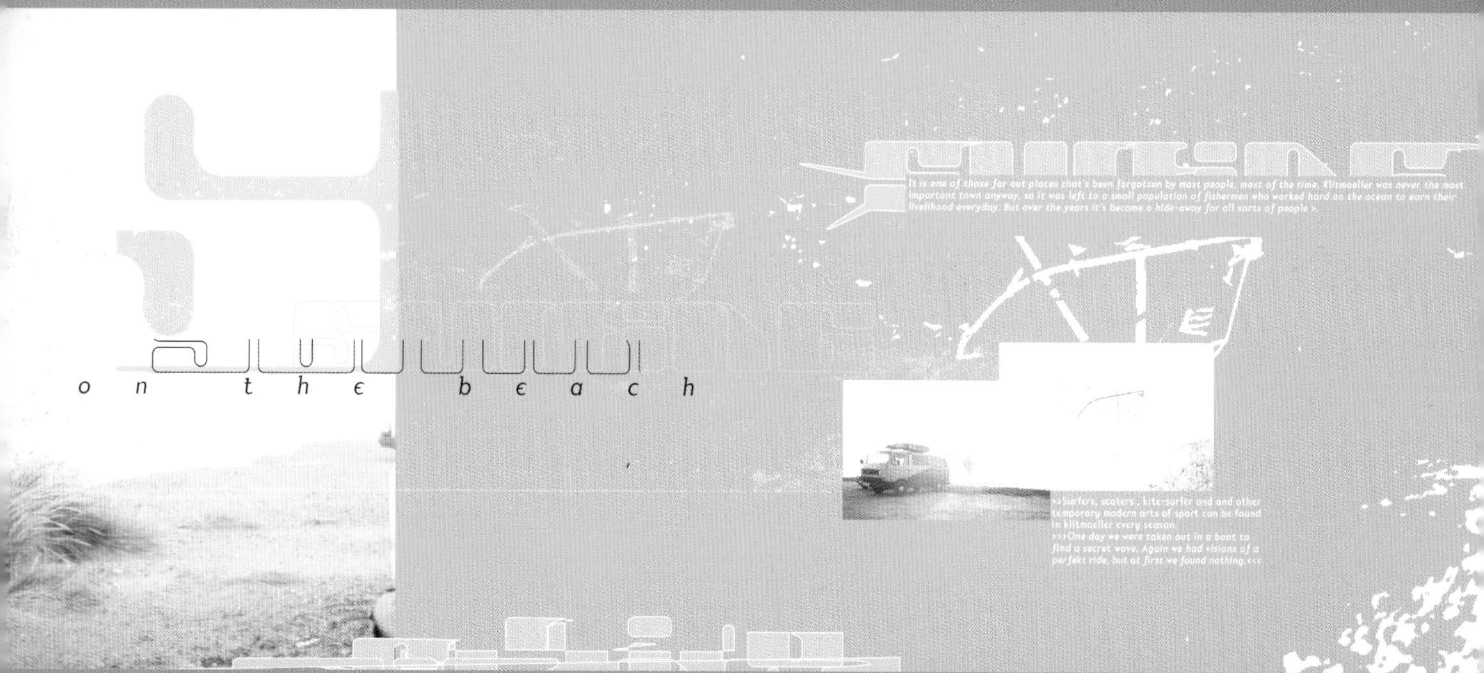

Klitmoeller Brochure

Although this evocative brochure, with its 'weathered' colors and rounded 'surfer' typography, alludes to the attractions of the beach in a rather abstract and oblique way, it is nonetheless quite clear. The text, which includes quotes from individual surfers and well-known pop songs, is sized and positioned to encourage closer scrutiny. Among the more obvious pictures, such as surfers on the water or a board strapped to the top of a van, there is an unexpected image with two animals (*opposite*, *top*) which immediately draws the viewer's attention.

The horizon is a key feature of this design. The photographic horizon is reinforced by a long line of text and the silhouette of a lone surfer looking out to sea, which align to create an alluring atmosphere.

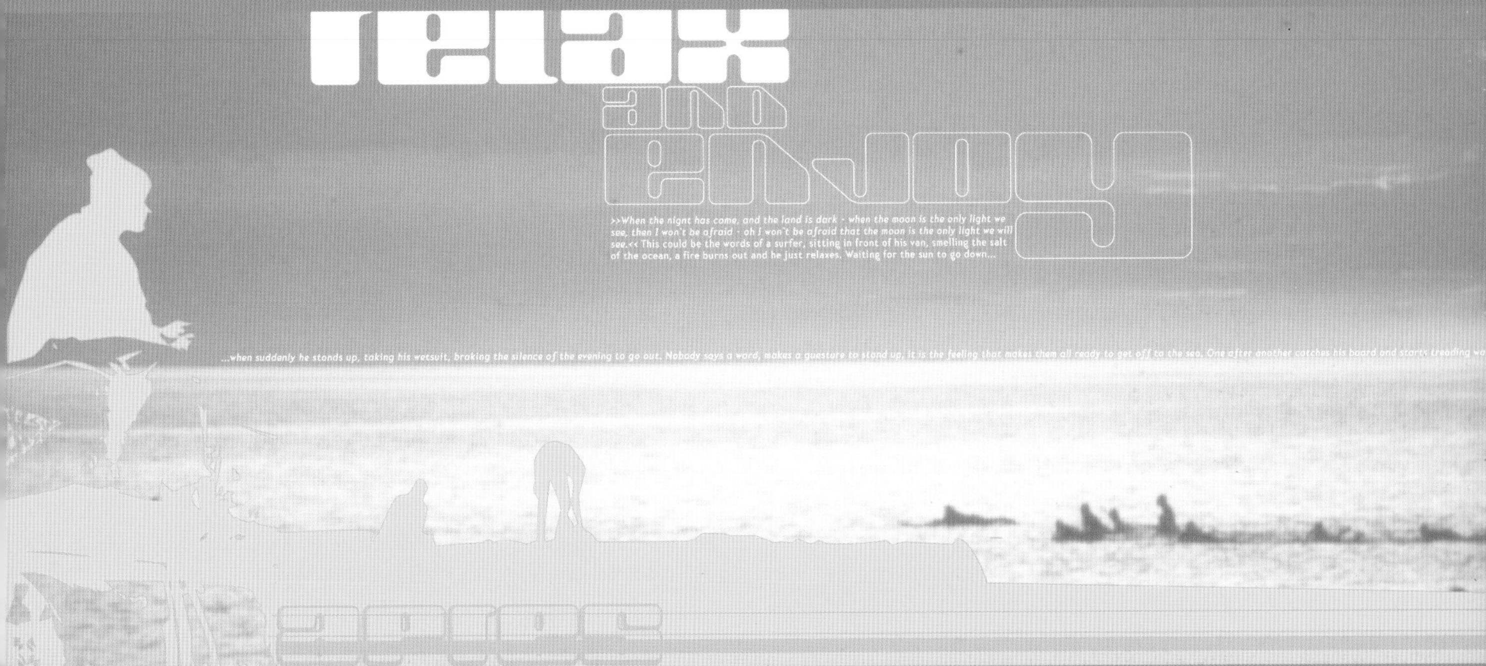

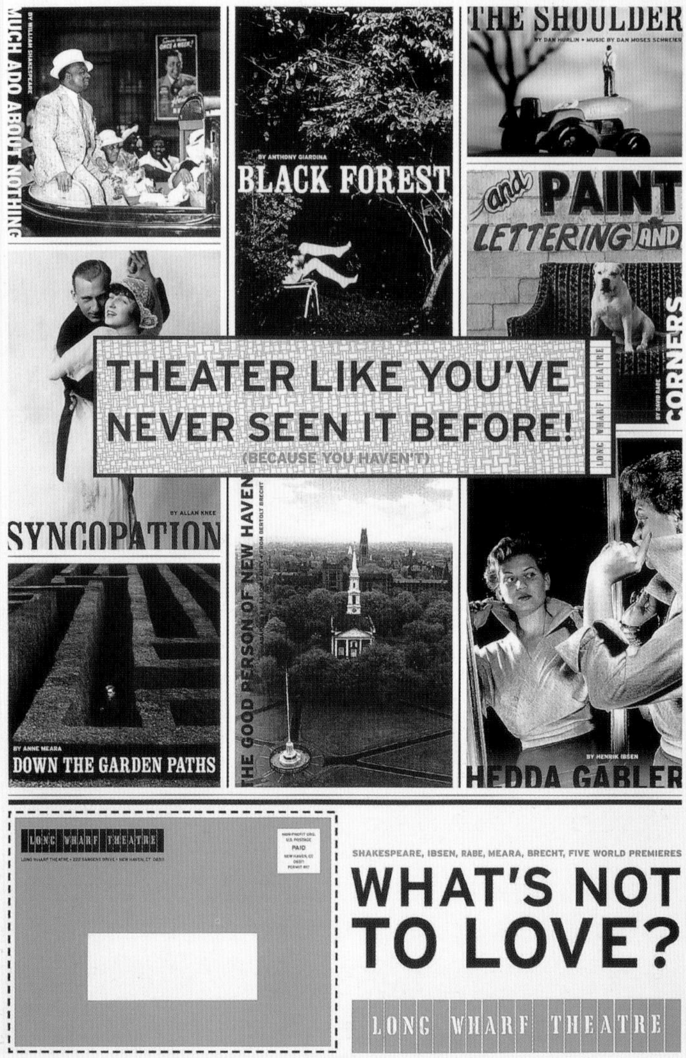

Long Wharf Theatre

To represent eight different elements (plays, in this case) in one piece is always difficult. However, an interesting and pleasing unity has been achieved by the clever use of duotone images (*above*). A different typeface or type size has been adopted for each play and this device has been repeated on the back (*opposite*) to help segregate a mass of information: individual production notes, special ticket deals, an introduction by the Artistic Director, a seating plan, and booking form. The mix-and-match approach to the typography and the use of a limited color palette gives this side the attractive period feel of a page of old advertisements.

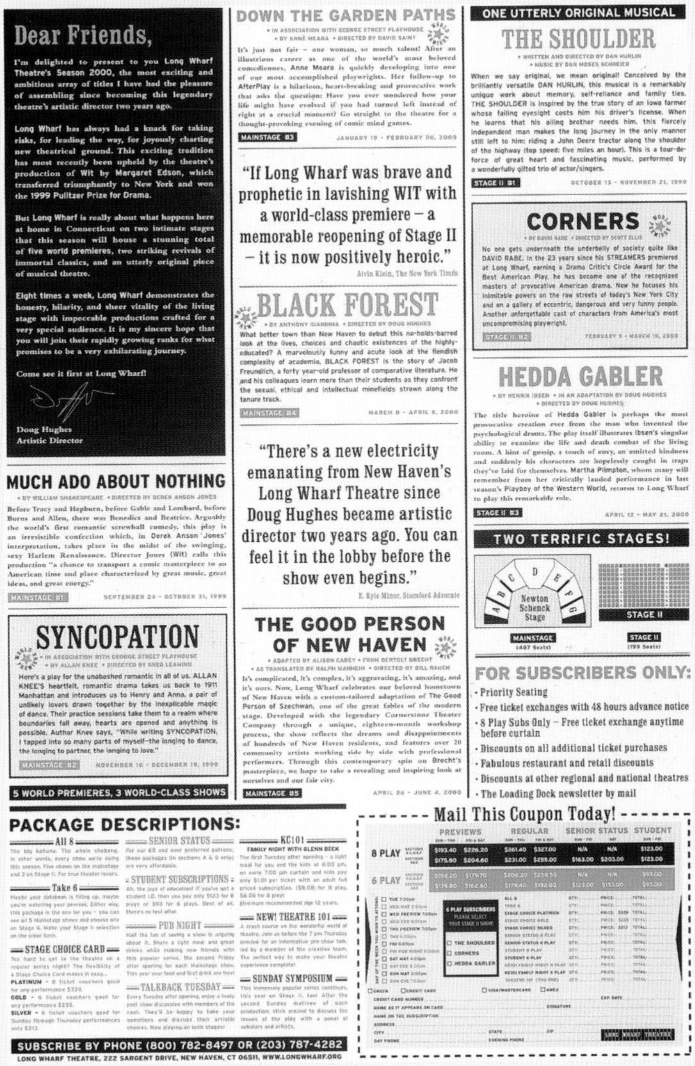

Dear Friends,

I'm delighted to present to you Long Wharf Theatre's Season 2000, the most exciting and ambitious array of titles I have had the pleasure of assembling since becoming this legendary theatre's artistic director two years ago.

Long Wharf has always had a knack for taking risks, for leading the way, for joyously charting new theatrical ground. This exciting tradition has most recently been upheld by the theatre's production of Wit by Margaret Edson, which transferred triumphantly to New York and won the 1999 Pulitzer Prize for Drama.

But Long Wharf is really about what happens here at home in Connecticut on two intimate stages that this season will house a stunning total of five world premieres, two striking revivals of immortal classics, and an utterly original piece of musical theatre.

Eight times a week, Long Wharf demonstrates the honesty, hilarity, and sheer vitality of the living stage with impeccable productions crafted for a very special audience. It is my sincere hope that you will join their rapidly growing ranks for what promises to be a very exhilarating journey.

Come see it first at Long Wharf!

Doug Hughes
Artistic Director

MUCH ADO ABOUT NOTHING

• BY WILLIAM SHAKESPEARE • DIRECTED BY DEREK ANSON JONES

Before Tracy and Hepburn, before Gable and Lombard, before Burns and Allen, there was Benedict and Beatrice. Arguably the world's first romantic screwball comedy, this play is an irresistible confection which, in Derek Anson Jones' interpretation, takes place in the midst of the swinging, sexy Harlem Renaissance. Director Jones (Wit) calls this production "a chance to transport a comic masterpiece to an American time and place characterized by great music, great ideas, and great energy."

MAINSTAGE #1 SEPTEMBER 24 - OCTOBER 31, 1999

SYNCOPATION

• IN ASSOCIATION WITH GEORGE STREET PLAYHOUSE • BY ALLAN KNEE • DIRECTED BY GREG LEAMING

Here's a play for the unabashed romantic in all of us. ALLAN KNEE'S heartfelt, romantic drama takes us back to 1911 Manhattan and introduces us to Henry and Anna, a pair of unlikely lovers drawn together by the inexplicable magic of dance. Their practice sessions take them to a realm where boundaries fall away, hearts are opened and anything is possible. Author Knee says, "While writing SYNCOPATION, I tapped into so many parts of myself–the longing to dance, the longing to partner, the longing to love."

MAINSTAGE #2 NOVEMBER 16 - DECEMBER 19, 1999

5 WORLD PREMIERES, 3 WORLD-CLASS SHOWS

DOWN THE GARDEN PATHS

• IN ASSOCIATION WITH GEORGE STREET PLAYHOUSE • BY ANNE MEARA • DIRECTED BY DAVID SAINT

It's just not fair – one woman, so much talent! After an illustrious career as one of the world's most beloved comediennes, Anne Meara is quickly developing into one of our most accomplished playwrights. Her follow-up to AfterPlay is a hilarious, heart-breaking and provocative work that asks the question: Have you ever wondered how your life might have evolved if you had turned left instead of right at a crucial moment? Go straight to the theatre for a thought-provoking evening of comic mind games.

MAINSTAGE #3 JANUARY 19 - FEBRUARY 20, 2000

"If Long Wharf was brave and prophetic in lavishing WIT with a world-class premiere – a memorable reopening of Stage II – it is now positively heroic."

Alvin Klein, The New York Times

BLACK FOREST

• BY ANTHONY GIARDINA • DIRECTED BY DOUG HUGHES

What better town than New Haven to debut this no-holds-barred look at the lives, choices and chaotic existences of the highly-educated? A marvelously funny and acute look at the fiendish complexity of academia, BLACK FOREST is the story of Jacob Freundlich, a forty year-old professor of comparative literature. He and his colleagues learn more than their students as they confront the sexual, ethical and intellectual minefields strewn along the tenure track.

MAINSTAGE #4 MARCH 8 - APRIL 9, 2000

"There's a new electricity emanating from New Haven's Long Wharf Theatre since Doug Hughes became artistic director two years ago. You can feel it in the lobby before the show even begins."

E. Kyle Minor, Stamford Advocate

THE GOOD PERSON OF NEW HAVEN

• ADAPTED BY ALISON CAREY • FROM BERTOLT BRECHT • AS TRANSLATED BY RALPH MANHEIM • DIRECTED BY BILL RAUCH

It's complicated, it's complex, it's aggravating, it's amazing, and it's ours. Now, Long Wharf celebrates our beloved hometown of New Haven with a custom-tailored adaptation of The Good Person of Szechwan, one of the great fables of the modern stage. Developed with the legendary Cornerstone Theater Company through a unique, eighteen-month workshop process, the show reflects the dreams and disappointments of hundreds of New Haven residents, and features over 20 community artists working side by side with professional performers. Through this contemporary spin on Brecht's masterpiece, we hope to take a revealing and inspiring look at ourselves and our fair city.

MAINSTAGE #5 APRIL 26 - JUNE 4, 2000

ONE UTTERLY ORIGINAL MUSICAL

THE SHOULDER

• WRITTEN AND DIRECTED BY DAN HURLIN • MUSIC BY DAN MOSES SCHREIER

When we say original, we mean original! Conceived by the brilliantly versatile DAN HURLIN, this musical is a remarkably unique work about memory, self-reliance and family ties. THE SHOULDER is inspired by the true story of an Iowa farmer whose failing eyesight costs him his driver's license. When he learns that his ailing brother needs him, this fiercely independent man makes the long journey in the only manner still left to him: riding a John Deere tractor along the shoulder of the highway (top speed: five miles an hour). This is a tour-de-force of great heart and fascinating music, performed by a wonderfully gifted trio of actor/singers.

STAGE II #1 OCTOBER 13 - NOVEMBER 21, 1999

CORNERS

• BY DAVID RABE • DIRECTED BY SCOTT ELLIS

No one gets underneath the underbelly of society quite like DAVID RABE. In the 23 years since his STREAMERS premiered at Long Wharf, earning a Drama Critic's Circle Award for the Best American Play, he has become one of the recognized masters of provocative American drama. Now he focuses his inimitable powers on the raw streets of today's New York City and on a gallery of eccentric, dangerous and very funny people. Another unforgettable cast of characters from America's most uncompromising playwright.

STAGE II #2 FEBRUARY 9 - MARCH 19, 2000

HEDDA GABLER

• BY HENRIK IBSEN • IN AN ADAPTATION BY DOUG HUGHES • DIRECTED BY DOUG HUGHES

The title heroine of Hedda Gabler is perhaps the most provocative creation ever from the man who invented the psychological drama. The play itself illustrates Ibsen's singular ability to examine the life and death combat of the living room. A hint of gossip, a touch of envy, an omitted kindness and suddenly his characters are hopelessly caught in traps they've laid for themselves. Martha Plimpton, whom many will remember from her critically lauded performance in last season's Playboy of the Western World, returns to Long Wharf to play this remarkable role.

STAGE II #3 APRIL 12 - MAY 21, 2000

TWO TERRIFIC STAGES!

A B C D E F G
Newton Schenck Stage
STAGE II
MAINSTAGE (487 Seats)
STAGE II (199 Seats)

FOR SUBSCRIBERS ONLY:

- Priority Seating
- Free ticket exchanges with 48 hours advance notice
- 8 Play Subs Only – Free ticket exchange anytime before curtain
- Discounts on all additional ticket purchases
- Fabulous restaurant and retail discounts
- Discounts at other regional and national theatres
- The Loading Dock newsletter by mail

PACKAGE DESCRIPTIONS:

All 8
The big kahuna. The whole shebang. In other words, every show we're doing this season. Five shows on the mainstage and 3 on Stage II. For true theater lovers.

Take 6
Maybe your datebook is filling up, maybe you're watching your pennies. Either way, this package is the one for you – you can see all 5 Mainstage shows and choose one on Stage II. Make your Stage II selection on the order form.

STAGE CHOICE CARD
Too hard to get to the theatre on a regular series night? The flexibility of a Stage Choice Card makes it easy...
PLATINUM - 8 ticket vouchers good for any performance $339.
GOLD - 6 ticket vouchers good for any performance $255.
SILVER - 6 ticket vouchers good for Sunday through Thursday performances only $213.

SENIOR STATUS
For our 65 and over preferred patrons, these packages (in sections A & G only) are very affordable.

STUDENT SUBSCRIPTIONS
Ah, the joys of education! If you've got a student I.D. then you pay only $123 for 8 plays or $93 for 6 plays. Best of all, there's no test after.

PUB NIGHT
Half the fun of seeing a show is arguing about it. Share a light meal and great drinks while making new friends with this popular series, the second Friday after opening for each Mainstage show. This year your food and first drink are free!

TALKBACK TUESDAY
Every Tuesday after opening, enjoy a lively post show discussion with members of the cast. They'll be happy to take your questions and discuss their artistic choices. Now playing on both stages!

KC101
FAMILY NIGHT WITH GLENN BECK
The first Tuesday after opening – a light meal for you and the kids at 6:00 pm, an early 7:00 pm curtain and kids pay only $1.01 per ticket with an adult full priced subscription. ($8.08 for 8 plays, $6.06 for 6 plays)
Minimum recommended age 12 years.

NEW! THEATRE 101
A crash course on the wonderful world of theatre. Join us before the 7 pm Thursday preview for an informative pre-show talk, led by a member of the creative team. The perfect way to make your theatre experience complete!

SUNDAY SYMPOSIUM
This immensely popular series continues, this year on Stage II, too! After the second Sunday matinee of each production, stick around to discuss the issues of the play with a panel of scholars and artists.

SUBSCRIBE BY PHONE (800) 782-8497 OR (203) 787-4282
LONG WHARF THEATRE, 222 SARGENT DRIVE, NEW HAVEN, CT 06511, WWW.LONGWHARF.ORG

Mail This Coupon Today!

	PREVIEWS		REGULAR		SENIOR STATUS		STUDENT
8 PLAY	$193.40	$226.20	$261.40	$327.00	N/A	N/A	$123.00
	$175.80	$204.60	$231.00	$255.00	$163.00	$203.00	$123.00
6 PLAY	$154.20	$179.70	$208.20	$259.50	N/A	N/A	$93.00
	$118.80	$162.60	$179.40	$192.00	$123.00	$153.00	$93.00

6 PLAY SUBSCRIBERS PLEASE SELECT YOUR STAGE II SHOW
THE SHOULDER
CORNERS
HEDDA GABLER

CHECK CREDIT CARD VISA/MASTERCARD AMEX
CREDIT CARD NUMBER EXP. DATE
NAME AS IT APPEARS ON CARD SIGNATURE
NAME ON THE SUBSCRIPTION
ADDRESS
CITY STATE ZIP
DAY PHONE EVENING PHONE

Designer
Sandra Planeta

Art Director
Drew Hodges

Design Company
Spot Design

Country of Origin
USA

Description of Artwork
A direct mailout program and booking form for the Long Wharf Theatre's 1999/2000 season.

Page Dimensions
152 x 204 mm
6 x 8 in

Format
Direct mailout

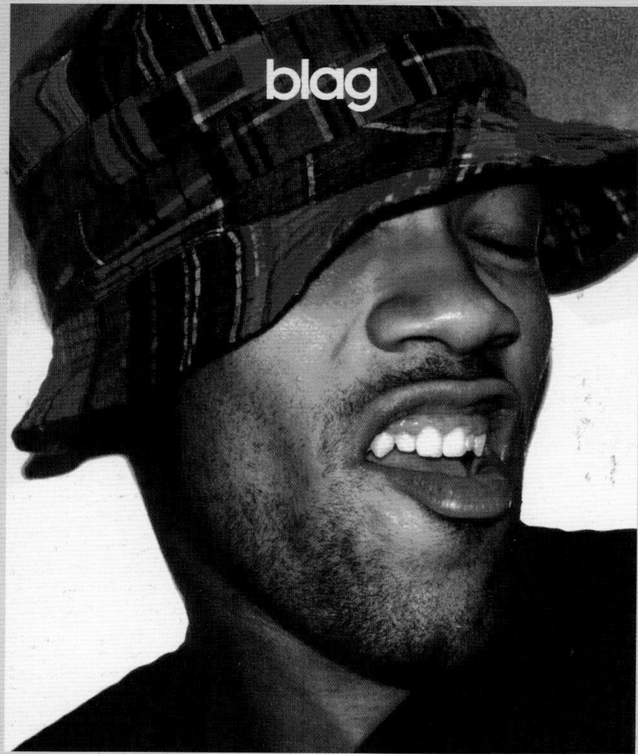

Designers
Yacht Associates and friends

Illustrator
Mark Thomson (departures spread)

Photographers
S. Edwards (cover), Red James (Japanese spread), Barnaby Wallace (departures spread)

Design Company
Yacht Associates

Country of Origin
UK

Description of Artwork
162-page book

Page Dimensions
245 x 303 mm
$9^5/_8$ x 12 in

Format
Book

Blag—The Book

This high-end fashion and style book treats the reader to a collage of verbal explanations and imagery on a diverse selection of subjects. The bewildering range in the style of images, along with the title, provokes the reader to assess and reassess the intention and meaning of the book. Printed on matt paper, in contrast to the usual glossy magazine stock, the whole book can be seen to be questioning the fashion-magazine-as-artifact status quo.

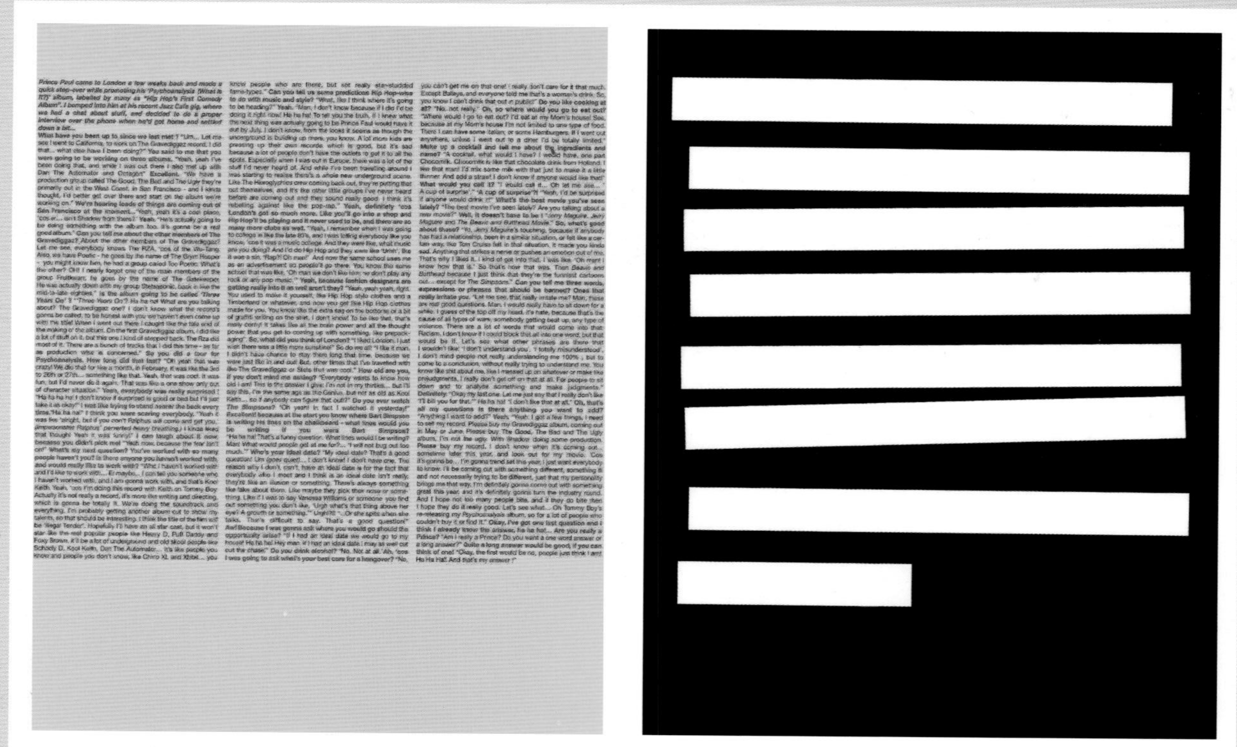

TOKYO [illegible] RED JAMES - www.redjam.com - red@redjam.com page 112 · 113

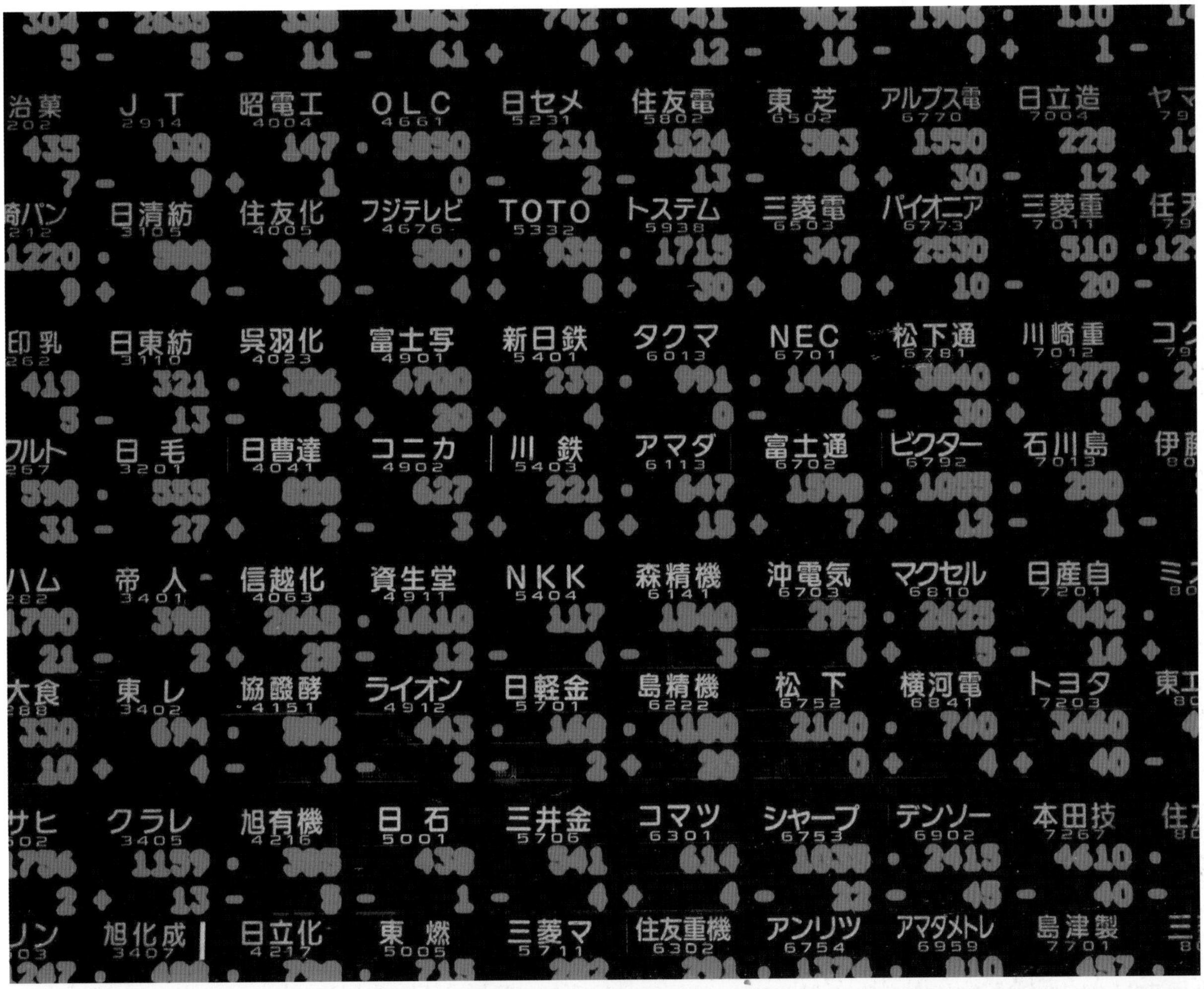

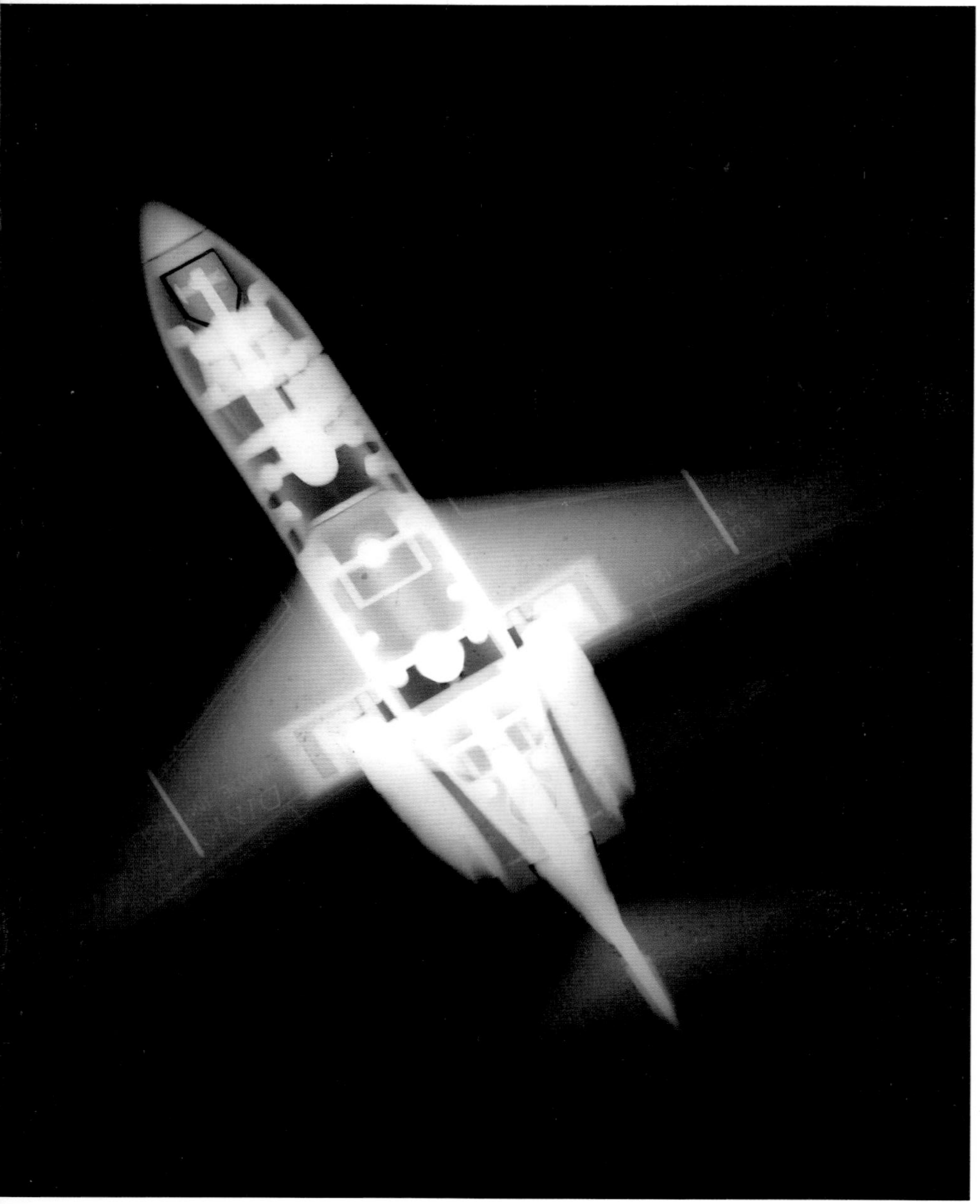

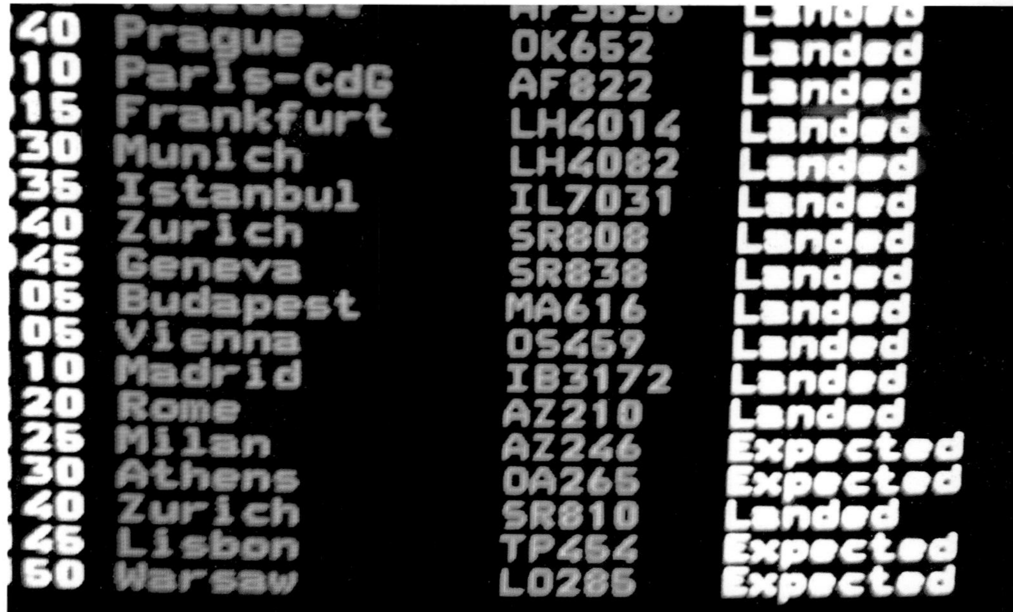
40 Prague OK652 Landed
10 Paris-CdG AF822 Landed
15 Frankfurt LH4014 Landed
30 Munich LH4082 Landed
35 Istanbul IL7031 Landed
40 Zurich SR808 Landed
45 Geneva SR838 Landed
05 Budapest MA616 Landed
05 Vienna OS459 Landed
10 Madrid IB3172 Landed
20 Rome AZ210 Landed
25 Milan AZ246 Expected
30 Athens OA265 Expected
40 Zurich SR810 Landed
45 Lisbon TP454 Expected
50 Warsaw LO285 Expected

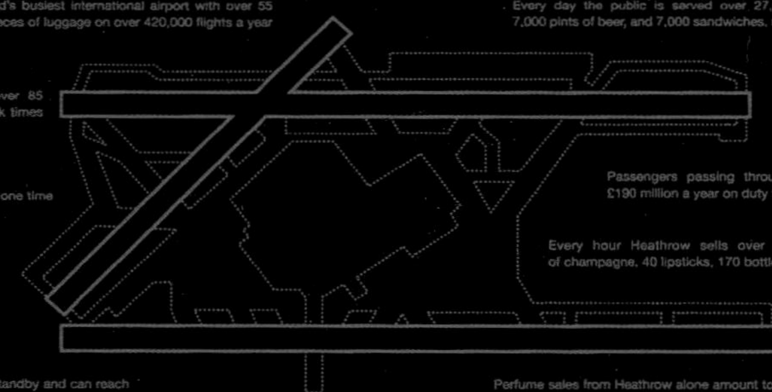
HEATHROW AIRPORT, LONDON is the world's busiest international airport with over 55 million passengers a year, taking 57 million pieces of luggage on over 420,000 flights a year
Every day the public is served over 27,000 cups of tea & coffee 7,000 pints of beer, and 7,000 sandwiches, making 1 tonne of litter daily
Open 24 hours, 365 days a year, over 85 aircraft land & take off per hour at peak times
Over 500 taxis are waiting at the airport at any one time
Passengers passing through Heathrow spend over £190 million a year on duty free, food, car hire & parking
Every hour Heathrow sells over 350 bottles of whiskey, 20 bottles of champagne, 40 lipsticks, 170 bottles of perfume & 60 bottles of aftershave
13 million vehicles a year enter the terminal and there are 16,800 parking spaces available
100 fire-fighters are on 24 hour standby and can reach any part of the 3,000 acre airport in less than 2 minutes
Perfume sales from Heathrow alone amount to 10% of the entire British market, book sales account for 6% of the national market
Grass on the airport is kept constantly at 8 inches high to avoid birds settling, at this height the birds can not spot predators so do not land
The Swatch Shop sells 78,000 watches a year from a space the size of an average sitting room

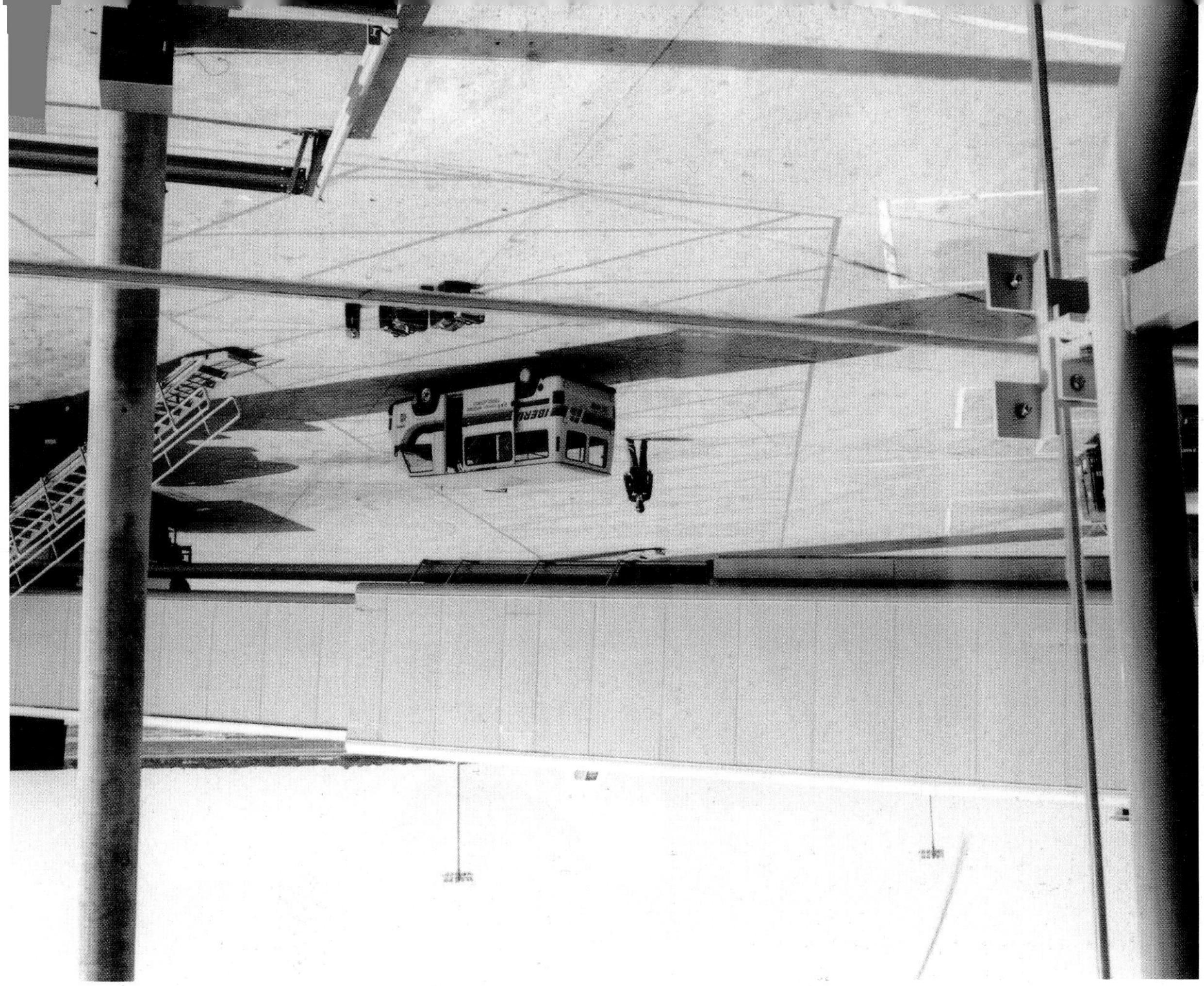

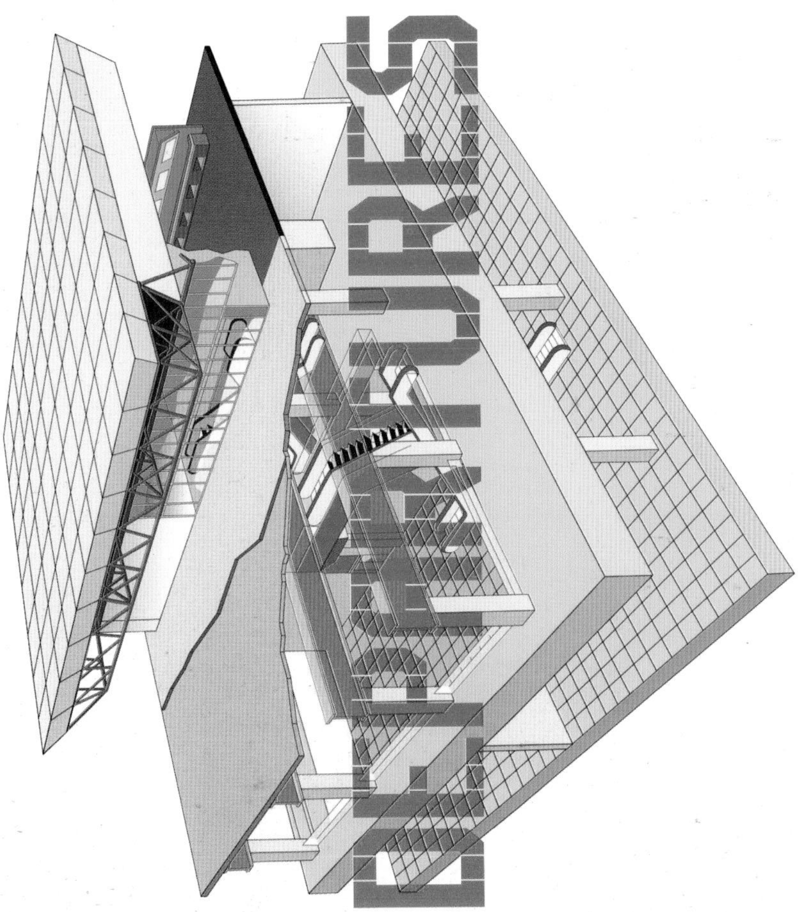
DEPARTURES

BAŞTAN AŞAĞI YEPYENİ NESNELER

Dünyanın ortasında bir Schuylkill'den çıkageldi
Küçük filolar, çağrılmış-arzulanmış, içlerinde taşıyarak

Dost gölgelerini, onun tanıdığı, herbiri getiriyordu
yaptığını, onun inandığı sudan ve arzudan,

Yerkürenin ortasında yaşayan, yarı insan
Ustalar, işlev neymiş bilmeyen, bilmek de istemeyen.

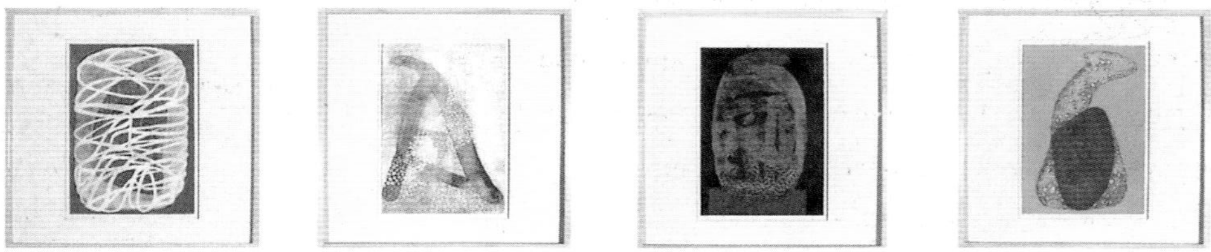

Bu adamcıklar zamanın pasıyla pas yeşili
Kanolarının küreklerini çeke çeke, binlerce binlerce.

Öyle biçimlerdeydiler ki, öyle derde deva biçimler,
Görünce bildi onların ince niyetini,

Anladı ki bu biçimler tam tamına biçimleriydi
Koskoca bir halkın, yaşlanmış düşüne düşüne...

Yatmış yıllanıyorlar belki de onların ataları
Tinicum'ın altında ya da küçük Cohansey'nin.

Wallace Stevens

Seçilmiş Şiirler. *Faber & Faber: Londra, 1965.*
(Çev: Fatih Özgüven - Nihal Koldaş)

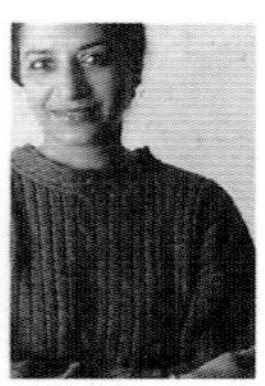

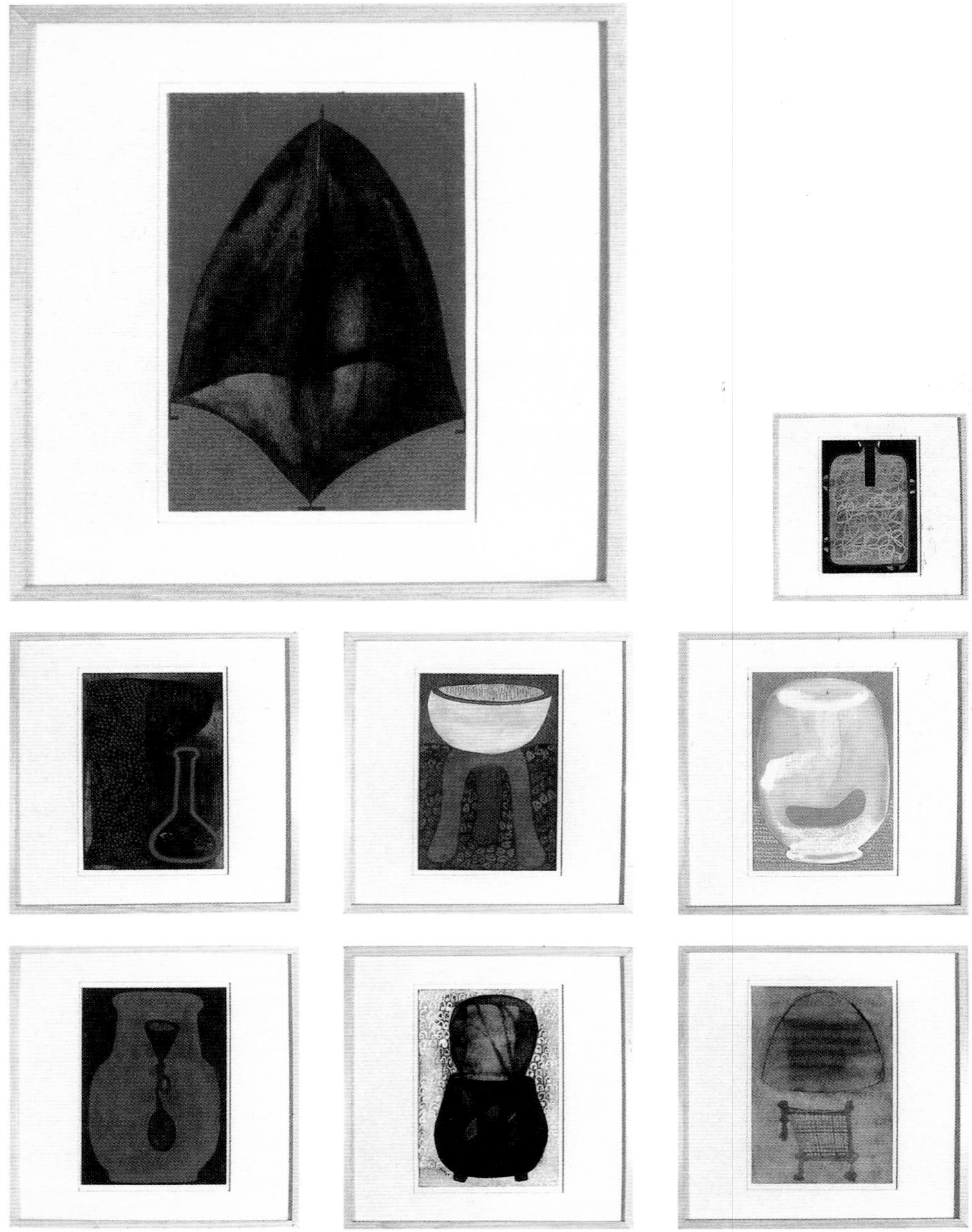

25 Dünya, 1996-1997. Kağıt üzerine suluboya. 17.8 x 12.4 cm. Milano, Studio Guenzani'nin izniyle.

25 Worlds, *1996-1997. Watercolor on paper. 17.8 x 12.4 cm. Courtesy Studio Guenzani, Milan.*

 1964 UTTARSANDA (GUJARAT), HİNDİSTAN DOĞUMLU. YENİ DELHİ'DE YAŞIYOR.

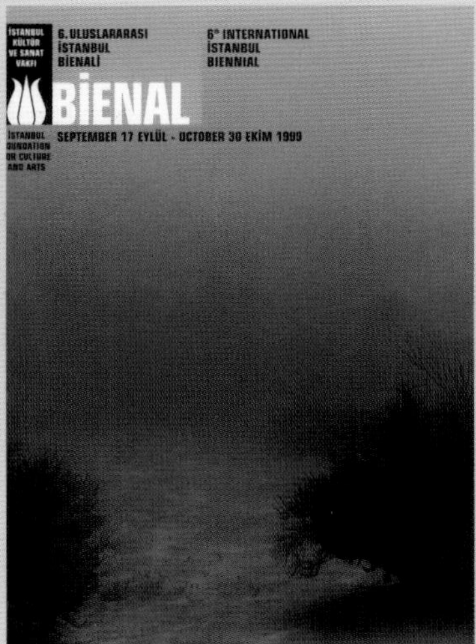

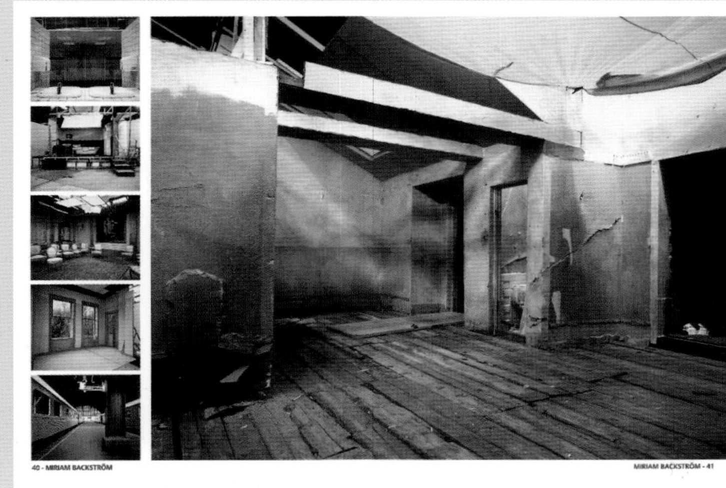

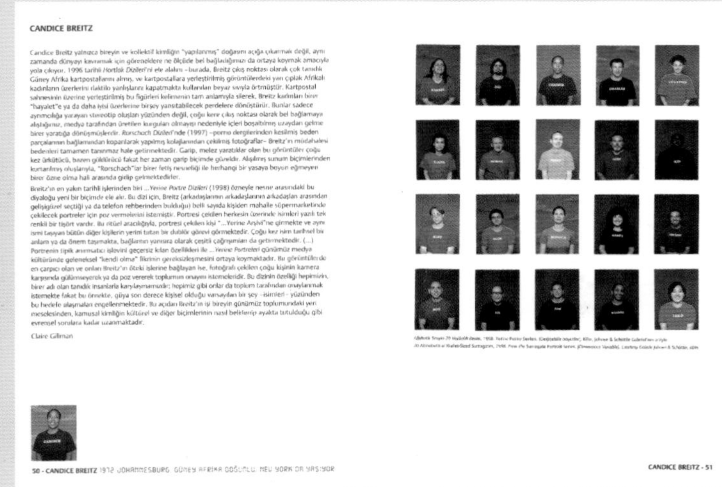

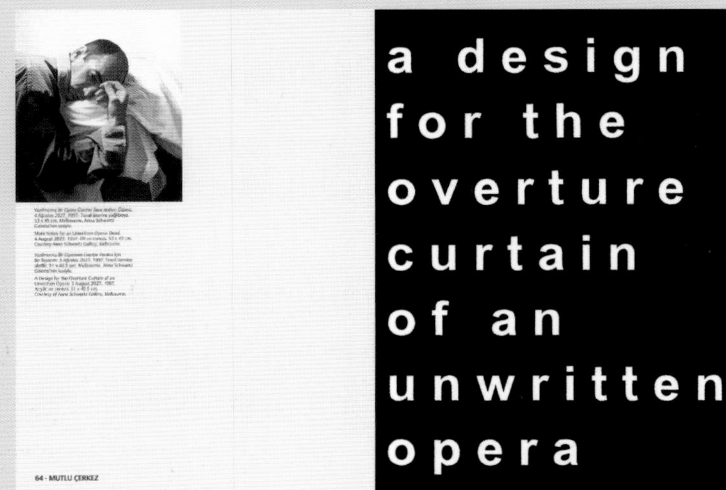

Designers
Gülizar Çepoğlu, Aysun Pelvan

Art Director
Gülizar Çepoğlu

Photographers
Various

Design Company
Gülizar Çepoğlu Graphic Design Co.

Country of Origin
Turkey

Description of Artwork
276-page book for the 6th International Istanbul Biennial fine-art festival. The first of two for each Biennial.

Page Dimensions
165 x 235 mm
$6^1/_2$ x $9^1/_4$ in

Format
Book

6th International Istanbul Biennial

When presenting the work of artists, the layout needs to serve the artworks without compromising the design itself. To anchor these layouts, the designers have used the consistent device of a 'running footer' at the base of each page which includes the folio number and the artist's name. The first page of each section has a small photograph of the artist, their year of birth, and address. Once established, such a layout allows framed images displayed as if in a gallery (*opposite page*) to sit comfortably alongside a more conceptual text-based work (*right*).

Designers
Brad Bartlett, Danielle Foushee

Art Directors
Brad Bartlett, Danielle Foushee

Photographer
Brad Bartlett (cover)

Art College
Cranbrook Academy of Art

Country of Origin
USA

Description of Artwork
144-page book documenting the work of 71 artists graduating from the Cranbrook Academy of Art.

Dimensions
241 x 165 mm
$9^1/_2$ x $6^1/_2$ in

Format
Book

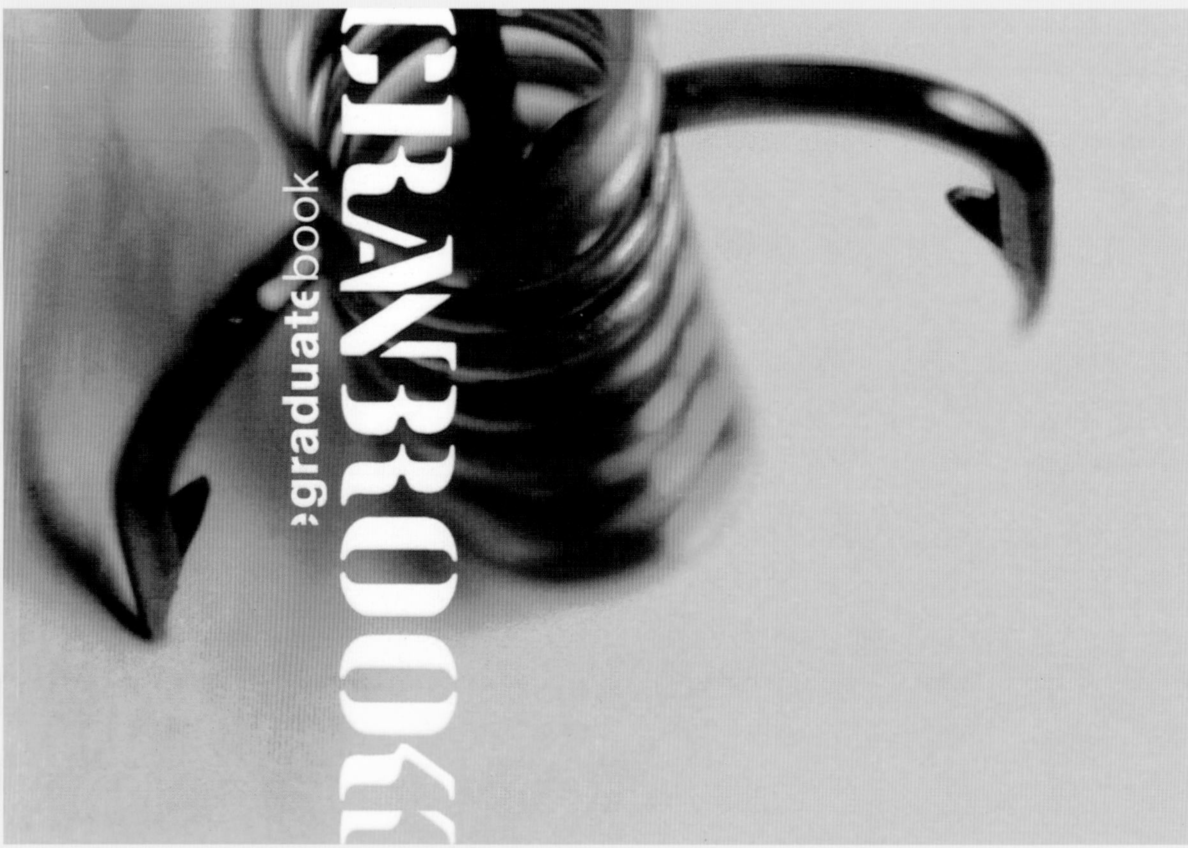

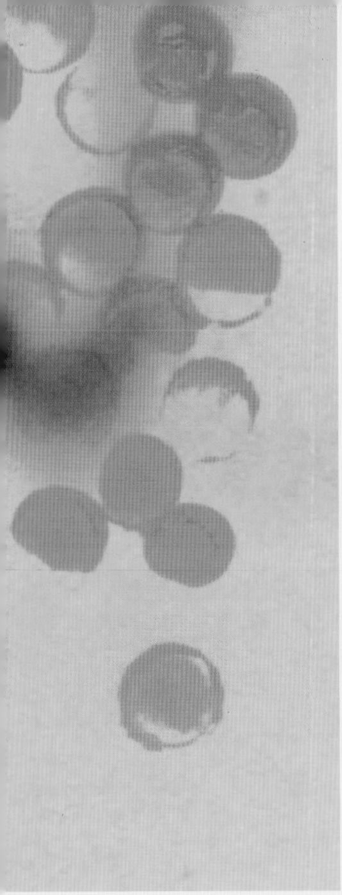

Cranbrook Graduate Book

The unsettling undercurrent generated by the ambiguously threatening image (*opposite, bottom*) contrasts with the clean typography of the word 'Cranbrook' to produce an arresting four-color cover. The inside spreads are economically monochrome yet nonetheless convey the individuality of each student's work.

Below and bottom: the freedom of composition in the first spread is a long way from the subtle formality of the squared-up images of flamingoes in the spread below it. This indicates that when a structure is needed it is there, and when it is less important it need not be imposed.

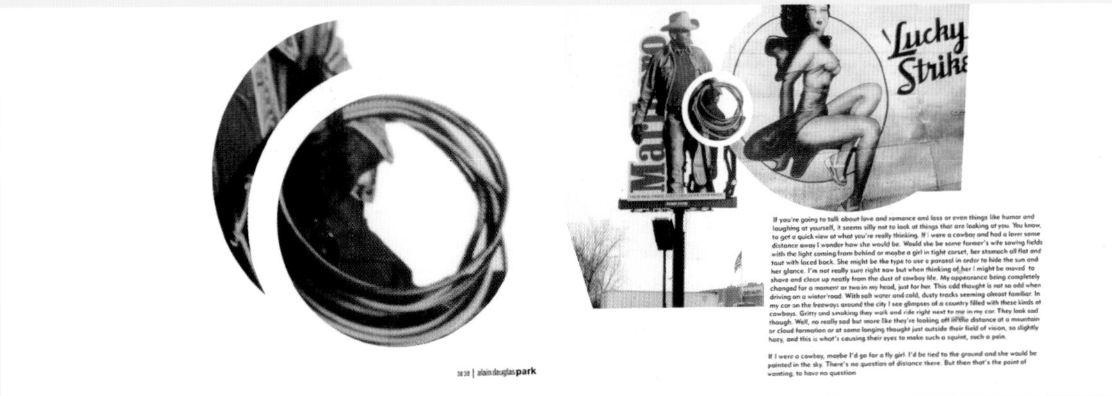

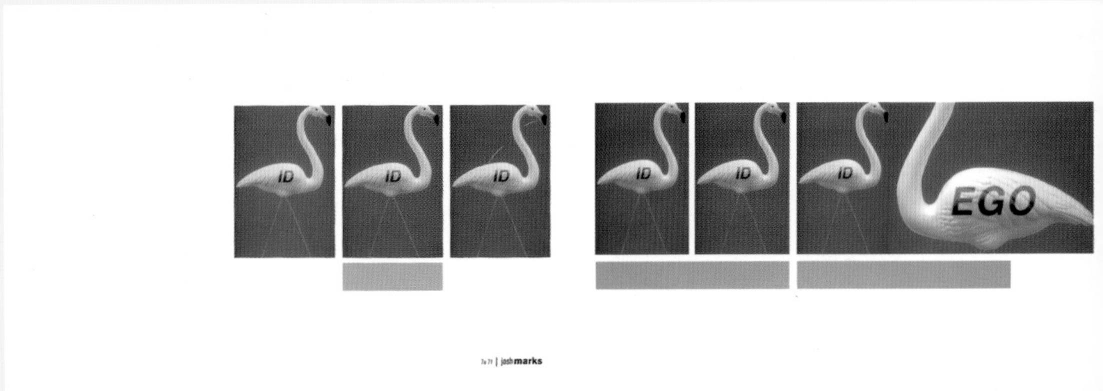

Designers
Dom Raban, Pat Walker

Illustrators
Dom Raban, Pat Walker, Andrew Wilson

Photographer
Mark Harvey

Design Company
Eg.G

Country of Origin
UK

Description of Artwork
Promotional brochure for the 'Year of the Artist'—the UK's largest ever nationwide arts festival.

Page Dimensions
210 x 297 mm
8¹/₄ x 11³/₄ in
Opening to a maximum width of: 940 mm, 37 in

Format
Brochure

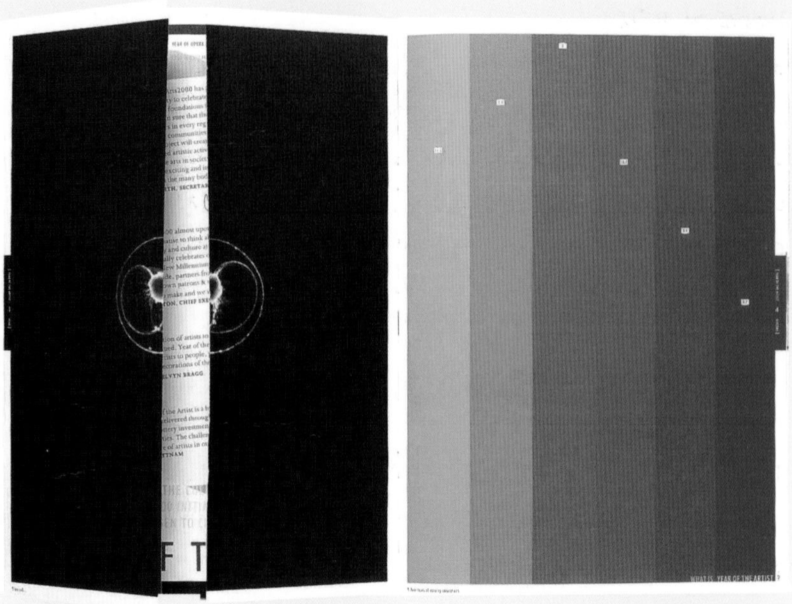

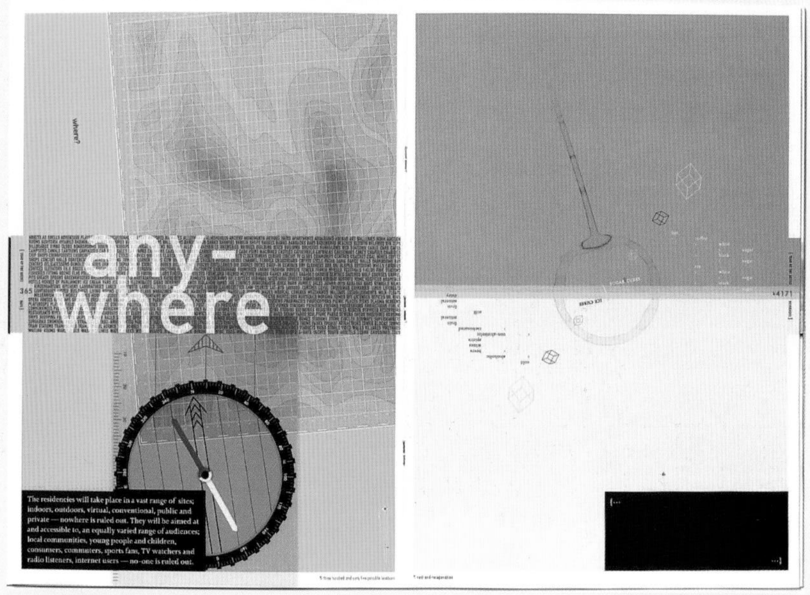

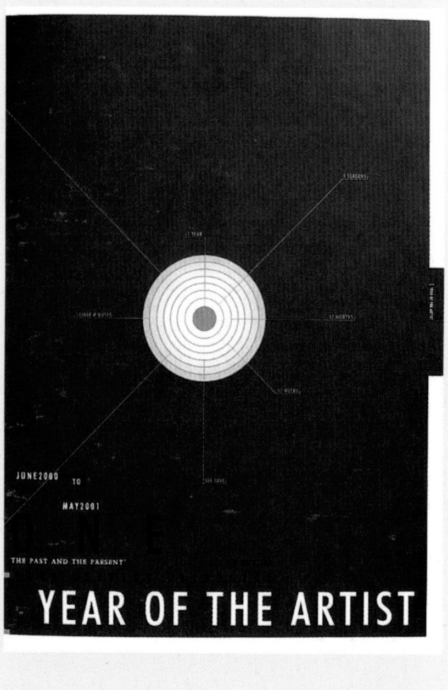

Year of the Artist

Based on the numerical sequence 1 (year), 4 (seasons), 12 (months), 52 (weeks), etc., this brochure is designed to promote the accessibility of contemporary art. Its visual appeal is enhanced by the use of vibrant colors indicating the different sections (*opposite, top right*) and the use of familiar imagery, such as the pull-out street scene. The accessible 'hands-on' nature of the project is shown by the inclusion of a do-it-yourself street cut-out kit (*bottom*).

Special Production Techniques

The use of fold-out pages has allowed the designers to create long landscape images which stretch the limitations of the brochure format and communicate the breadth of this arts festival.

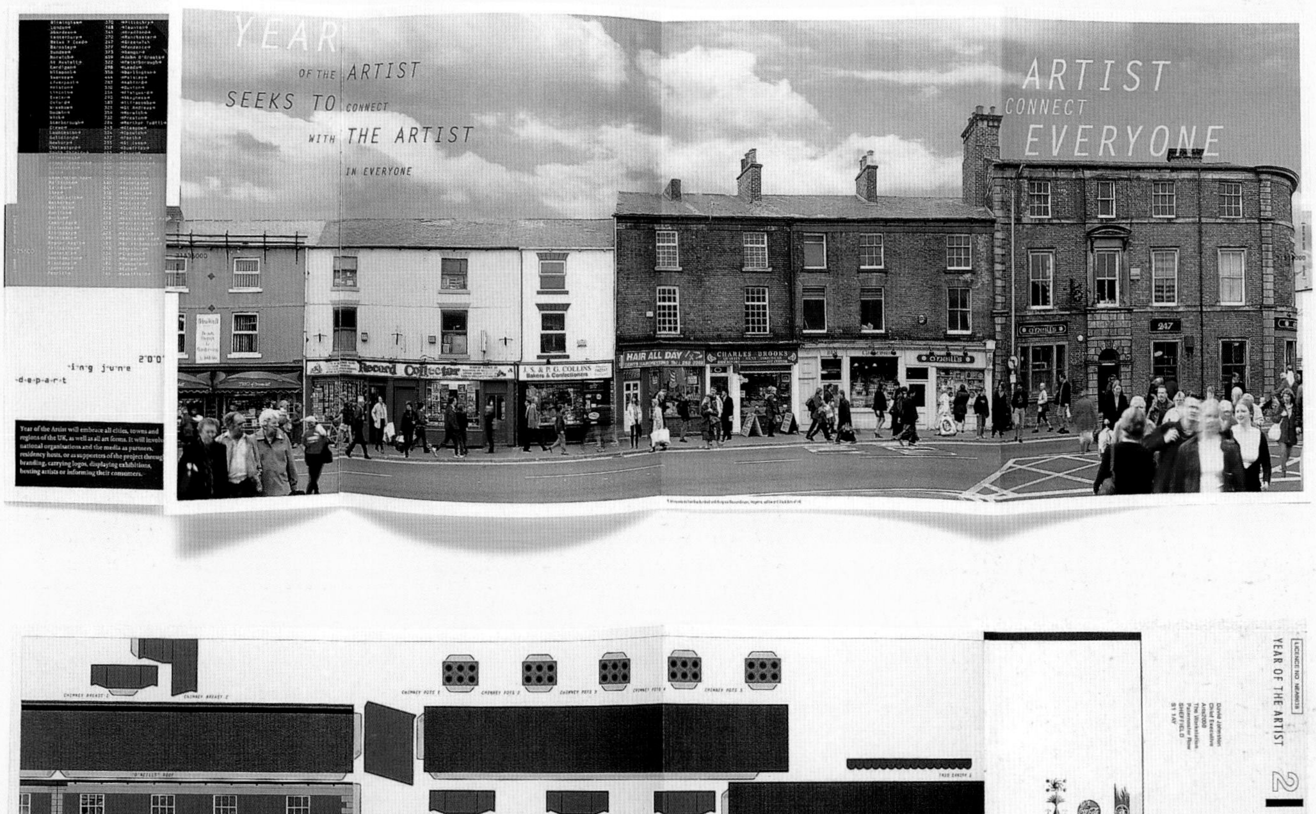

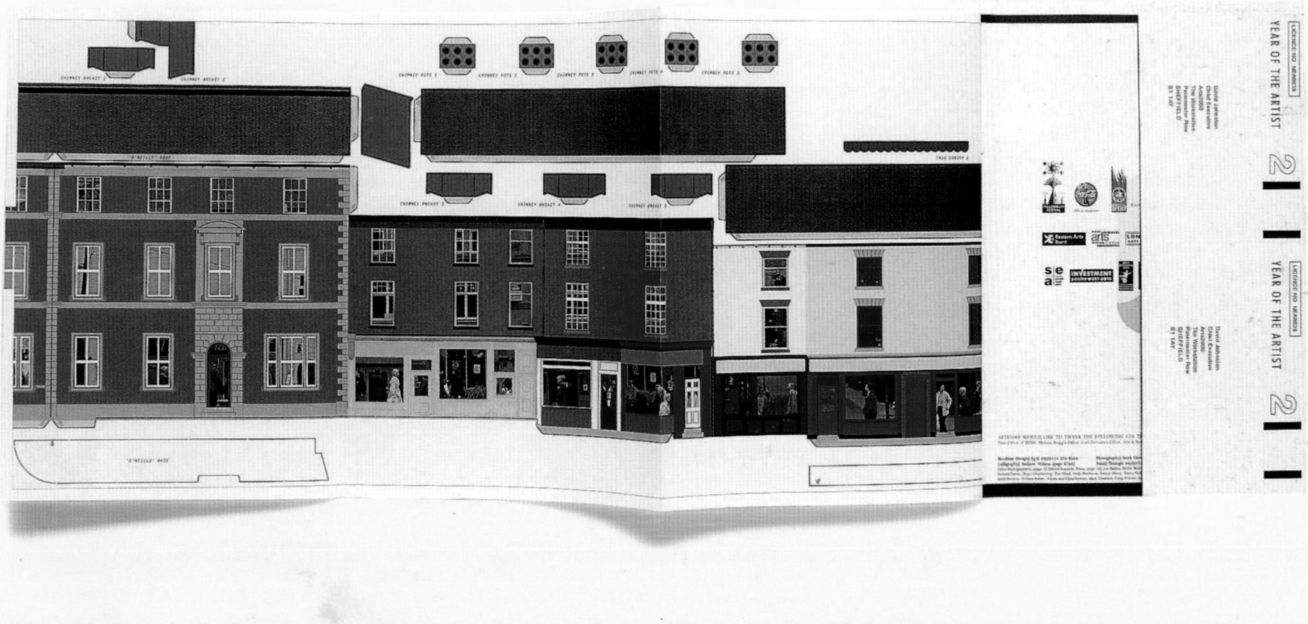

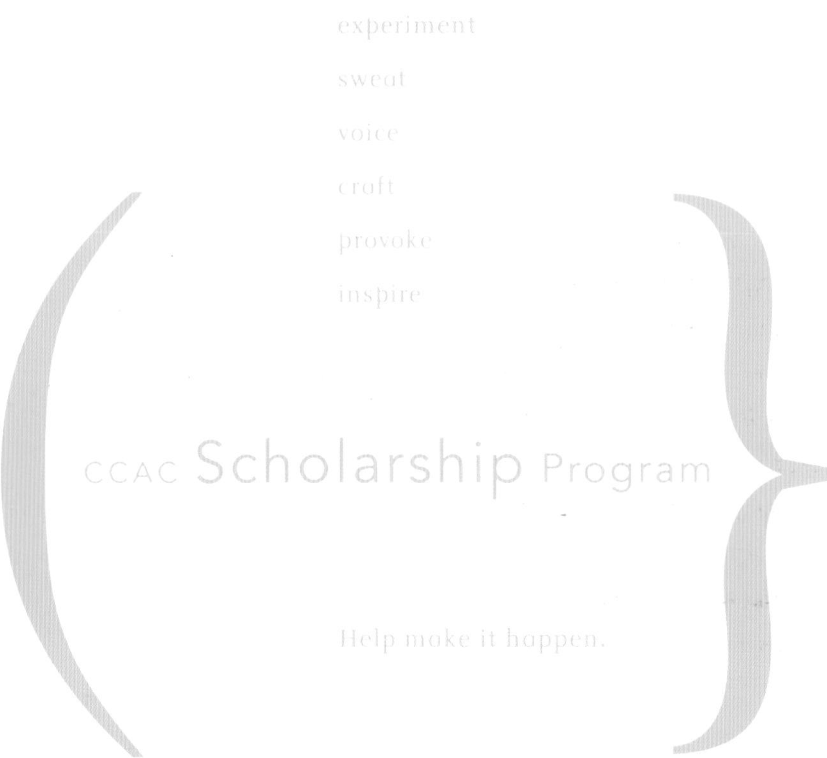

Designer
Bob Aufuldish

Art Director
Bob Aufuldish

Photographer
Douglas Sandberg

Hybrid Tool Designer
Karl Weiser

Design Company
Aufuldish & Warinner

Country of Origin
USA

Description of Artwork
A series of three postcards sent to alumni of the California College of Arts and Crafts to solicit donations to a scholarship fund.

Dimensions
152 x 229 mm
6 x 9 in

Format
Postcards

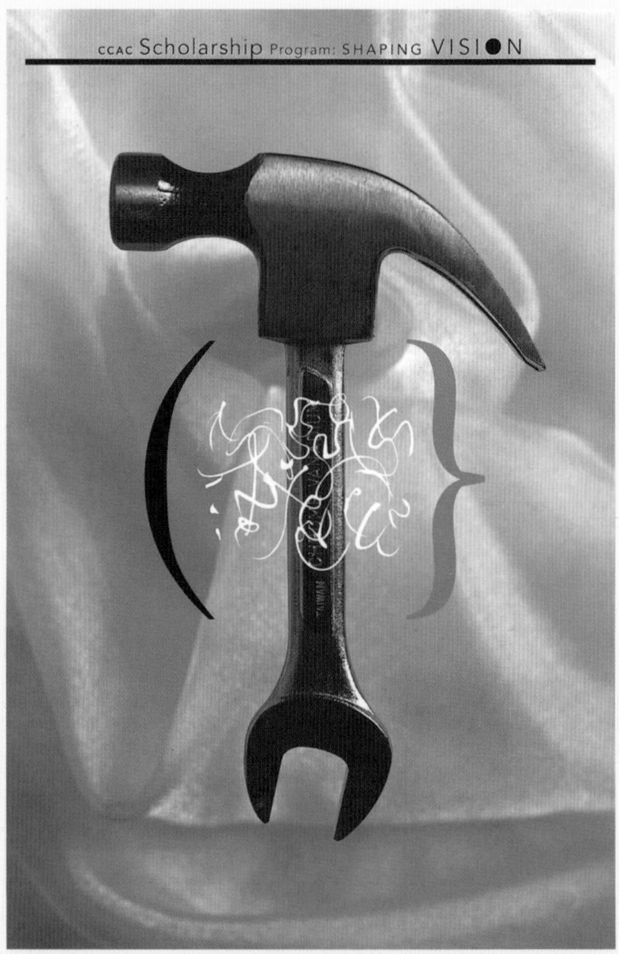

CCAC Scholarship Program

Here, direct and apparently simple imagery is used to make the complex and intangible theme of scholarship immediately accessible. The clarity and unity of the images is enhanced through the use of only two colors—black and metallic silver—and the recurring textile backdrop. The photograph on each card is subtly suggestive of a different process associated with learning—original and unexpected ideas (*left*), individual expression (*center*), and the receiving and understanding of information (*right*). These are reinforced through the use of the abstract, white, central graphic which is itself encapsulated and 'processed' within a variety of parentheses.

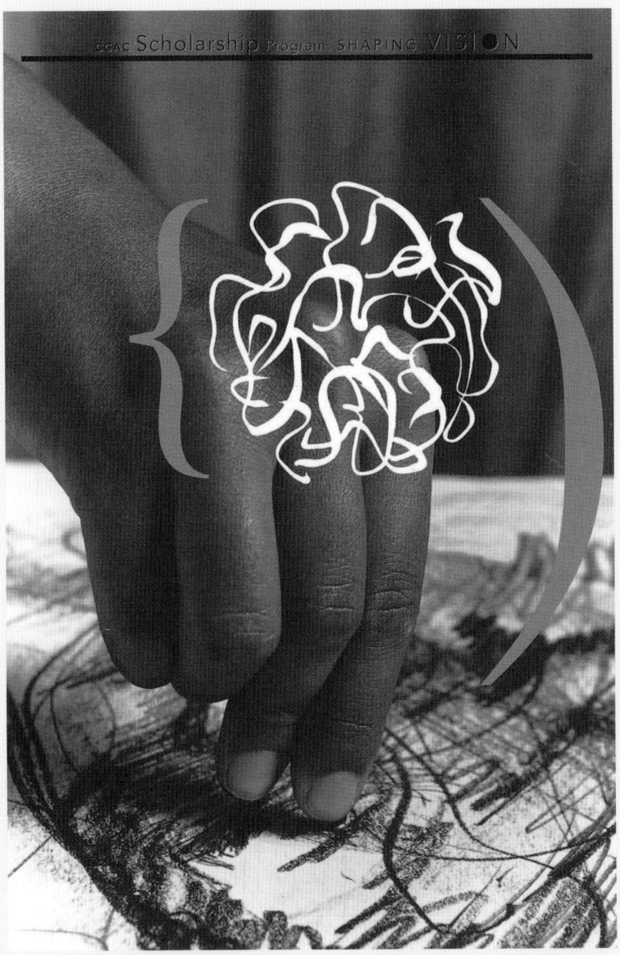

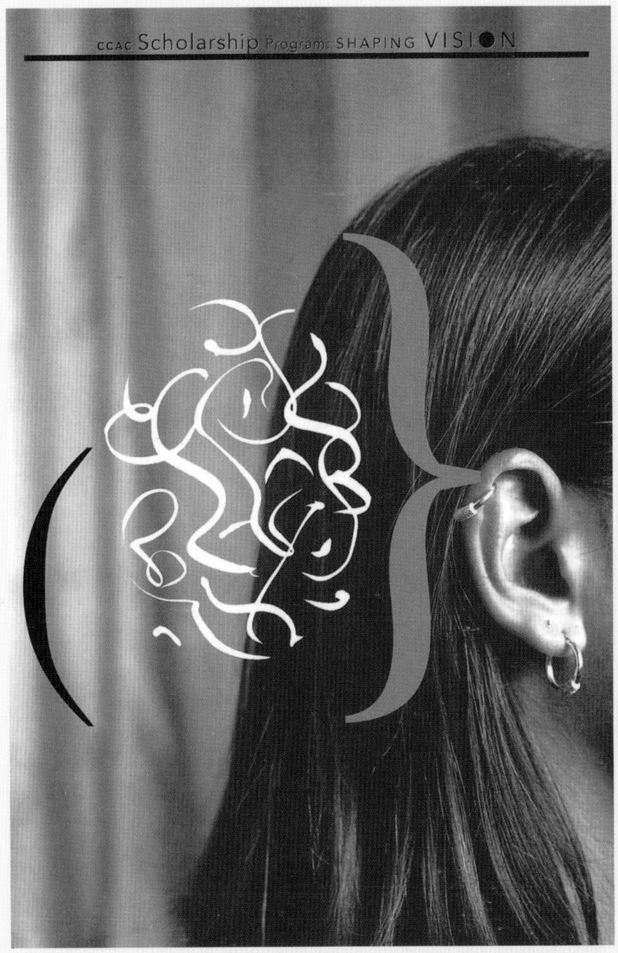

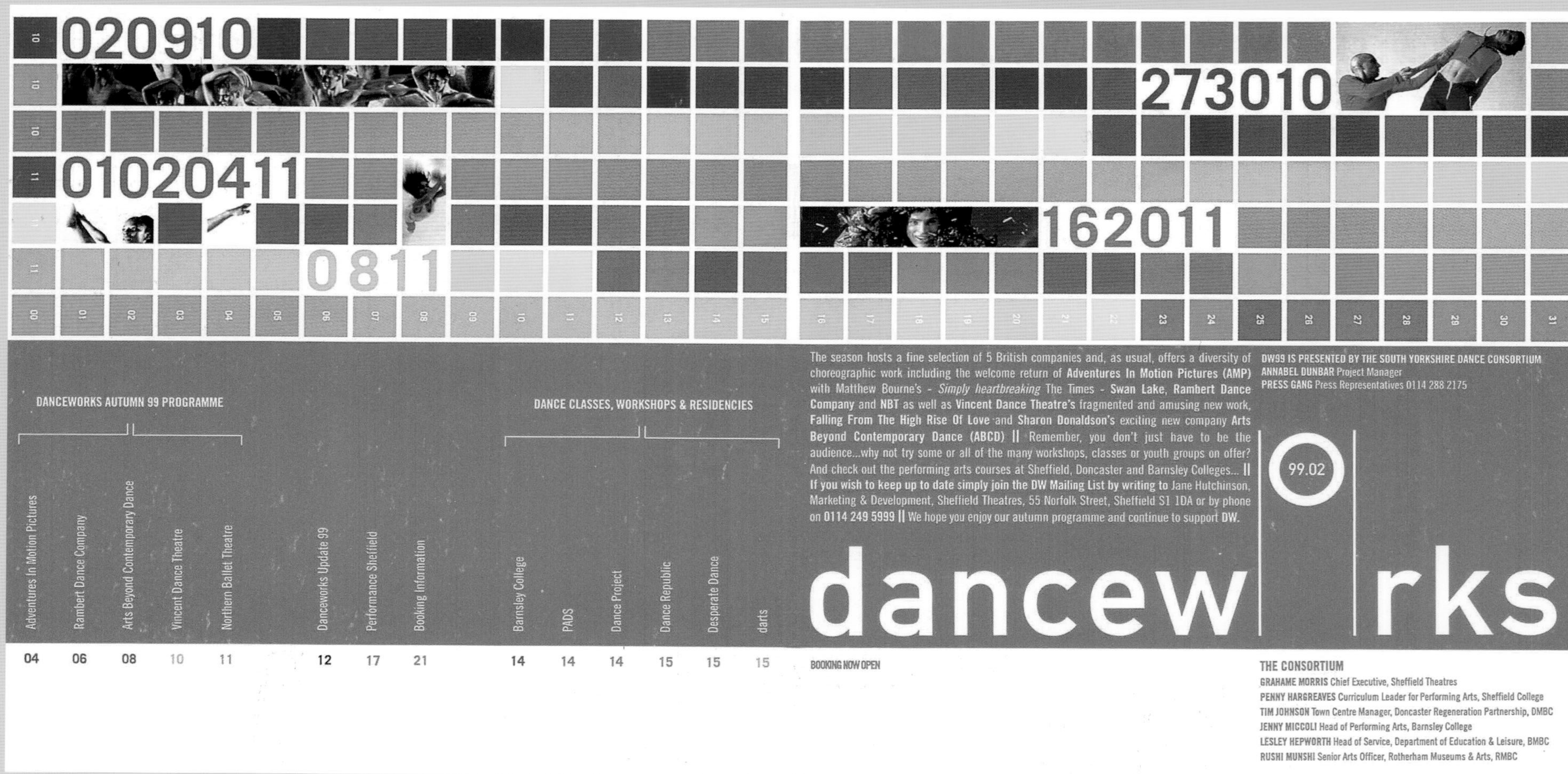

Designers
Dom Raban, Pat Walker

Photographers
Various

Design Company
Eg.G

Country of Origin
UK

Description of Artwork
24-page brochure for the South Yorkshire Dance Consortium.
Second in an annual series of three.

Page Dimensions
205 x 205 mm
8 x 8 in

Format
Brochure

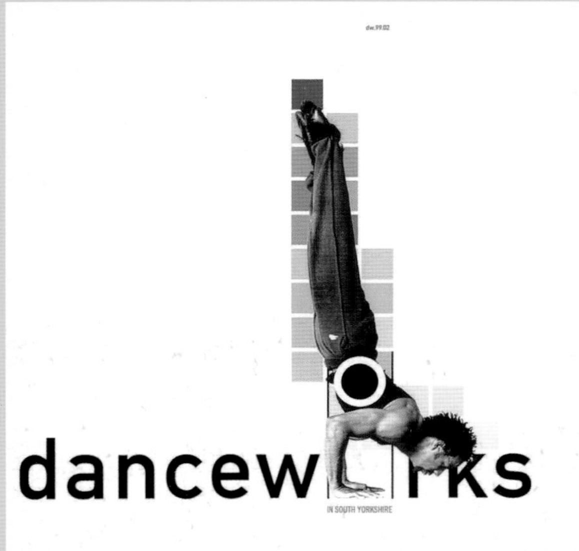

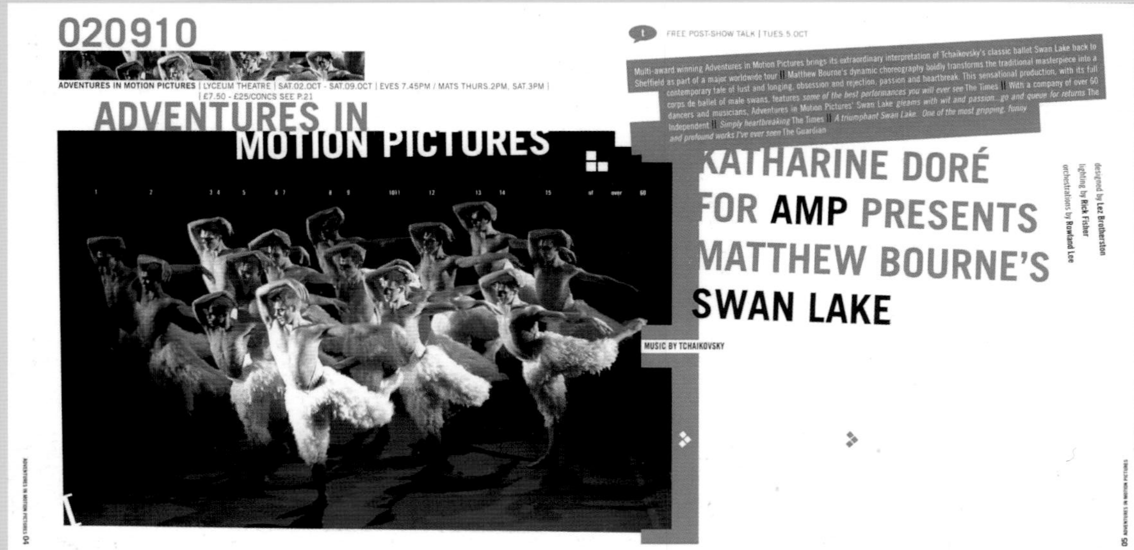

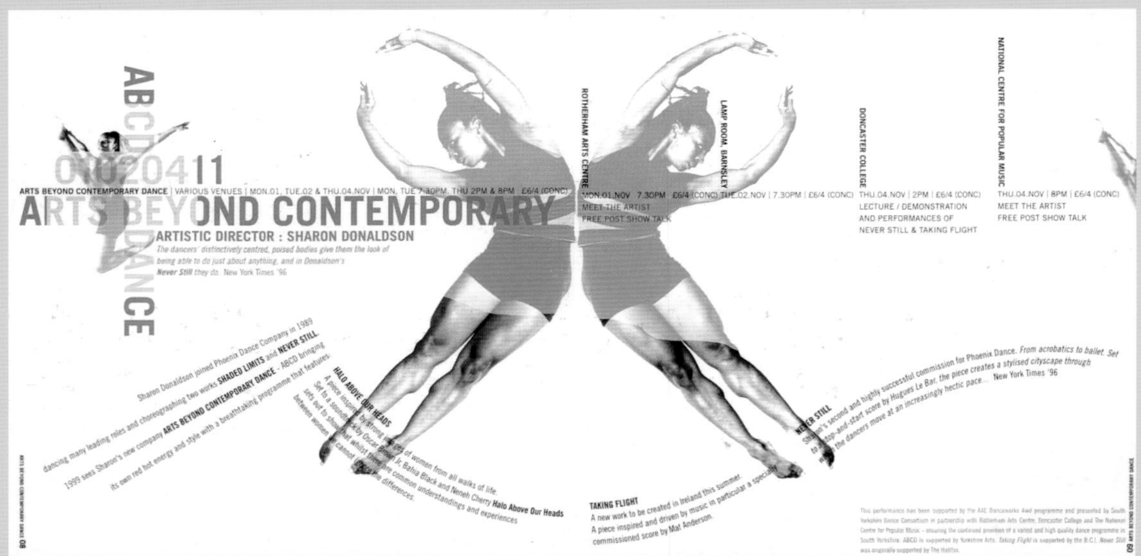

Danceworks

A powerful 'logo' (*above*), strong use of a colored grid (*above and opposite*), and consistent application of typeface and typesize have all been used to erect a framework within which the designers have then been able to play fast and loose with individual images. This approach allows a squared-up layout (*right, top*) to sit comfortably next to a free-flowing spread featuring cutouts (*right*), in which the typography reflects the motion in the leaping figure.

Special Production Techniques

The curved text (*right*) was produced with the use of two design programs: QuarkXPress and Illustrator.

CCAC INSTITUTE PROGRAMS

Unless otherwise noted, all CCAC Institute programs—exhibitions, opening receptions, film screenings, and lectures are free and open to the public. For more information, call 415.551.9210.

EXHIBITION: SAN FRANCISCO

SEARCHLIGHT: CONSCIOUSNESS AT THE MILLENNIUM
September 25–December 11, 1999
Logan Galleries and Carroll Weisel Hall
Montgomery Campus
1111 Eighth Street, San Francisco
Opening reception: Friday, September 24, 7–9 pm, featuring a special guest appearance by Deep Blue Jr.

This exhibition surveys thirty years of international contemporary art to reveal how consciousness has evolved as one of the most compelling artistic themes of our time. The exhibition includes over fifty works by more than thirty artists including Louise Bourgeois, Theresa Hak Kyung Cha, Stan Douglas, Douglas Gordon, Rodney Graham, Gary Hill, Robert Irwin, Iñigo Manglano-Oralle, Agnes Martin, Yoko Ono, Adrian Piper, Ad Reinhardt, Diana Thater, Bill Viola, Gillian Wearing, and La Monte Young and Marian Zazeela.

Logan Galleries
Hours: Monday, Wednesday, Thursday, Friday, and Saturday 11 am–5 pm Tuesday 11 am–9 pm; closed Sunday. Holiday closure: November 25–28

PUBLIC PROGRAMS: SAN FRANCISCO

SEARCHLIGHT: CONSCIOUSNESS AT THE MILLENNIUM PROGRAMS
Unless otherwise indicated, all *Searchlight* programs take place in Timken Lecture Hall on CCAC's Montgomery Campus in San Francisco. For more information, call the CCAC Institute at 415.5519210.

SEARCHLIGHT LECTURE SERIES
Artist Talk: Jörg Herold
Tuesday, September 7, 7:30 pm
In this *Searchlight* pre-opening talk, German conceptual artist and filmmaker Jörg Herold will discuss his work, including the video installation *Körper im Körper*, 1989, featured in the *Searchlight* exhibition. The talk will be followed by a screening of some of the artist's early film works including *Sportfest 69*, 1969–1988, *Beiwerk*, 1985, and *Der Wurstfilm*, 1987. Herold's work has been featured in documenta X (1997), the Venice Biennale (1990 and 1995), Prospect 93, and the Eighth Biennale of Sydney (1992). The *Searchlight* exhibition marks the first time his work has been shown in the United States.

Artist Talk: Stuart Sherman
Tuesday, September 21, 7:30 pm
Performer, video artist, and filmmaker Stuart Sherman will screen a selection of his works and discuss his unique approach to language, time, and mind. Sherman's films and videos

SEARCHLIGHT FILM SERIES
Seven evenings of experimental film explore the nature of conscious experience through the time-based medium of film. Presented by the San Francisco Cinemathèque, this film series was organized by Steve Anker, Irina Leimbacher, and David Sherman.

Dawning of Awareness
Tuesday, October 5, 7:30 pm
These films trace a journey from the origins of consciousness through the development of language to the social order of adulthood. Films include *Epilogue*, 1987, by Matthias Müller, Super-8mm, color, sound, 16 minutes; *Scenes from Under Childhood: Section No. 3*, 1970, by Stan Brakhage, 16 mm, color, silent, 27.5 minutes; *Peggy and Fred in Hell: Prologue*, 1985, by Leslie Thornton, 16mm, b/w, sound, 21 minutes; *Zorns Lemma*, 1970, by Hollis Frampton, 16mm, color, sound, 60 minutes.

Flows of Perception
Tuesday, October 19, 7:30 pm
This program explores the phenomenology of the mind through the experiential and structural possibilities of cinema. Films include *1997B (Departure)*, 1997, by Steve Polta, Super-8mm, color, sound, 7 minutes; *Opening the 19th Century: 1896*, 1896/1991, by Lumiere Brothers/Ken Jacobs, 16mm, b/w and color, sound, 9 minutes; *Short Film Series*, 1975-1998, by Guy Sherwin; 16mm, b/w, sound, 15 minutes; *Serene Velocity*, 1970, by Ernie Gehr, 16mm, color, 23 minutes; *Glass*, 1998, by Leighton Pierce, 16mm, color, sound, 7 minutes; *3.95 Untitled*, 1995, by Brian Frye, 16mm, b/w, silent, 3 minutes; *Don't Even Think*, 1992, by Scott Stark, Super-8mm, color, sound, 15 minutes; *S:TREAM:S:S:ECTION:S:ECTION:S:S:ECTIONED*, 1968-71, by Paul Sharits, 16mm, color, sound, 42 minutes.

In Search of Sense and Sequence
Tuesday, October 26, 7:30 pm
The creation/discovery/imposition of order and meaning is a ubiquitous urge of conscious life. The films in this program endeavor to make some "sense" of experience. Films include *Test*, 1996, by Kerry Laitala, 16mm, b/w, silent, 3 minutes; *An Algorithm*, 1977, by Bette Gordon, 16mm, color, sound, 10 minutes; *The Amateurist*, 1998, by Miranda July, video, color, sound, 17 minutes; *The Adventures of Blackie*, 1998, by Jeanne Finley and John Muse, video, color, sound, 9 minutes; *Poetic Justice*, 1972, by Hollis Frampton, 16mm, b/w, silent, 31.5 minutes; *Anatomy of Melancholy*, 1999, by Brian Frye, 16mm, b/w, sound, 12 minutes; *I'll Walk with God*, 1994, by Scott Stark, 16mm, color, sound, 8 minutes.

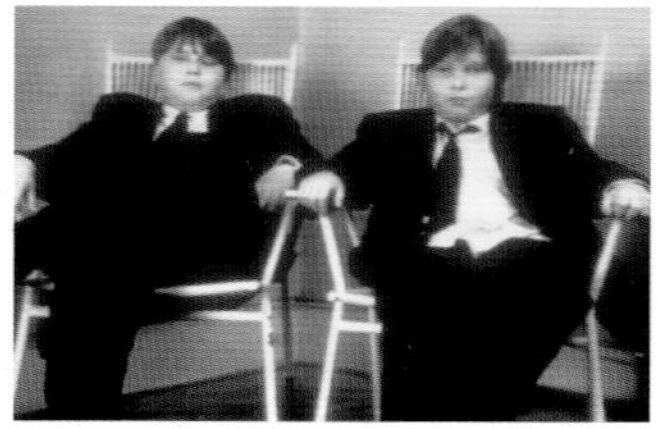

Gillian Wearing, *2 into 1*, 1997

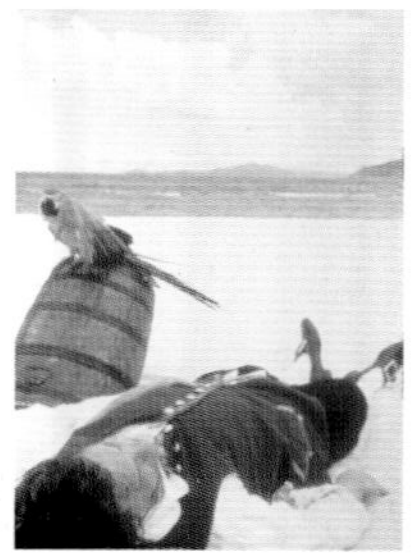

Rodney Graham, *Vexation Island*, 1997

EXHIBITION: OAKLAND

INTERWEAVINGS
October 2–November 24, 1999
Oliver Art Center
5212 Broadway, Oakland
Opening reception: Friday, October 1, 6–8 pm
Organized by Yves Sabourin and Lawrence Rinder, *Interweavings* presents works made through collaborations among contemporary international artists and practitioners of the classic French crafts of lacemaking, tapestry, and embroidery. Among the featured artists are Ghada Amer, John Armleder, Marie-Ange Guillerminot, Mona Hatoum, Fabrice Hybert, Annette Messager, and Jean-Michel Othoniel.

Oliver Art Center, Oakland campus
Hours: Monday, Tuesday, Thursday, Friday, and Saturday 11 am–5 pm Wednesday 11am–9 pm; closed Sunday. Holiday closure: November 25–28

PUBLIC PROGRAMS: OAKLAND

INTERWEAVINGS LECTURE SERIES
Unless otherwise indicated, all *Interweavings* programs take place in Nahl Hall on CCAC's Oakland campus. For more information, call the CCAC Institute at 415.551.9210.

Lecture: Yves Sabourin
Friday, October 1, 8 pm
Interweavings curator Yves Sabourin discusses

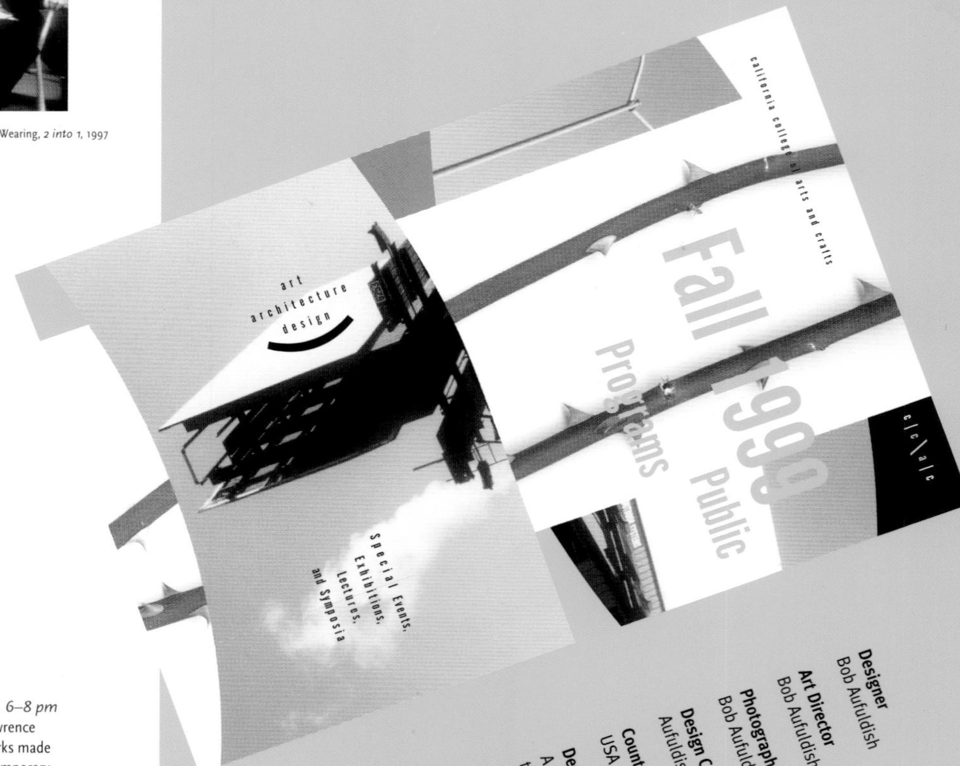

Designer
Bob Aufuldish

Art Director
Bob Aufuldish

Photographer
Bob Aufuldish

Design Company
Aufuldish & Warinner

Country of Origin
USA

Description of Artwork
A fold-out announcement of the public program offered by the California College of Art and Crafts during the fall semester 1999.

Page Dimensions
152 x 229 mm
6 x 9 in

Format
Self-mailing announcement

CCAC Public Programs, Fall 1999

The striking juxtaposition of natural and urban images on the cover draws attention to the experimental and conceptual nature of many of the films and events offered in the program. The clear typography on the inside, with the second color printed beneath the black text, reflects the preoccupations of many of the talks which have to do with contextualism and the overlaying of meanings.

Special Production Techniques

Two-color printing (pale green and black) has been used to good effect to add a subtle depth to the duotone images on the front cover and for the overlaying of text on the inside.

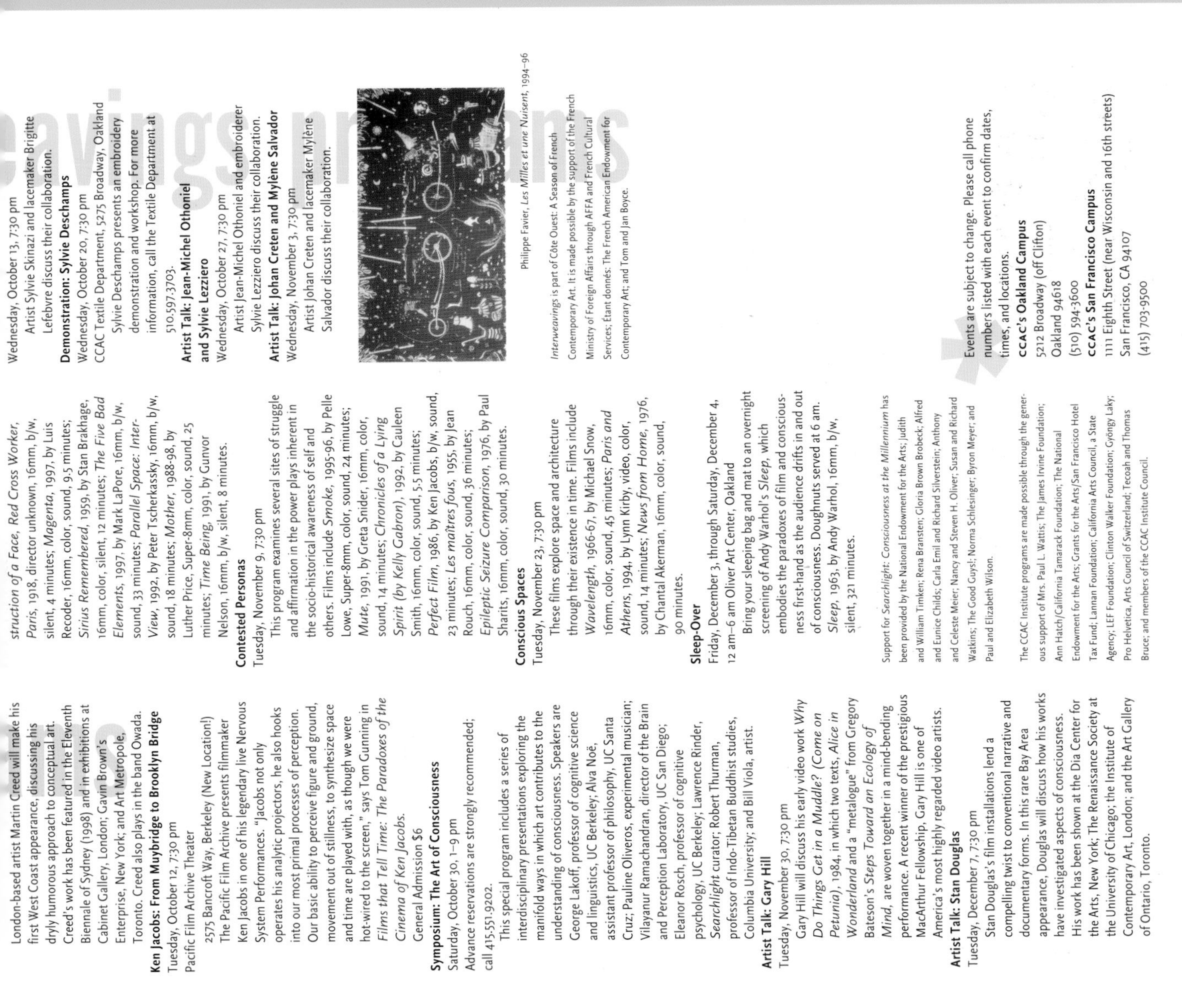

London-based artist Martin Creed will make his first West Coast appearance, discussing his dryly humorous approach to conceptual art. Creed's work has been featured in the Eleventh Biennale of Sydney (1998) and in exhibitions at Cabinet Gallery, London; Gavin Brown's Enterprise, New York; and Art Metropole, Toronto. Creed also plays in the band Owada.

Ken Jacobs: From Muybridge to Brooklyn Bridge
Tuesday, October 12, 7:30 pm
Pacific Film Archive Theater
2575 Bancroft Way, Berkeley (New Location!)
The Pacific Film Archive presents filmmaker Ken Jacobs in one of his legendary live Nervous System Performances. "Jacobs not only operates his analytic projectors, he also hooks into our most primal processes of perception. Our basic ability to perceive figure and ground, movement out of stillness, to synthesize space and time are played with, as though we were hot-wired to the screen," says Tom Gunning in *Films that Tell Time: The Paradoxes of the Cinema of Ken Jacobs.*
General Admission $6

Symposium: The Art of Consciousness
Saturday, October 30, 1–9 pm
Advance reservations are strongly recommended; call 415.551.9202.
This special program includes a series of interdisciplinary presentations exploring the manifold ways in which art contributes to the understanding of consciousness. Speakers are George Lakoff, professor of cognitive science and linguistics, UC Berkeley; Alva Noë, assistant professor of philosophy, UC Santa Cruz; Pauline Oliveros, experimental musician; Vilayanur Ramachandran, director of the Brain and Perception Laboratory, UC San Diego; Eleanor Rosch, professor of cognitive psychology, UC Berkeley; Lawrence Rinder, *Searchlight* curator; Robert Thurman, professor of Indo-Tibetan Buddhist studies, Columbia University; and Bill Viola, artist.

Artist Talk: Gary Hill
Tuesday, November 30, 7:30 pm
Gary Hill will discuss his early video work *Why Do Things Get in a Muddle? (Come on Petunia)*, 1984, in which two texts, *Alice in Wonderland* and a "metalogue" from Gregory Bateson's *Steps Toward an Ecology of Mind*, are woven together in a mind-bending performance. A recent winner of the prestigious MacArthur Fellowship, Gary Hill is one of America's most highly regarded video artists.

Artist Talk: Stan Douglas
Tuesday, December 7, 7:30 pm
Stan Douglas's film installations lend a compelling twist to conventional narrative and documentary forms. In this rare Bay Area appearance, Douglas will discuss how his works have investigated aspects of consciousness. His work has been shown at the Dia Center for the Arts, New York; The Renaissance Society at the University of Chicago; the Institute of Contemporary Art, London; and the Art Gallery of Ontario, Toronto.

struction of a Face, Red Cross Worker, Paris, 1918, director unknown, 16mm, b/w, silent, 4 minutes; *Magenta*, 1997, by Luis Recoder, 16mm, color, sound, 9.5 minutes; *Sirius Remembered*, 1959, by Stan Brakhage, 16mm, color, silent, 12 minutes; *The Five Bad Elements*, 1997, by Mark LaPore, 16mm, b/w, sound, 33 minutes; *Parallel Space: Inter-View*, 1992, by Peter Tscherkassky, 16mm, b/w, sound, 18 minutes; *Mother*, 1988-98, by Luther Price, Super-8mm, color, sound, 25 minutes; *Time Being*, 1991, by Gunvor Nelson, 16mm, b/w, silent, 8 minutes.

Contested Personas
Tuesday, November 9, 7:30 pm
This program examines several sites of struggle and affirmation in the power plays inherent in the socio-historical awareness of self and others. Films include *Smoke*, 1995-96, by Pelle Lowe, Super-8mm, color, sound, 24 minutes; *Mute*, 1991, by Greta Snider, 16mm, color, sound, 14 minutes; *Chronicles of a Lying Spirit (by Kelly Gabron)*, 1992, by Cauleen Smith, 16mm, color, sound, 5.5 minutes; *Perfect Film*, 1986, by Ken Jacobs, b/w, sound, 23 minutes; *Les maîtres fous*, 1955, by Jean Rouch, 16mm, color, sound, 36 minutes; *Epileptic Seizure Comparison*, 1976, by Paul Sharits, 16mm, color, sound, 30 minutes.

Conscious Spaces
Tuesday, November 23, 7:30 pm
These films explore space and architecture through their existence in time. Films include *Wavelength*, 1966-67, by Michael Snow, 16mm, color, sound, 45 minutes; *Paris and Athens*, 1994, by Lynn Kirby, video, color, sound, 14 minutes; *News from Home*, 1976, by Chantal Akerman, 16mm, color, sound, 90 minutes.

Sleep-Over
Friday, December 3, through Saturday, December 4, 12 am–6 am Oliver Art Center, Oakland
Bring your sleeping bag and mat to an overnight screening of Andy Warhol's *Sleep*, which embodies the paradoxes of film and consciousness first-hand as the audience drifts in and out of consciousness. Doughnuts served at 6 am. *Sleep*, 1963, by Andy Warhol, 16mm, b/w, silent, 321 minutes.

Support for *Searchlight: Consciousness at the Millennium* has been provided by the National Endowment for the Arts; Judith and William Timken; Rena Bransten; Gloria Brown Brobeck; Alfred and Eunice Childs; Carla Emil and Richard Silverstein; Anthony and Celeste Meier; Nancy and Steven H. Oliver; Susan and Richard Watkins; The Good Guys!; Norma Schlesinger; Byron Meyer; and Paul and Elizabeth Wilson.

The CCAC Institute programs are made possible through the generous support of Mrs. Paul L. Wattis; The James Irvine Foundation; Ann Hatch/California Tamarack Foundation; The National Endowment for the Arts; Grants for the Arts/San Francisco Hotel Tax Fund; Lannan Foundation; California Arts Council, a State Agency; LEF Foundation; Clinton Walker Foundation; Gyöngy Laky; Pro Helvetica, Arts Council of Switzerland; Tecoah and Thomas Bruce; and members of the CCAC Institute Council.

Wednesday, October 13, 7:30 pm
Artist Sylvie Skinazi and lacemaker Brigitte Lefebvre discuss their collaboration.

Demonstration: Sylvie Deschamps
Wednesday, October 20, 7:30 pm
CCAC Textile Department, 5275 Broadway, Oakland
Sylvie Deschamps presents an embroidery demonstration and workshop. For more information, call the Textile Department at 510.597.3703.

Artist Talk: Jean-Michel Othoniel and Sylvie Lezziero
Wednesday, October 27, 7:30 pm
Artist Jean-Michel Othoniel and embroiderer Sylvie Lezziero discuss their collaboration.

Artist Talk: Johan Creten and Mylène Salvador
Wednesday, November 3, 7:30 pm
Artist Johan Creten and lacemaker Mylène Salvador discuss their collaboration.

Philippe Favier, *Les Milles et une Nuisent*, 1994–96

Interweavings is part of Côte Ouest: A Season of French Contemporary Art. It is made possible by the support of the French Ministry of Foreign Affairs through AFFA and French Cultural Services; Étant donnés: The French American Endowment for Contemporary Art; and Tom and Jan Boyce.

Events are subject to change. Please call phone numbers listed with each event to confirm dates, times, and locations.
CCAC's Oakland Campus
5212 Broadway (off Clifton)
Oakland 94618
(510) 594-3600
CCAC's San Francisco Campus
1111 Eighth Street (near Wisconsin and 16th streets)
San Francisco, CA 94107
(415) 703-9500

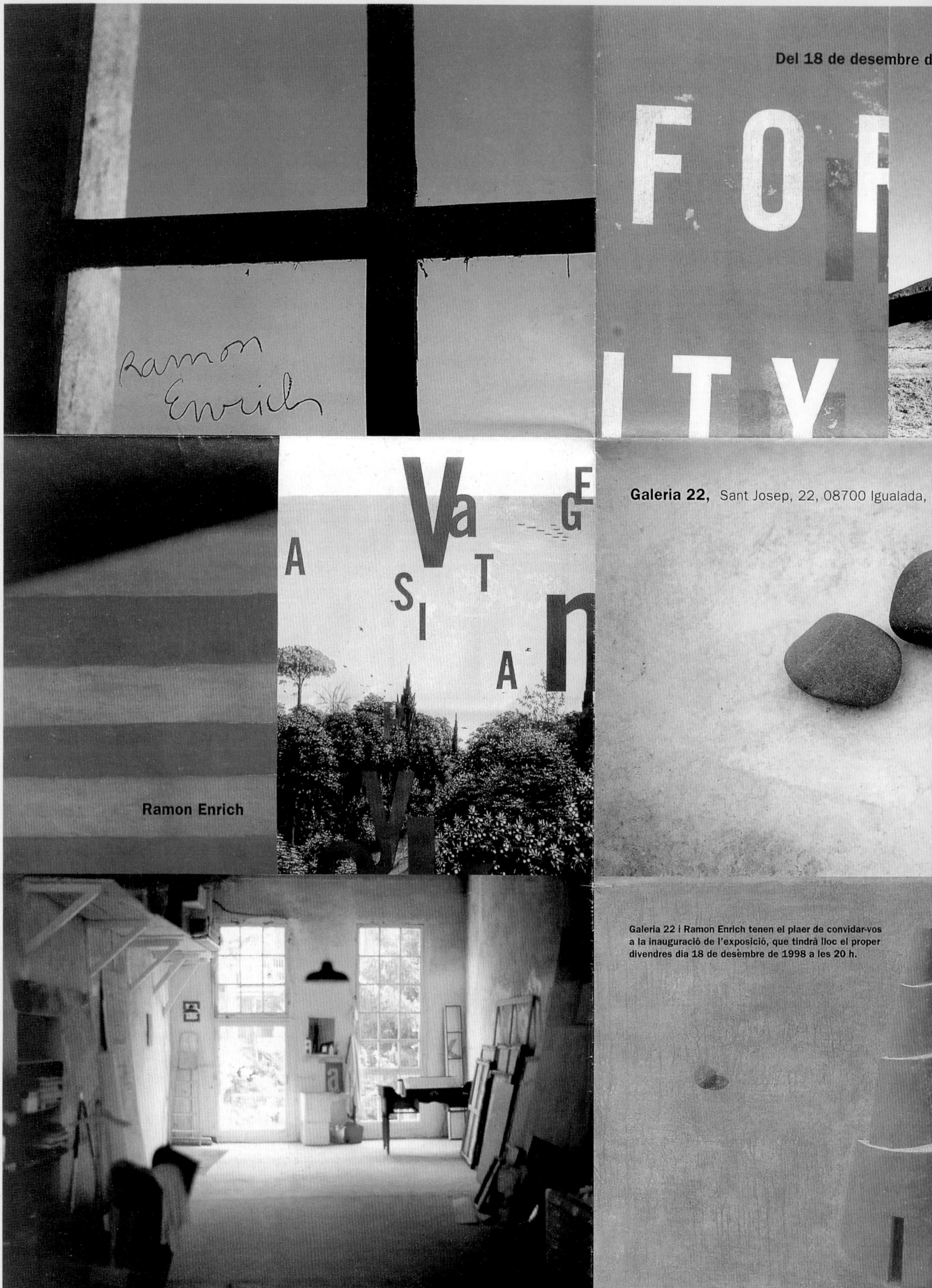
Del 18 de desembre d
FOR
ITY
Ramon Enrich
Ramon Enrich
Galeria 22, Sant Josep, 22, 08700 Igualada,
Galeria 22 i Ramon Enrich tenen el plaer de convidar-vos a la inauguració de l'exposició, que tindrà lloc el proper divendres dia 18 de desembre de 1998 a les 20 h.

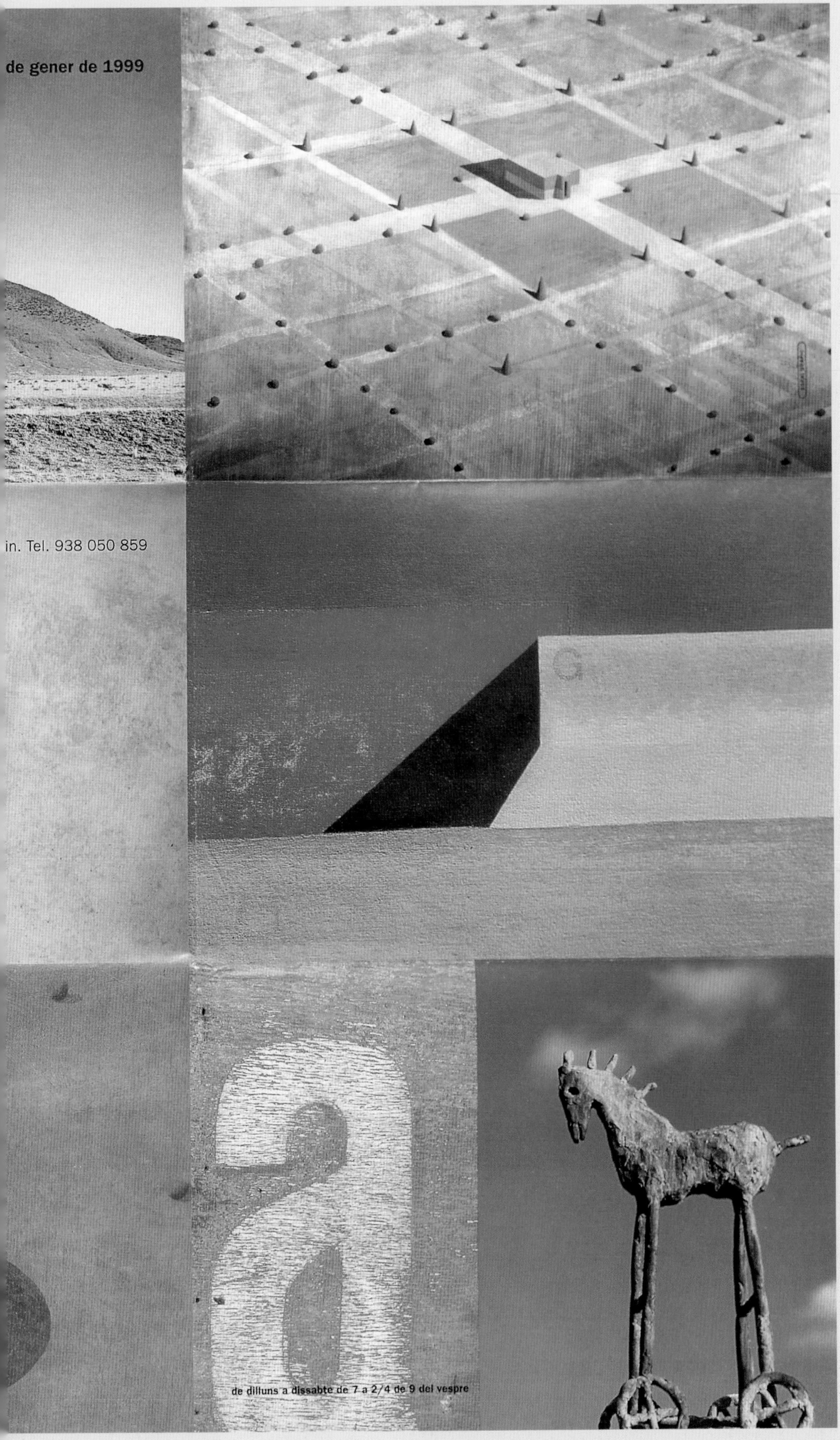

Galeria 22

Whether spread out as a poster (*left*), or folded to one ninth of its size to make an invitation, this eye-catching design gives a strong sense of the artist's preoccupations. The juxtaposition of rich imagery—photograph next to painting and close-up next to long-shot—reveals a concern with the geometric structure of images. This is something seen in the paintings themselves which, grouped together in this way, also show the extent to which the colors of landscape and sky have influenced the artist's color palette.

Designer
Lluis Jubert

Art Director
Ramon Enrich

Illustrator
Ramon Enrich

Photographer
Ramon Enrich

Design Company
Espai Grafic

Country of Origin
Spain

Description of Artwork
An invitation to an exhibition at a Barcelona art gallery, which can be unfolded to make a poster.

Dimensions
210 x 150 mm
8¼ x 5⅞ in (folded)
630 x 450 mm
24¾ x 17¾ in (unfolded)

Format
Invitation/Poster

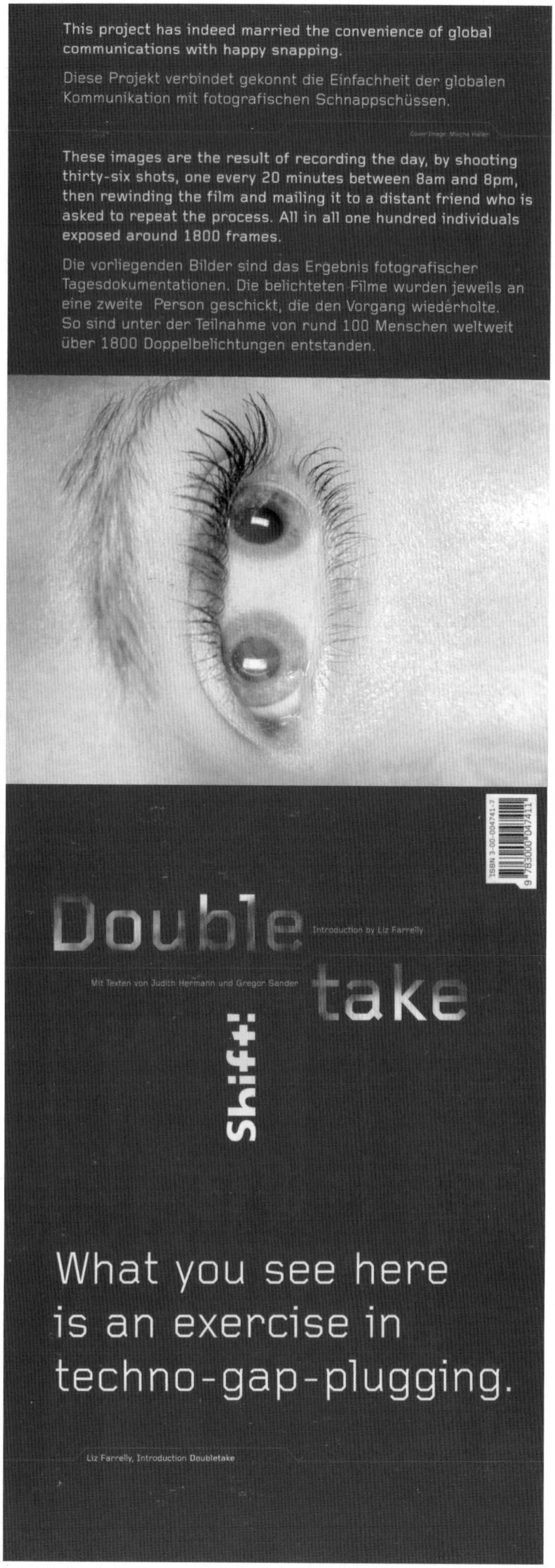

Shift! Doubletake

The originality of the initial idea (see jacket text, *above left*) and the intriguing nature of this international photographic project have been borne out by the resulting imagery. The layout of the spreads reflects the atmosphere of the double-exposed pictures and, critically, does not intrude upon them. This work stands for itself.

San Francisco

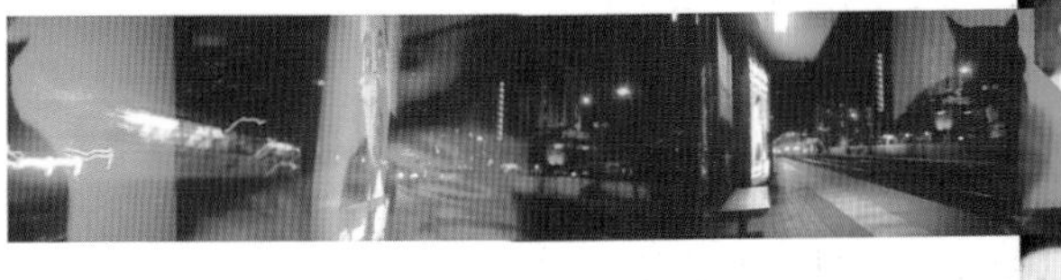

Barcelona

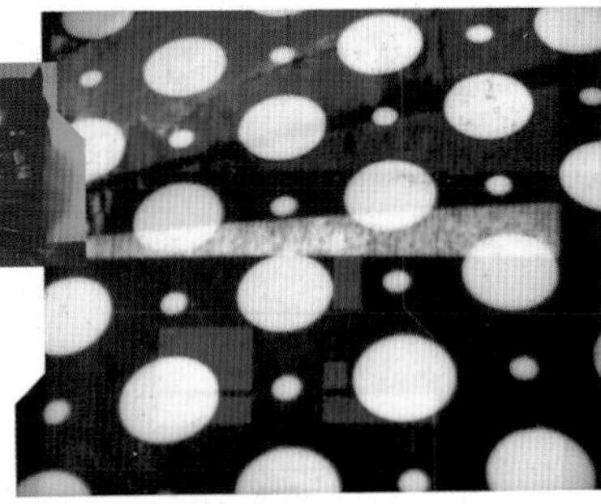

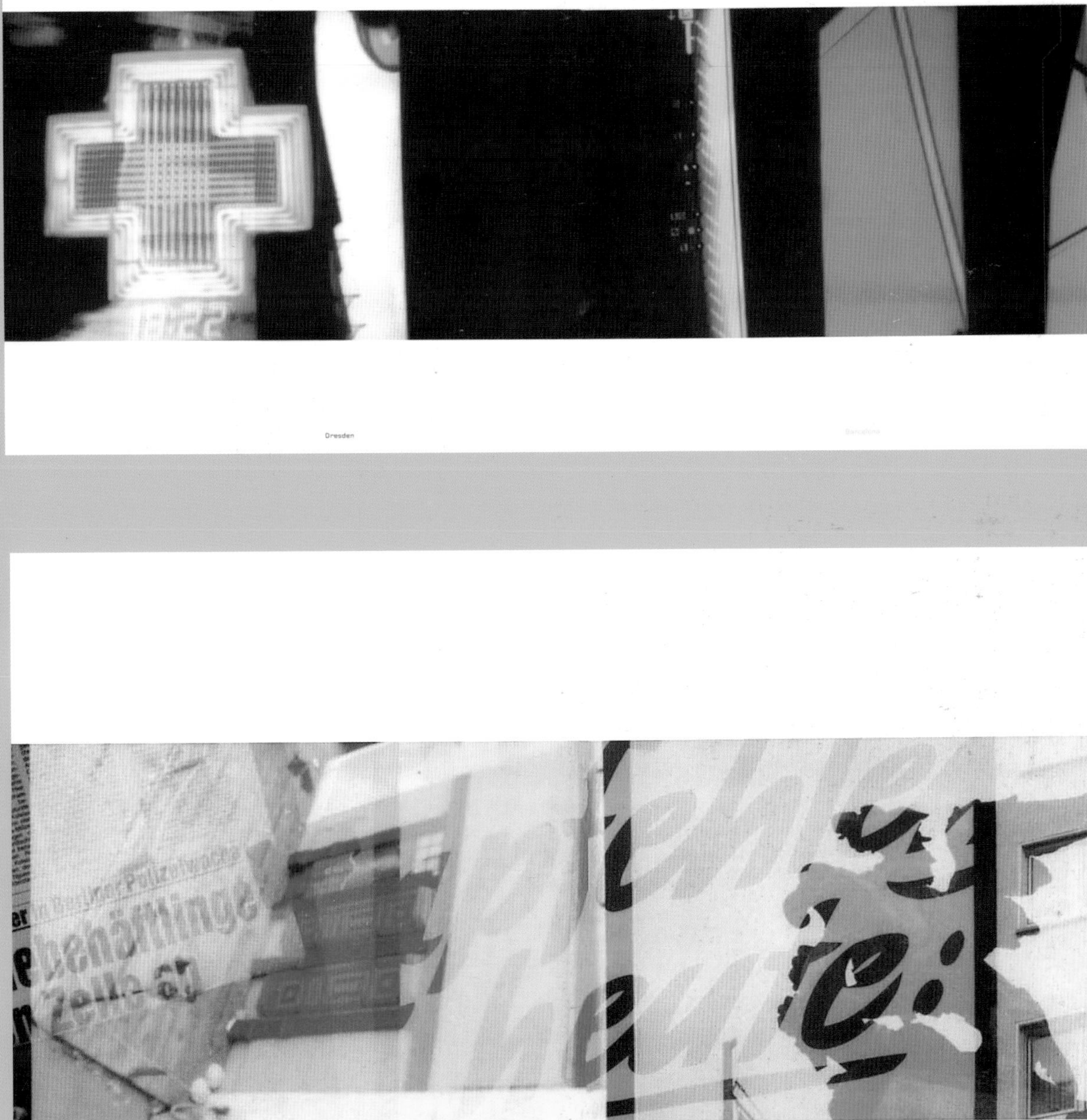

Dresden

Barcelona

New York

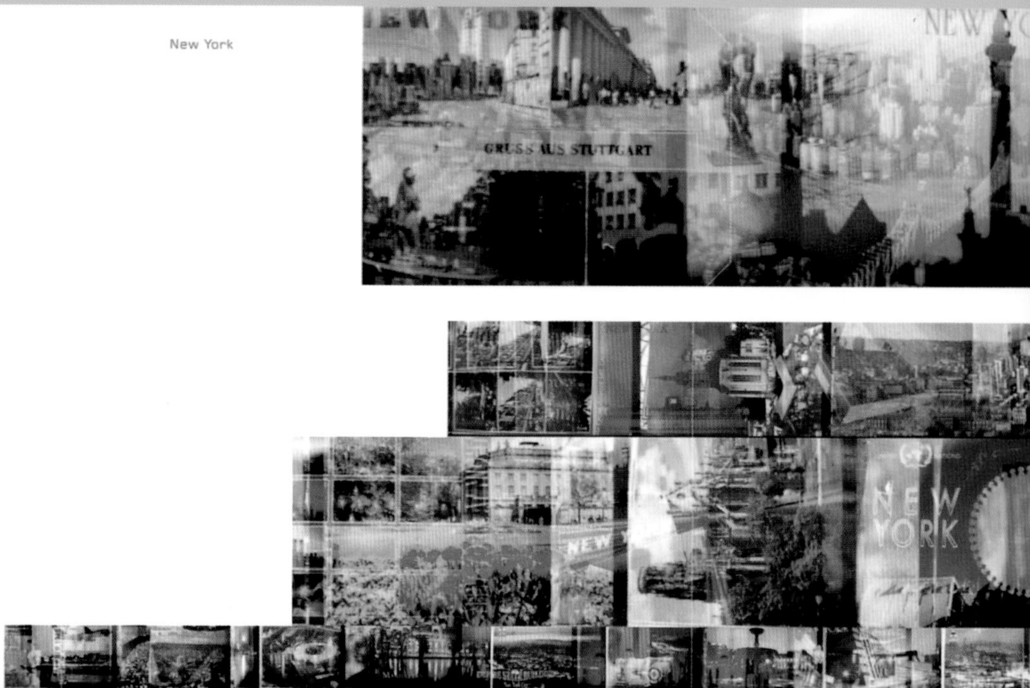

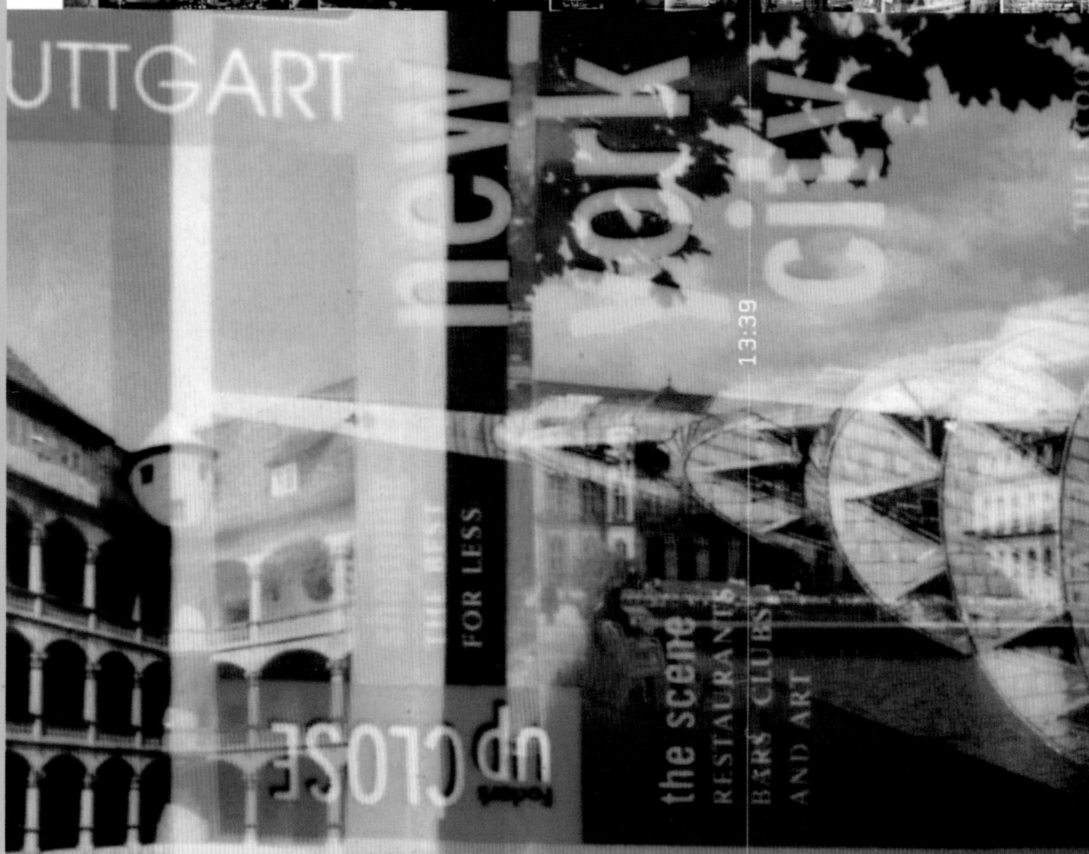

Stuttgart

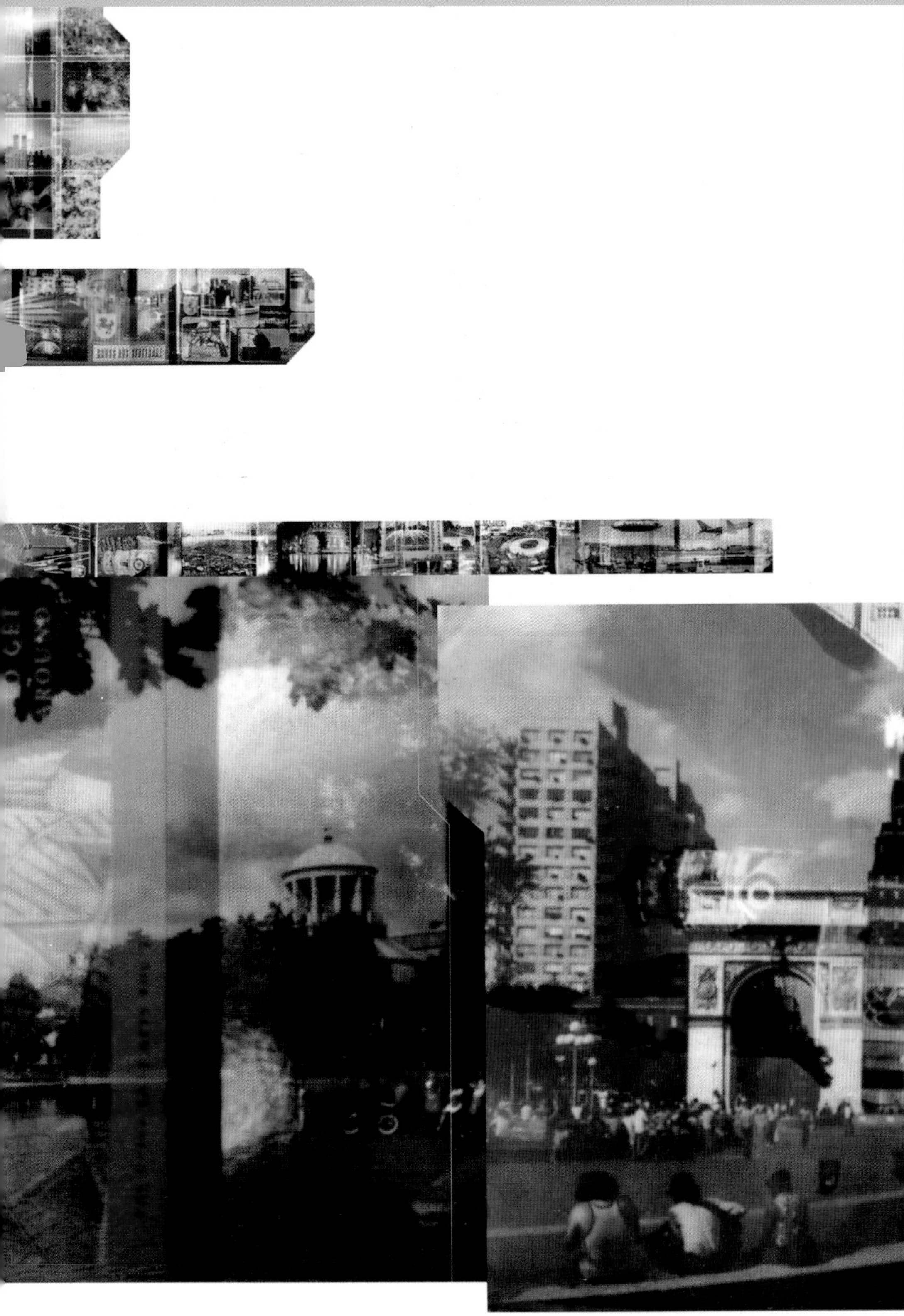

Concept
Anja Lutz, Christian Küsters

Designers
Anja Lutz, Christian Küsters, Julia Guther

Art Director
Anja Lutz

Photographers
Previous spread, right-hand page: Amy Auerbach and Tobias Melzer (*top, center*), Sergi and Lydia Carzola (*center and top, right*), Corinna Gab and Rudi Feuser (*bottom*). This spread: Anja Osterwauder and Oliver Krimmel.

Design Company
Shift!

Country of Origin
Germany

Description of Artwork
160-page book documenting a photography project involving double-exposed images from around the world. Introduction by Liz Farrelly and short stories by Judith Hermann and Gregor Sander.

Page Dimensions
225 x 168 mm
$8^{7}/_{8}$ x $6^{5}/_{8}$ in

Format
Book

GLOSSARY OF USEFUL TERMS

ADOBE ILLUSTRATOR
A popular graphic/illustration manipulation program used by many designers for both printed and electronic publication.

ADOBE PHOTOSHOP
The industry-standard image manipulation program used to prepare images for publication.

CMYK (COLOR PRINTING)
The printing of pages in full color through the application of four separate colors in succession: Cyan (blue), Magenta (pink), Yellow, and K (black). K is used for black, because using B could cause confusion between blue and black. It is possible to combine different types of color printing on the same sheet of paper by, for example, using four colors on one side and a single color on the reverse. This is referred to as 'four-back-one' printing. If this technique is used to produce a book then when the printed sheet, or signature, is folded the four- and one-color pages appear alternately throughout the publication.

CAP HEIGHT
The measuremant from the baseline to the top of a capital letter.

DUOTONE
The process by which the complete range of tones, from light to dark, is represented using two colors. Often, one of these two colors is black, but any two printer's inks can be used.

FOLIO
The page number in a book.

GUTTER
The line running along the center of a book where the pages are bound together. Gutter can also be used to refer to the space between two columns of type.

LEADING
The amount of space, measured from baseline to baseline, between two or more lines of type.

LITHOGRAPHIC PRINTING
The most common form of commercial printing process in which the text/image is first etched onto a metal plate. This plate is often curved and fits onto a fast-rotating drum. Ink is applied to the plate which is then pressed against a second rotating drum, usually covered in a rubber blanket, onto which the inked image is transferred. This second drum is then rolled over a sheet of paper printing the image onto the paper. This process is technically called Offset Lithographic Printing because the text/image is not printed directly but first 'offset' onto an intermediate surface before finally being printed onto the paper.

OVERPRINTING
The printing of one color on top of another.

PIXEL
The basic unit that makes up an image viewed on a TV or computer monitor. The ultimate size of an electronic image when viewed on a screen depends on its dimensions in pixels and the resolution of the screen. The higher the resolution of the screen, the smaller—and the more clearly defined—the image will appear.

POINT SIZE
In typography, still the most common unit of measurement used to denote the size of a typeface. There are approximately 72 points to the inch.

QUARK XPRESS
A page-layout computer program used in the production of all types of design.

REVERSE OUT/KNOCK OUT
In printing, the technique of creating text/outline/image by taking away the color from a particular area to allow the paper beneath, or another ink/inks, to show through without overprinting.

SERIF
In typography, a serif typeface is characterized by additional strokes at the extremities of each character. A typeface that lacks this is referred to as sans serif. Baskerville is an example of a serif face; Univers is a sans-serif face.

SIGNATURE
Books are often produced by printing a number of pages (usually 4, 8, 16, or 32) onto a single sheet of paper. Each of these sheets is then folded to form a section of the book. These sections are known as signatures.

SILK-SCREEN PRINTING
A method of printing in which the ink is forced through a mesh made from fine material (originally silk) onto the surface to be printed. It is often used in poster printing.

TYPEFACE
The style or design of the type.

X-HEIGHT
The measurement from the baseline to the top of a lower-case letter.

INDEX OF DESIGNERS, DESIGN COMPANIES, AND ART COLLEGES

A

ADIGARD, ERIK 76–9
AGRAPHE 20, 144
ALLEN, MARK 14, 68
AMBROSE, GAVIN 80
ART CENTER COLLEGE OF DESIGN 64
@RADICAL.MEDIA 100
AUFULDISH, BOB 128, 132
AUFULDISH & WARINNER 128, 132

B

BARIL, POL 40
BARTLETT, BRAD 104, 124
BEAUFONTS 18
BRAVENEC, DAVE 14
BROWN, MARTIN 62
BRUHN, PETER 84–7

C

CAYLOR, MARK 30
CEPOGLU, GULIZAR 122
CHENERY, ROB 92
CRANBROOK ACADEMY OF ART 104, 124
CRANE, ROB 32
CYAN 88–91

D

DE LOIA, ADRIANNE 14, 68
DULUDE, DENIS 40

E

EASTWOOD, JOSEPH 42
EG.G 94, 102, 126, 130
ENVISION+ 44–51
EPOXY 70–73
ESPAI GRAFIC 66, 134
ESQUER, RAFAEL 64, 100

F

FILIFOX 26–9
FOUNTAIN-BRUHN 84–7
FOUSHEE, DANIELLE 106, 124
FUEL 22–5

G

GARSIDE, SEEL 18
GEHLHAAR, JENS 22–5, 36–9

GLAHR, CHRISTINA 114
GLICKSMAN, CAROLINE 108–11
GRAPHIC HAVOC AVISUALAGENCY 16
GULIZAR CEPOGLU GRAPHIC DESIGN CO. 122
GUTHER, JULIA 136–9

H
HAGMANN, SIBYLLE 112
HAND, DAVID 18
HENSCHEL, ANTONIA 52–5
HGV DESIGN 62
HITCH 18

J
JARABO, ALEJANDRA 68
JOHNSON, CHAKARAS 100
JUBERT, LLUIS 66, 134

K
KICK MEDIA 14, 68
KO CREATION 40
KUSTERS, CHRISTIAN 136–9

L
LIQUID AGENTUR FUR GESTALTUNG 96–9
LLENADO, ARMANDO 14
LOREM IPSUM 114
LUTZ, ANJA 136–9

M
M.A.D. 76–9
MARK ROGERSON ASSOCIATES 34, 58–61
MARTINEZ, CHRIS 14, 68
MCSHANE, PATRICIA 76–9
MILDENBERGER, ESTHER 44–51
MITCHELL, IAN 18
MONO 80

O
ORSCHULKO, CARINA 96–9

P
PELVAN, AYSUN 122
PETTER, CATHERINE 70–73
PLANETA, SANDRA 116

R
RABAN, DOM 94, 102, 126, 130
RED DESIGN 10–13
ROGERSON, MARK 34, 58–61
ROYAL COLLEGE OF ART 44–51

S
SADDAKNI, MARIANA 100
SALLACZ, ILJA 96–9
SATELLITE 32
SAVOIR, PHILIPPE 26–9
SHIFT! 136–9
SPOT DESIGN 116
STYLOROUGE 30, 92
SWITZER, BRIAN 44–51

T
TYPOSTUDIO 112

U
UNIVERSITY OF BRIGHTON 108–11
UNIVERSITY OF SALFORD 42

W
WALKER, PAT 126, 130
WHY NOT ASSOCIATES 82

Y
YACHT ASSOCIATES 118–21
YATES, MARTIN 32

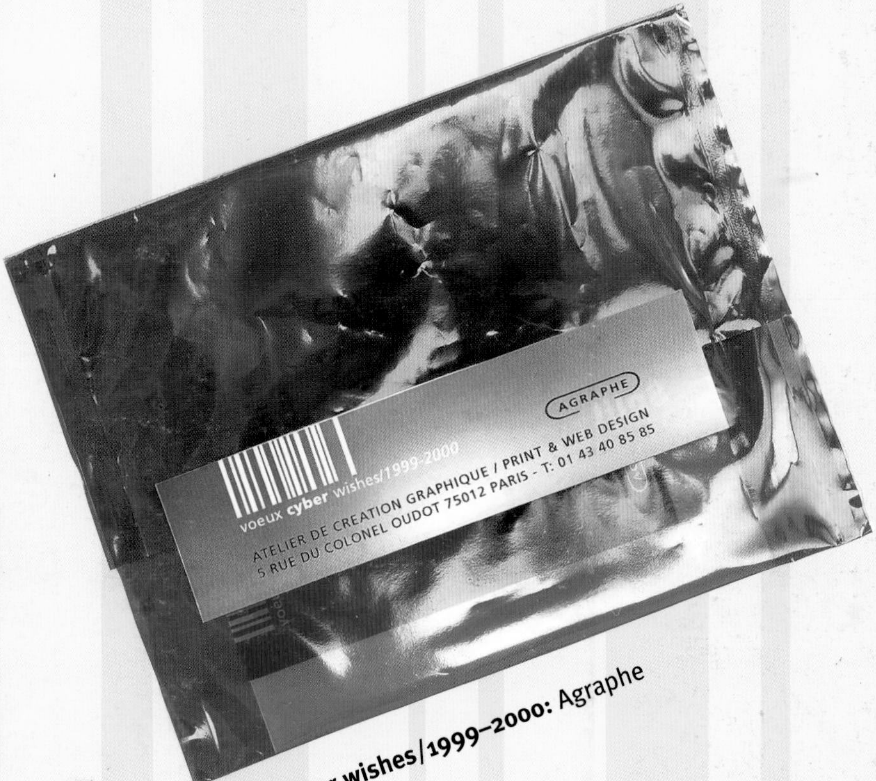

voeux cyber wishes/1999–2000: Agraphe